WORLD POETS

WORLD POETS

Ron Padgett

Editor in Chief

VOLUME 3

CHARLES SCRIBNER'S SONS
An Imprint of The Gale Group
New York

Text and photo credits begin on page 407 of volume 3.

Charles Scribner's Sons
1633 Broadway
New York, NY 10019

Library of Congress Cataloging-in-Publication Data

World poets / Ron Padgett, editor in chief.
     p. cm.
   "Mainly for use by students aged 14 to 18 . . . and for anyone interested in learning more about poetry"—Introd., vol. 1.
   Includes bibliographical references and index.
   Contents: v. 1. Apollinaire-Homer — v. 2. Hopkins-Shakespeare — v. 3. Shelley-Yeats.
   Summary: Alphabetically arranged articles on 107 poets from around the world, accompanied by fifteen essays on various genres and schools of poetry.
   ISBN 0-684-80591-X (set) — ISBN 0-684-80610-X (v. 1) — ISBN 0-684-80609-6 (v. 2) — ISBN 0-684-80592-8 (v. 3)
   1. Poetry—Bio-bibliography—Dictionaries—Juvenile literature. 2. Poets—Biography—Dictionaries—Juvenile literature. [1. Poets—Encyclopedias. 2. Poetry.] I. Padgett, Ron.

PN1021.W67 2000
809.1'003—dc21
[B]

00-024801

1 3 5 7 9 11 13 15 17 19 20 18 16 14 12 10 8 6 4 2

Printed in the United States of America.

The paper used in this publication meets the minimum requirements of the American National Standard for Information Sciences—Permanence of Paper for Printed Library Materials, ANSI Z39.48-1992.

CONTENTS

Thematic Essays

PERCY BYSSHE SHELLEY

(1792–1822)

by Anselm Berrigan

It would be hard not to be hypnotized by the details of Percy Bysshe (pronounced "Bish") Shelley's rich and fascinating life, which included his rejection of his family's class and cultural background; his friendship with another great Romantic writer, Lord Byron; his marriage to Mary Wollstonecraft Godwin (better known as Mary Shelley, author of *Frankenstein*); his atheism,* which helped cause his expulsion from Oxford University and, later, his self-imposed exile to Italy; his travels to Ireland in an attempt to incite revolution at the age of nineteen; and his tragic and untimely death by drowning off the coast of Italy at the age of thirty. As dynamic as Shelley's life may have been, at its core was a devotion to writing that was professional and passionate.

Shelley deeply believed in the capacity of poetry to inspire social change and fight oppression as well as to investigate the nature of humanity. One of Shelley's shorter poems, "Ozymandias," displays his hatred of tyranny and his ability to write a dramatic narrative:

*atheism disbelief in the existence of God

I met a traveller from an antique land
Who said: 'Two vast and trunkless legs of stone
Stand in the desert . . . Near them, on the sand,
Half sunk, a shattered visage* lies, whose frown,
And wrinkled lip, and sneer of cold command,
Tell that its sculptor well those passions read
Which yet survive, stamped on these lifeless things,
The hand that mocked them, and the heart that fed;
And on the pedestal these words appear:
"My name is Ozymandias, king of kings:
Look on my works, ye Mighty, and despair!"
Nothing beside remains. Round the decay
Of that colossal wreck, boundless and bare,
The lone and level sands stretch far away.'

*visage face

*sonnet a fourteen-line poem usually composed in iambic pentameter (each line has five feet, each foot consisting of an unstressed syllable followed by a stressed syllable).

The poem, a sonnet* written at the age of twenty-six, uses the voice of Ozymandias, the "king of kings," to represent the voice of tyrannical authority declaring, "Look on my works," as Shelley creates an image of a desert wasteland around the "shattered visage" of the king. The "works" are the works of oppression—the king has destroyed the civilization that he ruled. It is important when reading Shelley to be prepared for quick images that point to serious political and spiritual beliefs. Shelley's attention is constantly shifting, and that movement can make the poems seem difficult to understand on first reading. While Shelley, like most poets, makes use of the details of his life on all of its levels, he is also less outwardly autobiographical in his poems than some other poets. Many of his poems use characters from Greek mythology and other sources as protagonists,* and many are allegorical* in nature.

*protagonist the main character of a literary work

*allegorical having a story in which the fictional objects, characters, and actions are equated with meanings that lie outside the narrative itself

Early Life and Education

Shelley was born on 4 August 1792 near Horsham, Sussex, in England. His father was a country gentleman and member of Parliament, and Shelley was his privileged eldest son—a hot-headed, high-spirited practical joker (he once blew the top off of his desk at school as part of a chemistry "experiment") who had a tremendous appetite for reading. Early in life Shelley recognized the divide between himself and his family, his father in particular, in terms of political and religious beliefs. At home and at school, where he was mercilessly ridiculed by his fellow students for his refusal to conform, Shelley felt isolated from his family and peers. It is likely that during this period Shelley formulated the principles he presented in the introduction to a poem written later, called *Laon and Cynthna,* which was revised and retitled *The Revolt of Islam:*

> I will be wise,
> And just, and free, and mild, if in me lies
> Such power, for I grow weary to behold
> The selfish and the strong still tyrannize
> Without reproach or check.

Despite his removal from Oxford in 1811 for passing around an unsigned pamphlet entitled *The Necessity of Atheism,* written with his friend Thomas Hogg, Shelley continued his education on his own throughout his life. At the time of his death he was fluent in, and translating from, Italian, Spanish, German, Latin, and Greek and had even dabbled in Arabic. After eloping with sixteen-year-old Harriet Westbrook in 1811, Shelley made failed attempts in Ireland and Wales to circulate his prose writings on the oppression of the working classes and the poor. By the age of twenty-one, he had, however, written a long poem entitled *Queen Mab* (which, though published only now and then, was his one popular success while he was alive) as well as two books of prose (a romance and a thriller) and two volumes of Gothic* verse. These works were largely preludes* to the richer, more powerful writings that Shelley would begin to produce a few years later. Although Shelley is best known for his poetry, he was also an essayist, dramatist, pamphleteer, translator, reviewer, and correspondent. Writing was a full-time occupation for Shelley, the only occupation he truly took on.

In his brief thirty years, Shelley was subject to a great deal of personal tragedy and difficulty. His marriage to Harriet Westbrook failed, and in 1814 he met and ran away to Switzerland with Mary Wollstonecraft Godwin (Harriet committed suicide in 1816.) Although he and Mary remained together until his death in 1822, three of their children died, as did a number of other friends and relatives in a wide variety of painful circumstances. Shelley never made peace with his father after a bitter split around the time of his expulsion from Oxford, and until the death of his grandfather allowed him some inheritance, he was for the most part cut off from his

*****Gothic** characteristic of the medieval or Romantic period, as opposed to the classical period

*****prelude** an introduction or introductory piece (of music, poetry, etc.)

family's wealth. In his early twenties Shelley was often fleeing creditors and moving rapidly over the English countryside. His "scandalous" behavior—mainly his unwavering atheism, public disputes with his family, and controversial marriages—also caused him to become a figure of public scorn in London society. When published in England, Shelley's work was routinely trashed by critics. To top it off, in 1815 Shelley was diagnosed as having tuberculosis, and his health was a source of worry for the remainder of his life. Despite these trials, Shelley went on to produce an astonishing body of poetic work, much of it written in Italy, where he spent the last four years of his life.

Major Works

See the essay "Some Basic Poetic Forms" in volume 3 for further discussion of this topic.

Shelley's poetry blends his studies of literature, philosophy (the Greek philosopher Plato was a particular favorite), politics, nature, and physical science. He used a variety of forms—epic, elegy, ballad, tragedy, lyric, ode—to get his concerns across and maintained a vivid, imaginative music to propel the work regardless of what form he was using. In Italy, Shelley reached the height of his powers as a poet. His best-known poems, including "Ode to the West Wind," *Adonais,* "The Masque of Anarchy," and *Prometheus Unbound* were written while he lived in various parts of Italy but were largely unappreciated by those outside his immediate circle of friends and admirers. It was in Italy that Shelley's friendship with Byron blossomed, as the two poets developed a competitive but relatively friendly relationship as writers and thinkers. It is interesting to note that Byron was one of the most famous British poets of his time, while Shelley was known mainly for his disgraceful behavior and bizarre opinions.

Yet Shelley's poetry, in many ways, was intended for a large public audience. *Prometheus Unbound* is a dramatic lyrical poem in three acts based on the Greek myth of Prometheus, who gave fire to humankind and was punished by Jupiter, king of the gods, for doing so. Shelley presents Prometheus and Jupiter as opposing moral principles—light and dark, freedom and tyranny—in an attempt to demonstrate the change the human mind would have to undergo in order to create a truly just and liberated society. "Man must first dream the possible before he can do it," Shelley wrote in the poem's preface. Jupiter is cast as an oppressive villain who

Ode to the West Wind (excerpt)

O wild West Wind, thou breath of Autumn's being,
Thou, from whose unseen presence the leaves dead
Are driven, like ghosts from an enchanter fleeing,

Yellow, and black, and pale, and hectic red,
Pestilence-stricken multitudes: O thou,
Who chariotest to their dark wintry bed

The winged seeds, where they lie cold and low,
Each like a corpse within its grave, until
Thine azure sister of the Spring shall blow

Her clarion o'er the dreaming earth, and fill
(Driving sweet buds like flocks to feed in air)
With living hues and odours plain and hill:

Wild Spirit, which art moving everywhere;
Destroyer and preserver; hear, oh, hear!

punishes and tortures Prometheus not only for the "crime" of teaching humanity how to use fire but for introducing the arts and sciences as well.

"The Masque of Anarchy" was written in response to what became known as the Peterloo massacre, when a public meeting on 16 August 1819 of close to sixty thousand working men and women outside Manchester, England, had been attacked and driven away by British militiamen, resulting in hundreds of deaths. "The Masque of Anarchy" consists of ninety-one stanzas in ballad form using elements of satire,* shocking imagery, and the personification* of evils to create a blistering attack on the powers responsible for the massacre and for injustice in general:

> I met Murder on the way—
> He had a mask like Castlereagh—*
> Very smooth he looked, yet grim;
> Seven bloodhounds followed him:
>
> All were fat; and well they might
> Be in admirable plight,

*satire sarcastic, ironic criticism

*personification talking about an object or idea as if it were a person

*Castlereagh Viscount Castlereagh, the British foreign secretary and leader of the House of Commons from 1812 to 1822

For one by one, and two by two,
He tossed them human hearts to chew
Which from his wide cloak he drew.

Next came Fraud, and he had on,
Like Eldon,* an ermined* gown;
His big tears, for he wept well,
Turned to mill-stones* as they fell.

And the little children, who
Round his feet played to and fro,
Thinking every tear a gem,
Had their brains knocked out by them.

*Eldon John Scott, first earl of Eldon, a prominent English jurist and lord chancellor at the time of the Peterloo massacre

*ermined trimmed with ermine, a type of fur

*mill-stone a stone used for grinding

Later in the poem, Shelley lays out a description of true political freedom, focusing on protection against exploitation by the wealthy, justice available without cost, national peace, and distribution of wealth to improve the condition of the poor. Shelley also promotes a belief in the power of mass demonstration to bring political change:

Rise like Lions after slumber
In unvanquishable number
Shake your chains to Earth like dew
Which in sleep had fallen on you—
Ye are many, they are few.

"The Masque of Anarchy" remains a powerful inspirational force of the twentieth century; Allen Ginsberg, in particular, cited the poem as a strong influence on his poetry and political ideals.

Shelley's own life was often at odds with the values and beliefs he championed. He strongly supported the working class, yet he never had to work a day in his life at any kind of manual labor. He responded, often furiously, to political situations in England, yet spent the last five years of his life as an exile in Italy, writing, traveling, and dealing with domestic situations. He deeply believed that a close, strong family was vital to one's development into a freethinking person of principle but could never bring himself to reconcile his differences with his own family in England. But Shelley was not hypocritical; he was simply a young man still in the process of self-development at the time of his death.

Although his long poem *Prometheus Unbound* was written over the course of sixteen months, Shelley often wrote his poems quickly, dashing off lines at a frantic pace when the impulse struck him. On 25 October 1819, in Florence, Italy—according to one account—Shelley, in one sitting, penned "Ode to the West Wind," a beautiful, fiery testament to his belief in nature as a source of spiritual power unattached to organized faith. Here is the last section of the poem, in which Shelley calls on the west wind to carry his words out into the world:

> Make me thy lyre,* even as the forest is:
> What if my leaves are falling like its own!
> The tumult of thy mighty harmonies

*lyre a type of harp

> Will take from both a deep, autumnal tone,
> Sweet though in sadness. Be thou, Spirit fierce,
> My spirit! Be thou me, impetuous* one!

*impetuous impulsive and passionate

> Drive my dead thoughts over the universe
> Like withered leaves to quicken a new birth!
> And, by the incantation* of this verse,

*incantation a spell or chant

> Scatter, as from an unextinguished hearth
> Ashes and sparks, my words among mankind!
> Be through my lips to unawakened earth

> The trumpet of a prophecy! O Wind,
> If Winter comes, can Spring be far behind?

The poem, like many of Shelley's works, is visionary,* prophetic,* and cautiously optimistic. "Ode to the West Wind" was recognized as a poetic achievement only after Shelley's death.

*visionary given to idealistic speculation, dreams, or imaginary visions

*prophetic predicting the future

Shelley was strongly affected by the harsh treatment his work received from reviewers. His distaste for critics showed itself, oddly enough, in *Adonais,* the elegy he wrote after the death of the young poet John Keats in 1821.

Shelley and Keats were acquaintances and poetic peers, but they never came close to striking up a friendship. Shelley was a fan of Keats's poetry, however, and when Keats died of tuberculosis at the age of twenty-five, Shelley was moved to write a poem of fifty-five stanzas based on the Greek myth of Adonis, a boy—loved by the goddess Venus—who was killed by a boar while hunting. Shelley mistakenly believed that Keats's death had been caused in part by a bad review of a pamphlet of his poems. The poem both mourns Keats and attacks his critics, but perhaps the most striking aspect of *Adonais* is Shelley's image of Keats, through death, becoming a part of the beauty Keats's own work was often trying to communicate, as shown here in stanza forty-three:

> He is a portion of the loveliness
> Which once he made more lovely: he doth bear
> His part, while the one Spirit's plastic* stress
> Sweeps through the dull dense world, compelling there,
> All new successions to the forms they wear;
> Torturing th' unwilling dross* that checks its flight
> To its own likeness, as each mass may bear;
> And bursting in its beauty and its might
> From trees and beasts and men into the Heaven's light.

*plastic pliable

*dross scum; waste material

An Early Death

The last poem Shelley began before his death was to be called "The Triumph of Life." It is pointless, though tempting, to guess what Shelley's life and work might have produced if he had not drowned while sailing off the coast of Italy on 8 July 1822. A squall wrecked his boat as he was sailing home from a visit with friends in Leghorn, killing Shelley and two companions. (Shelley was an avid sailor throughout his life and even fantasized about the prospect of sailing down all the major rivers of the world.) It is easy to think of Shelley as a Romantic poet who died tragically before he could really blossom, but the body of work Shelley left behind is so rich that it seems unnecessary to become caught up in myth and speculation. After Shelley's death, Byron wrote in a letter to a friend, "There is thus another man gone about whom the world was ill-naturedly, and ignorantly, and brutally mistaken" (letter to Thomas Moore, 8 August 1822, in *The Selected Letters of Lord Byron,* edited by Jacques Barzun); but Shelley's poetry and writing remain vital, challenging, and thankfully received.

Selected Bibliography

IF YOU LIKE the poetry of Shelley, you might also like the poetry of George Gordon, Lord Byron, or of John Keats.

WORKS BY PERCY BYSSHE SHELLEY

Poetry

Queen Mab; A Philosophical Poem (1813).

Alastor; or, The Spirit of Solitude: and Other Poems (1816).

History of a Six Weeks' Tour throughout a Part of France, Switzerland, Germany, and Holland (1817).

The Revolt of Islam: A Poem in Twelve Cantos (1818).

Rosalind and Helen, a Modern Eclogue; with Other Poems (1819).

The Cenci: A Tragedy, in Five Acts (1819).

Prometheus Unbound: A Lyrical Drama in Four Acts, with Other Poems (1820).

Swellfoot the Tyrant, a Tragedy in Two Acts (1820).

Adonais: An Elegy on the Death of John Keats (1821).

Epypsychidion (1821).

Hellas: A Lyrical Drama (1822).

Available Collections

The Complete Poetical Works of Percy Bysshe Shelley. Edited by Neville Rogers. 2 vols. Oxford, U.K.: Clarendon Press, 1972–1975.

The Letters of Percy Bysshe Shelley. 2 vols. Edited by Frederick L. Jones. Oxford, U.K.: Oxford University Press, 1964.

The Poems of Shelley. Edited by Geoffrey Matthews and Kelvin Everest. London: Longman, 1989.

Posthumous Poems of Shelley. Montreal: McGill-Queen's University Press, 1969.

Prometheus Unbound: The Text and the Drafts. Edited by Lawrence John Zillman. New Haven, Conn.: Yale University Press, 1968.

Shelley: Selected Poems and Prose. Edited by G. M. Matthews. Oxford, U.K.: Oxford University Press, 1964.

Shelley's Adonais: A Critical Edition. Edited by Anthony D. Knerr. New York: Columbia University Press, 1984.

More About Shelley

You can find information about Shelley on the Internet at the Bartleby Archive at Columbia University:
http://www.columbia.edu/acis/bartleby/shelley/

Shelley's Poetry and Prose. Edited by Donald H. Reiman and Sharon B. Powers. New York: Norton, 1977.

Shelley's Prose; or, The Trumpet of a Prophesy. Edited by David Lee Clark. London: Fourth Estate, 1988.

WORKS ABOUT PERCY BYSSHE SHELLEY

Cameron, Kenneth Neill. *The Young Shelley: Genesis of a Radical.* London: Gollancz, 1951.

Chernaik, Judith. *The Lyrics of Shelley.* Cleveland: Press of Case Western University, 1972.

Holmes, Richard. *Shelley: The Pursuit.* New York: Dutton, 1975.

Rogers, Neville. *Shelley at Work.* Oxford, U.K.: Clarendon, 1967.

CHARLES SIMIC
(b. 1938)

by Karen Volkman

Beginnings

During World War II, when Charles Simic was three years old, German planes dropped bombs on the city of Belgrade in the former Yugoslavia, destroying the building next door to his home. The blast threw him out of bed and all the way across the room. On the following day, his family fled to the countryside. "I remember a beautiful meadow," he writes in *Wonderful Words, Silent Truth* (1990), "great clouds overhead, then suddenly a plane flying low."

This early memory, with its unexpected combination of violence and beauty, could almost be a moment in one of Simic's poems. Though he rarely writes "real" autobiographical poetry, the kind that sticks to the precise details of a writer's life, his poems often portray scenes of war-torn villages and bewildered characters trying to come to grips with a fantastic reality, almost as though they were living in a myth or fairy tale. By inventing a poetic world that is outside true history, Simic shows that violence, chaos, and mystery do not just occur from time to time but are part of a continuous human experience.

Simic's family scraped out a difficult existence in Belgrade during the war. While still a young child, he suffered extreme hunger and saw many shocking scenes, including the bodies of soldiers killed in air raids or shot by German soldiers. In 1944, his father, an engineer working for an American telephone company, escaped to Italy, intending to reach America and send for the family. It would be ten years before Simic saw his father again. In the meantime, his mother worked to support her two sons and schemed to arrange their flight from Yugoslavia. But when World War II ended, the country was again shaken by fighting, this time a civil war between supporters of a royalist* government and those who favored Communist rule. Within a short time, the Communists took power, establishing a repressive system of government and preventing citizens from emigrating.

As a child, Simic fell in love with books, first reading Westerns and adventure stories, then moving on to writers he discovered in his father's library, such as the novelists Charles Dickens and Fyodor Dostoyevsky. He also spent time with gangs of tough kids in the half-bombed city, sometimes taking part in petty thefts, and, at one time, skipping school for several months before he was caught. These two sides of the young Simic—reader and dreamer on the one hand, troublemaker on the other—were reflected in his family as well. His father's side was the rougher, more boisterous* one; his mother's, more cultivated, sophisticated, demure.* In the prose poem "I was stolen by the gypsies," Simic treats this conflicting legacy in his own distinctive way:

*royalist supportive of a monarchy

*boisterous rowdy

*demure reserved

> I was stolen by the gypsies. My parents stole me right
>   back. Then the gypsies stole me again. This went
>   on for some time. One minute I was in the caravan
>   suckling the dark teat of my new mother, the next
>   I sat at the long dining room table eating my break-
>   fast with a silver spoon.
> It was the first day of spring. One of my fathers was
>   singing in the bathtub, the other one was painting
>   a live sparrow the colors of a tropical bird.
>   (*The World Doesn't End*)

In this poem-fable, Simic depicts the two "fathers" as both being artists of a kind—one singing in the tub, the other painting. One art is spontaneous and natural, the other more exotic, ambitious, and even bizarre. But both arts are equally valuable and beautiful for the changes they make in the world around them: one father transforms the daily bath into an operatic occasion, while the other turns an ordinary sparrow into an exotic tropical bird. Finally, although the grammatical parallel with the "silver spoon" sentence suggests that the gypsy father is the singer and the more refined one is the painter, we can't be completely certain which is which. Simic loves to leave uncertainty and ambiguity* in his poems, reminding his readers that the world is a tricky place and that the truth—in this case, about identity or nature—can be shifting and elusive.

    ambiguity having more than one possible meaning

In 1948, Simic's mother made a brave attempt to escape with her sons, crossing the mountains into Austria in the hope of joining her husband in Italy. The family was caught by a British military patrol who, unaware of the harsh government policies in Yugoslavia, turned them over to the police. Simic and his younger brother spent a week in jail; their mother was imprisoned for several months. Finally, in 1953, she succeeded in obtaining a passport, and the three went to Paris to await approval of an immigration visa to America, where Simic's father had settled. Simic attended high school in Paris for a year, but, knowing little French, he found the schoolwork impossible and the teachers unsympathetic.

Escape to America

The family sailed for America in August 1954, and in New York, Simic, now sixteen, was reunited with his father, whom he had not seen since the age of six. Since the boy was nearly an adult, he and his father behaved more like friends than father and son, discussing literature and jazz and telling stories. Simic was fascinated by New York City, and his father encouraged his interest by taking him to jazz clubs and bookstores. After learning enough English to go to school, he began attending high school in Elmhurst, Queens. His family soon moved to Chicago, where he graduated from suburban Oak Park High

School in 1956. There he began writing poetry and painting, experimenting with a variety of styles based on the poets and artists he admired. After graduation, he worked as a proofreader for a newspaper while attending night classes at the University of Chicago. His first poems were published in the *Chicago Review* in 1959.

At the age of twenty, he moved back to New York and worked at a variety of jobs while taking night classes at New York University and living in Greenwich Village. Several poems in his 1990 collection, *The Book of Gods and Devils,* look back at the excitement of this time. In 1961, Simic was called up for army service. He was stationed first in Germany, then in eastern France in the town of Luneville, an experience he records in an autobiographical essay, "Luneville Diary." Finishing his service, he returned to New York and, in 1964, married Helen Dubin, a dress designer. His first book, *What the Grass Says,* was published in 1967, with other volumes quickly following.

Early Poetry

The poems in Simic's early collections are characterized by a literary quality known as *economy:* every word, line break, and pause works to important effect, and nothing is wasted. Though written with ordinary words, they are not simple poems; each of them suggests an underlying mystery, with the contrast between the plainness of their words and the strangeness of their images creating an eerie tension, as in the poem "Spoon," in which a common household object becomes strangely menacing:

> Eyeing you now
> From the table,
> Ready to scratch
>
> Today's date
> And your name
> On the bare wall.

(Selected Poems, 1963–1983,
revised and expanded edition, p. 35)

Simic's "thing poems," poems dealing with ordinary objects, were partly influenced by a group of poems by the Chilean poet Pablo Neruda called *Odas Elementales,* or *Elementary Odes.* Simic was delighted to find a poet writing about such untraditional poetic subjects as celery and a pair of socks. Simic's own efforts were not always appreciated, however. Here, the poet describes an editor's puzzled response to his poem "Fork": "I guess the editor's premise* was that there were things worthy of poetry and that the fork in my hand was not one of them. In other words, 'serious' subjects and 'serious' ideas make 'serious' poems, etc."

***premise** basis

But in Simic's poems, it is the very ordinariness of the fork or spoon which allows the process known as *defamiliarization,* in which the so-called ordinary object is looked at as though for the first time, with its strangeness suddenly recognized. Defamiliarization can also help poet and reader rise above their usual routines and feel the hidden mystery and interconnection that binds things together. Simic was influenced in this thinking by a group of European writers and artists called the surrealists,* who believed that great insights could be gained by placing seemingly unconnected words or objects near each other to show how the unconscious mind "arranged" them in significant ways.

***surrealist** an artist or poet involved in the art movement surrealism, which aimed (chiefly during the 1920s and 1930s) to express the workings of the unconscious or subconscious mind

Like virtually all of Simic's poetry, "Spoon" uses short lines and brief stanzas. Since his lines are frequently end-stopped—ending on punctuation or a natural syntactic* break between clauses—the reader must pause momentarily before going on to the next line. Meanwhile, the short stanzas also require a slight pause as the eye travels over the blank space that divides them. These small pauses add up to silences, which Simic regards as a crucial aspect of any poem. All poems are written over an underlying silence, but the pressure of that silence, as it resists the words that oppose it, can always be felt; it is in large part what gives the poem its shape and presence. In another early poem, "Dismantling the Silence," he imagines taking this overwhelming force to pieces:

***syntactic** related to the structure of a sentence; refers to word placement, as opposed to word choice

Take down its ears first.
Carefully, so they don't spill over.
With a sharp whistle slit its belly open.

Translations and Career Success

While working on his own poetry, Simic was also translating the work of other writers and introduced a number of important Yugoslavian poets to an American audience. In 1976, together with the poet Mark Strand, he edited an important anthology, *Another Republic,* featuring writers of Central and Eastern Europe (selected and often translated by Simic) and of Latin America (selected and translated by Strand). This anthology helped familiarize American readers with a number of writers already acclaimed in their own countries, such as Vasko Popa of Yugoslavia, Miroslav Holub of Czechoslovakia, and Czeslaw Milosz and Zbgniew Herbert of Poland. Simic has continued his translation projects and in 1992 published *The Horse Has Six Legs,* an anthology devoted exclusively to Serbian writers (one of the ethnic groups of the now divided Yugoslavia). This book includes work ranging from traditional songs to emerging poets of the present day. It is easy to see how this mischievous folk song, which Simic recalls singing as a child, may have influenced his own poetry:

> There smoke, sooty smoke,
> There is your door,
> And fried egg,
> And bread and butter,
> And your grandpa's bones
> With which to prick yourself.
>
> (*The Horse Has Six Legs,* p. 11)

Shortly after Simic's second collection, *Dismantling the Silence,* was published in 1971, he began receiving offers to teach at colleges and universities. At the time, many universities had introduced creative writing courses into the curriculum, and poets were in demand. Given his erratic educational history, Simic was at first amused by this development but eventually accepted a teaching position—and discovered that he enjoyed it.

After a few years, he settled into a job at the University of New Hampshire, where he teaches today. His books began appearing every three years or so, including *Return to a Place Lit by a Glass of Milk* (1974), *Charon's Cosmology* (1977), *Classic Ballroom Dances* (1980), and *Austerities* (1983). His *Selected Poems* (1986) featured work spanning twenty years. Each of the

Austerities

From the heel
Of a half loaf
Of black bread,
They made a child's head.

Child, they said,
We've nothing for eyes.
Nothing to spare for ears
And nose.

Just a knife
To make a slit
Where your mouth
Ought to be.

You can grin,
You can eat,
Spit the crumbs
Into our faces.

(*Collected Poems*)

title poems in these books gives a clue to one of his obsessions. "Return to a Place Lit by a Glass of Milk" depicts a haunting childhood memory and its uncanny persistence in the speaker's mind; "Charon's Cosmology" imagines the Greek mythic figure Charon, who takes newly dead souls across the river in the underworld, growing confused as to which side is which, a disturbing reflection of Simic's experience of life and death during the violence of the war; "Austerities" also recalls the hunger and desperation of wartime, in lines that are spare but startling.

The typical speaker in a Simic poem seems both naive and cynical, a simple asker of difficult questions. We can recognize here a quality of folklore or fable, but with a strange and contemporary turn at the end. Even in such a short poem as "Austerities" the images suggest an existence that is damaged and broken; the "child's head" is only one part of a strange being; the "heel" is just one part of the "half loaf"; the "mouth" is the only facial feature the strange creature can be given; and in the end he spits "crumbs," the tiniest fragments of bread. In this, as in many of his early and mid-career poems, the complex experience the poet wants to communicate comes to life through an image of shocking poverty or violence, a sudden leap to the grotesque—one made even more startling by the precision of the details.

In 1984, Charles Simic was awarded a prestigious MacArthur Foundation Fellowship for his sustained excellence as a poet.

The World Doesn't End

In 1990, Simic received another distinguished award, the Pulitzer Prize in Poetry, for a book of prose poems, *The World Doesn't End.* By the time Simic wrote his book of prose poetry, the form was nearly 150 years old and had produced a number of masterpieces, including Charles Baudelaire's *Paris Spleen,* Arthur Rimbaud's *Illuminations,* and Edmond Jabès's *The Book of Questions.* In spite of that, some American critics felt that only poems written in lines of verse could really be considered poetry. One critic, Hilton Kramer, wrote an editorial entitled "A Pulitzer for—What?" scoffing at the idea of the prose poem as a valid poetic form.

The World Doesn't End contains some of Simic's finest writing. The poem beginning with "Once I knew" is a haunting variation on one of his most common themes, the unknowability of the self: "Once I knew, then I forgot. It was as if I had fallen asleep in a field only to discover at waking that a grove of trees had grown up around me." The trees of the poem may be the complexity of the world, the huge variety of puzzling images from which the poet must create order. Later in the poem, the speaker, waking up in this chaotic reality, enters a drowsy state in which the possibility of making sense of the world appears tantalizing but ultimately elusive:

> I was already dozing off in the shade, dreaming that
> the rustling trees were my many selves explaining them-
> selves all at the same time so that I could not make out a
> single word. My life was a beautiful mystery on the verge
> of understanding, always on the verge! Think of it!

These "verge" moments are characteristic of Simic's speakers. The absolute, the elusive order, the solution to the beautiful mystery—all perpetually lurk just beyond the reach of the poetic imagination. They may be sensed, but they cannot be translated more fully into conscious thought or language. A momentary insight into that mysterious order, such as the speaker of the poem describes above, seems to prove just how far we are from reaching the absolute knowledge that is sensed as lost; instead of understanding, we have only confusing hints and clues. "The rustling trees," the world's multiplicity and the corresponding multiplicity of the self, offer up knowledge to the poet, but with so many possible explanations that a single meaning cannot be made out.

The attempt to decipher and order the many messages the world and the self offer are ongoing tasks in Simic's poetry. This may explain his interest in the visual artist Joseph Cornell, whose work he contemplates in the 1992 collection *Dime-Store Alchemy,* an unusual book that is part journal, part art criticism, and partly a series of prose poems inspired by Cornell's strange art. Cornell himself is equally hard to classify: his work is sometimes described as *assemblage,* in which the artist puts a variety of found objects together in unusual ways. Cornell often used small bottles filled with colored sand, feathers, marbles, newspaper clippings, old maps, dolls' heads, and other delicate objects, arranging them in old wooden boxes in combinations that seem like fragments of a half-remembered dream. Not surprisingly, Simic felt a kinship with Cornell's work and created a work that, like Cornell's, is hard to classify.

In the late 1990s, Simic continued to publish, translate, teach, and inspire young poets. His books of that period include the poetry collections *A Wedding in Hell* (1994), *Walking the Black Cat* (1996), and *Jackstraws* (1999), and a book of essays, *Orphan Factory* (1997). From a turbulent early life, full of dangers and uprootings, Charles Simic has created a poetry of dream images and mystery, humor and sometimes fear.

Selected Bibliography

WORKS BY CHARLES SIMIC
Poetry

What the Grass Says (1967).

Dismantling the Silence (1971).

IF YOU LIKE the poetry of Simic, you might also like the poetry of James Tate, Arthur Rimbaud, or Boris Pasternak.

🐦

Return to a Place Lit by a Glass of Milk (1974).

Charon's Cosmology (1977).

Classic Ballroom Dances (1980).

Austerities (1982).

Selected Poems, 1963–1983 (1985; revised and expanded, 1990).

Unending Blues (1986).

The World Doesn't End (1989).

The Book of Gods and Devils (1990).

Hotel Insomnia (1992).

A Wedding in Hell (1994).

Walking the Black Cat (1996).

Jackstraws (1999).

Prose

The Uncertain Certainty (1985).

Wonderful Words, Silent Truth (1990).

Dime-Store Alchemy: The Art of Joseph Cornell (1992).

The Unemployed Fortune Teller (1994).

Orphan Factory (1997).

Translations

The Little Box, Poems of Vasko Popa (1970).

Four Modern Yugoslav Poets (1970).

Another Republic: An Anthology of European and South American Poetry (edited with Mark Strand) (1976).

Selected Poems of Tomaz Salamun (1987).

The Horse Has Six Legs: An Anthology of Serbian Poetry (1992).

Night Mail: Selected Poems of Novica Tadic (1992).

WORKS ABOUT CHARLES SIMIC

Bedient, Cal. "Burning Alone." Review of *Selected Poems*. *Sewanee Review* 94: 657–668 (Fall 1986).

Bizarro, Patrick, ed. *Manassas Review: Essays on Contemporary Poetry, Charles Simic* 1 (winter 1978).

Hart, Henry. "Story-tellers, Myth-makers, Truth-sayers." Review of *The Book of Gods and Devils. New England Review* 15 (fall 1993): 192–206.

Haviaris, Stratis, ed. *Charles Simic at Large,* a special issue of the *Harvard Review* 13 (fall 1997).

McClatchy, J. D. "Figures in the Landscape." Review of *Classic Ballroom Dances. Poetry* 138 (July 1981): 231–241.

Rector, Liam. "Poetry Chronicle." Review of *Selected Poems. Hudson Review* 39 (autumn 1986): 501–515.

Stitt, Peter. "Staying at Home and Going Away." Review of *Selected Poems. Georgia Review* 40 (summer 1986): 557–571.

Vendler, Helen. "Totemic Shifting." *Parnassus: Poetry in Review* no. 18/no. 19, (1993): 86–99.

Weigl, Bruce, ed. *Charles Simic: Essays on the Poetry.* Ann Arbor: University of Michigan Press, 1996.

GARY SNYDER

(b. 1930)

by Michael Davidson

From the time that his two sons, Kai and Gen, were young, Gary Snyder took them backpacking in the mountains near their home in the Sierra Nevada* foothills. When they were four and five, they would go to nearby Bald Mountain and look back to their home on San Juan Ridge. When they were seven and eight, they went up to Grouse Ridge and looked back at Bald Mountain and beyond to their home. Later on, they went into the High Sierra, and from eight-thousand-foot English Mountain they could look back to Grouse Ridge, Bald Mountain, and home. When the boys were teenagers, they climbed Sierra Buttes and Mount Lassen, from which they could see Castle Peak, English Mountain, Grouse Ridge, Bald Mountain, and their home, in the far distance. "That is the way the world should be learned," Snyder says. "It's an intense geography that is never far removed from your body." (The above is based on an unpublished lecture by Snyder.)

*Sierra Nevada
mountains in eastern California, bordering western Nevada

The Beat Generation refers to writers who emerged in the 1950s and who attacked what they perceived as the conformism and conservatism of Cold War America. Allen Ginsberg, Jack Kerouac, and William Burroughs are the best known of the group.

This anecdote is a good introduction to Gary Snyder's poetry, since his work is always teaching the reader how to see the world more intensely, building from local details and looking back at what has already been learned. For instance, his poetry is sometimes crafted as a lesson in history in which he shows us how we can use what is valuable from a previous cultural tradition and apply it to current circumstances. At other times Snyder's poetry offers a lesson in geography, which for the poet means locating oneself in the present environment—knowing the names of plants, trees, land forms—yet always seeing the environment's relationship to other ecological systems and climates. The metaphor of walking is appropriate, too. Poetry, as Snyder has said, is like making trails in the mountains—the laying down of "riprap," that is, rocks placed to secure solid footing on unstable ground:

> Lay down these words
> Before your mind like rocks.
>   placed solid, by hands
> In choice of place, set
> Before the body of the mind
>   in space and time:
> Solidity of bark, leaf, or wall
>   riprap of things

"Riprap"(*Riprap*)

Although Gary Snyder is usually identified with the Beat Generation of writers, his work extends beyond group labels. His poetry is inspired by Asian literature (he has translated Chinese and Japanese poets) as well as by modern poets, such as Ezra Pound and William Carlos Williams. He has studied American Indian culture, drawing upon the lore of indigenous peoples* in formulating his theories of holistic* living. And whereas most of the principal Beat writers came from the urban East Coast, Snyder is a product of the Pacific Northwest, where he grew up. The influence of this region can be felt through his interest in mountaineering and backpacking, the love of the natural landscape, and his belief in the individualist, working-class spirit of the Industrial Workers of the World, the international labor union whose mission statement, "forming the structure of the new society within the shell of the old," could stand as Snyder's own.

*indigenous people the earliest human inhabitants of a place

*holistic concerned with how things interact and work as a complete system, as opposed to focusing on individual parts

Finding the Mountains

Gary Snyder was born in San Francisco on 8 May 1930. When he was two, his family moved to a small dairy farm outside Seattle, Washington, and later, when he was twelve, to Portland, Oregon. Like many depression*-era families, Snyder's parents, Harold and Lois Wilkie Snyder, had a hard time making ends meet, but he and his sister, Anthea, found plenty to occupy them in the Cascade and Olympic Mountains near their home. Backpacking and hiking provided Snyder with formative experiences with nature that became an important part of his writing. When, at age thirteen, he visited the Seattle Art Museum and saw its great collection of Chinese landscape paintings, he made an important link between the mountains depicted in Chinese scroll paintings and those of his own Pacific Northwest. It was a link that would reappear again and again in his writing.

depression the period of economic hardship in America in the 1930s following the stock market crash of 1929

In 1947, Snyder enrolled at Reed College in Portland. At Reed he met two other aspiring poets, Lew Welch and Philip Whalen, who became lifelong friends. All three poets were influenced by Lloyd Reynolds, a teacher of art history and Asian studies, who also taught them drawing and calligraphy, the Asian art of elegant penmanship. Snyder's bachelor's thesis, titled "Dimensions of a Myth," was an anthropological essay in which he focused on a traditional story told by the northwest Haida Indian tribe and showed how a single idea is expressed in multiple versions of the same tale: "Original mind speaks through little myths and tales that tell us how to *be* in some specific ecosystem of the far-flung world." (His thesis was published in 1979 as *He Who Hunted Birds in His Father's Village: The Dimensions of a Haida Myth.*) For the Haida people, as for Snyder, myths are not fantastic or unreal stories but guides for understanding the present. They provide models of community in balance with the natural environment.

Such interests inspired one of Snyder's earliest collections of poetry, *Myths and Texts.* Drawing from Northwest Indian mythology, Snyder explores the boundary between the reality of daily life and the myths created out of that life. Many of the poems in *Myths and Texts* are based on tales that the poet read in the U.S. Government–sponsored *Bureau of Ethnology Reports* and in Alfred Louis Kroeber's 1925 *Handbook of the Indians of California.* In his own book, Snyder attacks the misuse of land by modern industry and agricultural business. The book's three sections, "Logging," "Hunting," and "Burning" describe various ways in which the natural landscape is being despoiled. The forests sacred to primitive peoples are now being

> cut down
> Groves of Ahab, of Cybele
> Pine trees, knobbed twigs
>   thick cone and seed
>   Cybele's tree this, sacred in groves
> Pine of Seami, cedar of Haida . . .
> Cut down to make room for the suburbs
> *(Myths and Texts,* p. 14)

Ahab and Cybele are mythological figures associated with the destruction of nature; Seami and Haida represent Japanese and Native American traditions that celebrate nature in art and literature.

Against willful destruction of nature, Snyder contrasts Indian culture with its respect for the natural world. He criticizes modern hunters who track and kill deer from their cars. He then poses as an alternative the Native American hunter who sits for long hours imagining the condition of his prey:

> Deer don't want to die for me.
>   I'll drink sea-water
> Sleep on beach pebbles in the rain
> Until the deer come down to die
>   In pity for my pain
> *(Myths and Texts,* p. 26)

Myths and Texts represents the fruition of Snyder's anthropological studies in the early 1950s, but his first published book, *Riprap,* draws from his work as a trail builder, logger, and forest lookout. Poems in this volume seem formed out of natural landscape itself, lines consisting of hard, chiseled images with little commentary. Like his modernist masters, Ezra Pound and William Carlos Williams, Snyder pares away excess, leaving poems as stark and clear as a Japanese haiku.* "Mid-August at Sourdough Mountain Lookout," written while Snyder was a forest-fire lookout, condenses perceptions into short, compact lines:

Modernist poets rejected the ornamentation of much earlier poetry, and tried to infuse their work with immediacy and energy. See also the essay "Twentieth-Century Modernist Poetry" in these volumes.

***haiku** a Japanese poetic form, usually unrhymed and consisting of three lines of seventeen syllables. A haiku often contains only a single image.

> Down valley a smoke haze
> Three days heat, after five days rain
> Pitch glows on the fir-cones

Across rocks and meadows
Swarms of new flies.

(*Riprap*)

Journey to the East

Snyder read poems that were later published in *Riprap* at a famous poetry reading held in San Francisco in 1955 at a small art space called the Six Gallery. Among the writers present that evening was Jack Kerouac, who chronicled the Six Gallery reading in a passage in his 1958 novel *The Dharma Bums*. Kerouac's version of Snyder (called Japhy Ryder) as a Zen*-inspired, mountain-climbing scholar was a celebratory, if romantic, portrait that would follow Snyder throughout his life. During the Beat heyday, however, Snyder was far from San Francisco's bohemia,* living in Japan and studying Zen Buddhism at a monastery in Kyoto. During this period (1956–1968) Snyder devoted his time to Zen study, a discipline that involved reading and interpreting Buddhist scriptures and spending long hours sitting cross-legged (*zazen*) in meditation. Zen practice taught Snyder to concentrate on his immediate surroundings—including his own breathing and body—in an effort to become receptive to the larger patterns of natural and cosmic orders. Despite the strict regimen, Snyder's days in Kyoto were not spent exclusively in religious study. He traveled and backpacked throughout Japan, China, and India, part of the time with his second wife, the poet Joanne Kyger (he had been briefly married the summer of his senior year in college to Alison Gass), or with poets Allen Ginsberg and Peter Orlovsky. Snyder kept excellent records of his travels, and many of his journals from these years were published or else turned into poems.

***Zen Buddhism** a specific form of Buddhist religion that stresses meditation, zazen (sitting), and the interpretation of short parables or "koans."

***bohemia** a loosely grouped community of people (often writers, artists, and intellectuals) who share a nonconformist attitude toward mainstream society

Returning to the Mountains

Although Snyder returned often to Japan throughout his life, he moved back to California in the mid-1960s. It was during this period that he participated in the San Francisco youth culture movement, located in the city's Haight Ashbury district. He was present at the famous 1967 "Human Be-In" in Golden

Gate Park that launched the hippie movement,* and he became a well-known figure at poetry readings and political rallies. It was also during this period that he began to gain an international reputation through his environmental activism and his essays on ecology.

Snyder's four year marriage to Joanne ended in divorce in 1964, and he married his third wife, Masa Uehara, in 1967 on the rim of a volcano on a Japanese island. While the couple was still in Japan their first son, Kai, was born, in 1968. A second child, Gen, was born in San Francisco in 1969. When the family returned to the United States, they began work on their permanent home on the San Juan Ridge in the Sierra Nevadas. This home, with its Zen chapel (*Zendo*), sauna, and communal meeting place, surrounded by Douglas fir and black oak, became the center of a group of poets, artists, environmental activists, religious teachers, and naturalists. Called "Kitkitdizze," after a local shrub, this communal living experiment has persisted for decades and stands as the realization of many of Snyder's social goals.

Snyder's next major collection of verse, *The Back Country,* includes more poems that reflect his trail-making days of the 1950s and also writing from his Japanese sojourn and travels to India. The book's title reflects Snyder's love of the wilderness, but it also refers to the marginality* and wildness in human nature. Many of the poems could be described as "walking poems," charting the sights and sounds of a hike:

*marginality the social experience of people who live on the edges or within the margins of mainstream society

*skitter to skip, glide, or move lightly or rapidly along a surface

*stemmed in climbing, to plug or fill a narrow hole or crack

> Piute Creek—
> In steep gorge glacier-slick rattlesnake country
> Jump, land by a pool, trout skitter,*
> The clear sky. Deer tracks.
> Bad place by a falls, boulders big as houses,
> Lunch tied to belt,
> I stemmed* up a crack and almost fell
> But rolled out safe on a ledge
> and ambled on.
> "A Walk" (*The Back Country*)

Here, Snyder describes a hike to Benson Lake in the eastern Sierras. The irregular lines map the shifting changes of scenery, movement, and incident as the speaker moves along the trail. "Jump, land by a pool, trout skitter," registers the translation of human motion ("jump") into animal response

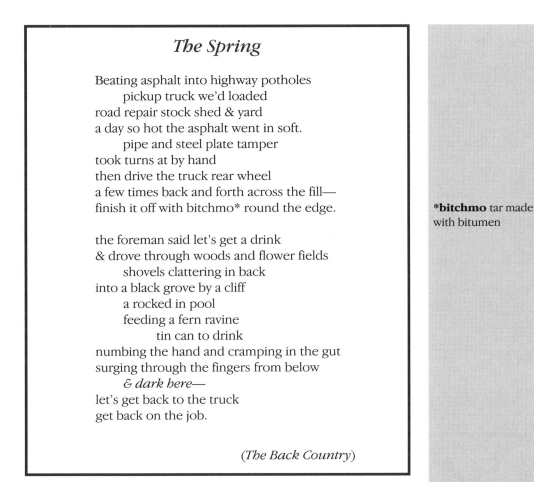

The Spring

Beating asphalt into highway potholes
     pickup truck we'd loaded
road repair stock shed & yard
a day so hot the asphalt went in soft.
     pipe and steel plate tamper
took turns at by hand
then drive the truck rear wheel
a few times back and forth across the fill—
finish it off with bitchmo* round the edge.

the foreman said let's get a drink
& drove through woods and flower fields
     shovels clattering in back
into a black grove by a cliff
     a rocked in pool
      feeding a fern ravine
        tin can to drink
numbing the hand and cramping in the gut
surging through the fingers from below
     & dark here—
let's get back to the truck
get back on the job.

(*The Back Country*)

bitchmo tar made with bitumen

("trout skitter"). The poem is less "about" what the poet sees on his walk than it is the embodiment of that walk through the poem's shifting rhythms. Snyder's care for natural detail plus his extraordinary ear for the acoustic* qualities of consonants and vowels mark his best work.

acoustic relating to sound

Rediscovering Turtle Island

With Snyder's settlement in the Sierra foothills in the late 1960s, issues involving community and family begin to pervade his work. Some of these concerns can be felt in his first collection of prose, *Earth House Hold,* published in 1969. This book contains sections from his mountain-lookout journal, his travels in India, and his lif in Japan. It also includes one of his most important essays on poetry, "Poetry and the

*Paleolithic relating
to the earliest period
of the Stone Age,
which was character-
ized by rough or
chipped stone imple-
ments

Primitive." Here Snyder states his belief that as a poet he shares values with the most ancient of people, going back to the Paleolithic*: "Poetry must sing or speak from authentic experience. Of all the streams of civilized tradition with roots in the paleolithic, poetry is one of the few that can realistically claim an unchanged function and a relevance which will outlast most of the activities that surround us today" (*Earth House Hold,* p. 118).

The increasing destruction of wild nature—the expansion of cities into suburbs, the pollution of the air and water through toxic waste—challenges our ability to learn from the primitive. Snyder's awareness of this challenge is powerfully invoked in his next two books, *Regarding Wave* and *Turtle Island,* the latter of which won the prestigious Pulitzer Prize in 1975. His poems of this period turn from the more objective depictions of natural landscape to what he calls "the real work" of building an alternate society. He yearns for the return of what Native Americans called "Turtle Island," the original name for the North American continent, and in *Turtle Island* he records signs that a new generation seeks a similar transformation:

*scat dung; excrement

> Turtle Island returned.
> my friend broke open a dried coyote-scat*
> removed a ground squirrel tooth
> pierced it, hung it
> from the gold ring
> in his ear.
>
> "Tomorrow's Song" (*Turtle Island*)

In other poems of this period, Snyder speaks directly to the reader, urging us to become aware of our surroundings. In "What You Should Know To Be a Poet" (from *Regarding Wave*), Snyder recommends local knowledge over abstract theories. One needs to know

> all you can about animals as persons.
> the names of trees and flowers and weeds.
> names of stars, and the movements of the planets
> and the moon.

Snyder always regarded his poetry as having an educational component, and his commitment as a teacher became more direct when he joined the University of California at Davis in 1986 as a professor of English literature and creative writing. In the 1990s he completed his epic poem, begun in the 1960s, *Mountains and Rivers Without End,* and published his selected poems in a book called *No Nature.* His various essays on the environment and wilderness have been collected in several volumes (*The Practice of the Wild; A Place in Space: Ethics, Aesthetics, and Watersheds*), and the Sierra Club has published a collection of essays on his life and work. His marriage to Masa having ended in divorce in 1987, he continued to live in the Sierra Nevada foothills, now with his fourth wife, Carole Koda, and their children.

Gary Snyder continued a distinctly American tradition in poetry that yoked the vocation of writer to that of social activist, teacher, and wanderer. From Henry David Thoreau and Walt Whitman to Adrienne Rich and Allen Ginsberg, poets like Snyder have regarded poetry as a vehicle of social change and education. More than any poet of the post–World War II era, Snyder has made us aware of the fragility of the natural landscape, its vulnerability to exploitation and neglect. He has also been singularly important in raising consciousness about the rights of the nonhuman—from gray whales to watersheds— and has tried to be a voice for natural forms and species that cannot speak for themselves. These environmental concerns, while significant in themselves, circulate the more powerfully because of Snyder's uncompromising clarity and rigor as a poet. His economical use of language and his spare imagery provide a verbal equivalent of the social balance he envisions for an ideal community. And his impact on subsequent poets has been substantial. Like the mountains that surround his home, Gary Snyder represents, for a younger generation of poets, a vantage from which to imagine the territory ahead.

Selected Bibliography

WORKS BY GARY SNYDER
Poetry

Riprap (1959).

Myths and Texts (1960).

Riprap, and Cold Mountain Poems (1965).

IF YOU LIKE the poetry of Snyder, you might also like the poetry of Walt Whitman, Allen Ginsberg, or Adrienne Rich.

❧

Six Sections from Mountains and Rivers Without End (1965).

A Range of Poems (1966).

The Back Country (1968).

Regarding Wave (1970).

Turtle Island (1974).

Axe Handles (1983).

Left Out in the Rain: New Poems 1947–1985 (1986).

No Nature: New and Selected Poems (1992).

Mountains and Rivers Without End (1996).

Prose

Earth House Hold: Technical Notes and Queries to Fellow Dharma Revolutionaries (1969).

The Old Ways: Six Essays (1977).

He Who Hunted Birds in His Father's Village: The Dimensions of a Haida Myth (1979).

Passage Through India (1983).

The Practice of the Wild: Essays (1990).

A Place in Space: Ethics, Aesthetics, and Watersheds: New and Selected Prose (1995).

Interviews and Talks

Faas, Ekbert. *Towards a New American Poetics: Essays and Interviews. Charles Olson, Robert Duncan, Gary Snyder, Robert Creeley, Robert Bly, Allen Ginsberg.* Santa Barbara, Calif.: Black Sparrow, 1978.

McLean, William Scott, ed. *The Real Work: Interviews and Talks 1964–1979.* New York: New Directions, 1980.

Robertson, David, "Practicing the Wild: Present and Future Plans. An Interview with Gary Snyder." In *Critical Essays on Gary Snyder.* Edited by Patrick D. Murphy. Boston: G. K. Hall, 1990.

WORKS ABOUT GARY SNYDER

Altieri, Charles. *Enlarging the Temple: New Directions in American Poetry During the 1960s.* Lewisburg, Pa.: Bucknell University Press, 1979.

Beach, Christopher. *The ABC of Influence: Ezra Pound and the Remaking of American Poetic Tradition.* Berkeley: University of California Press, 1992.

Davidson, Michael. *The San Francisco Renaissance: Poetics and Community at Mid-Century.* New York: Cambridge University Press, 1989.

Dean, Tim. *Gary Snyder and the American Unconscious: Inhabiting the Ground.* New York: St. Martin's Press, 1991.

Halper, Jon, ed. *Gary Snyder: Dimensions of a Life.* San Francisco: Sierra Club, 1991.

Kern, Robert. "Recipes, Catalogues, Open Form Poetics: Gary Snyder's Archetypal Voice." *Contemporary Poetry* 18, no. 2 (1977):173–197.

Molesworth, Charles. *Gary Snyder's Vision: Poetry and the Real Work.* Columbia: University of Missouri Press, 1983.

Murphy, Patrick, ed. *Critical Essays on Gary Snyder.* Boston: G. K. Hall, 1990.

Murphy, Patrick D. *Understanding Gary Snyder.* Columbia: University of South Carolina Press, 1992.

Norton, Jody. "The Importance of Nothing: Absence and Its Origins in the Poetry of Gary Snyder." *Contemporary Literature* 28 (spring 1987):41–66.

Parkinson, Thomas. "The Poetry of Gary Snyder." *Southern Review* 4 (summer 1968):616–632.

Steuding, Bob. *Gary Snyder.* Boston: Twayne, 1976.

✍

More About Snyder:

You can find information about Gary Snyder on the Internet at: http://wwwenglish.ucdavis.edu/faculty/snyder/snyder.htm

WILLIAM STAFFORD

(1914–1993)

by Peter Sears

Prose quotations throughout are taken from "William Stafford," *Contemporary Authors: Autobiography Series*, Vol. 3. Detroit, Mich.: Gale Research Company Book Tower, 1985. Sources for poetry are as noted.

ew North American poets of the twentieth century enjoyed genuine popularity during their lifetime. William Stafford is an exception. When two forest rangers were placed in charge of a series of signs about history and nature at seven sites along the Methow River in northern Washington, they wanted to ask William Stafford to write poems for these plaques. Forest rangers? Poems? What a novel idea! And what a testament to the popularity of William Stafford! This water-planning project is also noteworthy for another reason: the poems on the signs are not about the project, or about events that took place at the sites, or even about the particular sites themselves. What, then, are they about? One of the poems, "Time for Serenity, Anyone?" (from *The Methow River Poems*), starts simply with what the poet likes:

> I like to live in the sound of water,
> in the feel of mountain air. A sharp
> reminder hits me: this world is still alive.
> it stretches out there shivering toward its own

creation, and I'm a part of it. Even my breathing
enters into this elaborate give-and-take,
this bowing to sun and moon, day or night,
winter, summer, storm, still—this tranquil
chaos, that seems to be going somewhere.
This wilderness with a great peacefulness in it.
This motionless turmoil, this everything dance.

The first two lines of the poem make it clear that the poet likes nature: "I like to live in the sound of water, / in the feel of mountain air." This experience serves for him as a "sharp reminder" that "this world is still alive. / . . . and I'm a part of it." The following lines are less easy to understand right away. Not all lines in poetry are easy; that is the chance the poet takes. Stafford continues, "Even my breathing / enters into this elaborate give-and-take." He describes "this tranquil / chaos" and "this motionless turmoil"; these two phrases are very much alike—both combine calmness and wild motion. Why do that? Probably to bring attention to the point, which is that the calmness and the wild motion of this world exist at the same time. At the end of the poem Stafford calls it "this everything dance."

> *I like to imagine William Stafford standing at the site of the poem, at a roadside pull-off, looking out over the river. . . .*

I like to imagine William Stafford standing at the site of the poem, at a roadside pull-off, looking out over the river, noting "the sound of water, / . . . the feel of mountain air" and writing the poem. More likely, though, he stood there and absorbed the scene—and later, at home, reimagined it and wrote the poem. Once he had put those few details from the scene down on paper, off he went into his imagination: the poem changes at line four from descriptive to philosophical. That most of the lines are philosophical is not characteristic of Stafford's poems, which usually include more physical details of an actual scene and, sometimes, someone else in the scene. This someone else may be you, the reader. Stafford liked the idea of a poem as a sharing with the reader. Another of the *Methow River Poems* is "Ask Me" (in *Stories That Could Be True: New and Collected Poems*):

Some time when the river is ice ask me
mistakes I have made. Ask me whether
what I have done is my life. Others
have come in their slow way into
my thought, and some have tried to help

or to hurt: ask me what difference
their strongest love or hate has made.

I will listen to what you say.
You and I can turn and look
at the silent river and wait. We know
the current is there, hidden; and there
are comings and goings from miles away
that hold the stillness exactly before us.
What the river says, that is what I say.

At the outset, the reader is invited into the poem to ask the poet some interesting questions—for example, "what difference / their strongest love or hate has made." Stafford adds that he "will listen to what you say." If you as a reader are thinking of questions to ask, the poem has become a sort of conversation.

Stafford takes the poem further without fanfare. Note how slowly the poem moves. He just lets you assume that if you were indeed there with him, he would not only "listen to what you say" but also respond to what you say. Then he shifts ever so slightly, saying,

You and I can turn and look
at the silent river and wait. We know
the current is there, hidden . . .

It is hidden under the ice—we know that from the first line. The river is frozen, that is why it is "silent." So what are we waiting for?

Does the poem further reveal itself? Yes, it does. What come next are "comings and goings from miles away / that hold the stillness exactly before us." Here, we are helped by having read another of Stafford's poems. We know from the previous poem that the poet cherishes nature for its "great peacefulness." So here is the poet telling his guest that he or she is welcome to ask him revealing questions about his life and that he will encourage his guest to join him and "turn and look / at the silent river and wait." But if the guest is waiting for him to speak, the guest will be disappointed. He, the poet, is there to experience "the stillness." You—the reader, the guest—are welcome to join him.

*sublime situated or rising high up; produc-ing a sense of awe or high emotion
*maudlin overly emo-tional or sentimental

Stafford focuses attention on "the stillness" by using the word "exactly," which is precisely chosen and placed: "the still-ness exactly before us." With that word, Stafford almost makes "the stillness" stand still. For the entire poem, there is no mo-tion, no sound. Here, before the frozen river, questions about one's life pale in importance in the face of the vastness of life. The poet opts for the sublime* experience of silence: "What the river says, that is what I say." The river says nothing; I say nothing. With a lesser poet, this last line might have been a maudlin* suggestion of the babbling brook of greeting-card verse. But in Stafford's poem, "What the river says" is nothing, is silence. The poem ends in an embodiment of "stillness."

"Ask Me" is one of my favorite Stafford poems. It is soft and simple and reads easily, yet for me it remains eerie, almost haunting, each time I read it. I marvel that the poet suggests you ask him about "mistakes I have made" and whether "what I have done is my life." I am disarmed by these questions. I would love to ask him these questions. At the same time, I know there is sleight of hand going on here, that I am being set up for a deflection, that the poet does not intend to dis-cuss these questions with the reader. Yet I like the poem more for being set up. And I am entranced by the way the poem moves so quietly down to the only emphatic word in it, the word "exactly." This word makes me feel that this moment of the poem is the moment of actually sensing "the stillness." That Stafford even conceived of writing another line after that next-to-last line amazes me. By sharing my experience of the poem with you, I am acting in accord with the poem. The con-versation in it goes on. The life of the poem goes on.

William Stafford's Life

William Stafford was born in Hutchinson, Kansas, on 17 January 1914. The oldest of three children, he found plenty of adven-ture in the little town. He wrote in his memoir, *Down in My Heart:* "Beyond that edge [of town] was adventure, fields for-ever, or rivers that wended over the horizon, forever. And in the center of the town was a library, another kind of edge, out there forever, to explore." Because his parents loved to read, he did too. As for writing: "The territory of the book looms so much in our lives that it seems natural we would write, engag-ing in the other half of the transaction." He liked growing up in

Traveling Through the Dark

Traveling through the dark I found a deer
dead on the edge of the Wilson River road.
It is usually best to roll them into the canyon:
that road is narrow; to swerve might make more dead.

By glow of the tail-light I stumbled back of the car
and stood by the heap, a doe, a recent killing;
she had stiffened already, almost cold.
I dragged her off; she was large in the belly.

My fingers touching her side brought me the reason—
her side was warm; her fawn lay there waiting,
alive, still, never to be born.
Beside that mountain road I hesitated.

The car aimed ahead its lowered parking lights;
under the hood purred the steady engine.
I stood in the glare of the warm exhaust turning red;
around our group I could hear the wilderness listen.

I thought hard for us all—my only swerving—
then pushed her over the edge into the river.

(*The Darkness Around Us Is Deep*)

Hutchinson. The poem "One Home" opens, "Mine was a Midwest home—you can keep your world." And it ends, "Wherever we looked the land would hold us up." The flat land of the Midwest, the prairie, was land Stafford loved. In his memoir he recalls a camping trip out along the Cimarron River:

How slow and majestic the day was, and the sunset. No person was anywhere, nothing, just space, the solid earth, gradually a star, the stars. . . . That encounter with the size and serenity of the earth and its neighbors in the sky has never left me. The earth was my home; I would never feel lost while it held me.

William Stafford was a teenager during the 1930s, the dark years of the Great Depression, when the family moved from one small Kansas town to another as his father followed the work crews. Stafford had many jobs before graduating from high school. To attend the University of Kansas he waited on tables. But he was excited to be away at college, and his writing developed there. As he recalls:

> Once in the evening in the library something happened that linked to my dream-vision night along the Cimarron. . . . It was winter; a strange, violet light was in the sky—a color typical of clear prairie evenings. . . . Something about the light, and the quiet library, and my being away from home—many influences at once—made me sit and dream in a special way. I began to write. What came to me was a poem, with phrases that caught the time, my feelings. I was as if in a shell that glowed.

Early on, Stafford experienced a deep connection between nature and writing. They both gave him an opportunity to explore his inner being. A third source of inspiration was his home, for it was at home, through his family, that he first experienced love and devotion. Stafford was nurtured by his parents to have a strong sense of personal integrity and responsibility. Although the family did not belong to a particular church or regularly attend services, the parents encouraged in their children a sense of justice, integrity, and tolerance.

This inner strength was tested soon after Stafford arrived at the University of Kansas. Activist students took part in protests against the segregative* policy of the university dining hall. Stafford was one of these students. "I didn't have to be black to be bitter about it [the policy]," he noted in his memoir.

At the same time, World War II was drawing near. "History was stalking us," Stafford recalled. His experience in this "kind of social action was a new feeling for me." He was drawn to the pacifists: "That fit my feelings." He became a CO (conscientious objector*) and served in civilian public service from 1942 to 1946 in Arkansas and California, doing forest service work and soil conservation. "Life as a conscientious objector in a popular war," Stafford wrote in his memoir, "was an intensive lesson in certain ways to live." In the CO camp, "we were surrounded by challenges that had to do with that tension between open, daily life and the interior life that distinguishes individuals from each other. The two parts of my life that blended or clashed in making my writing were in constant

segregative separating, especially of people of different races

conscientious objector a pacifist; someone whose religious, philosophical, or ethical beliefs prevent him or her from willingly going to war

alertness." Stafford experienced what it meant to live by one's convictions. His fictionalized version of these four years was the subject of his first book, *Down in My Heart,* his master's "creative thesis" at the University of Kansas in 1946.

In 1943, William Stafford met Dorothy Frantz, the daughter of a minister, in a church at a CO camp outside Santa Barbara, California. They were married in 1944. Their "big break," as the poet describes it, took place in 1948, when he was offered a teaching position at Lewis and Clark College in Portland, Oregon. There they stayed and raised a family of four children in Lake Oswego, a town outside Portland.

Their one prolonged absence from Oregon was a 1950–1952 sojourn at the Iowa Writers Workshop at the University of Iowa. "Those years," wrote Stafford, "remain the principal reference point I have for the literary life as lived by others." The comment is interesting for the way it reveals how solitary Stafford saw his literary life up to that point. It was another eight years before "my first collection [of poems], *West of Your City. . . .* This was 1960, and I was forty-six years old." He was turning out poems at a fast clip: "An average of fifty were in the mail to editors [at any one time] all through the fifties, sixties, and seventies." Did he ever burn out or fear that he might? Regarding this question he is known for the following advice: "Lower your standards." More to the point, though, he kept up a practice he had developed during his CO years, getting up very early in the morning to write, and he never lacked subject matter: "Because my writing was an ongoing linking of the inner river of my life to my emergent realizations that daily experience brought, I was never without material. It seemed that even if I wrote as fast as I could I would never catch up to my life."

His first book had been published by a small press. His second book of poems, *Traveling Through the Dark,* was from a large publisher, Harper and Row. It won the National Book Award and brought Stafford's poetry closer to a generation that had to contend with questions of conscience, such as the Vietnam War. Because of his background of protest, Stafford was invited by students to many college campuses to read his poems. He delighted in these engagements but was uneasy because students often made mistaken assumptions about his stance. As he put it in his memoir, "Another little quirk isolated me, a reluctance to put my writing to work for any cause."

*chapbook a small book of ballads, poems, tales, or the like

Seven other collections followed from Harper and Row, among many other books and chapbooks.* In 1964, Stafford was awarded the Shelley Memorial Award from the Poetry Society of America, and in 1970 he was named Poetry Consultant to the Library of Congress, becoming a poetry ambassador of sorts, reading his poems all over the world. Back home, he was named the first poet laureate of the state of Oregon. By the time he died, in 1993, William Stafford, through his person, his poetry, and his teaching, may have come as close as a poet of his century could to creating a public role for poetry in the United States.

IF YOU LIKE the poetry of Stafford, you might also like the poetry of Gary Snyder.
✑

Selected Bibliography

WORKS BY WILLIAM STAFFORD
Poetry

Winterward (1954).

West of Your City (1960).

Traveling Through the Dark (1962).

The Rescued Year (1966).

Eleven Untitled Poems (1968).

Weather: Poems (1969).

Allegiances (1970).

Temporary Facts (1970).

Someday, Maybe (1973).

In the Clock of Reason (1973).

That Other Alone (1973).

Going Places: Poems (1974).

The Earth (1974).

North by West (1975).

Braided Apart (1976).

Late, Passing Prairie Farm (1976).

Stories That Could Be True: New and Collected Poems (1977).

The Design and the Oriole (1977).

Two About Music (1978).

All About Light (1978).

Tuned in Late One Night (1978).

Passing a Creche (1978).

Tuft by Puff (1978).

The Quiet of the Land (1979).

Around You, Your House and a Catechism (1979).

Things Happen Where There Aren't Any People (1980).

Absolution (1980).

Passwords (1980).

Wyoming Circuit (1980).

Sometimes Like a Legend: Puget Sound Poetry (1981).

A Glass Face in the Rain: New Poems (1982).

Segues: A Correspondence in Poetry (with Marvin Bell) (1983).

Roving Across Fields: A Conversation and Uncollected Poems, 1942–1982 (1983).

Smoke's Way: Poems from Limited Editions, 1968–1981 (1983).

Stories and Storms and Strangers (1984).

Listening Deep (1984).

Wyoming (1985).

Brother Wind (1986).

An Oregon Morning (1987).

You and Some Other Characters (1987).

Writing the World (1988).

Annie-Over (with Marvin Bell) (1988).

A Scripture of Leaves (1989).

Fin, Feather, Fur (1989).

Kansas Poems (1990).

How to Hold Your Arms When It Rains (1990).

Passwords (1991).

The Long Sigh the Wind Makes (1991).

History Is Loose Again (1991).

My Name Is William Tell (1992).

Seeking the Way (1992).

Even in Quiet Places (includes *The Methow River Poems;* 1996).

Prose

Down in My Heart (1947). A memoir.

Writing the Australian Crawl: Views on the Writer's Vocation (1978). Essays and interviews.

You Must Revise Your Life (1986). Essays and interviews.

The Animal That Drank Up Sound (1992). Children's book with illustrations by Debra Frasier.

WORKS ABOUT WILLIAM STAFFORD

Andrews, Tom, ed. *On William Stafford: The Worth of Local Things.* Ann Arbor: University of Michigan Press, 1995.

Carpenter, David A. *William Stafford.* Boise, Idaho: Boise State University Western Writers Series, no. 72, 1986.

Holden, Jonathan. *The Mark to Turn: A Reading of William Stafford's Poetry.* Lawrence: University Press of Kansas, 1976.

Kitchen, Judith. *Understanding William Stafford.* Columbia: University of South Carolina Press, 1989.

More About Stafford

You can write to:
Friends of William Stafford
P.O. Box 592
Lake Oswego, OR 97034

GERTRUDE STEIN

(1874–1946)

by Lyn Hejinian

I n the twentieth century, people often expressed admiration for newness and originality. A lively tradition of experimentation is a major part of the history of all the modern arts. As a result, people have been able to experience the things around them in new and exciting ways. For example, MTV introduced radical visual experiences to a wide audience, and people learned to see differently. They discovered ways to make quick and unusual connections between things. They, in essence, learned a new artistic "grammar."

Despite our culture's wide exposure to experimentation, however, the inventive work of Gertrude Stein remains for many people difficult to understand. Even if people know that Stein wrote sentences like "A tiny violent noise is a yellow happy thing" or "A balance in a sentence makes it state that it is staying there" or "A rose is a rose is a rose," they rarely understand what she meant.

In part, this is because people fail to make a distinction between the everyday uses of language and its artistic or *poetic* uses. They approach every piece of writing expecting to get a

Quotations from Stein's work throughout are taken from the editions listed in the bibliography under "Available Collections and Editions."

message from it—a piece of information. One cannot read the work of Gertrude Stein as one reads a newspaper article, however. Instead one must view each sentence of her work as representing the *shape* and *flow of thought*. Stein's writing is "experimental," but not because it looks or sounds strange. Stein was an experimental writer because she made her writing into a laboratory for studying thought and language. This took considerable heroism on her part, since the results were often ridiculed.

Stein began writing when she was in college, but her main interest was science, particularly psychology, and that is primarily what she studied. From early childhood she had been observing human nature. As she grew into adulthood, she became especially interested in the ways in which we perceive the world. In order to study perception, Stein found that she also had to study language, since for most of us language is the ever-present and natural medium for discovering, testing, defining, and asserting reality.

Early Life

Gertrude Stein was born to Jewish-Bavarian parents, Daniel and Amelia Stein, on 3 February 1874, in Allegheny, Pennsylvania, the baby of the family. "One should always be the youngest member of the family," she said. "It saves you a lot of bother everybody takes care of you" (*Everybody's Autobiography*, p. 70). When Stein was still an infant, the family moved to Austria. Three years later the family moved again, this time to France. As a result, Stein spoke German and French before she spoke English. Even at a very young age, Stein seemed fascinated by language. Her aunt Rachel, who lived with the family in Vienna, wrote, "Our little Gertie is a little Schnatterer.* She talks all day long and so plainly. . . . [She] toddles around the whole day & repeats everything that is said or done" (Brinnin, p. 6).

Schnatterer German word meaning chatterbox; someone who talks all the time

When Stein was five, the family returned to the United States, first to Baltimore and then to Oakland, California. Her brother, Leo, was her closest companion, and frequently they went to art museums or to the theater or opera together. They loved to read, and they would often read the same books and discuss them with each other: books by writers like Jules Verne and Mark Twain and all of Shakespeare. They also read history books and books about science, and they adored encyclopedias. This period came to an end in 1888, when Stein was fourteen years old. That year her mother died. Three years later her father also died, leaving Michael Stein, the oldest of the children, to take over responsibility for the family.

When Stein was eighteen years old, she moved back to Baltimore to live "with a whole group of very lively little aunts" (*Lectures in America,* p. 168). Living with these aunts, Stein's fascination with language was reawakened.

> If they had to know anything and anybody does they naturally had to say and hear it often, anybody does, and as there were ten and eleven of them they did have to say and hear said whatever was said and any one not hearing what it was they said had to come in to hear what had been said. That inevitably made everything said often. I began then to consciously listen to what anybody was saying and what they did say while they were saying what they were saying (*Lectures in America,* p. 169).

Listening to "the way everybody has to tell what they have to say," Stein began to imagine making portraits in words (*Lectures in America,* p. 135). She believed that she could grasp the essence of people through their manner of speaking and especially from their ways of repeating things.

> I began to get enormously interested in hearing how everybody said the same thing over and over again with infinite variations but over and over again until finally if you listened with great intensity you could hear it rise and fall and tell all that that there was inside them, not so much by the actual words they said or the thoughts they had but the movement of their thoughts and words endlessly the same and endlessly different (*Lectures in America,* p. 138).

In 1893, Stein entered Harvard Annex (today known as Radcliffe), a college for women. There she began her studies with the great psychologist and philosopher William James, the brother of the novelist Henry James. James was particularly interested in the way language gives us a view of the workings of human consciousness. He believed that we become aware of the world by speaking or writing about it. The shapes of language shape our perceptions; there is a "grammar" of perception. These ideas had a lasting effect on Stein.

Stein's use of language may seem unconventional, but it was not careless. In her essay "Poetry and Grammar" (in

Lectures in America), for example, she gives an account of her discoveries and opinions about punctuation and about the parts of speech (nouns, verbs, adjectives, prepositions, etc.). Her thoughts on punctuation are often witty.

> When I first began writing, I felt that writing should go on, I still do feel that it should go on but when I first began writing I was completely possessed by the necessity that writing should go on and if writing should go on what had colons and semi-colons to do with it, what had commas to do with it. . . . What had periods to do with it. Inevitably no matter how completely I had to have writing go on, physically one had to again and again stop sometime and if one had to again and again stop some time then periods had to exist. Beside I had always liked the look of periods and I liked what they did. . . . I did believe in periods and I used them (*Lectures in America*, p. 217).

After graduating from Harvard Annex in 1898, Stein entered medical school in Baltimore. She expected to have a career in psychology, but after a time there, "she was bored, frankly openly bored" (*The Autobiography of Alice B. Toklas*, p. 81), and she failed four of her courses. For Stein, medical school was not the best place to study language and the mind, and she left without receiving a medical degree.

Paris Before the War

In 1903, Stein moved to Paris to live with her brother Leo in an apartment at 27 rue de Fleurus. This was to be her address for the next thirty-four years. In Paris, Gertrude Stein found her real life's work.

Leo and Gertrude began to purchase paintings by exciting young artists. Conversations with the painters, and especially with Pablo Picasso, influenced Gertrude Stein's writing. "I was a little obsessed by words of equal value. Picasso was painting my portrait at that time, and he and I used to talk this thing over endlessly. . . . I began then to want to make a more complete picture of each word, and that is when the portrait business started" (*A Primer for the Gradual Understanding of Gertrude Stein,* pp. 17–18).

Stein had been working on *The Making of Americans* (the writing of it began in 1903 and ended in 1911; it was not published until 1925), and she had already written the stories called *Three Lives* (published in 1909). For the portraiture she was now interested in, however, she had to invent new ways to use language. Words would not tell stories or give descriptions; instead they would convey color and shape directly. One of the first portraits of this period is "Ada" (first published in *Geography and Plays*), a rapturous view of Alice B. Toklas, who had just arrived in Paris.

> **Ada was then one and all her living then one completely telling stories that were charming, completely listening to stories having a beginning and a middle and an ending. Trembling was all living, living was all loving, some one was then the other one. Certainly this one was loving this Ada then. And certainly Ada all her living then was happier in living than any one else who ever could, who was, who is, who ever will be living (*A Stein Reader*, p. 103).**

The admiration was mutual, and the friendship between the two women developed into a lifelong relationship. Meanwhile, Gertrude's relations with her brother became increasingly difficult. He disliked her writing, and worse, he tried to convince her that she was stupid. In 1913 Leo moved out. Gertrude stayed on in the rue de Fleurus apartment with Alice B. Toklas. Details from their daily life together appear in many of the poems. In the long love poem titled "Lifting Belly," (written in 1917 but not published until 1953), for example, we find lines capturing the rhythms of intimate conversation:

> We do not need butter.
> Lifting belly enormously and with song.
> Can you sing about a cow.
> Yes.
> And about signs.
> Yes.
> And also about Aunt Pauline.
> Yes.
> . . .
> In the midst of writing there is merriment.
>
> (*Bee Time Vine*)

"Aunt Pauline" was what Gertrude and Alice called their beloved Ford motor car, which they bought in 1916.

> ## *Stanza XV* (excerpt)
>
> I have thought that I would not mind if they came
> But I do.
> I also thought that it made no difference if they came
> But it does
> I also was willing to be found that I was here
> Which I am
> I am not only destined by not destined to doubt
> Which I do.
> Leave me to tell exactly well that which I tell.
> This is what is known.
>
> (*Stanzas in Meditation*)

*prose poem a short piece of creative prose that provides a glimpse of an imagined scene or character, or an unexpected view of a real scene or person. Prose poems do not use rhyme or meter.

In 1914, just before World War I erupted, Stein had completed *Tender Buttons,* one of her most radical works. Writing the work had demanded intense concentration. "I had to feel anything and everything that for me was existing so intensely that I could put it down in writing as a thing in itself without at all necessarily using its name" (*Lectures in America*, pp. 242–243). The resulting prose poems* are beautifully evocative and always puzzling. Perhaps Stein recognized that any actual reality, even of something as ordinary and familiar as a handkerchief, will always remain mysterious:

A Handkerchief.
A winning of all the blessings, a sample not a sample because there is no worry.

World War I and After

During World War I, Stein and Toklas traveled all over France as volunteers with the American Fund for the French Wounded, taking medical supplies to the soldiers and delivering blankets and clothing to civilians. "It was during these long trips that she began writing a great deal again. The landscape, the strange life stimulated her" (*The Autobiography of Alice B. Toklas*, p. 185).

By 1921 Stein had accumulated an enormous amount of writing. As she said, "If you write not long but practically every day you do get a great deal written" (*Lectures in America*, p. 200). *Geography and Plays*, a large collection of Stein's writings, was published in 1922, but despite its size, the collection represented only a small part of the work she was producing. It was not until after Stein's death that all of her work was published.

In 1923, Toklas and Stein spent the first of their summers in the country, where Stein began her observations of landscape. She often wrote outdoors, like a painter at an easel. Her friend, the American composer Virgil Thomson, recalled watching her at work one day.

> The scene took place in a field, its enactors being Gertrude, Alice, and a cow. Alice, by means of a stick, would drive the cow around the field. Then at a sign from Gertrude, the cow would be stopped; and Gertrude would write in her copybook. After a bit she would pick up her folding stool and progress to another spot, whereupon Alice would again start the cow moving around the field till Gertrude signaled she was ready to write again (Thomson, p. 70).

During this period, 1923–1929, Stein wrote many of her major works, including *Four Saints in Three Acts*, which she completed in 1927. The drama appeared in various published forms before it was turned into an opera by Virgil Thomson and published as an independent volume in 1934.

Tours and Triumphs

In 1926, Stein's friend, the British poet Edith Sitwell, had decided that Stein needed more publicity, and she had arranged for Stein to give a lecture tour in England. Stein wrote out her lecture as the essay *Composition as Explanation* and went to England. For days before the first lecture, Stein was desperately nervous, but her appearance was immediately successful, and after that she enjoyed the lecture tour.

Composition as Explanation was Gertrude Stein's first attempt to offer her opinions about writing. In the essay she speaks for the first time of her interest in what she calls the "continuous present." She wanted her writing to be based not on memory but on present observation. And she was discovering a relationship between landscape and writing. Both might be seen as compositions. The way thoughts move in a sentence might be similar to the way things move in a landscape.

Out of these simple observations, Stein began *How to Write,* a collection of writings about writing. Many people regard them as among the twentieth century's most profound studies of language. They are complex, but they are also delightful. "It makes me smile to be a grammarian and I am," she says (p. 107). "I return to sentences as to a refreshment" (p. 26). "This is a sentence" (p. 31). "Sentences are made wonderfully one at a time" (p. 34).

How to Write was published by Plain Edition, Alice B. Toklas's new publishing company. Both Alice and Gertrude had become increasingly frustrated by cowardly publishers who were afraid to publish experimental writing. Over the next two years (1931–1933), Plain Edition published seven of Stein's previously unpublished works. After that, Plain Edition became unnecessary. Gertrude Stein had become famous.

Publication of *The Autobiography of Alice B. Toklas* in 1933 brought a new level of success to Gertrude Stein. Easier to understand than her other works, the book became a bestseller in the United States, where readers were charmed by Stein's stories of her famous friends and acquaintances. People enjoyed her conversational style; it resembled gossip. Stein wrote *The Autobiography of Alice B. Toklas* for the public, but as she was working on it she was also writing another work. This one, *Stanzas in Meditation,* is considered by many to be her most private and difficult work, and it was not published until 1956, ten years after Stein's death.

In the wake of the success of *The Autobiography of Alice B. Toklas,* Stein began to make money and to receive invitations to visit the United States. In October 1934, Stein and Toklas arrived in New York. They were met by friends and swarms of reporters and were immediately swept up into a whirlwind of parties, sightseeing, and public appearances. Everywhere they went, Stein gave lectures. She and Toklas had tea at the White House, they attended a college football game, and in Chicago, they finally had a chance to see Virgil Thomson's production of *Four Saints in Three Acts,* which had been performed on Broadway earlier in the year by an all–African-American cast and was an enormous success. For Stein, who always loved reading detective novels, the high point of her visit was the opportunity to spend an evening riding around in a patrol car with two detectives from the Chicago homicide squad.

> *The high point of her visit was . . . riding around . . . with two detectives from the Chicago homicide squad.*

Return to France

Traveling all over the United States as a celebrity was exciting but tiring. When Stein returned to Paris, she was exhausted, and her fame seemed to have plunged her into depression. She recognized that in becoming more of a public personage, she had become less of a private person. She felt confused about herself and wondered if "I am I" only "because my little dog knows me" (*Four in America,* p. 119).

Meanwhile, events were beginning to change life in Europe. Adolph Hitler had come into power in Germany, attacks on Jews were under way, and in September 1939 war broke out. Because of the danger to Jews, the American consulate warned Stein that she and Toklas should leave France, but they refused to do so. Instead they closed up their Paris apartment and moved to the village of Bilignin, getting out just ahead of the invading Germans.

They were safe for a while, but in 1943 they were forced to leave Bilignin too. They moved to another village, but within months German and then Italian troops occupied the area. This time there was nowhere for them to go. Luckily, the villagers protected them. Despite danger and difficulties, Stein continued to write. She finished *Mrs. Reynolds,* a novel about a woman in Nazi-occupied France, and then she began the autobiographical *Wars I Have Seen.* After American troops liberated France in 1944, Stein and Toklas moved back to Paris.

On 27 July 1946, Gertrude Stein died of cancer. Her grave is in the famous Père-Lachaise cemetery in Paris. Alice B. Toklas, who lived until 1967, lies beside her. In an interview, Stein repeated advice that she had learned from her teacher William James. "Never reject anything. Nothing has been proved. If you reject anything, that is the beginning of the end" (*A Primer for the Gradual Understanding of Gertrude Stein,* p. 34). Following this advice, Stein turned writing into an adventure.

"Never reject anything. Nothing has been proved."

Selected Bibliography

WORKS BY GERTRUDE STEIN

Three Lives: Stories of the Good Anna, Melanctha, and the Gentle Lena (1909).

Tender Buttons: Objects, Food, Rooms (1914).

Geography and Plays (1922).

The Making of Americans: Being a History of a Family's Progress (1925).

Composition as Explanation (1926).

Useful Knowledge (1928).

Lucy Church Amiably (1930).

How to Write (1931).

Operas and Plays (1932). Includes *Four Saints in Three Acts*.

The Autobiography of Alice B. Toklas (1933).

Four Saints in Three Acts (1934).

Lectures in America (1935).

The Geographical History of America; or, The Relation of Human Nature to the Human Mind (1936).

Everybody's Autobiography (1937).

The World Is Round (1939).

What Are Masterpieces (1940).

Wars I Have Seen (1945).

Brewsie and Willie (1946).

Four in America (1947).

Last Operas and Plays (1949).

Mrs. Reynolds (1952).

Bee Time Vine, and Other Pieces, 1913–1927 (1953).

As Fine as Melanctha, 1914–1930 (1954).

Painted Lace (1955).

Stanzas in Meditation (1956).

A Novel of Thank You (1958).

Blood on the Dining-Room Floor (1982).

AVAILABLE COLLECTIONS AND EDITIONS

The Autobiography of Alice B. Toklas. New York: Vintage Books, 1961.

Everybody's Autobiography. New York: Vintage Books, 1973.

Gertrude Stein: Writings 1903–1932. Edited by Catherine R. Stimpson and Harriet Chessman. New York: The Library of America, 1998.

Gertrude Stein: Writings 1932–1946. Edited by Catherine R. Stimpson and Harriet Chessman. New York: The Library of America, 1998.

How Writing Is Written: Volume 2 of the Previously Uncollected Writings of Gertrude Stein. Edited by Robert Bartlett Haas. Santa Barbara, Calif.: Black Sparrow, 1974.

Lectures in America. Boston: Beacon Press, 1985.

A Primer for the Gradual Understanding of Gertrude Stein. Edited by Robert Bartlett Haas. Santa Barbara, Calif.: Black Sparrow, 1971.

Reflection on the Atomic Bomb: Volume 1 of the Previously Uncollected Writings of Gertrude Stein. Edited by Robert Bartlett Haas. Santa Barbara, Calif.: Black Sparrow, 1973.

A Stein Reader. Edited by Ulla E. Dydo. Evanston, Ill.: Northwestern University Press, 1993.

The Yale Gertrude Stein. Edited by Richard Kostelanetz. New Haven, Conn.: Yale University Press, 1980.

Writings and Lectures, 1909–1945. Edited by Patricia Meyerowitz. Baltimore: Penguin, 1971.

WORKS ABOUT GERTRUDE STEIN

Bridgman, Richard. *Gertrude Stein in Pieces.* New York and London: Oxford University Press, 1970.

Brinnin, John Malcolm. *The Third Rose: Gertrude Stein and Her World.* Reading, Mass.: Addison-Wesley, 1987.

Hemingway, Ernest. *A Moveable Feast.* New York: Charles Scribner's Sons, 1964.

Mellow, James R. *Charmed Circle: Gertrude Stein and Company.* New York: Avon, 1974.

Simon, Linda, ed. *Gertrude Stein Remembered.* Lincoln: University of Nebraska Press, 1994.

Sprigge, Elizabeth. *Gertrude Stein: Her Life and Work.* New York: Harper, 1957.

More About Stein:

You can find information
about Gertrude Stein on
the Internet at:

http://www.sappho.com/poetry
/g_stein.htm

http://www.tenderbuttons.com

http://www.columbia.edu/acis
/bartleby/stein/

Stendhal, Renate, ed. *Gertrude Stein in Words and Pictures: A Photobiography.* Chapel Hill, N.C.: Algonquin, 1994.

Sutherland, Donald. *Gertrude Stein: A Biography of Her Work.* New Haven, Conn.: Yale University Press, 1951.

Thomson, Virgil. *A Virgil Thomson Reader.* Boston: Houghton Mifflin, 1981.

Toklas, Alice B. *What Is Remembered.* New York: Holt, Rinehart, and Winston, 1963.

Wagner-Martin, Linda. *"Favored Strangers": Gertrude Stein and Her Family.* Piscataway, N.J.: Rutgers University Press, 1995.

WALLACE STEVENS

(1879–1955)

by John Koethe

On an ordinary morning when he was in his fifties or sixties, Wallace Stevens would get up early and dress in a conservative three-piece business suit. He would have breakfast and then set out on foot for his office at the Hartford Accident and Indemnity Company, an insurance firm where he was a vice president. As he walked the several miles from the house on Westerly Terrace where he lived with his wife, Elsie, in an affluent neighborhood in Hartford, Connecticut, he would begin composing a poem in his head. Sometimes there would be a glancing reference in the poem to the trees, streets, and other sights he passed as he walked, but on the whole his gaze was turned inward, for the poem was usually abstract and the process of composing it an intense and private meditation. When he arrived at his office, he would write out the poem and then revise it.

Some writers are reclusive,* but many live in the company of other writers, from whom they often draw encouragement and support. Stevens was no recluse, but the people he saw in his daily life were his fellow executives at the insurance

Quotations from Stevens's poetry throughout are taken from *Collected Poetry and Prose,* 1997.

*reclusive** withdrawn from society

company. They were aware of his poetry but had little interest in it or understanding of it. His relations with his wife were distant, and she discouraged visitors to their house. Stevens really inhabited two worlds, which had almost no connection with each other. He knew other poets and met and corresponded with them, but his day-to-day world was the social world of a conventional businessman. His other world was the world of his poems; he entered it on his walks to work, but it was contained almost entirely in his mind, in his imagination.

Stevens's Life

Wallace Stevens was born on 2 October 1879 in Reading, Pennsylvania. His father was a lawyer and his mother a former schoolteacher. He attended Harvard University from 1897 to 1900, where he studied French and German, served as president of the *Harvard Advocate* (the undergraduate literary magazine), and became friends with the philosopher George Santayana. After leaving Harvard without a degree, he worked for a while as a reporter for the *New York Tribune* but decided he did not care for journalism. He enrolled in New York Law School, from which he graduated in 1903. He practiced law with a number of firms, at the same time reading and writing poetry. In 1908 he began working as a lawyer for the first of several insurance firms, an occupation that he felt suited him. In 1916 he joined the Hartford Accident and Indemnity Company and moved to Connecticut, where he lived and worked for the rest of his life.

In 1904, Stevens met Elsie Kachel Moll on a summer trip to Reading, and they married four years later. A strikingly beautiful woman, she posed for the figure on two United States coins, the dime and the half-dollar (these coins were not the same as those in circulation today). In later years their marriage was not a close one, a fact that may be reflected in the sense of loneliness that runs through many of Stevens's late poems. He once recounted to a friend: "Mrs. Stevens and I went out for a walk yesterday afternoon. We walked to the end of Westerly Terrace, and she turned left and I turned right" (Brazeau, p. 43).

Stevens began publishing significant poems in 1914, and his first book, *Harmonium,* came out in 1923. Although it is now regarded as one of the most important American poetry books of the twentieth century, it sold few copies and was not well received by critics. T. S. Eliot's *The Waste Land* had been published the previous year, and some critics found Stevens's work light and frivolous by comparison with Eliot's dark and pessimistic vision. In retrospect, this judgment was unfair, for while *Harmonium* does display Stevens's playful and aesthetic* side, it also contains a number of major poems of great intensity and gravity.

Whether because of the reception of *Harmonium* or simply owing to the increased demands of family life following the birth of his daughter, Holly, in 1924, Stevens wrote and published very little during the remainder of the decade. In the 1930s he began writing again, and he remained prolific* for the rest of his life. *Ideas of Order* came out in 1935, followed by *Owl's Clover* (1936), *The Man with the Blue Guitar* (1937), *Parts of a World* (1942), *Transport to Summer* (1947), *The Auroras of Autumn* (1950), and *The Collected Poems of Wallace Stevens* (1954). His reputation grew steadily, and he received most of poetry's major awards and honors. These included the Bollingen Prize in 1950, an award that had become very well known as a result of a public controversy surrounding its previous recipient, the poet Ezra Pound. Stevens also received the National Book Award in 1951 and the National Book Award and Pulitzer Prize for his collected poems in 1955.

Stevens was a proper and reserved businessman and could sometimes seem aloof, but there was also an emotional and boisterous side to his personality. He enjoyed winter vacations with his friends (none of them writers) in the Florida Keys, vacations that often involved a good deal of drinking. On one occasion in 1936, he got into a fistfight with the novelist Ernest Hemingway, who knocked him down several times. Stevens hardly landed a punch, and when he did finally connect, he broke his hand on Hemingway's jaw. The two writers made peace before Stevens left Florida, but he was worried that word of the fight would reach his co-workers at the insurance company. Stevens also had strong enthusiasms and appetites. He never visited Europe, but he had a passion for French paintings, which he arranged to have sent to him in Hartford, along with other art objects. He loved exotic fruits, sausages, fine wines, and French cheeses, and he would stock up on these items when he visited New York.

In April 1955, Stevens was discovered to have inoperable stomach cancer. He was not told of it, but no doubt he realized

*aesthetic relating to ideas about art or beauty

*prolific producing many works; fertile; productive

Pound had made radio broadcasts supporting Italy and Germany during World War II. At the end of the war he was arrested, charged with treason, and imprisoned in a cage in Pisa, Italy, where he wrote *The Pisan Cantos*, which received the Bollingen Prize. He was found mentally unfit to stand trial and confined to St. Elizabeth's Hospital in Washington, D.C., until his release in 1958. See separate essay on Pound in these volumes.

he was dying. During his last weeks in the hospital he was baptized into the Catholic Church, though it is unlikely that he fully accepted the church's doctrines. His baptism is probably best seen as an affirmation of the powerful but diffuse spirituality that pervades his poetry. He died on 2 August 1955.

Stevens's Poetry

For more information on the modernists, see the article on Twentieth-Century Modernist Poetry in volume 3.

Wallace Stevens was one of the poets known as modernists, whose work transformed American poetry early in the twentieth century. Other important modernists include Eliot, Pound, William Carlos Williams, Marianne Moore, and Robert Frost. Their poetry is sometimes obscure and challenging to readers, but what sets Stevens apart from most of the others is the strong strain of romanticism* in his work. Some of the main influences on Stevens's poetry are William Shakespeare, the English Romantic poet John Keats, the nineteenth-century English poet Alfred Lord Tennyson, and the French symbolist poet Stéphane Mallarmé.

*romanticism a literary outlook that emphasized the imagination, powerful emotions, and the primacy of the individual.

The poems in *Harmonium* display two distinctive aspects of Stevens's style, both of which can be seen in "Sunday Morning," the first of many major long poems he wrote over the course of his life. One of these aspects is a fondness for lush and decorative language, to which some critics of *Harmonium* objected. Here are the poem's opening lines:

*peignoir a loose woman's garment; a dressing gown

> Complacencies of the peignoir,* and late
> Coffee and oranges in a sunny chair,
> And the green freedom of a cockatoo

*hallmark a distinguishing feature

*cadence the rhythms of the flow of language or verse music

A second hallmark* of Stevens's poetry is the sustained cadences* of a solemn and serious style of meditation, a style with a richness sometimes reminiscent of Shakespeare. Here is the famous ending of "Sunday Morning":

> We live in an old chaos of the sun,
> Or old dependency of day and night,
> Or island solitude, unsponsored, free,
> Of that wide water, inescapable.
> Deer walk upon our mountains, and the quail
> Whistle about us their spontaneous cries;

Sweet berries ripen in the wilderness;
And, in the isolation of the sky,
At evening, casual flocks of pigeons make
Ambiguous undulations* as they sink,
Downward to darkness, on extended wings.

After *Harmonium,* Stevens's language becomes barer and his poetry more abstract. Certain words recur throughout his poems, words like "idea," "world," "real," "mind," "summer," "winter," "imagination," "poem," "green," "sun," and "snow." These usually signify different conditions or states of being, which his poems roam through and explore without ever settling on any single one. Stevens is especially engaged by the opposition between the world of the senses and the solitary inner world of the mind and the imagination (two worlds paralleling the two worlds of his personal life). He is drawn to each but finds each disappointing and unequal to his deepest desires and aspirations, and so his poems move back and forth between them.

Stevens's meandering explorations of different states of being are carried out most powerfully in his long poems, which, in addition to "Sunday Morning," include "The Comedian as the Letter C," "Le Monocle de Mon Oncle," "The Man with the Blue Guitar," "Examination of the Hero in a Time of War," "Esthétique du Mal," "Credences of Summer," "Notes Toward a Supreme Fiction," "The Auroras of Autumn" and "An Ordinary Evening in New Haven." "The Auroras of Autumn," for instance, is in part an exploration of what the German philosopher Immanuel Kant called the experience of the sublime. This is an experience that can be both frightening and exhilarating, and which we often have in the presence of something huge and enormously powerful in nature, but which ultimately drives us inward. In Stevens's poem the phenomenon that triggers the experience is the spectacle of the northern lights:

It is a theatre floating through the clouds,
Itself a cloud, although of misted rock
And mountains running like water, wave on wave,

Through waves of light. It is of cloud transformed
To cloud transformed again, idly, the way

*undulation a wave-like pulsation or motion

A season changes color to no end,

Except the lavishing of itself in change,
As light changes yellow into gold and gold
To its opal elements and fire's delight,

Splashed wide-wise because it likes magnificence
And the solemn pleasures of magnificent space.

Stevens is sometimes called a philosophical poet, but this
is only half true. If a philosophical poet is one whose poems
address very general and abstract concepts and themes that
apply to all human beings, then he certainly is one. But if by a
philosophical poet we mean a poet whose work embodies a
consistent set of doctrines or theories, then he is not. Stevens
had no formal training in philosophy—unlike Eliot, whose
Four Quartets really is a philosophical poem—and in his
poems he explores, tries on, and plays with various ideas and
concepts but comes to no settled conclusions. The true importance of his work lies in the way it conveys what it is like to
be a person engaged by the entire range of thought and feeling, the experience of being fully human. The best way to read
Stevens, especially at first, is not to try to "figure out" his
poems but to let their music and language carry you along as
they flow from one thought to the next.

Stevens is also sometimes considered a "pure" or aesthetic poet, whose main subject is art itself rather than human
life. This, too, is a distortion, as his very late poems make clear.
These poems bring out the human themes present in his work
from the start. They are alive with a sense of longing, loss, and
the pain of unsatisfied desire, and in this they undoubtedly reflect the disappointments of his personal life. In "As You Leave
the Room," which may be the last poem he wrote, Stevens
looks back at his whole life, and while he alludes* to several of
his poems, he is frightened by the thought that he may have
simply neglected the real world he is about to leave. He seems
to find reassurance in the thought that the facts of the world
have been imaginatively transformed and incorporated into
what he has achieved in his life through his poetry. Yet in the
end he finds this consolation ambiguous, for as complete as
his achievement may be, poetry, he says, changes only what is
"unreal, as if nothing had been changed at all," and leaves the
world as it was.

*allude to refer to,
often indirectly

As You Leave the Room

You speak. You say: Today's character is not
A skeleton out of its cabinet. Nor am I.

That poem about the pineapple, the one
About the mind as never satisfied,

The one about the credible hero, the one
About summer, are not what skeletons think about.

I wonder, have I lived a skeleton's life,
As a disbeliever in reality,

A countryman of all the bones in the world?
Now, here, the snow I had forgotten becomes

Part of a major reality, part of
An appreciation of a reality

And thus an elevation, as if I left
With something I could touch, touch every way.

And yet nothing has been changed except what is
Unreal, as if nothing had been changed at all.

Stevens's Legacy

Wallace Stevens received wide recognition and many honors in his lifetime. Even so, his reputation has grown enormously since his death, and he is now widely regarded as one of the most important poets of the twentieth century. The critic Harold Bloom, for instance, has argued that the main tradition of poetry in English starts with Shakespeare and John Milton; runs through English Romantic poets like William Wordsworth, Percy Bysshe Shelley, and John Keats; through the nineteenth-century American poet Walt Whitman; and then, in the twentieth century, through Stevens.

Stevens's influence on American poetry can be seen both in our poetry's general character and in the work of many individual poets. One of the characteristic styles in the poetry of the last several decades of the twentieth century combines an

*diction choice of words

elegant finish with a natural diction* and tone. This style comes largely from Stevens, whose poems give the impression of a person talking about serious matters in a precise but casual tone of voice. Another characteristic of American poetry is its inwardness and self-absorption. Stevens is not a self-absorbed poet, but he is the poet who, perhaps more than any other, made individual human consciousness itself, rather than the particular things a person might think about, the true subject of his work. The idea that a poem could be simply about what it feels like to think and imagine has had a profound influence on the way we now conceive of poetry.

Stevens's poetry has also strongly influenced the work of many contemporary poets. These include James Merrill, Mark Strand, A. R. Ammons, Robert Creeley, and John Ashbery. Ashbery is probably the poet whose work most clearly resembles Stevens's in the way it conveys the feeling of the mind's movements. When Ashbery's first book, *Some Trees,* was published in 1956, the poet Frank O'Hara described it in a review as the most beautiful first book of poems published by an American since Stevens's *Harmonium.*

It is fair to say that Stevens's work represents a high, or elite, conception of art. His poetry is extremely polished, and it makes intellectual demands of the reader. It has few social or political overtones, and it is not intended to appeal to a broad popular audience. American poetry is much more various now than it was in Stevens's lifetime, and there is a strong populist element in the work of many poets. It will be interesting to see how Stevens's work comes to be regarded in the future.

IF YOU LIKE the poetry of Stevens, you might also like the poetry of John Ashbery.
❧

Selected Bibliography

WORKS BY WALLACE STEVENS
Poetry

Harmonium (1923).

Ideas of Order (1935).

Owl's Clover (1936).

The Man with the Blue Guitar (1937).

Parts of a World (1942).

Transport to Summer (1947).

The Auroras of Autumn (1950).

Available Collections

The Collected Poems of Wallace Stevens. New York: Knopf, 1954.

Collected Poetry and Prose. New York: Library of America, 1997. Contains all of Stevens's writings.

Letters. Edited by Holly Stevens. New York: Knopf, 1966. A selection of Stevens's letters edited by his daughter.

WORKS ABOUT WALLACE STEVENS

Bates, Milton. *Wallace Stevens: A Mythology of Self.* Berkeley: University of California Press, 1985. A critical and biographical study.

Bloom, Harold. *Wallace Stevens: The Poems of Our Climate.* Ithaca, N.Y.: Cornell University Press, 1977.

Brazeau, Peter. *Parts of a World: Wallace Stevens Remembered.* New York: Random House, 1983. An oral biography of Stevens, with reminiscences from people who knew him.

Richardson, Joan. *The Early Years, 1879–1923,* vol. 1 of *Wallace Stevens.* New York: William Morrow, 1986. An account of Stevens's life up to the publication of *Harmonium.*

Vendler, Helen. *On Extended Wings: Wallace Stevens' Longer Poems.* Cambridge, Mass.: Harvard University Press, 1969. A study of Stevens's long poems.

More About Stevens:

For information on Wallace Stevens, sites to visit, and related events, you can contact:
Hartford Friends and Enemies of Wallace Stevens
500 Main St.
Hartford, CT 06103
http://www.wesleyan.edu /wstevens/stevens.html

MAY SWENSON

(1913–1989)

by Katharine Coles

A reader might imagine the young May Swenson playing in the yard of her childhood home in the mountain town of Logan, Utah, where she was born Anna Thilda May Swenson on 28 May 1913. The oldest of ten children, May enjoyed playing with her first three siblings, her brothers Roy, Dan, and George. When the next three children—Grace, Ruth, and Beth—arrived, May quickly switched roles from playmate to helper and began assisting her mother with chores ranging from cooking to laundry.

As a child May spent much of her rare free time outside. Her brother Paul remembers the yard as being overgrown with flowers, berry brambles, and fruit trees that provided pollen for the bees kept by their father. Here, May observed nature, wrote in the journal she began to keep at a young age, daydreamed, and rode on her imaginary horse, Rob Roy.

May often pretended that she was a natural creature. In her poem "The Centaur"* she remembers herself at ten cutting a willow switch and mounting the creature. As she gallops around the yard, the switch becomes a horse; then, there is

Quotations of Swenson's poetry throughout are taken from *New and Selected Things Taking Place.*

*centaur a mythical creature that is half human and half horse

67

another transformation. One might imagine young Swenson's round face flushed with heat and her very pale hair, cut in bangs across her forehead, flying:

> My head and my neck were mine,
>
> yet they were shaped like a horse.
> My hair flopped to the side
> like the mane of a horse in the wind.
>
> My forelock swung in my eyes,
> my neck arched and I snorted.
> I shied* and skittered* and reared,
>
> stopped and raised my knees,
> pawed at the ground and quivered.

*__shied__ reacted in fright

*__skittered__ glided quickly or skipped

Like many of Swenson's lines, these are packed with active verbs like "flopped," "shied," and "skittered," verbs that help the reader see this girl-horse in motion. Swenson also uses verbs to show how the girl first loses control of her body—she doesn't arch her neck; her neck arches as if on its own—and then regains that control as she becomes a new creature.

A few years later, from the time she was about thirteen, one might as often have found Swenson inside as out, typing poetry at her father's typewriter. Like "The Centaur," these early poems often had their roots in nature and in Swenson's imaginative sympathy with its creatures. Both places—the natural world outside and the poems that came from within—provided this oldest child with a necessary refuge from nine younger brothers and sisters she often had to take care of. In fact, though she loved her family, she later recollected in an interview that she was always struggling to be alone.

Spirituality

This need for escape might be one of the reasons Swenson left Utah after graduating from Utah State University, where her father taught mechanical engineering. Another reason was her desire to escape the influence of the church in which she was raised. Her parents, Anna Margaret and Dan Arthur Swenson, had converted to Mormonism in Sweden before emigrating to the United States. "I was brought up very strictly in a religious way," she observed (*Made with Words*, p. 115), and this strictness made her "turn away" from the religion of her childhood.

The fact that she had no organized religion, however, does not mean that her poetry is without spiritual content. Although her brother Paul thinks she may have embraced agnosticism* as early as her teenage years, her poems often show a deep spirituality, associated sometimes with nature, sometimes with objects, and sometimes with words themselves. Poetry, Swenson says in her essay "The Poet as Antispecialist," "amounts to a virtual compulsion to probe with the senses into the complex actuality* of all things, outside and inside the self, and to determine relationships between them" (*Made with Words*, p. 92). Often, then, her poems seem like efforts to use words to get beyond the materiality, or physical being, of things to their essence. In her poem "October" she talks about light in this way:

> Surely it is godly,
> that it makes all things
> begin, and appear, and become
> actual to each other.

As these lines unfold, their words behave very much as does light itself, revealing word by word both the "things" and their gradual appearance to the eye. It is interesting to notice how the line break changes the meaning of the verb "makes": In reading that light "makes all things," one might suppose that light itself is a kind of creating god; the following line shows that this making is more an act of revelation, or uncovering, than of creation.

Science

In a way, Swenson replaced her childhood religion with an interest in the visible world. Like a scientist, she seemed to notice the smallest details of the objects around her. Her brother recalls a visit she paid him during the 1960s, when the entrance into his home was through a back alley lined with garbage cans. Of all the people who visited him there, he remembers that only two, May and the bluegrass musician Doc

*__agnosticism__ a refusal to believe in any religious tenet for which one has no evidence

*__actuality__ reality; existing in fact

Watson, noticed and identified the numerous birds living in the alley and not only the odors that attracted them.

Science appears in Swenson's work in many forms. She wrote poems about the rotation of the earth, poems observing animals or the sky or geology in detail, and poems about the Apollo space program, including the first walk on the moon, which she found extremely exciting. In fact, according to Swenson, "the impulses of the scientist and the poet . . . are parallel," in that both attempt to get "beyond the flat surface of appearances" in their investigations of reality. However, in spite of what they have in common, Swenson also believed that the scientist and the poet have different methods and objects of investigation. According to Swenson, "the scientist has an actual moon under observation," while the poet's moon is "not in the sky but within [her] psyche" and also "within the psyche of every man" as an archetype* or symbol* (*Made with Words,* pp. 93–96).

Swenson enjoys using some of these differences. Her poem "Pure Suit of Happiness," in which she imagines climbing into her own space suit, designed for survival not in outer space but in the equally strange space of this planet, shows both her interest in science and her pleasure in playing with language and ideas. The fun begins with the title, which plays with the phrase "pursuit of happiness," but the poem also has something serious to say about the virtues of the different ages of life.

*archetype the original form of something

*symbol anything that stands for or represents something else, for example, "The dove is a symbol of peace"

The pure suit of happiness,
not yet invented. How I long
to climb into its legs,

fit into its sleeves, and zip
it up, pull the hood
over my head. It's got

a face mask, too, and gloves
and boots attached. It's
made for me. It's blue. It's

not too heavy, not too
light. It's my right.
It has its own weather,

which is youth's breeze,
equilibrated* by the ideal
thermostat of maturity,

and built in, to begin with,
fluoroscopic* goggles of
age. I'd see through

everything, yet be happy.
I'd be suited for life. I'd
always look good to myself.

Playing with Language

Swenson's pleasure in language play emerges even more clearly in the two kinds of poems for which she is perhaps best known: her riddles and her iconographs, poems whose shape on the page amplify the subject matter. Nowadays, we tend to think of a riddle as a silly child's joke. The riddle is actually an ancient form, and it was originally a much darker one. In the traditional riddle, an object is described, often in a way that gives it a dark, mysterious quality, while its name is held back.

In this way, the riddler is also a little like the scientist, whose job is to describe a thing with as much accuracy as possible. Swenson says, "If I'm observing something, I don't think about its name or its label to begin with," because the label can get in the way of accurate observation. Instead, she says, "I think about how [the object is] affecting me." By removing the name, Swenson allows us to see the thing behind it freshly, as if for the first time. The attention we bring to it allows us, the readers, to be touched and transformed, as the poet's attention has allowed her to be changed as well. In "Living Tenderly," Swenson describes an animal. Later, she says, she realized she was also describing herself (*Made with Words,* p. 105). It is not difficult to solve the riddle, but by withholding the name of the animal, Swenson allows its human qualities to emerge.

My body a rounded stone
with a pattern of smooth seams.
My head a short snake,
retractive,* projective.*

equilibrated brought into equilibrium or balance

fluoroscope an instrument that uses X-rays to see inside nontransparent objects

retractive having the ability to retract or pull in

projective having the ability to extend or push out

My legs come out of their sleeves
or shrink within,
and so does my chin.
My eyelids are quick clamps.

My back is my roof.
I am always at home.
I travel where my house walks.
It is a smooth stone.
It floats within the lake,
or rests in the dust.
My flesh lives tenderly
inside its bone.

While the riddle has been around for thousands of years, the iconograph, or "picture writing," is a form Swenson invented and named herself. Because iconographs depend on the way the poem looks on the page, some readers have mistaken them for "concrete poems,"* which also depend on the visual arrangement of words. For Swenson there was a crucial difference. According to her, concrete poems begin with a shape, which the words are written and arranged to fulfill. In the iconograph, the words come first. They then determine the shape the poem is to take, as in the form of this poem:

> You give yourself such funny
> > > > looks
> > > when you
> > > > look
> > in the mirror. You're
> > > > looking
> > at yourself, but you're not
> > > > looking
> > > at yourself
> > > > looking.
> > > You
> > > > look
> > at a pimple on your brow. You
> > > bare your teeth. I'm
> > > > looking
> > > > at you
> > > > > looking

*concrete poem** a poem that looks like the thing it describes, such as a poem about a fish that is written in the shape of a fish. See also separate essay on Calligrammatic and Concrete Poetry in volume 3.

funny at yourself in the mirror.
                    You're not
                              looking
                    at me. I
                              look
                    at you. I
                              look
              in the mirror at you
                              looking
          in the mirror. In the mirror I
                              look
                    at me,
                              looking
                    at you
                              looking
    at a pimple and baring your teeth.
                    You don't
                              look
              at me in the mirror
                              looking
                    at myself
                              looking
                    at you
                              looking
          at a pimple on your brow.
                    You give yourself funny
                              looks,
                    not
                              looking
              at me in the mirror.
                              Look!
              I bare my teeth!

                                        "Looks"

The form, in which the right side of the poem acts as a mirror catching all the different kinds of "looks" being cast on the left side, grows out of the action of the poem itself. The speaker keeps trying to capture the attention of "you," who is fully absorbed in looking at her own pimple. The last "Look!" of the poem, and the last action, demand that the "you" return the speaker's attention. "Don't look in the mirror," the speaker is saying. "Look at me."

In making her iconographic poems, Swenson tries to make language do more than it usually can in a poem. She doesn't want to just "talk *about* something," she says; she wants "to *build* a poem with language as the material." If she can do this, she can make the poem project to the reader "something more actual, more graspable by his senses than just words on the page" (*Made with Words*, pp. 65–66).

Sometimes Swenson's poems are simply playful, without necessarily following a form like that of a riddle or an iconograph. "Painting the Gate" becomes crazier and more playful as it goes, so that when it finally comes around full circle, it seems to end at a very different place from the one where it began.

The Complete Person

The poem "The Centaur" suggests that Swenson was an active child. Later, she says, "I think I began to be a feminist at age three-and-a-half." As in every aspect of her life, however, she was independent in her relationship to feminism: "I don't like the word [feminism] if it means to cut out the male." The male and female are different, she believed, but they both "exist in every person." Although she always "felt complete" as a person herself, she "sometimes felt that some of the rest of the world didn't find [her] as complete or capable as if [she] had been born male." When she says she was "annoyed" by such treatment, it is hard not to read the word as an understatement (*Made with Words*, p. 62).

Swenson was indeed known for independence and stubbornness—in her poetry, which, though always interesting, rarely did whatever was fashionable in poetry at the moment, and in her life. As a young woman of twenty, she borrowed two hundred dollars from her father for a "visit" to New York City, but she had already decided to stay there and make her way as a poet even though it was during the Great Depression and times were hard. May had to struggle to make ends meet, mostly working as a freelance editor and ghostwriter;* she was too proud to take money from her family, especially since they did not approve of her life. She became increasingly desperate, and at one point her clothes were so worn she turned to shoplifting so she would have something to wear when she

****ghostwriter** a writer who writes a book for another person who is named as the author

Painting the Gate

I painted the mailbox. That was fun.
I painted it postal blue.
Then I painted the gate.
I painted a spider that got on the gate.
I painted his mate.
I painted the ivy around the gate.
Some stones I painted blue,
and part of the cat as he rubbed by.
I painted my hair. I painted my shoe.
I painted the slats, both front and back,
all their beveled* edges, too.
I painted the numbers on the gate—
I shouldn't have, but it was too late.
I painted the posts, each side and top,
I painted the hinges, the handle, the lock,
several ants and a moth asleep in a crack.
At last I was through.
I'd painted the gate
shut, me out, with both hands dark blue,
as well as my nose, which,
early on, because of a sudden itch,
got painted. But wait!
I had painted the gate.

*beveled slanted, as when an edge or groove is cut at a slant rather than at ninety degrees

went to apply for relief. On her relief application she said she was an orphan so that she could receive a winter coat.

In 1938 May got a job collecting oral histories for the Federal Writers Project, a federal government program set up to give jobs to writers, who would tell the story of America through interviews with ordinary people about their jobs and their lives. She was fired from this project when the administrators discovered the lie on her relief application.

Slowly, May began to receive recognition for her poetry. She won fellowships to Yaddo, a writers' colony, where she met influential writers. She was introduced to the powerful poetry editor of the *New Yorker*, Howard Moss, who was to publish many of her poems. She also became friends with the poet Elizabeth Bishop. As she became increasingly well known and highly regarded as a poet, she won a number of awards, including a Guggenheim fellowship. She even went on book tours, which took her to the West Coast as well as to her hometown of Logan, where she was received as a literary heroine.

Swenson's independence and stubborness, her need to do things alone, had caused some difficulty in her early life, but these same qualities also helped her to overcome those difficulties. Even her face, her friend Richard Wilbur remembered after her death, was "capable of pugnacity" (that is, combativeness). Mostly, though, he said it displayed "forthrightness, independence, good nature, and a great power of attention," qualities also evident in her writing ("May Swenson," p. 81). One might wonder which her old friend was reading: the poems, the person, or both?

The "I" There

*lyric a kind of poetry characterized by musical and personal expression

Even though Swenson appears in many of her poems as a speaker, the poems are not autobiographical in the sense that we often associate with lyric* poetry today. They reveal little about the poet's personal life: who her friends and family are, how she gets along with them, what she thinks about their habits, how they may have hurt her or made her happy. Much of the impersonal quality of the poems comes from subject matter and technique: the close, almost scientific attention to detail; the riddling; the language play.

It is also through subject matter and technique that a reader might feel she is "getting to know" the poet in some small way. From the poet's subjects and close attention to objects, the reader knows that the poet is deeply interested in nature and the world, in the mysterious qualities of things, plants, and animals. From the language play the reader knows that Swenson is equally interested in words and what they can do and that the poet has a charming, often quirky sense of humor. From the originality and oddness of the poems, the reader can sense the poet's determination to be true to herself and her own vision. And from the impersonal tone of the poems, the reader gets the sense of a person who is intensely private. A reader can know something about places Swenson visited and lived in, because she wrote many poems about place, but the reader must infer or guess at most information about the poet's life within those places, because the poems give very little directly personal information. Some readers would read "Looks" as a love poem, but the poem has none of the language that one usually expects to see in a love poem. The only piece of personal information the poem gives is that the beloved has a pimple.

One reason for Swenson's deep sense of privacy may have been her lesbianism. Although she received several marriage proposals from young men during her early years in New York, her passionate attachments were to women. Like so many aspects of Swenson's life, her refusal to marry and have a family was at odds with her Mormon background. When her parents decided to compile a family history and sent out questionnaires to all family members, in the space reserved for listing the names of children, Swenson wrote in the titles of thirty-nine of her poems.

Swenson lived a stormy decade with Anca Vrbovska, a Czech refugee and poet. Although Swenson would later champion Vrbovska's poems to her own publisher, James McLaughlin, she herself was able to write only a few dozen poems during their turbulent years together. More peaceful was her relationship with Pearl Schwartz, with whom she established a stable domestic partnership. But her longest relationship was with Roxanne Knudson, known as Zan. The two were together for nearly thirty years, and Swenson appointed Knudson to oversee her papers and unpublished works after her death. For Swenson, this was like making Knudson the guardian of her children.

The Westerner

In 1936, Swenson left Utah for New York City. Eventually she settled in Seabrook, Connecticut, in a house on the ocean. The landscapes and seascapes of the eastern United States appear as frequently in Swenson's poems as the landscape of her childhood. She died of a heart attack on 4 December 1989 in Oceanview, Delaware. Though she never returned to Utah to live, Swenson visited often, and she is buried in the cemetery in Logan. Throughout her life she retained many of her Western habits, especially in her love of nature and wild creatures. Richard Wilbur remembers that when Swenson toured Europe she carried a tent and did most of her sleeping "under canvas." Perhaps most important, Wilbur notes, Swenson retained her sense of Westernness in her poems, "in their openness of tone and diction" and in the way that, "even at their trickiest, they are made out of plain American words" ("May Swenson," p. 81).

Selected Bibliography

WORKS BY MAY SWENSON
Poetry

Another Animal (1954).

A Cage of Spines (1958).

To Mix with Time (1963).

Poems to Solve (1966).

Half Sun Half Sleep (1967).

Iconographs (1970).

More Poems to Solve (1971).

In Other Words (1987).

Translations

Windows and Stones: Selected Poems by Tomas Tranströmer. Translated by May Swenson in collaboration with Leif Sjöberg. Pittsburgh: University of Pittsburgh Press, 1972.

Editions for Children

The Guess and Spell Coloring Book. Illustrated by Lise Gladstone. New York: Scribners, 1976.

Available Collections

The Love Poems of May Swenson. Edited by Richard Wilbur. Boston: Houghton Mifflin, 1991.

Made with Words. Edited by Gardner McFall. Ann Arbor: University of Michigan Press, 1998.

New and Selected Things Taking Place. Boston: Little, Brown, 1978.

IF YOU LIKE the poetry of Swenson, you might also like the poetry of Marianne Moore or Elizabeth Bishop.

⋅⁀§

WORKS ABOUT MAY SWENSON

Howard, Richard. "May Swenson: Turned Back to the Wild by Love." In his *Alone with America.* New York: Atheneum, 1969.

Knudson, R. R. *The Wonderful Pen of May Swenson.* New York: Macmillan, 1993.

Schulman, Grace. "Life's Miracles: The Poetry of May Swenson." *American Poetry Review* 23:9–13 (Sept.–Oct. 1994).

Swenson, Paul. "May in October: Life and Death as Existential Riddles in May Swenson's Poetry." *Weber Studies* 8:18–21 (Spring 1991).

Wilbur, Richard. "May Swenson: A Memorial Tribute." *Gettysburg Review* 5:81–85 (Winter 1992).

More About Swenson

Though her childhood home has been torn down, you can visit May Swenson's grave in the cemetery in Logan, Utah.

JAMES TATE

(b. 1943)

by Claudia Keelan

Many people fall in love with people they have never met, like movie stars or singers. The fourteenth-century Italian poet Petrarch never knew Laura, the woman for whom he wrote more than five hundred sonnets; the twelfth-century troubadour* poets rarely knew the ladies to whom their poems were dedicated. In fact, a lot of poetry is devoted to the idea of womanhood, with little attention to any actual woman. Often, the pursuit of the mysterious "unknown" can be a prime motive for writing poetry. This is certainly the case for James Tate, whose thirteen books of poetry speed through surreal* dreamscapes toward the unrevealed, intent on the quest. In *The Lost Pilot,* the book that made James Tate at twenty-three the youngest winner ever of the prestigious Yale Younger Poets' Prize, the poet seeks the origins of his own life as he searches for a man he never met—his father.

*troubadour a traveling poet. Troubadours were common in France in the Middle Ages.

*surreal characterized by fantastic, irrational images

Basic Facts

James Tate was born on 8 December 1943 in Kansas City to Betty Jean Whitsitt and Samuel Vincent Appleby. He attended the University of Missouri in 1963–1964 and graduated from Kansas State College with a bachelor's degree in 1965. He then attended the University of Iowa Writers' Workshop and received his master of fine arts in poetry in 1967. Tate has taught at many universities, including the University of Iowa; the University of California, Berkeley; Columbia University; and the University of Massachusetts at Amherst, where he has taught English since 1971. A prolific writer, Tate has won many awards, including a Guggenheim Fellowship, the National Book Award, the Tanning Prize, and the William Carlos Williams Award. His *Selected Poems* received the Pulitzer Prize for poetry in 1992.

The Search

James Tate's father, Samuel Appleby, was a pilot who was shot down (and never found) over Stettin, Germany, on 9 April 1944, during World War II. Tate was only one year old at the time, and he grew up trying to imagine the man whom, as he says, "we talked about . . . so much when I was a child, my mother and all her family that we lived with my first seven years, that I didn't really think he was dead" (*Durak,* pp. 22–38).

> Your face did not rot
> like the others—the co-pilot,
> for example, I saw him
>
> yesterday. His face is corn-
> mush: his wife and daughter,
> the poor ignorant people, stare
>
> as if he will compose soon.
> He was more wronged than Job.
> But your face did not rot
>
> like the others—it grew dark,
> and hard like ebony;
> the features progressed in their

distinction. If I could cajole*
you to come back for an evening,
down from your compulsive

orbiting, I would touch you,
read your face as Dallas
your hoodlum gunner, now,

with the blistered eyes, reads
his braille* editions. I would
touch your face as a disinterested

scholar touches an original page.
However frightening, I would
discover you, and I would not

turn you in; I would not make
you face your wife, or Dallas,
or the co-pilot, Jim. You

could return to your crazy
orbiting, and I would not try
to fully understand what

it means to you. All I know
is this: when I see you,
as I have seen you at least

once every year of my life,
spin across the wilds of the sky
like a tiny, African god,

I feel dead. I feel as if I were
the residue of a stranger's life,
that I should pursue you.

My head cocked toward the sky,
I cannot get off the ground,
and, you, passing over again,

fast, perfect, and unwilling
to tell me that you are doing
well, or that it was mistake

cajole to coax or
convince

braille a system of
writing for the blind
that uses raised dots

that placed you in that world,
and me in this; or that misfortune
placed these worlds in us.

"The Lost Pilot"

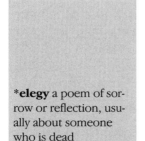

elegy a poem of sorrow or reflection, usually about someone who is dead

epitaph writing on a tombstone; the term can be used to mean any words written in memory of the dead

"The Lost Pilot" redefines the purpose of elegy.* The poet cannot sum up his father's life with a fitting epitaph* and so is forced to follow the lost pilot through the skies of his imagination, begging him to return, vowing that "however frightening, I would / discover you." But how can we ultimately "discover" the unknown? The lost pilot, unreachable through the traditional channel of memory, is as mysterious as a "tiny, African god," his facial features growing "dark, / and hard like ebony." The father in "The Lost Pilot" remains a stranger. The poet-son who seeks his father is ultimately denied the consolation an elegy gives because he "cannot get off the ground," and the father remains a mystery

. . . passing over again,

fast, perfect, and unwilling
to tell me that you are doing
well, or that it was mistake

that placed you in that world,
and me in this . . .

Talking about the poem, Tate says:

> The real source of the poem came during an afternoon nap. . . . A mystical experience swept through me, really shook me, and left the image of my father circling the earth in his B-17 continuously, refusing to come down. I understand that it is some kind of shame that keeps him there the past twenty-two years. And in the dream I somehow sensed that I was passing him in flight, I was changing roles with him, I was becoming his father, he was becoming my son. . . . The point of this is that, as far as I can ascertain, the dream took place literally at the time I passed the age of my father when his plane was shot

down. . . . At twenty-two I was passing him on the clock (*Durak,* pp. 22–38).

A devotee of the "mystical experience," Tate also avows that he often would "go into trances" when he wrote (*Poetry Observed,* p. 149).

Increasingly, after *The Lost Pilot,* Tate's emphasis is on seeking what he does not know, and whether it is his father, love, or answers to the meaning of life, it is the quest, not the answers themselves, that preoccupies him. His poems confuse and sometimes anger critics. Many complain that Tate's poems are set in landscapes that are too bizarre and surreal. Others complain about Tate's writing style itself, as Philip Dacey did in *American Book Review:* "Tate writes as if he were translating from a foreign language he did not understand, relying solely on word-association for method. . . . He has fun at the expense of language, rather than vice versa, acting less to employ it than to expose it." In his willingness to seek the truths of the irrational or subconscious world and in his determination to "expose" the falsehoods of conventional language use, Tate is the premiere American descendent of the surrealists.

Surrealism

Surrealism, founded by the French poet André Breton, was one of the chief branches of modernism in the twentieth century. In his *Manifesto* (1924), Breton called for a break with existing modes of communication and perception. In order to create new ways of writing and perceiving, Breton prescribed "psychic automatism" (automatic writing), through which the writer would gain access to the otherwise repressed activities of the mind. The surrealist movement consisted of both painters and poets, including Max Ernst, Salvador Dali, Joan Miró, Louis Aragon, Antonin Artaud, and Robert Desnos. Under Breton's definition, the surrealist must pay special attention to the dream state, when the mind is involved in the free play of thought, so that the dreamer can open new vistas for the arts and "help solve the principal problems of life." Because surrealism was situated between the two world wars, it

. . . It is the quest, not the answers themselves, that preoccupies him. His poems confuse and anger some critics.

is possible to view the surrealist experiment as a proposed antidote to the misuses of language in wartime.

The Oblivion Ha-Ha, Hints to Pilgrims, Absences, Viper Jazz

Tate, along with many of his contemporaries, is sometimes ironically, sometimes angrily, sometimes sadly aware that poetry may not "help solve the principal problems of life." Despite that, he is still willing to make the attempt. Although his imagery is often fantastical and the "turns" in the poems resemble the irrational logic of dreams, Tate's poetry is most deeply imbedded in ordinary human emotion. The titles of his books often indicate his concerns. Destined by nature and historical circumstance to be a "pilgrim"—a wanderer seeking a homeland—he must laugh at the oblivion and absence he finds instead of answers. His poetry travels toward a "homeland" but fails to find one, so he must be content with the journey itself. The central theme of all his poetry is the pursuit of meaning in its endless disguises, and in *The Oblivion Ha-Ha* and following books, that pursuit often leads to fear. Traveling through his customary surreal landscapes, the poet desperately seeks connection to nature, lovers, and language. In "Up Here," the reader is introduced to a dream motel, where two lovers meet and "the right word is not needed." Since language is invariably needed to communicate, however, the man tries to describe his lover as "supple," "svelte," "wholesome." Instead of helping him, these words place him "one / or two thousand feet above" her, where he can see only the

> bubble,
> which rises and rises into
> my hand: inside it is a word:
> *Help.*

Neither lover hears the other; the words they use separate them further, and the poem ends with the poet saying:

> I would like to help,
> believe me, but up here nothing
> is possible, nothing is clear . . .

Dear Reader

I am trying to pry open your casket
with this burning snowflake.

I'll give up my sleep for you.
The freezing sleet keeps coming down
and I can barely see.

If this trick works we can rub our hands
together, maybe

start a little fire
with our identification papers.
I don't know but I keep working, working

half hating you,
half eaten by the moon.

(*The Oblivion Ha-Ha*)

Like "The Lost Pilot," the speaker in "Up Here" is unavailable, separated from the loved one not by death but by the words they speak hoping to reach each other.

Tate's subjects are the pursuit of love, belief, and mortality and, most important, the ultimate inability of language to capture the world. For while the speakers in Tate's poems are always

> surrounded by the pieces of this huge
> puzzle: here's a piece I call my wife, and
> here's an odd one I call convictions . . .

he is always willing to "leap head-first like a diver into the wretched confusion" ("Prose Poem"). As a pilgrim, Tate is ultimately committed only to the activity of the crusade, that activity for a poet, the process of finding the poem's occasion:

> But there is only one poem,
> why do I try to disguise that beautiful fact!
> This year the poem is falling in love

not with itself for a change
but with innumerable swaggering bipeds,*

with last night and today,
the scent of it, a lemon blossom.
("Bennington," *The Oblivion Ha-Ha*)

Who are the "innumerable swaggering bipeds"? Humanity, of
course, and it is a tribute to his faith in his pilgrimage that oc-
casionally Tate is able to find love for his fellow humans and a
connection to the actual world, where "last night and today
. . . a lemon blossom" makes it possible to appreciate the
world he usually cannot reach. While Tate insists that the "I" in
his poems is the speaker, not himself, the poems do come
from the central occasions of a real life and from those of a life
in poetry in particular. Opposing the tradition that places the
emphasis on craft and the poem—sonnet, villanelle, sestina,
and so forth—as object, Tate follows the path of the troubadour (from the French *trouver,* "to find"), who finds (or fails
to find) the subject / lady he seeks. Believing only in the journey, he is unable in advance to know anything at all. This is
made clear by Guillaume IX of Aquitaine, a twelfth-century
troubadour whose poem Tate offers as an epigraph* to the
title poem of *Absences:*

> I'll write a song about nothing at all,
> Not about myself, not about anything else.
> Not about love, nor about the joys of youth,
>   Nor anything else.
> I wrote it just now as I slept
>   In the saddle.
> I do not know at which hour I was born;
> I am not joyful and yet not sad;
> I am neither reserved nor intimate
>   And can do nothing about it:
> I was put under a spell one night
>   On a high hill.

Securely grounded in the lack at the heart of the world, "Absences" sets forth on a journey whose destination cannot be
anticipated by its beginning. Like the surrealists who came before him, Tate is "put under a spell" of his own making, and
the charm of his poetry is found in his verbal energy and a

deadly serious sense of play. Far from Breton's hope for a poetry "helping to solve the principal problems of life," however, Tate's experiment with his subconscious unleashes nightmare landscapes. "Toto, I don't think we're in Kansas," begins the last section of "Absences," and if you think this is Oz, think again. In Tate's spectral* land, nature and myth have lost all power, "the voice of the leaf . . . poisons the dowry" while the "eleven elves drop dead / in the basin of gold trousers." And, while in *The Wizard of Oz,* Dorothy never forgets Aunt Em and the possibility of safety, the speaker in "Absences" forgets to wave as an island is reached, wryly but exhaustedly admitting, "it is too beautiful to excite me with the idea / of accessibility." In other words, the island is "too beautiful" to let him enter— so this speaker is different from Dorothy, whose idea of home is firmly rooted in Kansas no matter how many adventures she has. The poems in *Absences* express an urban and urbane emptiness, where

*spectral ghostly

> hotels, hospitals, jails
> are homes in yourself you return to
> as some do to Garbo movies . . .
> "The Private Intrigue of Melancholy"

Viper Jazz takes up where *Absences* leaves off, continuing Tate's exploration into the unconscious, the illogical, the surreal, the "viper jazz" that is language—forcing laughter even as its poisons move the speaker into death and oblivion.

A Softer Terror

After winning the Pulitzer Prize for his *Selected Poems* in 1992, James Tate published two books of poems, *Worshipful Company of Fletchers,* which won the National Book Award, and *Shroud of the Gnome.* Tate is still a seeker, but age and success have softened the terror of his previous books as well as given him perspective on his initial desire to reach the unknowable. A fletcher is, after all, only a maker of arrows, not the bowman himself; and in these later works there is a new humility, still wry and funny for all that, but as measured and steady as someone who has asked a question of the darkness and lived on without its answer:

*miscellany a hodge-
podge or mixture of
different things

In time I will heal, I know this, or I believe this.
The contents and furnishings of my secret room will be
    labeled
and organized so thoroughly it will be a little fright-
    ening.
What I thought was infinite will turn out to be just a
    couple
of odds and ends, a tiny miscellany,* miniature stuff,
    fragments
of novelties, of no great moment. But it will also be
    enough,
maybe even more than enough, to suggest an immense
    ritual and tradition.
And this makes me very happy.

"Happy as the Day Is Long"
(*Worshipful Company of Fletchers*)

IF YOU LIKE the poetry of
Tate, you might also like the
poetry of André Breton or
Charles Simic.
⮴§

Selected Bibliography

WORKS BY JAMES TATE
Poetry

The Lost Pilot (1967).

The Oblivion Ha-Ha (1970).

Hints to Pilgrims (1971).

Absences (1972).

Hottentot Ossuary (1974).

Viper Jazz (1976).

Riven Doggeries (1979).

Constant Defender (1983).

Reckoner (1986).

Distance from Loved Ones (1990).

Selected Poems (1991).

Worshipful Company of Fletchers (1994).

Shroud of the Gnome (1997).

Prose

The Making of Poetry. New Haven, Conn.: Yale University Press, 1967.

Lucky Darryl: A Novel (with Bill Knott) Brooklyn, N.Y.: Release Press, 1977.

"A Box for Tom." In *Fifty Contemporary Poets.* Edited by Alberta Turner. New York: David McKay, 1977. Essay.

Interviews

"Interview with James Tate." *Durak,* May 1979:22–39.

Poetry Observed. Interviewer and editor, Joe David Bellamy. Urbana: University of Illinois Press, 1984.

WORKS ABOUT JAMES TATE

Degruson, Eugene H. *James Tate: A Descriptive Bibliography.* Westport, Conn.: Meckler, 2000.

Gardener, Stephen. "James Tate." In *American Poets Since World War II,* Vol. 2. Edited by Donald J. Greiner. Detroit: Gale, 1980.

Shaw, Robert B., ed. *American Poetry Since 1960: Some Critical Perspectives.* Chester Springs, Penn.: Dufour Editions, 1974.

✍️
More About Tate

You can write to:
James Tate
16 Jones Road
Amherst, MA 01002

ALFRED LORD TENNYSON

(1809–1892)

by Rachel Hadas

Alfred Tennyson was born on 6 August 1809 at Somersby, Lincolnshire, in England. He was the fourth son of the Reverend George Clayton Tennyson, rector of Somersby, and Elizabeth (née Fytche) Tennyson. The Reverend George Tennyson had been virtually disinherited by his father in favor of a younger brother, and Alfred Tennyson's youth was overshadowed by this family feud.

Quotations from Tennyson's poetry throughout are taken from Ricks, ed., *The Poems of Tennyson.*

Life and Reputation

Tennyson wrote poetry from an early age with the fluency that would be his all his life. An average student, he nevertheless had a deep and enduring love for the classics. He studied at Trinity College, Cambridge, from 1827 to 1831 and left without taking a degree. One of Tennyson's lifelong friends from his university days was Edward FitzGerald (1809–1883), now known as the translator of the *Rubáiyát of Omar Khayyám*; his best friend was Arthur Henry Hallam.

*precocious talented or mature at an early age

*irony a situation in which the actual outcome is opposite or contrary to what was expected

*elegy a poem of sorrow or reflection, usually about one who is dead

*poet laureate in England, an outstanding poet, once appointed for life as a paid member of the royal household and expected to write poems for certain national occasions. In other countries, the term refers to a poet honored and recognized for his or her achievements

*blank verse unrhymed verse in iambic pentameter

*prolific producing many works; fertile; productive

*Victorian era the time of Queen Victoria (1837–1901)

Precocious* and productive, Tennyson wrote and published poetry while still very young (two volumes dated 1830 and 1832) and traveled in Europe with Hallam. When Hallam died suddenly in 1833 at age 22, Tennyson's whole life was changed; hope gave way to bitter and prolonged grief. It is one of the characteristic ironies* of art that without his anguish at the loss of a friend, Tennyson would never have written what may be his greatest poem, *In Memoriam,* an elegy* to Hallam that was published in 1850. In the same year, Tennyson married Emily Sellwood and was also named poet laureate* by Queen Victoria following the death of the previous laureate, William Wordsworth. In 1851 Emily gave birth to a stillborn son. The Tennysons' son Hallam was born in 1852; Lionel followed in 1854.

With his marriage and his new official poetic status, Tennyson became established not only as a family man but as a celebrity; for many years he enjoyed tremendous popular success and respect. He died at home on 6 October 1892 and was buried in Poets Corner, Westminster Abbey, in London.

Throughout his long life, Tennyson was an inventive and prolific poet. Master of many meters and stanza forms, he was also skillful and inventive on the level of the individual stanza or even the individual line. Sonnets, blank verse,* stanzaic lyrics with various elaborate rhyme schemes—Tennyson used them all with authority, fluency, and often great beauty.

Much of the abundant work of this versatile poet has been unfamiliar for most readers since his death. Some of Tennyson's most ambitious long poems, such as *The Princess, Maud,* and *Enoch Arden,* seem stilted and melodramatic now, despite many beautiful lines or passages. *Idylls of the King,* hugely popular in its own day, remains very readable but is read only in excerpts, if at all. This turn in taste is partly due to the fact that many readers are now unwilling to read long poems. Even in Tennyson's time, the novels of Charles Dickens, William Makepeace Thackeray, and George Eliot satisfied the popular appetite for stories far more than a long poem was able to do.

The ups and downs of poetic taste make it difficult to be sure what portion of a prolific* poet's work will last the longest. Tennyson's legacy is further complicated by the fact that his career squarely coincided with and indeed seemed to exemplify the Victorian era,* culminating in his being named the poet laureate. Subsequent reaction, whether against Tennyson's official success or his flowery language, has sometimes had the personal zeal of an adolescent's rebellion against parents who are behind the times. Now that this excessive reaction has run its course, Tennyson is simply one among several excellent Victorian poets. We can see him in all his human unevenness—versatile, prolific, ambitious, restless, and probably aware of his own weaknesses. Like that of most poets, Tennyson's achievement was uneven, but this need not detract from the richness and appeal of his best work.

Dramatic Monologues

Much of Tennyson's most enduring and accessible poetry can be found in his dramatic monologues.* Rarely more than a few pages long, these poems feature characters from other sources, most often Greek mythology (Tithonus, Oenone, Demeter, Ulysses). Some are not true dramatic monologues in that instead of being spoken by the title character, they are spoken by someone else ("The Lady of Shalott," "The Lotos-Eaters," and "Mariana" are examples). But all these poems are dramatic, charged with the predicament of the protagonist,* for the people in them are always in some kind of trouble. Tithonus, who has been granted eternal life without the eternal youth that should accompany it, laments:

> The woods decay, the woods decay and fall,
> The vapours weep their burthen* to the ground,
> Man comes and tills the field and lies beneath,
>   And after many a summer dies the swan.
> Me only cruel immortality*
> Consumes; I wither slowly in thine arms.
>
> "Tithonus"

After wandering for many years, Ulysses has reached home safely but is bored and restless. The poem named for him has become a classic expression of the human determination to keep exploring, whatever the cost.

> . . . Come, my friends,
> 'Tis not too late to seek a newer world.
> . . . .
> One equal temper of heroic hearts,
> Made weak by time and fate, but strong in will
> To strive, to seek, to find, and not to yield.
>
> "Ulysses"

*dramatic monologue a poem written as a speech by one character

*protagonist the main character of a literary work

*burthen burden

*immortality deathlessness; eternal life

*vessel a ship

*mariner a sailor

*furrow a groove; in this case, the trough of a wave

*Achilles legendary hero of Greek mythology; protagonist of Homer's *Iliad*

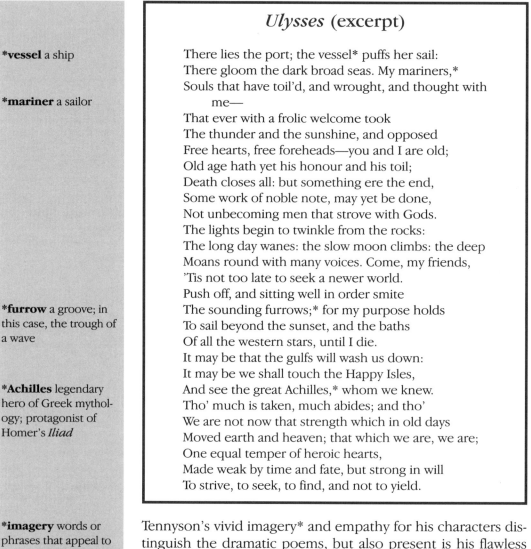

Ulysses (excerpt)

There lies the port; the vessel* puffs her sail:
There gloom the dark broad seas. My mariners,*
Souls that have toil'd, and wrought, and thought with
    me—
That ever with a frolic welcome took
The thunder and the sunshine, and opposed
Free hearts, free foreheads—you and I are old;
Old age hath yet his honour and his toil;
Death closes all: but something ere the end,
Some work of noble note, may yet be done,
Not unbecoming men that strove with Gods.
The lights begin to twinkle from the rocks:
The long day wanes: the slow moon climbs: the deep
Moans round with many voices. Come, my friends,
'Tis not too late to seek a newer world.
Push off, and sitting well in order smite
The sounding furrows;* for my purpose holds
To sail beyond the sunset, and the baths
Of all the western stars, until I die.
It may be that the gulfs will wash us down:
It may be we shall touch the Happy Isles,
And see the great Achilles,* whom we knew.
Tho' much is taken, much abides; and tho'
We are not now that strength which in old days
Moved earth and heaven; that which we are, we are;
One equal temper of heroic hearts,
Made weak by time and fate, but strong in will
To strive, to seek, to find, and not to yield.

*imagery words or phrases that appeal to one or more of the five senses in order to create a mental picture

Tennyson's vivid imagery* and empathy for his characters distinguish the dramatic poems, but also present is his flawless ear for how the words sound when read aloud.

Short Lyrics

*lyric a kind of poetry dominated by musical and personal expression

Tennyson's attention to the musical effects of language evident in the dramatic poems also marks many of his shorter lyric* poems. Unlike the monologues, these lyrics do not feature characters or events; instead, they seem to express pure feeling, so that the meaning of the words in the poem is secondary to their sound and mood. Like music, these short poems can be packed with emotion, but just what that emotion refers to or springs from is difficult to pin down. "Sweet and Low" is clearly a lullaby:

> Sweet and low, sweet and low,
>   Wind of the western sea,
> Low, low, breathe and blow,
>   Wind of the western sea!
> Over the rolling waters go,
> Come from the dying moon, and blow,
>   Blow him again to me;
> While my little one, while my pretty one, sleeps.

Several of the lyrics do not deal in human relationships at all:

> The splendour falls on castle walls
>   And snowy summits old in story;
> The long light shakes across the lakes,
>   And the wild cataract* leaps in glory.
> Blow, bugle, blow, set the wild echoes flying,
> Blow, bugle; answer, echoes, dying, dying, dying.
>   "The Splendour Falls"

*cataract waterfall

Although the imagery is clear and appealing, the chief virtue of these poems lies in their beautiful sounds and their tantalizing vagueness; the latter quality makes them, like music, more universal than any specific story.

In Memoriam

This long poem began as a series of brief, disconnected elegies that Tennyson began to write after Hallam's death. These poems accumulated for seventeen years (1833–1850) before they were combined and published; the resulting long poem, entirely composed of quatrains,* has a unique structure. *In Memoriam* is tight, even rigid, on the scale of the individual stanza. Tennyson adheres to the *abba* iambic tetrameter* quatrains and yet avoids monotony, for he manages not only to sustain the form—finding endless rhymes, for example—but also to vary its pace and tone. Furthermore, despite the predictable compactness of the individual unit, *In Memoriam* is loose in its overall structure. The poem moves back and forth

*quatrain a stanza of four lines

*iambic tetrameter a line of verse consisting of four metrical feet, each of which has one unstressed syllable followed by one stressed syllable

in time and space as it records the zigzags of emotion and the loopings of memory. In this combination of precision in individual stanzas and a loose overall structure, the poem resembles the translation of the *Rubáiyát* made a few years later by Tennyson's friend FitzGerald; both poems are hypnotic in their formal predictability and yet fluid in their twists and turns.

In Memoriam came entirely from Hallam's death. Its subject matter, grief, is both intensely personal and universal. By giving this intimate and emotional theme so much room to develop, Tennyson created a remarkably honest work of art, one that tells many enduring truths about the experience of sorrow over time. Reading straight through *In Memoriam* is probably the best way to appreciate the poem's emotional ups and downs, its echoes and revisiting, such as the references to successive Christmases following Hallam's death. *In Memoriam* is also a poem into which readers can profitably dip. Each person will find different places where the poem speaks directly to her or him. Some remarkable passages describe the writer's impatience with banal* letters of condolence:

> One writes, that 'Other friends remain,'
>   That 'Loss is common to the race'—
>   And common is the commonplace,
> And vacant chaff* well meant for grain.
>
> That loss is common would not make
>   My own less bitter, rather more:
>   Too common! Never morning wore
> To evening, but some heart did break.

Tennyson's honest recording of the roller-coaster ups and downs of grief is evident in this passage:

> What words are these have fallen from me?
>   Can calm despair and wild unrest
>   Be tenants of a single breast,
> Or sorrow such a changeling be?

A precise and beautiful evocation* of the motion and effect of Tennyson's chosen verse form is "Short swallow-flights of song, that dip / Their wings in tears, and skim away." Such comments on the poet's own writing give *In Memoriam* a personal, unguarded intimacy that adds to the appealing frankness of the poem as a whole.

*__banal__ commonplace; unoriginal

*__chaff__ worthless husks of grains (such as wheat) separated out during the process of threshing

*__evocation__ a calling to mind

Although it is the source of many famous phrases, such as "nature red in tooth and claw" or " 'Tis better to have loved and lost / Than never to have loved at all," *In Memoriam* does not lend itself to summary. The poet reaches no hard and fast conclusions about life, death, God, or immortality; as he himself wrote, he touches down only to fly away. In addition, the poem refuses to sentimentalize Hallam; the dead man is evoked chiefly as an absence whose pain grows gradually more bearable. In our own age this remarkable poem, monumental in scale and yet intimate in tone, continues to compel.

Idylls of the King

This sequence of twelve short-story-length poems, or idylls, retelling the familiar tale of King Arthur, occupied Tennyson from 1833 to 1889, when the entire poem was published in its final order. Tennyson's blank-verse narrative version of this richly powerful material has his characteristic virtues of musical language, vivid imagery, and raw emotion. Perhaps because of its scope, *Idylls of the King* has been more sharply criticized than the shorter dramatic poems. Tennyson's literary peers found the poem too Victorian and moralistic, not medieval enough. To readers now, the allegorical* structure of the poem may seem too obvious. King Arthur appears to represent mankind's higher nature, and the other main characters fall predictably into symbolic slots, so that his wife, Guinevere, and her lover, Lancelot, represent temptation and betrayal. Rather than crudely insisting on such symbolism, Tennyson chooses to stress the scenic aspect of the poem, its backdrops and weather and their appropriate moods. Thus the early idylls,* such as "Gareth and Lynette," set in the early days of Camelot, are springlike and hopeful, but as the years pass the idylls move steadily toward winter. At the end of the wintry conclusion, "The Passing of Arthur," a faint hope is indicated by the sunrise of a new year. The Arthurian legend clearly continues to exert a fascination: the image of Camelot* was frequently invoked to describe the presidency of John Kennedy.

*allegorical having a story in which the fictional objects, characters, and actions are equated with meanings that lie outside the narrative itself.

*idyll a long narrative poem on a major theme

*Camelot legendary site of King Arthur's palace and court

Less-Known Works

In order to appreciate the restless reach of Tennyson's career, readers should be aware of the range of some of the poet's less-known works. Tennyson was a master of poems written in dialect; "Owd Roä" (Old Rover) is the touching story of a faithful dog. Another kind of dramatic monologue, "Walking to the Mail," in its capturing of conversation in blank verse, surprisingly anticipates the work of Robert Frost:

> *John.*   And when does this come by?
> *James.* The mail? At one o'clock.
> *John.*   What is it now?
> *James.* A quarter to.
> *John.*   Whose house is that I see?

As a lover of Greek and Latin poetry, Tennyson paid tribute to the old masters with skillful imitations of their demanding meters: alcaics, dactylic hexameters, hendecasyllabics (see glossary in volume 3):

> O you chorus of indolent reviewers,
> Irresponsible, indolent reviewers,
> Look, I come to the test, a tiny poem
> All composed in a meter of Catullus*
>   "Hendecasyllabics"

*Catullus (84 B.C.–54 B.C.) Roman lyric poet

In Tennyson's early poem "The Epic," a young poet, probably Tennyson himself, is asked by his friends to read aloud from his work. Before he consents to read them his brand-new "Morte d'Arthur" ("The Death of Arthur"), the poet hesitates, confessing his uneasiness about the appropriateness of epic in this day and age:

> 'Nay, nay,' said Hall,
> 'Why take the style of those heroic times?
> For nature brings not back the Mastodon,*
> Nor we those times; and why should any man
> Remodel models? these twelve books of mine
> Were faint Homeric* echoes, nothing-worth,
> Mere chaff and draff, much better burnt.'

*mastodon an extinct elephant-like mammal

*Homeric characteristic of Homer's long heroic epics, the *Iliad* and the *Odyssey* (ca. 750 B.C.)

The self-questioning here and elsewhere in Tennyson's work suggests that his sustained success had not blinded him to the poetic risks he ran. His greatest challenge may well have been the haunting feeling that the great age of poetry was over. Tennyson's late sonnet "Poets and Their Bibliographies" ends by wondering whether the modern world, with its cult of celebrity, is actually harmful to the art of poetry.

> If, glancing downward on the kindly sphere
>   That once had rolled you round and round the Sun,
>   You see your Art still shrined in human shelves,
> You should be jubilant* that you flourished here
>   Before the Love of Letters, overdone,
>   Had swampt the sacred poets with themselves.

*jubilant joyful; exultant; triumphant

Tennyson's reverence for poetry stayed with him all his life. Even if as a much-honored poet he shrank from adverse criticism, Tennyson may have remained, in private, his own most severe critic.

Selected Bibliography

WORKS BY ALFRED LORD TENNYSON

Poems (1833).

Poems (1842).

The Princess (1847).

In Memoriam (1850).

Maud and Other Poems (1855).

Idylls of the King (1859, 1862, 1874).

Enoch Arden (1864).

Available Collection

The Poems of Tennyson. Edited by Christopher Ricks. 2d ed. 3 vols. Berkeley and Los Angeles: University of California Press, 1987.

WORKS ABOUT ALFRED LORD TENNYSON

Buckley, Jerome H. *Tennyson: The Growth of a Poet.* Cambridge, Mass.: Harvard University Press, 1960.

Culler, Arthur Dwight. *The Poetry of Tennyson.* New Haven, Conn.: Yale University Press, 1977.

Henderson, Philip. *Tennyson, Poet and Prophet.* London: Routledge and Kegan Paul, 1978.

IF YOU LIKE the poetry of Tennyson, you might also like the poetry of Robert Browning or Henry Wadsworth Longfellow.

Hughes, Linda K. *The Manyfaced Glass: Tennyson's Dramatic Monologues.* Athens: Ohio University Press, 1987.

Joseph, Gerhard. *Tennysonian Love: The Strange Diagonal.* Minneapolis: University of Minnesota Press, 1969.

Jump, John D., ed. *Tennyson: The Critical Heritage.* London: Routledge and Kegan Paul, 1967.

Kincaid, James R. *Tennyson's Major Poems: The Comic and Ironic Patterns.* New Haven, Conn.: Yale University Press, 1975.

Kissane, James D. *Alfred Tennyson.* New York: Twayne, 1970.

Martin, Robert Bernard. *Tennyson: The Unquiet Heart.* New York: Oxford University Press, 1980.

Richardson, Joanna. *The Pre-eminent Victorian: A Study of Tennyson.* London: Jonathan Cape, 1962.

Rosenberg, John D. *The Fall of Camelot: A Study of Tennyson's* Idylls of the King. Cambridge, Mass.: Harvard University Press, 1973.

Tucker, Herbert F. *Tennyson and the Doom of Romanticism.* Cambridge, Mass.: Harvard University Press, 1988.

✍

More About Tennyson:

You can find information about Alfred Lord Tennyson on the Internet at:
http://www.stg.brown.edu /projects/hypertext/landow /victorian/tennyson /tennyov.html
http://charon.sfsu.edu /tennyson/tennyson.html

DYLAN THOMAS

(1914–1953)

by Douglas Oliver

As Swansea, Wales, schoolboys in the 1920s, Dylan Thomas and the future composer Daniel Jones would broadcast to each other upstairs and downstairs at the Jones's house via a radiogram.* Program titles included "The Rev. Percy will play three piano pieces, Buzzards at Dinner, Salute to Admiral Beattie, and Badgers Beneath My Vest"; "Locomotive Bowen, the one-eyed cowhand, will give a talk on the Rocking Horse and Varnishing Industry"; and "Zoilredb Pogoho will read his poem Fiffokorp" (the Russian composer Sergei Prokofiev's name reversed). Thomas's adult poetry included such verbal creations as "man-iron," "bagpipe-breasted," "seaspindle," and "bonerailed"; complex puns such as "corset the boneyards"; subconscious associations like "man of leaves" and "wood of weathers"; and nouns-as-verbs or mixed-sense adjectives, such as "brassy orator" and "tear-stuffed time" (Francis Scarfe, "Dylan Thomas: A Pioneer," Tedlock, *Dylan Thomas,* pp. 96–112).

At the Kaufmann Auditorium in New York on 14 May 1953, Thomas first presented his play for voices, *Under Milk Wood,* set

*radiogram a predecessor of the audio cassette recorder, combining a record player (gramophone) and a radio

Quotations from Thomas's poetry throughout are taken from Davies and Maud, ed., *Collected Poems 1934–1953.*

*bard a poet and singer

*ecstatic extreme delight; also a person who continually feels a divine presence

*lyrical having a musical quality

in the mythical Welsh village of Llareggub (reversed, it is a mildly impolite term for "nothing") modeled on the real Laugharne, a village in southwest Wales. That bubbling schoolboyish delight in the fun of words had never left him. That November, on his fourth and last tour of the United States, Thomas died in St. Vincent's Hospital, New York, leaving a mystery about his death and a double legend: first, of the word-drunk genius dreaming in his boathouse in Laugharne (now a museum) overlooking the tidal sands, and, second, of the literally drunk, inspired, chanting, traveling bard* ruined by excessive admiration.

The legends have been harmful. In Britain after his death, Thomas's ecstatic,* lyrical* poetry ran smack into a reaction, with mainstream British poets favoring modesty and honesty over the grandiose "new apocalypse" style of Thomas and his poetic colleagues. (New apocalypse poetry can be characterized as having great faith in imaginative powers, spiritual aspirations, and, sometimes, grandiose imagery.) If the academic community has sometimes slighted him, book sales show that he has never lost his wider public.

Between boyhood and death, a lifetime of exploiting anyone who could contribute to his upkeep drained innocence from Thomas, but in vision, language, and poetic craft he remained incorruptible. Never a profound philosopher, he read poetry deeply, sensing that to envision clearly enough and to let words well up to create wonderful sounds produce another kind of depth. His extraordinary use of words, as he would say, enabled him to "see."

Country and Town Boy

Born on 27 October 1914, he first lived at 5 Cwmdonkin Drive, Uplands, Swansea, on the southern shores of Wales. His mother, Florence, came from a farming family with the surname Williams. His father, D. J. Thomas, a stern, embittered English teacher at Swansea Grammar School, loved poetry fiercely and let young Dylan range among his magazines and books. Before D. J. died in 1952, Dylan had already written the celebrated villanelle* "Do not go gentle into that good night," a poem showing pride in his difficult father, who was a lifelong influence. Dylan had one sister, Nancy.

Although his parents spoke Welsh together, Dylan, a neglectful student in everything except literature, never learned

*villanelle a rigorously formal poem in which whole lines and only two rhyming sounds are repeated

his native language. Yet few writers in English have had a more Welsh lilt,* and the stuff of his imagination is Welsh: village eccentrics, family life, biblical imagery, the seashore, small farms, and, above all, the rolling seaside hills surmounted by hawks and estuary* sands stalked by herons—these make the fuller romance of many of his best poems.

There were two early Thomases: town boy and country boy. The town boy scribbled away at childhood poems, first published them in his school magazine at the age of eleven, failed most of his graduation exams, and left school in 1931. Shunning university studies, he became a junior reporter for the *South Wales Daily Post* and reviewed for the weekly *Herald of Wales.* The country boy would visit relatives in the rural area northwest of Swansea, especially his aunt Ann Jones's farmstead, and absorb deep into his spirit the life he later portrayed in romantic elegy* or in lovely comic burlesque.*

When Ann Jones died in 1933, the teenage Thomas began a celebrated elegy eventually revised for publication in 1938.

> After the funeral, mule praises, brays,
> Windshake of sailshaped ears, muffle-toed tap
> Tap happily of one peg in the thick
> Grave's foot
> "After the funeral"

The most entertaining guides to Thomas's early life are his own stories and radio broadcasts, notably the autobiographical *Portrait of the Artist as a Young Dog* and the collection *Quite Early One Morning.* They are not factually reliable, however, because Thomas mythologizes both himself and the local populace into comic grotesques.*

The Prodigy

Thomas's work was so advanced, adventurous, and musical that he had poems accepted by Welsh and London publications when he was still a teenager. An early version of "And death shall have no dominion" was published in the *New English Weekly* in London as early as 1933. By 1934 his publishing credits included many influential London literary journals, and the youthful work already included what are now anthology

*__lilt__ rhythmic swing

*__estuary__ a water passage where the tide of the ocean meets a river current

*__elegy__ a poem of sorrow or reflection, usually about one who is dead

*__burlesque__ a character or work of art that is ridiculously exaggerated for comic purposes; a caricature

*__grotesque__ with absurdly exaggerated characteristics; also someone or something grotesque

pieces: "I see the boys of summer," "The force that through the green fuse," and "Light breaks where no sun shines," the last of which was absurdly judged obscene by readers of the British Broadcasting Corporation's magazine, the *Listener.* The BBC's apology only increased Thomas's renown.

The poet Pamela Hansford Johnson liked Thomas's early poems; they corresponded, visited, and contemplated marriage, but the Thomas mentality was too immature for Hansford Johnson. His life was doomed to be messy. Thomas won the *Sunday Referee* poetry book prize, which led to the 1934 publication of his first book, *Eighteen Poems*. Hansford Johnson had been the previous year's winner. While this collection was charged with being too interested in words as sounds alone, critics quickly hailed the twenty-year-old poet as a new force. The magazine *Time and Tide* proclaimed: "It is more probably the sort of bomb that bursts not more than once in three years" (Desmond Hawkins, *Time and Tide,* 9 February 1935, in Tremlett, *Dylan Thomas,* p. 49).

Some critics in the 1930s wrongly associated Thomas with surrealism,* but he hotly denied this connection. True, he read his poetry at the 1936 International Surrealist Exhibition in London with Paul Éluard and David Gascoyne, French and English surrealist poets, respectively. (The painter Salvador Dali posed in a sweaty diving suit.) He could not read French, however, and his poetry's difficulty had a simpler origin: that boyhood love of tricks with words had changed into a sophisticated adult practice.

Nowadays, a beginning reader of Thomas is helped by Walford Davies and Ralph Maud's edition of the *Collected Poems* or William York Tindall's *Reader's Guide to Dylan Thomas.* With this guidance, new readers can enter Thomas's unusual world with greater ease.

Thomas's early themes derived from his reading of the eighteenth-century poet William Blake: the poet's imagination like, it is supposed, the divine mind, can see as a harmonious unity aspects of existence more normally regarded as contraries or opposites—birth and death, good and evil, male and female, human and natural worlds, and so on.

> The force that through the green fuse drives the flower
> Drives my green age; that blasts the roots of trees
> Is my destroyer.
> > "The force that through the green fuse"

*surrealism an artistic movement that aimed (chiefly during the 1920s and 1930s) to express the workings of the unconscious or subconscious mind

Thomas inherited an occultism* coming down through Blake from the Renaissance. In Thomas, the strain does not always run deep; many superficially entrancing poems are not finally satisfying. When a further element enters the poetry, what the poet Gerard Manley Hopkins called "inscape," the natural world seen through the poet's imagination becomes a shining presence. Then, his fine poetic voice, crafted with extreme care into syllable, line, rhyme, cadence,* and stanza, creates a poetry that is unique.

Meeting Caitlin

In 1936 the Dent edition of *Twenty-Five Poems* was published. That year Thomas also met Caitlin Macnamara, a mistress of the fiery English painter Augustus John, and spent five nights with her at a hotel. Later, Thomas turned up when John and Macnamara were visiting the novelist Richard Hughes at Castle House, in Laugharne. The aging painter, jealous of this ill-kempt, dwarfish Welshman with his angelic brown-blond curls and lobster-like eyes, knocked the poet down in a fistfight. Later, John painted an inspiring image of the young Thomas; Dylan and Caitlin returned several times to live in Laugharne.

In 1937, young and impoverished, Dylan married Caitlin in Cornwall. The stormy marriage was beset by money problems and complicated by alcohol, Dylan's slyness, and Caitlin's hot temper. Thomas had become a boyish figure in the London literary avant-garde,* shuttling between Wales and the English capital, a bubbling and very funny storyteller, but also a hustler for publication and friendly "loans," which rarely were repaid.

In November of that year, the avant-garde's high priestess, the English poet and critic Edith Sitwell, reviewed *Twenty-Five Poems* in the *Sunday Times* newspaper. She wrote that she "could not name one poet of this, the youngest generation, who shows so great a promise, and even so great an achievement" (quoted in Davies, *Reference Companion,* p. 43). Her judgment finally launched Thomas into fame as Britain's inescapable prodigy.* *Twenty-Five Poems* contains a brilliant, obscure sequence of ten sonnets, "Altarwise by owl-light," and other poems, such as the revised "And death shall have no dominion," that became favorites. In 1939 Thomas

*occultism belief in or study of the action or influence of supernatural or supernormal powers

*cadence the rhythms of the flow of language or verse music

*avant-garde advanced or cutting-edge; experimental; normally applies to the arts

*prodigy one who is highly talented

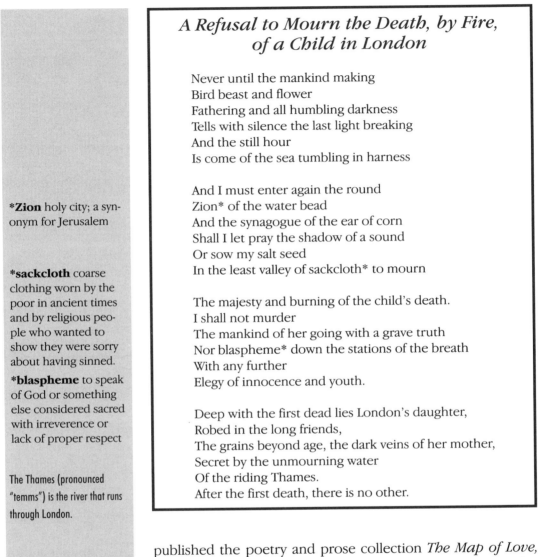

A Refusal to Mourn the Death, by Fire, of a Child in London

Never until the mankind making
Bird beast and flower
Fathering and all humbling darkness
Tells with silence the last light breaking
And the still hour
Is come of the sea tumbling in harness

And I must enter again the round
Zion* of the water bead
And the synagogue of the ear of corn
Shall I let pray the shadow of a sound
Or sow my salt seed
In the least valley of sackcloth* to mourn

The majesty and burning of the child's death.
I shall not murder
The mankind of her going with a grave truth
Nor blaspheme* down the stations of the breath
With any further
Elegy of innocence and youth.

Deep with the first dead lies London's daughter,
Robed in the long friends,
The grains beyond age, the dark veins of her mother,
Secret by the unmourning water
Of the riding Thames.
After the first death, there is no other.

***Zion** holy city; a synonym for Jerusalem

***sackcloth** coarse clothing worn by the poor in ancient times and by religious people who wanted to show they were sorry about having sinned.

***blaspheme** to speak of God or something else considered sacred with irreverence or lack of proper respect

The Thames (pronounced "temms") is the river that runs through London.

published the poetry and prose collection *The Map of Love,* which includes the Ann Jones funeral poem and "I make this in a warring absence." It is as if a hint of early marital difficulties had been transformed into a vision of love that can harmonize the contrary impulses of male and female.

Thomas made his first adult radio broadcast for the BBC Welsh Service in 1937. He lived with Caitlin in Laugharne in 1938, and their first child, Llewelyn, was born in 1939. Later, they would have two other children, Aeronwy and Colm. In the United States, New Directions published a prose and poetry selection, *The World I Breathe* in 1939, and *New Poems* in

1943; in England, Dent published the *Portrait of the Artist as a Young Dog* stories in 1940.

Maturity and War

Wartime was difficult: the poet, who was horrified by the killing, escaped military service, perhaps by faking his medical examination. Unmoored, he scrounged for grants or loans or sold his notebooks. He lived in Laugharne until July 1940 and then with friends in southern England, much of the time in London, during the German air raids, and later with his parents in Wales. In 1944 he moved to the bungalow* Majoda at New Quay, Wales, to begin one of his most productive periods. The following year, an intoxicated commando officer, believing his wife was having intimate relations with Dylan and Caitlin, raked the bungalow with machine-gun fire. The officer was acquitted, but the episode underlined the precariousness* of the Thomases' life.

> ***bungalow** a type of house, usually one story with a low-pitched roof

> ***precariousness** uncertainty; insecurity

Thomas's wartime writing includes fine elegies about deaths caused by the German bombing of London and scripts for Ministry of Information documentaries and for film companies. "A Refusal to Mourn the Death, by Fire, of a Child in London," the finest of elegies, reads like a response to a newspaper story, and was sent in a letter to Vernon Watkins on 28 March 1945. An able scriptwriter, Thomas wrote his best film scenario for Donald Taylor in 1944, *The Doctor and the Devils*. His 1944 radio script "Quite Early One Morning" was a foretaste of his later international success with *Under Milk Wood*.

With *Deaths and Entrances* in 1946, Thomas emerged as a mature talent. The collection included "The Hunchback in the Park," a rewritten teenage poem about his Swansea boyhood, as well as the bombing elegies, "A Winter's Tale," "When I woke," the quirky "Ballad of the Long-Legged Bait," and two anthology pieces to fall in love with: "Poem in October" and "Fern Hill," each in intricate stanzas:

> It was my thirtieth year to heaven
> Woke to my hearing from harbour and neighbour wood
> And the mussel pooled and the heron
>   Priested shore
>   The morning beckon

With water praying and call of seagull and rook
And the knock of sailing boats on the net webbed wall
"Poem in October"

Reading these lines aloud will help convey the swing, syncopation,* and intense vowel and consonant echoing (see the second line's *w,h,h,w,* somewhat similar to the ancient Welsh technique of *cynghanedd,* or consonant chiming). Further, Thomas frequently used Blake's device of repeating vocabulary from poem to poem. The common "heron" recurs, transformed, for example, into "Herons spire and spear" ("Poem on his Birthday"), where "Priested" now suggests a church "spire" (heron stretching its neck) mutating into "spear" as the fisher-bird stabs the water.

The post–World War II poems sometimes imply spiritual unease and self-doubt; their claim to happiness can seem willful, supported by biblical imagery, imprecise mysticism,* or pagan mythology. They achieve grandeur when he trusts the words themselves, as they form in his imagination, to create full meaning, rather than trusting to a more conscious control over intelligibility. Then the poem's narrative moves onwards to the ornate sound of verbal music that matches both the meaning and emotional significance of what is said.

After World War II, Thomas was a frequent radio broadcaster and film scriptwriter, though he was writing poetry more slowly, more carefully. He had a travel grant to Italy, went to Prague as an honored poet-guest, and finally moved back to Laugharne.

Fame and Tragedy

Margaret Taylor, whose husband, A. J. P. Taylor, was a well-known historian, had taken up the Thomases as a cause. After the Majoda incident, the Taylors lodged the couple in a wooden summerhouse on their grounds; in 1947 they provided an Oxfordshire manor house that the Thomases quickly became dissatisfied with; and in 1949, they moved to the Boat House at Laugharne, which Margaret had acquired for them.

Soon after moving there, Thomas was invited to read in New York by John Malcolm Brinnin, who was the director of the Poetry Center of the Young Men's and Young Women's Hebrew Association in New York, and who acted as Dylan's U.S.

tour organizer. A hectic, forty-reading tour followed in 1950; Brinnin's anguished account of this and of Thomas's subsequent U.S. tours (*Dylan Thomas in America*) promoted an image of the poet as drunken victim of his success. Thomas seems to have behaved professionally before and during performances, only descending into late-night drinking afterward. It was the poet as rock star, as George Tremlett has suggested: huge audiences, great humor and good feeling, and the rolling voice soaring over everything.

His marriage was in trouble, partly because Caitlin suspected him of having affairs in the United States. He was contemplating a long poetic sequence to be called *In Country Heaven.* It would have included "In Country Sleep," the grand "Over Sir John's Hill" (the headland across from his boathouse), and "In the White Giant's Thigh." In a 1950 radio broadcast he said the work would be about happiness and would include the godhead, the author, the milky-way farmer, the first cause, architect, lamp-lighter, quintessence, the beginning Word, the anthropomorphic* bowler-out and blackballer, the stuff of all men, scapegoat, martyr, maker, woe-bearer . . . and so forth. He talked of Blakean light and tears gliding down together, the godhead weeping, Country Heaven dark. The earth has killed itself. Ultimately the poem would stand as "an affirmation of the beautiful and terrible worth of the Earth."

*anthropomorphic having human qualities but not human

Little clear sense can be made out of this hodgepodge of often obscure terms but they are nevertheless vaguely suggestive and should not be sneered at, for the sequence could well have been a great one. Its water imagery and hints of ecological disaster strike a modern environmentalist reader as prophetic.* The sometimes wintry, frosty clarity of these late poems is some measure of what British poetry lost by his death, for he was at the height of his powers.

*prophetic predicting the future

Accounts of that death vary. On 19 October 1953 Thomas arrived in New York for his fourth U.S. tour, and he was excited about working with the composer Igor Stravinsky on a libretto.* His last public reading was at City College, New York, on 29 October, and on 5 November, probably as the result of alcohol consumption compounded with cortisone and morphine injections, he collapsed at the Chelsea Hotel, having earlier told his companion, Liz Reitell, "I've had eighteen straight whiskies. I think that's a record." He had alcohol-induced pneumonia and perhaps a cerebral complication. When Caitlin arrived on 8 November he was still in a coma. He

*libretto the text of an opera or other musical narrative

*stereotypical based on preconceived categories rather than actual facts

died the next day as the poet John Berryman was watching a nurse bathe him. Caitlin took the body back home, and Dylan Thomas was buried in Laugharne on 24 November.

The stereotypical* image of Thomas in beer-soaked corduroys propping up a favorite bar, such as New York's White Horse Tavern, is misleading. His bardic voice and his enchanted eye for scenery, eccentric character, and magical combinations of words, haunt us yet. He left a select group of poems whose high position in twentieth-century British poetry seems secure.

IF YOU LIKE the poetry of Thomas, you might also like the poetry of Gerard Manley Hopkins or John Donne.

₰

Selected Bibliography

WORKS BY DYLAN THOMAS
Poetry

Eighteen Poems (1934).

Twenty-Five Poems (1936).

The World I Breathe (1939).

The Map of Love (1939). Poems and stories.

New Poems (1943).

Deaths and Entrances (1946).

Selected Writings of Dylan Thomas (1946).

In Country Sleep and Other Poems (1952).

Short Stories and Essays

Portrait of the Artist as a Young Dog (1940). Autobiographical short stories.

Adventures in the Skin Trade and Other Stories (1953).

Quite Early One Morning (1954). Includes radio broadcasts.

A Prospect of the Sea, and Other Stories and Prose Writings (1955). Edited by Daniel Jones.

Film Scripts

The Doctor and the Devils. (1953).

The Beach of Falesa (1963). Based on a short story by Robert Louis Stevenson.

A Film Script of Twenty Years A-Growing: From the Story by Maurice O'Sullivan (1964).

The Doctor and the Devils, and Other Scripts (1966). Introduction by Ralph Maud.

Selected Sound Recordings

Selections from the Writings of Dylan Thomas (1952–1960). Caedmon TC-1005, 1018, 1043, 1061, 1132. Five records; includes works by other authors, too.

Under Milk Wood: A Play for Voices (1954). Argo RG 21–22. Two records.

An Evening with Dylan Thomas, Reading His Own and Other Poems (1963). Caedmon TC-1157.

Dylan Thomas Reading His Complete Recorded Poetry (1963). Caedmon TC-2014. Two records.

The Complete Recorded Stories and Humorous Essays (1972). Caedmon TC-3006.

Available Collections

Collected Essays, 1934–1952. London: Dent, 1957.

Collected Poems, 1934–1952. London: Dent, 1953. Also published as *The Collected Poems of Dylan Thomas*. New York: New Directions, 1953.

Collected Poems, 1934–1953. Edited with notes by Walford Davies and Ralph Maud. London: Dent, 1988. The best edition.

The Collected Prose of Dylan Thomas. 3 vols. New York: New Directions, 1969.

The Collected Stories. London: Dent, 1983; New York: New Directions, 1984.

Early Prose Writings of Dylan Thomas. Edited with an introduction by Walford Davies. New York: New Directions, 1971.

Letters to Vernon Watkins. Edited with an introduction by Vernon Watkins. New York: New Directions, 1957.

The Notebooks of Dylan Thomas. Edited by Ralph Maud. New York: New Directions, 1967.

WORKS ABOUT DYLAN THOMAS

Ackerman, John. *Dylan Thomas: His Life and Work*. London: Oxford University Press, 1964. Illuminating.

Ackerman, John. *A Dylan Thomas Companion*. Basingstoke, U.K.: Macmillan, 1989.

Brinnin, John Malcolm. *Dylan Thomas in America*. Boston: Little, Brown, 1955. Started the controversy about his later days.

Davies, James A. *A Reference Companion to Dylan Thomas*. Westport, Conn.: Greenwood, 1998.

Davies, Walford. *Dylan Thomas*. New York: St. Martin's Press, 1990.

Ferris, Paul. *Dylan Thomas*. London: Hodder and Stoughton, 1977. One of the best studies.

FitzGibbon, Constantine. *The Life of Dylan Thomas*. London: Dent, 1965. Much detail.

Jones, Daniel. *My Friend Dylan Thomas*. London: Dent, 1977. By his close childhood friend.

Jones, Richard. "Introductory Note to Dylan Thomas's 'Poetic Manifesto.'" *Texas Quarterly* 4 (Winter 1961): 4. Followed by Thomas's responses to Jones's questions, pp. 45–53.

Moynihan, William T. *The Craft and Art of Dylan Thomas*. Ithaca, N.Y.: Cornell University Press, 1966. A good examination of the poetic technique.

Olson, Elder. *The Poetry of Dylan Thomas*. Chicago: University of Chicago Press, 1954. Excellent study, still of value.

Tedlock, E. W., ed. *Dylan Thomas: The Legend and the Poet*. London: Heinemann, 1960; Westport, Conn.: Greenwood, 1975. Useful collection of essays, many by those who knew the poet.

Thomas, Caitlin. *Leftover Life to Kill*. London: Putnam, 1957. A fierce lament by his widow.

Tindall, William York. *A Reader's Guide to Dylan Thomas*. London: Thames and Hudson, 1962; Syracuse, N.Y.: Syracuse University Press, 1996. Still the best overall guide to the poetry.

Treece, Henry. *Dylan Thomas: Dog Among the Fairies*. London: Lindsay Drummond, 1949. Early coverage by a fellow "New Apocalypse" poet.

Tremlett, George. *Dylan Thomas, In the Mercy of His Means*. London: Constable, 1991. An interesting corrective to previous biographies.

TU FU

(712–770)

by David Hinton

Tu Fu is generally considered to be the greatest poet in the Chinese poetic tradition, which is the longest continuous poetic tradition in world literature. Given that he lived more than 1,200 years ago in a very distant culture, one would expect his poems to be difficult and foreign, but like the poems of all ancient Chinese poets, Tu Fu's writing feels familiar and contemporary. Consider the poem "Impromptu," which one might almost imagine being written by someone canoeing on a Vermont lake:

> A river moon cast only feet away, storm-lanterns
> Alight late in the second watch. . . . Serene
>
> Flock of fists on sand— egrets asleep when
> A fish leaps in the boat's wake, shivering, cry.

Quotations from Tu Fu's work throughout are taken from Hinton, ed. *The Selected Poems of Tu Fu.*

In ancient China, the night was divided into five two-hour "watches."

A Short Lesson in Chinese Poetics

*characters Chinese
words that are in the
form of pictograms or
ideograms

The experience conveyed by this poem survives intact, but the experience of reading it in English in this book today bears little resemblance to the experience of reading it in China a thousand years ago. Obviously the poem looked and sounded very different in the original. Even if we could read modern Chinese, it would not help very much, because classical Chinese, used for ancient literary texts, is a language all its own. Tu Fu would have written this poem in couplets (two-line stanzas), with exactly seven characters* to a line. The second lines of each couplet would have rhymed. Within the couplets, Tu Fu would have carefully chosen the characters so that each word in the first line is paired with the matching word in the second line, thus establishing contrasting but parallel elements. Here is a literal, word-for-word translation:

> (bank)
> sand head / sleep egrets // gather fists / tranquil
>
> boat tail / jump fish // spread out / cry (sound)
> (wake)

*resonate to have significance and relevance

In addition, he would have chosen characters that would call up other poems in the reader's mind. Thus, each character would resonate* with its own sound and meaning and the sound and meanings it created in relation to its line, its couplet, and other poems in which it had appeared.

Chinese provides little connecting material between characters. There are no conjunctions or prepositions. Chinese sentences generally do not have subjects and often lack verbs. Verbs do not have tenses. This means that if you read Tu Fu's poem in the original, you would be actively engaged in making all these connections yourself. In a very vital way, your reading would be another step in the poem's ongoing creation.

Early Years

Tu Fu was born in 712 near the then-capital of China, Ch'ang-an (Xi'an). He was born into the lower levels of the Chinese aristocracy, that class of society which served as scholar-officials for the government. His mother died shortly after his birth. His father remarried, and Tu Fu had three stepbrothers and one stepsister. We do not know very much about Tu Fu's early life, except that he received a full classical education and showed great promise as a student. In his teens and early twenties, he traveled extensively, which was not at all customary for young men of his age and class, especially because he apparently traveled alone, without his family.

Working in the government assisting the emperor to rule the people wisely was the only proper place for a man of his class in ancient China. In his mid-twenties, Tu Fu took the imperial examinations, which were the means by which men of his class secured government appointments (at this time in China, all government positions were reserved for men). He was one of the empire's star candidates, but to his great disappointment and everyone's surprise, Tu Fu failed these exams. Tu Fu soon left the capital city and spent the next eight years unsettled. It was during this time that he met his illustrious* contemporary Li Po in a country wineshop. This was a legendary meeting, for Tu Fu and Li Po are traditionally acclaimed as China's two greatest poets. After meeting several times during this period, the two poets never met again, but Tu Fu wrote many poems to Li Po, whom he admired a great deal. A particularly fine example of these poems is "Dreaming of Li Po," written when Tu Fu heard that Li Po had been banished to a dangerous section of southern China:

*illustrious well-regarded; famous for one's talents

> Death at least gives separation repose.
> Without death, its grief can only sharpen.
> You wander out in malarial* southlands,
> and I hear nothing of you, exiled*
>
> old friend. Knowing I think of you
> always now, you visit my dreams, my heart
> frightened it is no living spirit
> I dream. Endless miles— you come
>
> so far from the Yangtze's* sunlit maples
> night shrouds the passes when you return.
> And snared as you are in their net,
> with what bird's wings could you fly?
>
> Filling my room to the roof-beams, the moon
> sinks. You nearly linger in its light,

*malarial infected with malaria, a disease caused by parasites in the blood and transmitted by mosquitoes

*exiled forced out of one's homeland

*Yangtze the major river through southern China

but the waters deepen in long swells,
unfed dragons— take good care old friend.

Because his great talent was so apparent, Tu Fu was eventually offered a government position. But before he could settle his wife and children in the capital, his success fell victim to the major political event of his time: the devastating An Lu-shan Rebellion.*

Tu Fu's China

One of Tu Fu's great achievements was that he wrote poems about any subject, lofty or mundane, private or public. The poems are tied closely to his life, but they are also tied to history, for the momentous historical events of his time largely shaped his life. And so he came to be known as the "poet-historian."

Tu Fu was lucky to be born into one of the great periods of Chinese civilization. The ruling emperor was frugal and devoted. His military kept the country safe from "barbarian"* invasions, and within China the people knew peace and prosperity. This was a good time for the arts and letters, to which the emperor lent his strong support, and Chinese culture flourished. It is not by accident that the High T'ang period (ca. 713–755) produced two of China's best-known poets, Tu Fu and Li Po.

Such good fortune was not to last, however. By midcentury, about the time Tu Fu had returned to the capital, the empire was already in decline. The emperor's interests had turned from governing his people well to pleasing his favorite concubine* and pursuing immortality* through occult* methods. Affairs of state were left to the corrupt prime minister, and the military network soon escaped imperial control. In 755, An Lu-shan, a non-Chinese military governor on the frontier, rebelled. Within two years his rebel forces controlled most of northern China, including the capital. The emperor fled, and his concubine and prime minister were killed by his own armies.

The T'ang dynasty never recovered from the An Lu-shan Rebellion, and its repercussions* would last through the rest of Tu Fu's lifetime. The statistics are staggering. The census lists a population figure of fifty-three million prior to the rebellion and only seventeen million after it, which means that

*An Lu-shan Rebellion** a catastrophic civil war (A.D. 755–763) that devastated China during Tu Fu's life

*barbarians** term used by Chinese to refer to aboriginal people who lived on the borders of China

*concubine** a mistress

*immortality** deathlessness; eternal life

*occult** related to supernatural or supernormal powers

*repercussion** effect or result

about two-thirds of the Chinese people were either dead or homeless refugees. Tu Fu would never again know his country free of fighting: either rebellions from within or invasions from without, or both. Never would his Confucian* desire to serve the empire be uncomplicated by imperial* corruption, and never in his wanderings could he ignore the devastation caused by continuous political and social turmoil.

The terrible times that Tu Fu lived through often served as a backdrop to his poetry. Sometimes, as in "Moonlit Night Thinking of My Brothers" they are also its subject:

Warning drums have ended all travel.
A lone goose cries across autumn
Borderlands. White Dew begins tonight,
This bright moon bright there, over

My old village. My scattered brothers—
And no home to ask *Are they alive or dead?*
Letters never arrive. War comes
And goes— then comes like this again.

Tu Fu Makes a Decision

Tu Fu served as an adviser to the emperor during this war and was at one point trapped for a year in the rebel-occupied capital. The emperor did not always welcome Tu Fu's forthright and honest advice, so Tu Fu's career in government was a rocky one. Finally, in 759, when he was forty-seven years old and the rebel armies appeared to be defeated, Tu Fu resigned his post and moved with his wife and children three hundred miles west to Chin-chou (Jinzhou). Tu Fu's decision was remarkable for several reasons. First, it showed his willingness to give up his public life and his identity as a scholar-official, all to devote himself to poetry. Second, unlike most men who left government positions, Tu Fu had no means of support.

This decision brought much hardship for himself and his family. The years that followed were full of poverty and wandering, often driven by the need to escape from local fighting, which was constantly breaking out all over the empire. All of this was compounded by Tu Fu's chronic illnesses, such as asthma, diabetes, and malaria. After only two months

*Confucian** relating to the teaching of the Chinese philosopher Confucius (551–479 B.C.)

*imperial** related to an emperor or empire

in Chin-chou, the family traveled another five hundred miles south to Ch'eng-tu (Chengdu). There they spent a few happy and peaceful years living in a comfortable "thatched hut" beside a gentle river in a small farming village outside the city. During this period Tu Fu wrote many lovely poems about the simple pleasures of quiet family life in the country, poems, such as "The River Village," that are especially cherished because Tu Fu is admired for being such a devoted father and husband:

> In one curve, cradling our village, the clear river
> Flows past. On long summer days, the business of solitude
>
> Fills this river village. Swallows in the rafters
> Come and go carelessly. On the water, gulls nestle
>
> Tenderly together. My wife draws a paper *go** board,
> And tapping at needles, the kids contrive fishhooks.
>
> Often sick, I need drugs and herbs— but what more,
> Come to all this, what more could a simple man ask?

*go a board game that originated over four thousand years ago in India or China

Eventually, local rebellions and fighting sent the family north again, and then in 765, down the Yangtze (Chang) River to Kuei-chou (Guizhou). Kuei-chou was situated where the Yangtze cuts through the Wu Mountains, forming the Three Gorges, a spectacular site with steep, narrow canyons; towering cliffs; violent white water; and shrieking gibbons. The aboriginal* peoples there spoke dialects* Tu Fu could not understand. For the Chinese, this was the very edge of the civilized world. In spite of, or perhaps more likely because of this dramatic situation, the two years that Tu Fu spent in the Kuei-chou area were to be his most productive period. Not only were more than a quarter of his surviving poems written there, but they also open a new dimension of stark, elemental experience. "Night at the Tower" is a good example:

*aboriginal of or relating to the first ethnic group to live in a region

*dialect provincial, rural, or socially distinct variety of a language that differs from the standard language

> *Yin* and *yang* cut brief autumn days short. Frost and snow
> Clear, leaving a cold night open at the edge of heaven.
>
> Marking the fifth watch, grieving drums and horns erupt as

Yin (dark, female) and yang (light, male) are, according to Chinese philosophy, opposite forces that fit together in balance and harmony.

A river of stars, shadows trembling, drifts in Three
    Gorges.

Pastoral* weeping— war heard in how many homes?
    And tribal
Songs drifting from the last woodcutters and
    fishermen. . . .

Chu-ko Liang, Pai-ti: all brown earth in the end. And it
Opens, the story of our lives opens away . . . vacant, silent.

Tu Fu left Kuei-chou in 768, sailing east and then south, never settling anywhere for very long. By 770, when Tu Fu was fifty-eight, the family had decided to return to his home in Changan. But another invasion by the Tibetans in the fall delayed their return. Before autumn was over, Tu Fu's baby daughter had fallen ill and died. And that winter, Tu Fu died as well.

Tu Fu the Poet

Tu Fu's human life was difficult and tragic, but his poetic life was quite the opposite. His range allowed him to write poems of great beauty and joy, such as "8th Month, 17th Night: Facing the Moon." In the eleven years after his momentous decision to devote himself to poetry, he wrote about 80 percent of his surviving works. And in them he succeeded in making himself into a poet capable of a poetry unlike anything that preceded it. The range and power of his poems was so great that virtually all modes of Chinese poetry that followed him found their source in his work.

His innovations* are too many to list here, except for the most important ones. First, Tu Fu brought every aspect of experience into poetry's domain, rather than limiting his writing to certain accepted themes and occasions. Second, as we see in "Moonlit Night Thinking of My Brothers," he addressed real, immediate social concerns. Third, departing entirely from tradition, he allowed his poems to combine widely varying moods, tones, and images—all part of a compression and complexity that was unknown in Chinese poetry. And fourth, more difficult for us to recognize in translation, he worked the Chinese language into elegant, distilled* structures never before imagined by earlier poets.

*pastoral dealing with rural life and tending to portray nature as sweet and beautiful

Chu-ko Liang and Pai-ti are Historical figures, one noble and one villainous.

*innovation a new development

*distilled concentrated in its purest essence

> ## *8th Month, 17th Night: Facing the Moon*
>
> The autumn moon is still full tonight.
> In a river village, a lone old wanderer
> Raising the blinds, I return to moonlight.
> As I struggle with a cane, it follows.
>
> And bright enough to rouse hidden dragons,
> It scatters roosting birds from trees. All
> Around my thatched study, orange groves
> Shine: clear dew aching with fresh light.

More important than all these innovations, though, is the sensibility Tu Fu brought to poetry, because that is why his poems are still compelling. Tu Fu is at once deeply in love with the world and profoundly detached from it. Through his poems, exile, that state in which we find ourselves at a distance from what we know and love best, becomes the human condition. And it gives rise to a variety of human responses, of which longing is certainly one, but wonder, even delight, is another, as in the poem "Returning Late":

> After midnight, eluding tigers on the road, I return
> home below dark mountains. My family asleep inside,
>
> the Northern Dipper drifts nearby, sinking low
> over the river. Venus blazes— huge in empty space.
>
> Holding a candle in the courtyard, I call for two
> torches. A gibbon in the gorge, startled, shrieks once.
>
> Old and tired, my hair white, I dance and sing out.
> Goosefoot cane, no sleep. . . . *Catch me if you can!*

Of his poems, Tu Fu once said: "If my words aren't startling, death itself is without rest." Oddly enough, death was without rest for Tu Fu—it took forty-three years for his remains finally to be buried in his family graveyard near Lo-yang. But we can assume he has been resting peacefully since, as his words have been moving and startling readers now for well over a thousand years.

Selected Bibliography

WORKS BY TU FU

The Selected Poems of Tu Fu. Translated by David Hinton. New York: New Directions, 1989.

WORKS ABOUT TU FU

Davis, A. R. *Tu Fu.* New York: Twayne, 1971.

Hawkes, David. *A Little Primer of Tu Fu.* Oxford, U.K.: Clarendon Press, 1967.

Hung, William. *Tu Fu: China's Greatest Poet.* Cambridge, Mass.: Harvard University Press, 1952.

Owen, Stephen. *The Great Age of Chinese Poetry: The High T'ang.* New Haven, Conn.: Yale University Press, 1980.

WORKS BY OTHER MAJOR ANCIENT CHINESE POETS

Han Shan (Cold Mountain). *Cold Mountain: 100 Poems from Cold Mountain.* Translated by Burton Watson. New York: Columbia University Press, 1970.

Lu Yu. *The Old Man Who Does as He Pleases: Selections from the Poetry and Prose of Lu Yu.* Translated by Burton Watson. New York: Columbia University Press, 1973.

Meng Chiao. *The Late Poems of Meng Chiao.* Translated by David Hinton. Princeton, N.J.: Princeton University Press, 1996.

Po Chü-i. *The Selected Poems of Po Chü-i.* Translated by David Hinton. New York: New Directions, 1999.

Su Tung-p'o. *The Selected Poems of Su Tung-p'o.* Translated by Burton Watson. Port Townsend, Wash.: Copper Canyon, 1994.

T'ao Ch'ien. *The Selected Poems of T'ao Ch'ien.* Translated by David Hinton. Port Townsend, Wash.: Copper Canyon, 1993.

Wang Wei. *Laughing Lost in the Mountains: Poems of Wang Wei.* Translated by Willis Barnstone and Tony Barnstone. Hanover, N.H.: University Press of New England, 1991.

IF YOU LIKE the poetry of Tu Fu, you might also like the poetry of Li Po.

VIRGIL

(70–19 B.C.)

by James Gibbons

Poets have idolized him for centuries. He has been called "the best poet" (John Dryden, "Dedication to the Georgics," in *The Poems of John Dryden,* Vol. 2, edited by James Kinsley, London: Oxford University Press, 1958, p. 913) and "the classic of all Europe" (T. S. Eliot, *What Is a Classic?,* p. 31). He was chosen as Dante's wise and trustworthy guide through the rings of hell in the *Inferno.* Inspired by the drama and intensity of his poetry, some of the world's greatest artists have painted scenes from his epic, the *Aeneid.* Who was Virgil, and why has he earned such praise?

Verse quotations throughout are from the editions of Virgil listed in the bibliography. For the *Eclogues,* the first numeral in the citation is the number of the eclogue. For the *Georgics* and the *Aeneid,* which are divided into books, this first numeral is the book number. Numbers after the period in each case are lines.

Life and Career

In Virgil's case, it is hard to separate fact from legend. We know that he was born Publius Vergilius Maro on 15 October 70 B.C. at Andes, in a northern province of Roman Italy. His father owned a farm and was wealthy enough to provide for

*rhetoric the art of persuasion with written or spoken language

Virgil's education in rhetoric* and law, as preparation for a political career. Virgil went to Cremona, Milan, and Rome to study but did not enter politics as planned. He made just one court appearance as a lawyer before going to Naples to study philosophy. When civil war broke out in 49 B.C., he probably did not have to fight—his health was poor.

After the war, land in Italy was awarded to veterans, and many landowners, including Virgil's father, were forced off their estates. Judging from a poem that Virgil wrote after the war, his father's estate seems to have been returned to him. In that poem, the good fortune of the aging shepherd Tityrus is contrasted with that of the shepherd Meliboeus:

> Tityrus, you lie beneath the spreading beech
> and practice country songs upon a slender pipe.
> I leave my father's fields and my sweet ploughlands,
> an exile from my native soil.
>
> (*Eclogues* 1.1–4)

If the estate was saved, it is evidence of Virgil's influence with Roman officials. His most important supporter was the minister Maecenas, who was at the center of a literary circle in Rome that included Virgil's fellow poet Horace (with whom Virgil journeyed to Brindisium in 37 B.C.). Virgil's poetry was admired by Augustus (Octavian), emperor of Rome, who became his patron. In return, Virgil praised the emperor in verse on several occasions.

Virgil wrote three great poems: the *Eclogues* (45–37 B.C.), the *Georgics,* (36–29 B.C.), and the *Aeneid* (27–19 B.C.). (Several other works have been rather unconvincingly attributed to him.) Every morning he would dictate to a scribe, and in the afternoon he would revise the morning's work. Because he was a perfectionist, Virgil's output seems small. For the *Georgics* he finished an average of only one line of poetry per day. The elegance of his poems is impossible to translate; it came from painstaking effort. His verses were flawless.

We know that he was tall, with a dark complexion. He was also sickly and painfully shy. He never married. His poetry was widely admired, and he lived his later years as a wealthy man in a country villa. He died on 21 September 19 B.C. after falling ill on a journey to Greece. More important than the biographical facts, however, are Virgil's poems, which testify to the richness of his poetic world.

The *Eclogues*

Virgil's *Eclogues* is an imitation of the *Idylls* (sometimes spelled *Idyls*) of the Greek poet Theocritus. Regarding themselves as heirs to the Greek legacy, Romans often imitated the Greeks and sometimes sought to outdo them. Later, in the *Georgics,* Virgil boldly claimed:

> I will be first, if life is granted me,
> To lead in triumph from Greek Helicon*
> To my native land the Muses.
>
> (*Georgics* 3.11–13)

*Helicon a mountain in Greece, often celebrated in classical literature as a favorite residence of the Muses, the nine goddesses of the arts and sciences

The *Eclogues* imitated Theocritus's work but also added to it, giving birth to the genre of pastoral poetry. The conventions, or rules, for pastoral poetry were established by Virgil. Its countryside setting is shaped more by fantasy than by close observation of reality. The fantasy world of pastoral poetry—called "Arcadia"—is peopled by shepherds and shepherdesses, who sing of their loves, engage in singing contests, and praise nature's beauty. The "simple life" is praised, while the hardships of rural life are ignored. An actual shepherd would not recognize himself in a poem like the *Eclogues,* or even read it.

Why should *we* read pastoral poetry? For one thing, its longing for the "simple life" represents a strong human urge. (Who has not daydreamed about a life of ease?) Pastoral poetry also examines the pretensions of society and particularly those of city dwellers, preferring simplicity and communion with nature. As the shepherd Corydon proclaims:

> Gods too have lived
> in the woods, and Paris of Troy.* Let Pallas Athene*
>   dwell
> inside the citadels she builds. Let us enjoy
> the woods.
>
> (*Eclogues* 2.63–65)

*Paris of Troy in Greek legend, the son of the king of Troy. His kidnapping of a woman named Helen led to the Trojan War.

*Pallas Athene the Greek goddess of wisdom (also known as Pallas Athena)

And because the shepherds in pastoral poems are humble, we identify with them fairly easily. We can put ourselves in the place of Corydon, frustrated in love, when he says:

> Desire draws each one on.
> Look, the oxen carry their plows aslant from the yoke,

and the setting sun doubles all the shadows' length.
But love burns me still. What help is there for love?

(*Eclogues* 2.67–70)

The *Eclogues* is not only about shepherds. In the fourth eclogue, the poet assumes the role of prophet and predicts a new golden age, heralded by the birth of a royal son:

> He will consort* with the gods and see heroes mingling
> with them and he himself will appear to heroes and
>   gods
> and rule a world his father's virtues have brought to
>   peace.
>   For you, little child, spontaneously, as first gifts,
> the earth will lavish creeping ivy and foxglove,
> everywhere, and Egyptian lilies with smiling acanthus,
> Goats will come home by themselves with udders full
> of milk, nor will the oxen fear the lion's might.

(*Eclogues* 4.15–22)

*consort associate, socialize

Later, some Christians, including Dante, believed that Virgil had been mystically granted a premonition of the birth of Christ. The poem, however, certainly has a Roman child in mind.

Prophecy might seem unexpected in a poem about shepherds, as would a description of the origin of the universe. But in eclogue 6, such a description occurs. Virgil uses the pastoral genre to write about all sorts of subjects—political, mythological, and philosophical. An ambitious poet, Virgil wanted to write about more than just Arcadia. His ambitions would be fulfilled by his next two works, the *Georgics* and the *Aeneid*.

The *Georgics*

Virgil's *Georgics* also borrowed from a Greek source, the poet Hesiod's *Works and Days,* written at the end of the eighth century B.C. It is an example of "didactic poetry"—poetry that aims to instruct, in this case about farming. Didactic poetry is one of the earliest forms of literature, perhaps because poetry provides powerful aids to memory. Virgil's *Georgics* claims to be an instruction manual in farming, divided into books devoted to crop production, trees, animals, and beekeeping.

The *Georgics* is fascinating in what it tells us about ancient views of nature. Some of those beliefs—that horses can
be impregnated by the wind or that honey falls like dew from
heaven—seem utterly fantastic. Sometimes it expresses folk
wisdom and superstitions. About the weather, for example,
Virgil writes:

> Rain never catches men without some warning:
> Either its surge has driven the skyey* cranes
> Before it deep down valleys, or a heifer
> Looked up to heaven and spread her nostrils wide
> To catch the breeze, or round and round the pond
> The twittering swallow has flitted, and in the mud
> Frogs have struck up their ancient croaking protest.
> (*Georgics* 1.373–379)

skyey like the sky; heavenly

Note the closely observed description, which does not occur
in the *Eclogues;* there nature is represented as a paradise of
leisure. Indeed, the *Georgics* celebrates human labor—the
work that actual farmers do—and the rich variety of nature.
Clearly Virgil delighted in his subject matter: in the passage
quoted, notice how quickly the poem moves, as if on the wind
it describes, from the cranes to the heifer to the swallows to
the frogs. Even the most harrowing* passages, such as this description of a plague, are alive with terrible enthusiasm:

harrowing disturb-ing; intense

> The very birds
> Find in the air no favour: even they
> Plunge headlong, leaving life beneath the clouds.
> Changes of pasture now gave no relief.
> New treatments made things worse; renowned
>   physicians—
> Chiron the son of Phillyra, Melampus
> The son of Amythaon—owned defeat.
> Let loose from the Stygian* darkness into daylight
> Tisiphonê* the ghastly Fury raged
> Driving before her Terror and Disease,
> And daily higher reared her hungry head.
> (*Georgics* 3.545–553)

Stygian like the Styx, a river of the Under-world (Hades)

Tisiphonê one of the Furies, who pursue and punish sinners on Earth

The poem is supposed to teach farming; what is such a description, which conveys no "useful" information, doing here?
The Roman statesman and philosopher Seneca was probably

After the death of his wife, Eurydice, Orpheus went to the underworld (Hades) and, because of his skillful lyre-playing, persuaded Pluto to allow Eurydice to return to Earth with him. Orpheus was commanded to walk in front of her without glancing back. When he yielded to temptation and looked at her, she vanished.

*utopia an imaginary, ideal place

*exalted noble; impressively high

*invocation plea for help or divine intervention

The Greeks' siege of Troy, led by the warrior Achilles, was the subject of Homer's *Iliad*. The poet declares at the outset of the poem that his theme will be the "wrath of Achilles."

*demigod a mythological being that has less power than a god, but more power than a mortal

right to say that Virgil wrote the *Georgics* to delight his readers, most of whom were not farmers anyway. The poem's ending, for example—the story of Orpheus's descent into the underworld—is hardly practical advice for a working farmer.

The descriptions of animals, too, are often more than just descriptions. Book 4, concerning beekeeping, shows how Virgil uses animals to examine the human condition. The society of bees is portrayed as harmonious and rational, even utopian. The behavior of the bees, who are self-sacrificing and loyal to their leader, sets a moral example for humans. Or does it? Their society is orderly, but it is also joyless and lacks poetry or art. Here Virgil's charming fable asks an important question: Would such a utopia* be desirable, even if we could achieve it? The value of sacrifices demanded by the state—to ensure the smooth running of its "hive"—was one of the main concerns of Virgil's next work, the *Aeneid*.

The *Aeneid*

Virgil is best remembered for the *Aeneid,* his epic. Epic, like pastoral, is a type of poetry—a long poem that tells stories of heroic acts. Its tone is exalted,* to stress the importance of its events and themes. All epics thus begin with an invocation* to the muse, or source of inspiration, and also an announcement of the poem's theme:

> I sing of warfare and a man at war.
> From the sea-coast of Troy in early days
> He came to Italy by destiny
>
> (*Aeneid* 1.1–3)

Epic poetry is set in the distant past ("in early days") and begins *in medias res* ("in the middle of things") at some key moment in the story, to heighten the drama of what is being told. Gods and goddesses intervene in the action, in biased and often petty ways.

Virgil's greatest predecessor in epic poetry, not surprisingly, was Greek—Homer. Homer's *Iliad* tells of the Greek victory in the Trojan War and the "wrath of Achilles," the demigod* Greek warrior. Homer's *Odyssey* relates the adventures of its hero, Odysseus, in his ten-year voyage home from the war. Virgil based his *Aeneid* on these two poems. His hero,

The Aeneid (excerpt)

Now came the sound of thrashed seawater foaming;
Now they were on dry land, and we could see
Their burning eyes, fiery and suffused* with blood,
Their tongues a-flicker out of hissing maws.*
We scattered, pale with fright. But straight ahead
They slid until they reached Laocoön.*
Each snake enveloped one of his two boys,
Twining about and feeding on the body.
Next they ensnared the man as he ran up
With weapons: coils like cables looped and bound him
Twice round the middle; twice about his throat
They whipped their back-scales, and their heads towered,
While with both hands he fought to break the knots,
Drenched in slime, his head-bands black with venom,
Sending to heaven his appalling cries
Like a slashed bull escaping from an altar,
The fumbled axe shrugged off. The pair of snakes
Now flowed away and made for the highest shrines,
The citadel of pitiless Minerva,*
Where coiling they took cover at her feet
Under the rondure of her shield.

(Book 2, lines 286–306)

suffused filled; soaked

maw the throat, stomach, or jaws of an animal

Laocoön a Trojan priest

Minerva the Roman goddess of wisdom, medicine, the arts, dyeing, science, trade, and war

the Trojan warrior Aeneas, is a character in the *Iliad,* surviving combat with Achilles through the intercession of the sea god Poseidon, who proclaims: "Aeneas and his sons, and theirs, / will be lords over Trojans born hereafter" (Homer, *Iliad,* book 20, lines 307–308). The *Aeneid* grows out of Poseidon's prophecy, as Aeneas flees Troy's smoking ruins and, after many trials, founds Rome. The first part of the *Aeneid,* which recounts Troy's destruction from the Trojan point of view and tells of the Trojans' journey to Italy, relies heavily on Homer's epics. Aeneas, like Odysseus, is searching for a home. The *Aeneid*'s final books tell of a war between Aeneas's Trojans and the Rutulians, led by the warrior Turnus. This war mirrors the Trojan War in the *Iliad*. Achilles battles the Trojan Hector in the *Iliad;* Turnus battles Aeneas in the *Aeneid*. There are other parallels, too: the disputed marriage of Helen of Troy (the

"Disputed marriage": Both Helen and Lavinia are eagerly sought in marriage; wars were fought to decide who would be the husband of each woman.

cause of the Trojan War) is echoed by the disputed marriage of Lavinia in the *Aeneid.*

The *Aeneid,* though indebted to Homer, also brought something new to epic poetry. Homer's poems had glorified past events but did not connect them with the present. Virgil sought to explain Rome's present greatness through the heroism involved in its founding. Aeneas's destiny is emphasized continually in the *Aeneid*—the gods, despite their bickering, all know that Aeneas has been chosen by fate to found a great empire. In book 8, Aeneas's mother, the goddess Venus, persuades the god of fire, Vulcan, to forge a dazzling shield for her son. On it are scenes portraying Rome's triumphs:

> All these images on Vulcan's shield,
> His mother's gift, were wonders to Aeneas.
> Knowing nothing of the events themselves,
> He felt joy in their pictures, taking up
> Upon his shoulder all the destined acts
> And fame of his descendants.
> (*Aeneid* 8.987–992)

The poem seeks to glorify Rome. Is it, then, merely a work of political propaganda? No, because propaganda simplifies its characters and situations, something Virgil never does. In their complexity, Aeneas's behavior and feelings represent those of an intensely human man of action. The *Aeneid* also shows the great cost of Aeneas's destiny. After fleeing Troy, the Trojans land at Carthage, where Dido, the queen of Carthage, falls in love with Aeneas:

> The queen, for her part, all that evening ached
> With longing that her heart's blood fed, a wound
> Or inward fire eating her away.
> The manhood of the man, his pride of birth,
> Came home to her time and again; his looks,
> His words remained with her to haunt her mind,
> And desire for him gave her no rest.
> (*Aeneid* 4.1–7)

Aeneas and Dido soon become lovers, but in a vision Aeneas is reminded of the prophecy that he will found Rome. His destiny must take precedence over anything else, including his passion. Telling Dido, "I sail for Italy not of my own free will"

(4:499), he leads the Trojans out of Carthage. "So broken in mind by suffering, Dido caught / Her fatal madness and resolved to die," Virgil writes (4:656–657). She climbs a huge flaming altar, heaped with the burning remnants of Aeneas's clothes and the bed the couple had shared, and kills herself with Aeneas's sword, crying:

> "I die unavenged," she said, "but let me die.
> This way, this way, a blessed relief to go
> Into the undergloom. Let the cold Trojan,
> Far at sea, drink in this conflagration*
> And take with him the omen of my death!"
> (*Aeneid* 4. 915–919)

"Unavenged": Although Aeneas has wronged her, he will not be punished.
*conflagration** a huge disaster, usually a fire or war

In the logic of the poem, Dido's death is necessary, because Aeneas's public duties outweigh his private passions. Aeneas later encounters Dido's ghost in the underworld and is mad with longing. The ghost disappears, and Aeneas is left with his grief. This episode suggests that the glories of the Roman Empire came at a high price. The *Aeneid* is not just about what Rome has gained through its triumphs and conquests but also about what Rome has lost.

When Virgil died, the *Aeneid* was not quite finished. He planned to spend three more years polishing his poem and asked that the manuscript be burned because the poem was not yet equal to his high standards. The emperor himself ordered that Virgil's wishes be ignored, and the manuscript was edited carefully by Virgil's friends and literary advisers, Varius Rufus and Plotius Tucca. If the poem had been burned according to Virgil's wishes, much of European literature would have been different. Without it, Virgil would still be regarded as a fine poet, but he would not have had the same impact on the literature that followed. It is no exaggeration to say that the *Aeneid* has influenced most of the subsequent poetry—and narrative literature—of Europe.

Selected Bibliography

IF YOU LIKE the poetry of Virgil, you might also like the poetry of Homer or Ovid.
❧

WORKS BY VIRGIL

The Aeneid. Translated by Robert Fitzgerald. New York: Random House, 1983.

The Georgics. Translated by L. P. Wilkinson. New York: Penguin, 1982.

Vergil's Eclogues. Translated by Barbara Hughes Fowler. Chapel Hill: University of North Carolina Press, 1997.

Virgil in English. Edited by K. W. Grandsen. New York: Penguin, 1996.

WORKS ABOUT VIRGIL

Alpers, Paul. *The Singer of the Eclogues.* Berkeley: University of California Press, 1979.

Eliot, T. S. *What Is a Classic?* London: Faber and Faber, 1945.

Griffin, Jasper. *Virgil.* Oxford, U.K.: Oxford University Press, 1986.

Hardie, Philip R. *The Epic Successors of Virgil: A Study in the Dynamics of a Tradition.* Cambridge, U.K.: Cambridge University Press, 1993.

Heinze, Richard. *Virgil's Epic Technique.* Translated by Hazel and David Harvey and Fred Robertson. Berkeley: University of California Press, 1993.

Leach, Eleanor Winsor. *Vergil's Eclogues: Landscapes of Experience.* Ithaca, N.Y.: Cornell University Press, 1974.

Marindale, Charles, ed. *The Cambridge Companion to Virgil.* Cambridge, U.K.: Cambridge University Press, 1997.

Perkell, Christine. *The Poet's Truth: A Study of the Poet in Virgil's Georgics.* Berkeley: University of California Press, 1989.

Wilkinson, L. P. *The Georgics of Virgil: A Critical Survey.* Cambridge, U.K.: Cambridge University Press, 1969.

✍🏻
More About Virgil

You can find information about Virgil on the Internet at:
http://www.virgil.org/

WALT WHITMAN

(1819–1892)

by Ed Folsom

Except where otherwise noted, quotations from Whitman's work throughout are taken from Kaplan, ed., *Walt Whitman: Poetry and Prose*.

At age eleven, Walt Whitman finished going to school and started to work full-time. Before that, he had attended the one and only public school in what was then the village of Brooklyn, New York. Whitman did not mind quitting the public school at such a young age and going to work: since wealthier parents sent their children to private schools, only the children of the working class and the poor attended the public school, where students of a wide variety of ages shared the same crowded classroom (and where African American children were taught separately on the top floor). Students spent most of their time memorizing and reciting facts and were often whipped or paddled.

First Walt became a messenger boy. When he was twelve, he began to learn the printing and newspaper trades. He lived much of the time away from his family, rooming with other apprentices* in Brooklyn and Manhattan. He read books from a lending library and often went to museums, where he learned many things he had not been taught in school. Most of Whitman's education, then, came from teaching himself, by taking

*apprentice a student who is learning the skills of a trade through hands-on experience, often working in exchange for a practical education (and sometimes room and board) rather than for pay

135

advantage of opportunities in the quickly growing and ethnically diverse city of New York.

Although it would still be twenty-five years until he published *Leaves of Grass,* the book that would make him famous, Whitman was already gaining the kind of experience that would allow him to create a radically new kind of American poetry. The essayist and poet Ralph Waldo Emerson once described Whitman's poetry as "a remarkable mixture of the Bhagvat Ghita* and the *New York Herald*"* (Myerson, p. 144). Emerson meant that Whitman's work blended religious, philosophical, and mystical insights with the gritty, down-to-earth details of daily life. And young Walt Whitman, working on newspapers before he was even a teenager, saw firsthand the often sordid details of life in urban America. He wrote many newspaper articles about the challenges and corruptions of city life—poverty, prostitution, filth, and violence. And when he began writing poetry, he produced something new by mixing this realistic detail with his idealistic notions about America and democracy. The result was a poetry that celebrated the grand possibilities of America while never losing sight of its actual people who worked and struggled with their daily lives.

*Bhagvat Ghita refers to the *Bhagavadgita,* a portion of the Hindu epic *Mahabharata.* This part of the *Mahabharata* is a discussion between the god Krishna and the warrior Arjuna.

*New York Herald a popular newspaper of the mid-nineteenth century, founded and edited by James Gordon Bennett

Early Years: Long Island, Brooklyn, and Manhattan

Whitman spent two decades as a typesetter, newspaper reporter, rural schoolteacher, and newspaper editor before he suddenly bloomed into the author of *Leaves of Grass,* his great book of poetry that he would spend his adult lifetime adding to and revising. It is a book that grew out of the many influences that made Whitman who he was. One of those influences was Long Island, where he was born on 31 May 1819 in the farming community of West Hills. The Long Island shore was always one of his favorite landscapes, and it appears in some of his best-known poems, like "Out of the Cradle Endlessly Rocking," where he recalls his boyhood "on the sands of Paumanok's shore gray and rustling." He always preferred to call Long Island by its Native American name, "Paumanok," and he named one of his poems "Starting from Paumanok," to indicate the importance that this place had in forming his personality: "Starting from fish-shape Paumanok where I was born, / Well-begotten, and rais'd by a perfect mother." His parents were from families that had lived for several generations on Paumanok. His mother, Louisa Van Velsor Whitman, was of Dutch heritage and came from a Quaker background. His father, Walter Whitman, Sr., was of English Puritan* heritage and was a fiercely independent political thinker, proud of America's revolutionary heritage. The names of three of Whitman's brothers—George Washington Whitman, Andrew Jackson Whitman, and Thomas Jefferson Whitman—suggest Whitman's parents' devotion to the new Republic.

Walter Whitman, Sr., was a farmer and carpenter, and young Walt (with his two sisters and five brothers) grew up in a working-class family. He became one of the first major poets in America to emerge from a working-class background. While most poets of his time were college-educated and from well-to-do families and had formal-sounding names (like Ralph Waldo Emerson, Henry Wadsworth Longfellow or James Russell Lowell), Whitman chose to shorten his name to the informal "Walt" and to celebrate his identity with the common people. His poems are filled with long lists of American workers engaged in their lives of labor. When he published *Leaves of Grass* in 1855, he designed the book himself and even set the type for several of the pages. He decided not to put his name on the title page, to suggest that the book was not just his voice but the representative voice of a democratic America. The opening words of the first poem of *Leaves of Grass*, a poem he later entitled "Song of Myself," captured the proud and confident tone of a young nation announcing its commitment to a democratic way of thinking that included the equal acceptance of everyone:

> I celebrate myself,
> And what I assume you shall assume,
> For every atom belonging to me as good belongs to you.

Some readers find Whitman's celebration of himself egotistical,* but he insisted that he was singing an inclusive, democratic song, and he was inviting everyone in the nation to join in. America, he believed, had to overcome discriminatory and antidemocratic ways of thinking and acting: it was crucial for Americans to learn to share beliefs ("what I assume you shall assume") instead of being divided by them. And it was important not to value people on the basis of what they owned ("every atom belonging to me as good belongs to

*Puritan a Protestant Christian who opposed the traditions and forms of the Church of England. Most Puritans opposed elaborate ceremony and church hierarchy, believing that God's will was directly revealed to individuals through Bible reading. Puritans believed that only a few "elect" were chosen in advance by God for heaven.

*egotistical self-centered; arrogant

you"). Rather, everyone—rich and poor, male and female, slave and master—must be valued for the unlimited potential that lives in each individual soul. Whitman's poetry insists on a radical leveling of people in a democracy, a breaking down of the differences and hierarchies* that organize most societies. His poetry, however, does not encourage *sameness* of people so much as an *equal valuing* of differing beliefs, backgrounds, and experiences. Everyone in a democracy has a self worth celebrating, he believed, and democracy is the political and philosophical system that insists on placing an equal value on every single human being.

*hierarchy a system that ranks some individuals more highly than others

Teacher and Journalist

As a young man, Whitman had already gained a great deal of experience with the nation's fragile new institutions of democracy. If democracy was going to work, it had to have a strong and universally available educational system that would produce a well-informed citizenry. So, when he was only seventeen years old, and with only five years of schooling himself, Whitman became a schoolteacher, traveling from one Long Island village to another, teaching in crowded one-room schoolhouses, and rooming with students' families. Whitman quickly became disillusioned* with this kind of education, which required teachers to be strict disciplinarians and required students to obey unquestioningly. Whitman believed that in order for students to become responsible citizens in a democracy, they needed instead the lessons of resistance and independence. He went back to newspaper work, because he knew that newspapers were also a crucial institution in the development of America—a free press encouraged open debate about all the issues that were important to the country.

*disillusioned disenchanted; no longer viewing things idealistically

Hundreds of new newspapers started up at this time, and Whitman became a successful newspaper editor in the 1840s on Long Island and in the cities of New York and Brooklyn. In 1848, he even went to New Orleans to edit a newspaper there, an experience that allowed him to see the expanse of the nation for the first time and offered him a direct encounter with Southern culture. He was impressed with many of the people he met in the South, but his most lasting impression was of the inhumanity of the slave auctions that he witnessed. After only three months, Whitman was glad to return to New York.

During these years, Whitman was actually more interested in writing fiction than in writing poetry. He published a number of short stories in well-known magazines, and he even wrote a novel that explored the destructive effects of alcohol. He wrote many nonfiction essays about everything from the history of Brooklyn to the sights of Long Island. The poetry he wrote during the 1840s was ordinary, rhymed, and sentimental. But by 1850, he had begun to focus on a different kind of writing. In small notebooks that he carried with him, he wrote drafts of what would become his unusual new kind of poetry—stripped of rhyme and meter, flowing in a free verse* that incorporated the rhythms and words of everyday speech, and absorbing the sights and sounds of America while recording the simple pleasure of living in a body that was keenly responsive to the world around him.

As he was working on this innovative kind of writing, Whitman was becoming increasingly active in politics, too, and supported the Free Soil Party, which fought the extension of slavery into America's Western territories. Whitman knew that slavery was a huge problem for America because it made a mockery of the young democracy's claim of equality for all people. Whitman also believed, however, that it was vital for the United States to remain unified and strong, so he did not agree with many abolitionists* who were willing to allow the South to break away from the Union in order to rid the nation of the hypocrisy* of slavery. He wanted to find a way that would both preserve the Union and eventually make slavery disappear. In *Leaves of Grass,* he wrote compassionately about slaves and sought to give voice to (actually to *embody*) the horrors that they endured:

> I am the hounded slave . . . . I wince at the bite of the
>   dogs,
> Hell and despair are upon me . . . . crack and again crack
>   the marksmen,
> I clutch at the rails of the fence . . . . my gore dribs*
>   thinned with the ooze of my skin,
> I fall on the weeds and stones,
> The riders spur their unwilling horses and haul close,
> They taunt my dizzy ears . . . . they beat me violently
>   over the head with their whipstocks.

*free verse** poetry that does not follow traditional forms, meters, or rhyme schemes

*abolitionist** a person who believed that slavery should be made illegal

*hypocrisy** saying one thing and doing another

*gore dribs** drips of blood

Camaraderie and Competition: Approaching the Civil War

When Whitman published a new edition of *Leaves* in 1856, and then again in 1860, he added poems that wove images from the various regions of the country——North, South, and West—into single unified poems, as if he were trying somehow to hold the country together even as it was plunging toward civil war. The Civil War began in 1860, and during the first two years of the conflict, Whitman stayed in New York, spending time with artists and writers at a beer hall named Pfaff's, where he discussed politics and writing and the war. By this time, Whitman had experienced intimate friendships with young men, and he wrote about this affection between males in a group of poems he entitled "Calamus":

> We two boys together clinging,
> One the other never leaving,
> Up and down the roads going, North and South excursions making,
> Power enjoying, elbows stretching, fingers clutching,
> Arm'd and fearless, eating, drinking, sleeping,
>   loving . . .

Some critics and biographers believe that the "Calamus" poems are the first expression in American literature of what later would be called homosexual, or gay, relationships, even though few readers in Whitman's day seemed to find the poems objectionable (readers, on the other hand, often found many of his poems about explicit male-female sexual relationships to be obscene). Whitman did write powerfully about the need for men to care more deeply for each other and to express affection more openly than cultural customs generally allowed. Whitman sensed that America was becoming a colder, more capitalistic country, where competition rather than camaraderie was encouraged between men. For democracy to flourish, he believed, love would have to move beyond traditional romantic models, not be limited to husbands and wives, and become more available among all citizens and across social barriers. Whitman decided to use his poetry to encourage a new culture based on widespread affection that broke the bounds of traditional love.

Calamus is a kind of grass, which Whitman described as "very large and aromatic. . . . The biggest and hardiest kind of spears of grass" (Miller, ed., *The Correspondence*, p. 347).

The War Years: Nursing Soldiers, Mourning Lincoln

When wounded soldiers from the Civil War began to be brought to New York hospitals, Whitman started to visit them and to sense an even more desperate need for his "Calamus" emotions: not only were young men competing against each other, brother against brother, they were also killing each other in a horrible war. The need for love between men never seemed greater. No major American writer responded more passionately to the Civil War than Whitman. More than forty years old when the war began, Whitman never served as a soldier, but he volunteered as a nurse in the war hospitals. Two of his brothers served in the Union Army, and when one of them was wounded at the Battle of Fredericksburg, Whitman rushed to the Virginia battlefield to help out. One of the first sights to greet him was "a heap of amputated feet, legs, arms, hands, &c., a full load for a one-horse cart" (p. 736) stacked outside a makeshift hospital. Caring for both Confederate and Union soldiers in the hospitals, Whitman offered his own arms and legs in the service of those young Americans who had given theirs: he wrote letters for them, ran errands, and held many of them as they died. Working as a government clerk during the day, Whitman spent every evening and many nights in the hospitals. The young soldiers called the prematurely gray poet "Old Man," and he became a father and comrade to thousands of them. His unique perspective on the war allowed him to see that America, "though only in her early youth," was "already to hospital brought" (p. 969), and he wrote a book of poems, *Drum-Taps*, about the devastating effects of the war and his hopes for a national reconciliation. His commentary recentered the war in the hospital rather than on the battlefield, focusing on the need for healing instead of revenge.

As the war came to an end in 1865, President Abraham Lincoln was assassinated, and Whitman wrote his great meditation on Lincoln's death, "When Lilacs Last in the Dooryard Bloom'd," along with his popular ballad* about the assassination, "O Captain! My Captain!" These poems would forever link his name to that of the president he so deeply admired. Whitman spent the final twenty-five years of his life trying to reconcile the horrifying experiences of the Civil War with his

*ballad rhythmic verse that tells a story and is often meant to be sung

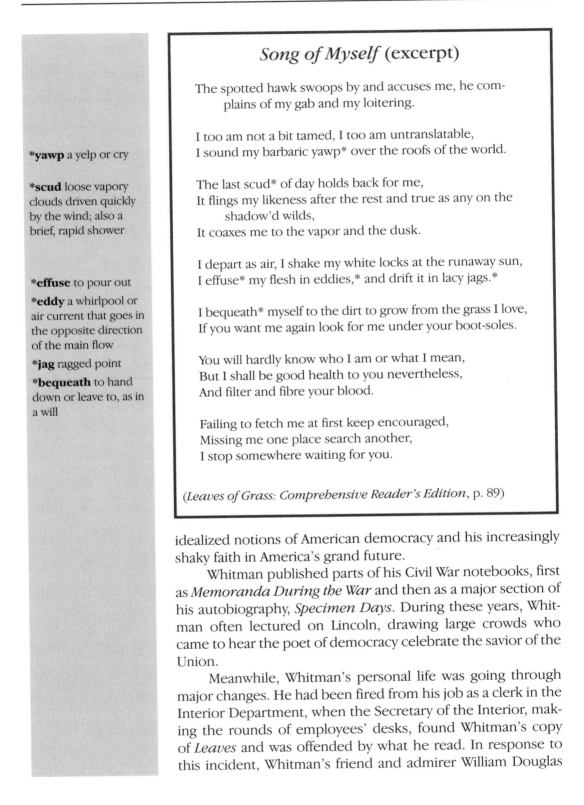

Song of Myself (excerpt)

The spotted hawk swoops by and accuses me, he complains of my gab and my loitering.

I too am not a bit tamed, I too am untranslatable,
I sound my barbaric yawp* over the roofs of the world.

The last scud* of day holds back for me,
It flings my likeness after the rest and true as any on the
shadow'd wilds,
It coaxes me to the vapor and the dusk.

I depart as air, I shake my white locks at the runaway sun,
I effuse* my flesh in eddies,* and drift it in lacy jags.*

I bequeath* myself to the dirt to grow from the grass I love,
If you want me again look for me under your boot-soles.

You will hardly know who I am or what I mean,
But I shall be good health to you nevertheless,
And filter and fibre your blood.

Failing to fetch me at first keep encouraged,
Missing me one place search another,
I stop somewhere waiting for you.

(*Leaves of Grass: Comprehensive Reader's Edition*, p. 89)

*yawp a yelp or cry

*scud loose vapory clouds driven quickly by the wind; also a brief, rapid shower

*effuse to pour out

*eddy a whirlpool or air current that goes in the opposite direction of the main flow

*jag ragged point

*bequeath to hand down or leave to, as in a will

idealized notions of American democracy and his increasingly shaky faith in America's grand future.

Whitman published parts of his Civil War notebooks, first as *Memoranda During the War* and then as a major section of his autobiography, *Specimen Days*. During these years, Whitman often lectured on Lincoln, drawing large crowds who came to hear the poet of democracy celebrate the savior of the Union.

Meanwhile, Whitman's personal life was going through major changes. He had been fired from his job as a clerk in the Interior Department, when the Secretary of the Interior, making the rounds of employees' desks, found Whitman's copy of *Leaves* and was offended by what he read. In response to this incident, Whitman's friend and admirer William Douglas

O'Connor wrote a passionate and expressive tract defending Whitman against charges of immorality, blasting the government, and praising Whitman's hospital service during the war. Appearing in 1866, O'Connor's *The Good Gray Poet* helped change Whitman's image in the public mind, from immoral young radical to loving old patriot. He got a new government job, and he continued to write new poetry, to revise and rearrange *Leaves of Grass,* and to write prose essays (including the extended essay *Democratic Vistas,* a severe critique of the failures of American democracy).

After the War

In the post–Civil War years, Whitman became involved in a complex and intimate relationship with Peter Doyle, a young former Confederate soldier whom the poet met at the end of the war while Doyle was driving an omnibus* in Washington. Whitman's relationship with Doyle was the perfect "Calamus" affair: crossing barriers of age, gender, and regional loyalties, it became the strongest and most sustained caring bond of his life. Doyle was a loyal companion to Whitman when the poet suffered a stroke in early 1873. Soon after his stroke, Whitman went to the working-class city of Camden, New Jersey, where his beloved mother was dying. She had been living with Whitman's brother George. Finding himself comfortable in a city of laborers and grateful to be cared for by members of his family, Whitman first moved into his brother's home and later purchased his own small house, where he lived out the remaining years of his life.

    While in Camden, he received visits from famous writers, including the Irish poet and playwright Oscar Wilde, and he continued to write poetry and prose while working on the final edition of *Leaves of Grass.* He took frequent trips to stay with friends in Philadelphia and New York and made two extended trips—one to London, Ontario, to visit his admirer, the Canadian psychiatrist Richard Maurice Bucke, and one by rail out West, getting as far as the Rocky Mountains. Back in Camden, he used his savings to build a tomb large enough to contain not only his own remains but those of his parents and several of his siblings; he would try to use his death to reunite his large and scattered family under one roof. After many years of deteriorating health, he died on 26 March 1892 at his home in

*omnibus a horse-drawn vehicle for public transportation

Camden. Thousands of Americans, most of them just average citizens, came to his modest house to pay their final respects to the "good gray poet" who had so powerfully turned the American common people into poetry.

Selected Bibliography

WORKS BY WALT WHITMAN
Poetry and Prose

Leaves of Grass (1855).

Leaves of Grass (1856).

Leaves of Grass (1860–1861).

Walt Whitman's Drum-Taps (1865).

Leaves of Grass (1867).

After All, Not to Create Only (1871).

Democratic Vistas (1871).

Passage to India (1871).

Leaves of Grass (1871).

As a Strong Bird on Pinions Free, and Other Poems (1872).

Memoranda During the War (1876–1876).

Two Rivulets, Including Democratic Vistas, Centennial Songs, and Passage to India (1876). Author's Edition.

Leaves of Grass (1881–1882).

Specimen Days and Collect (1882–1883).

November Boughs (1888).

Complete Poems and Prose of Walt Whitman 1855 . . . 1888 (1888).

Good-Bye My Fancy (1891).

Leaves of Grass (1891–1892).

Complete Collection

The Collected Writings of Walt Whitman. Gay Wilson Allen and Sculley Bradley, general editors. A forty-five-year project, still in progress, to collect all of Whitman's writings, including his notebooks, manuscripts, newspaper

IF YOU LIKE the poetry of Whitman, you might also like some of the poets who were very much influenced by his work, such as Allen Ginsberg, Langston Hughes, Galway Kinnell, Vachel Lindsay, Federico García Lorca, Pablo Neruda, Fernando Pessoa, Carl Sandburg, or William Carlos Williams.

⮤

articles, and letters. The 23 volumes thus far are: *The Correspondence,* 6 vols., edited by Edwin Haviland Miller (New York: New York University Press, 1961–1977); *The Early Poems and the Fiction,* edited by Thomas L. Brasher (New York: New York University Press, 1963); *Prose Works 1892,* 2 vols., edited by Floyd Stovall (New York: New York University Press, 1963–1964); *Leaves of Grass: Comprehensive Reader's Edition,* edited by Harold W. Blodgett and Sculley Bradley (New York: New York University Press, 1965); *Daybooks and Notebooks,* 3 vols., edited by William White (New York: New York University Press, 1978); *Leaves of Grass: A Textual Variorum of the Printed Poems,* 3 vols., edited by Sculley Bradley, Harold W. Blodgett, Arthur Golden, and William White (New York: New York University Press, 1980); *Notebooks and Unpublished Prose Manuscripts,* 6 vols., edited by Edward F. Grier (New York: New York University Press, 1984); and *Journalism,* vol. 1 (of 6 vols. in progress), edited by Herbert Bergman, Douglas A. Noverr, and Edward J. Recchia (New York: Peter Lang, 1998).

Available Collections

Selected Letters of Walt Whitman. Edited by Edwin Haviland Miller. Iowa City: University of Iowa Press, 1990. A large selection of letters, including some recently discovered letters not in the *Correspondence* volumes of the *Collected Writings.*

The Walt Whitman Archive. 6 vols. Edited by Joel Myerson. New York: Garland, 1993. Gathers facsimiles of Whitman's poetry manuscripts and corrected proofs from collections at the Library of Congress, Duke University, University of Texas, and University of Virginia.

Walt Whitman: Poetry and Prose. Edited by Justin Kaplan. New York: Library of America, 1996. The most complete single-volume edition of Whitman's work, containing the 1855 edition of *Leaves of Grass,* the final "deathbed" edition of *Leaves,* all of *Specimen Days,* and additional prose.

ELECTRONIC RESOURCES

Major Authors on CD-ROM: Walt Whitman and *Major Authors Online: Walt Whitman.* Edited by Ed Folsom and Kenneth M. Price. Woodbridge, Conn.: Primary Source

Media, 1997, 1998. Searchable electronic resources, containing all of *The Collected Writings of Walt Whitman,* facsimiles of Whitman manuscripts and first editions, Whitman photographs, early reviews of Whitman's work, and more.

WORKS ABOUT WALT WHITMAN

Allen, Gay Wilson. *The New Walt Whitman Handbook*. New York: New York University Press, 1975. Excellent overview of Whitman's biography, of the growth of *Leaves of Grass,* of the range of Whitman's ideas, of Whitman's style, and of his international influence.

Allen, Gay Wilson. *The Solitary Singer: A Critical Biography of Walt Whitman.* Rev. ed. Chicago: University of Chicago Press, 1985. Excellent critical biography.

Allen, Gay Wilson, and Ed Folsom, eds. *Walt Whitman and the World.* Iowa City: University of Iowa Press, 1995. Gathers responses to Whitman from writers around the world.

Erkkila, Betsy. *Whitman the Political Poet.* New York: Oxford University Press, 1989. Careful examination of Whitman's changing political views.

Folsom, Ed. *Walt Whitman's Native Representations.* Cambridge, U.K.: Cambridge University Press, 1994. Examines how Whitman was influenced by various cultural developments in the nineteenth century.

Greenspan, Ezra, ed. *The Cambridge Companion to Walt Whitman.* Cambridge, U.K.: Cambridge University Press, 1995. Solid group of essays on different aspects of Whitman's work.

Kaplan, Justin. *Walt Whitman: A Life.* New York: Simon and Schuster, 1980. Not the most detailed, but one of the most readable, biographies of Whitman.

Krieg, Joann P. *A Whitman Chronology.* Iowa City: University of Iowa Press, 1998. Detailed year-by-year account of Whitman's life and publications.

Kummings, Donald D., ed. *Approaches to Teaching Whitman's* Leaves of Grass. New York: Modern Language Association, 1990. Essays about how Whitman is taught at the college and graduate levels.

LeMaster, J. R., and Donald D. Kummings, eds. *Walt Whitman: An Encyclopedia.* New York: Garland, 1998. Hundreds of entries on all aspects of Whitman's life, times, and works.

Loving, Jerome. *Walt Whitman: The Song of Himself.* Berkeley: University of California Press, 1999. Careful critical biography, based on the latest scholarship.

Myerson, Joel, ed. *Whitman in His Own Time: A Biographical Chronicle of His Life, Drawn from Recollections, Memoirs, and Interviews by Friends and Associates.* Detroit: Omnigraphics, 1991. Gathers contemporary accounts of visits with and conversations with Whitman.

Padgett, Ron, ed. *The Teachers & Writers Guide to Walt Whitman.* New York: Teachers & Writers, 1991. Wide-ranging group of essays on Whitman, many focusing on innovative ways of teaching his poetry.

Perlman, Jim, Ed Folsom, and Dan Campion, eds. *Walt Whitman: The Measure of His Song.* Duluth, Minn.: Holy Cow! Press, 1981; rev. ed., 1998. Large collection of responses to Whitman by poets from his time to the present.

Price, Kenneth M., ed. *Walt Whitman: The Contemporary Reviews.* Cambridge, U.K.: Cambridge University Press, 1996. Gathers all the reviews of Whitman's work published during Whitman's lifetime.

Reynolds, David S. *Walt Whitman's America: A Cultural Biography.* New York: Knopf, 1995. Examines Whitman's life in relation to the culture of nineteenth-century America.

Zweig, Paul. *Walt Whitman: The Making of the Poet.* New York: Basic Books, 1984. Lively account of Whitman's transformation from a newspaper editor into America's greatest poet.

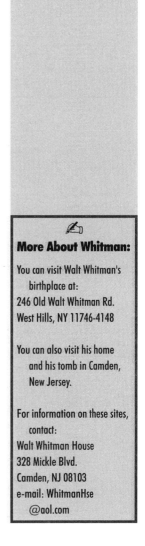

More About Whitman:

You can visit Walt Whitman's birthplace at:
246 Old Walt Whitman Rd.
West Hills, NY 11746-4148

You can also visit his home and his tomb in Camden, New Jersey.

For information on these sites, contact:
Walt Whitman House
328 Mickle Blvd.
Camden, NJ 08103
e-mail: WhitmanHse
@aol.com

RICHARD WILBUR

(b. 1921)

by Dana Gioia

Richard Purdy Wilbur was born on 1 March 1921 in New York City. In a nation famously composed of immigrants, Wilbur had unusually deep native roots—he was an eleventh-generation American descended from the original settlers of Massachusetts and Rhode Island. His family, however, was not especially affluent and his parents reflected an unusual mixture of artistic and middle-class values. His Nebraska-born father, Lawrence Wilbur, had run away to New York City at sixteen to study art. He became a successful commercial artist and later a portrait painter. Richard's mother, Helen Purdy Wilbur, came from a family of newspaper journalists. Not surprisingly, the future poet's earliest ambitions combined his parents' backgrounds; the young Wilbur hoped to be a newspaper cartoonist.

Wilbur had an odd but idyllic childhood. In 1923 his family moved to North Caldwell, New Jersey, where they rented a pre-Revolutionary stone house on a four-hundred-acre estate owned by a charming, eccentric English millionaire. Few other

Quotations from Wilbur's work throughout are taken from *New and Collected Poems* (1988).

149

children lived nearby, so the poet and his younger brother Lawrence amused themselves by wandering the farm and countryside. This pleasant rural boyhood surely helped form the imagination that later created such memorable nature poems as "Hamlen Brook" and "The Beautiful Changes."

The Amherst Radical

In 1938 Wilbur entered the then all-male Amherst College, where he majored in English. The young poet was a self-styled radical. Although he once dutifully attended a Marx* study group (where he fell asleep), his real political passions were for the progressive New Deal* programs fostered by President Franklin Roosevelt. During two summers he hitchhiked and rode the rails across Depression-era America, an adventure he recounts wryly in the poem "Piccola Commedia." Today, no one looking at the exceptionally well-groomed and dignified adult poet would guess that he was the only United States poet laureate to have been a hobo.

At Amherst, Wilbur became chairman of the student newspaper, to which he contributed both drawings and articles. He also fell in love with Charlotte Ward, a student at nearby Smith College, an all-women college then considered one of Amherst's sister schools. The poet often walked the nine miles separating the two schools to visit "Charlee." They married in June 1942 following the poet's graduation.

War Years

The young couple were wed in the shadow of World War II, which the United States had entered in December 1941. Several of Wilbur's Amherst classmates, who had enlisted before graduation, had already been killed in action. Wilbur hoped to become a cryptographer—a specialist in deciphering enemy codes—and he even spent part of his honeymoon practicing Morse code. Joining the United States Army, he briefly studied at a secret military installation in Virginia, learning to transcribe and translate radio codes. Midway through this training, however, Wilbur was abruptly transferred to infantry. He had been classified "Suspected of Disloyalty" after a security check discovered his leftist views and radical friends.

*Marx, Karl Heinrich** (1818–1883) German politician, philosopher, and socialist whose writings, along with F. Engels', are the basis for the type of socialism called Marxism

*New Deal** the umbrella turm for the 1930s measures designed to foster economic recovery and reform

In his new unit, Wilbur joined the Allied forces that invaded Italy and France to fight the German army. His division saw combat for three years, from the dangerous amphibious landing on the beaches of Anzio and the brutal assault on Monte Cassino (both in Italy) to the final collapse of the fortified Siegfried line guarding Germany's border. Having seen many of his fellow soldiers killed in combat, Wilbur left the army in 1945 with the rank of staff sergeant.

Coming to Harvard

After the end of World War II, Wilbur joined the millions of United States veterans who furthered their education on the GI Bill.* Now with a small daughter (the first of four children—all the rest boys), he entered Harvard's graduate school to study English. After receiving his master's degree in 1947, he spent three years as a junior fellow, the university's highest academic honor for a young scholar, and then joined the Harvard faculty in 1950. In Cambridge, Wilbur met many writers who influenced his intellectual development. He also served as a teaching assistant for two of Harvard's most eminent literary scholars—F. O. Matthiessen, the intellectual historian of *American Renaissance* and editor of *The Oxford Book of American Verse,* and I. A. Richards, the literary linguist and author of *Practical Criticism.*

Wilbur's most important literary friendship at Harvard, however, was with Robert Frost. Although there was nearly a half-century difference in their ages, the two poets became fast friends. The often cantankerous Frost recognized the admiring younger poet's talent, but what initially caught his attention was Charlee Ward Wilbur's maiden name. Her grandfather had in 1894 been the first editor to publish Frost's poems. This early friendship had a lifelong impact on Wilbur. Frost's poetic style—with its balance of formal music and conversational tone, its engaging surface sense and disturbing depths—deeply influenced Wilbur's notion of lyric poetry.

Soon Wilbur's promising scholarly career took an unexpected turn. Although he had written poems since childhood, he had never thought of himself primarily as a poet. During the war he began writing regularly and sent the poems to his wife. She showed one poem to a friend who was an editor at the *Saturday Evening Post,* one of the nation's biggest

*GI Bill post–World War II legislation enabling members of armed forces to receive a college education paid for by the government

magazines, which published it. Wilbur published no other verse during the war (only a column for his army division's newspaper). At Harvard, he continued writing and published a few poems in small magazines. One day he gave a group of his poems to an Amherst friend who worked as an editor. A few hours later the man returned, and according to Wilbur, "wrapped his arms around me, kissed me on both cheeks, and declared me a poet" (Butts, p. 20). The friend quickly convinced the New York firm of Reynal and Hitchcock to publish the manuscript. Few poets have had an easier debut.

Early Critical Success

In September 1947, Wilbur's first book, *The Beautiful Changes and Other Poems* appeared. The poet was twenty-six years old, a remarkably early age for so definitive a debut. *The Beautiful Changes* received excellent reviews, with critics praising Wilbur as an especially gifted member of "the war generation" of writers. By the time his second book, *Ceremony and Other Poems,* arrived in 1950, Wilbur had become the poet of his generation. Babette Deutsch exclaimed in the *New York Times Book Review,* "Here is poetry to be read with the eye, the ear, the heart and the mind" (Salinger, p. 37). Even the notoriously tough Joseph Bennett declared in *The Hudson Review,* "Wilbur's is the strongest poetic talent I can see in America below the generation now in their fifties" (Salinger, p. 41). Heady praise for a poet not yet thirty.

After the publication of *Ceremony,* Wilbur's artistic stature was never seriously challenged. His work not only demonstrated his unsurpassed individual gifts, but it also exemplified a new formal style emerging among the mid-century generation of poets. Sometimes called the "New Critical" style, this approach usually employed rhyme and meter, elaborate wordplay (especially puns and paradoxes), and intricate argument to create subtle and intelligent—but rarely highly emotional—poems. The poems were complex but comprehensible, and they often seemed to cry out for critical analysis, especially the line-by-line examination called "close reading" practiced by the New Critics.*

One sees the features of the "New Critical" style in the opening stanza of "Ceremony," which describes a painting of a woman in a forest by the French impressionist Jean-Frédéric

*__*New Critics__ a group of twentieth-century American literary critics who believed that poetry should be studied through its specifically literary features like form and language rather than its historical or biographical sources

Bazille. The dry wit and quiet control of the first five lines hardly prepare one for the magic of the stanza's final line:

> A striped blouse in a clearing by Bazille
> Is, you may say, a patroness of boughs
> Too queenly kind toward nature to be kin.
> But ceremony never did conceal,
> Save to the silly eye, which all allows,
> How much we are the woods we wander in.

Is it any wonder that critic Clive James praised Wilbur's genius for the "killer-diller line" (Salinger, p. 111)?

If *Ceremony* cemented Wilbur's reputation, it also raised what became a critical issue surrounding his work. There was no question that his poetry was immensely accomplished—musically phrased, intelligently conceived, and imagistically memorable. Wilbur seemed incapable of writing a bad poem. The question was whether he was sufficiently ambitious. Did Wilbur achieve perfection on a small scale at the expense of larger accomplishment? Was he unwilling to risk failure by tackling big themes and extended forms? Poet-critic Randall Jarrell most succinctly expressed this creative quandary in an otherwise positive review of *Ceremony:* "Mr. Wilbur never goes too far, but he never goes far enough" (Salinger, pp. 48–49). This critical reservation would follow Wilbur across his entire career.

Wilbur's next volume, *Things of This World* (1956), however, momentarily silenced his critics and dazzled his admirers. The collection won both the Pulitzer Prize and the National Book Award. His academic career was also happily settled. In 1957 Wilbur accepted a professorship at Wesleyan University in Middletown, Connecticut, where he taught for the next twenty years.

A Poet in the Theater

While Wilbur wrote the poems that eventually made up *Things of This World,* he began to explore a new form of artistic expression—verse drama. In 1952 Wilbur had won a Guggenheim Fellowship, which provided funds for a year free from teaching to write full-time. Verse drama had experienced a huge revival in the years after World War II, with successful productions in London and New York of poetic plays by T. S.

Eliot and Christopher Fry. A new drama company, the Poets' Theatre, had just started in Cambridge, Massachusetts, dedicated to producing new verse plays or foreign classics in contemporary translations. Wilbur spent his fellowship year in New Mexico trying to write poetic plays. "They didn't come off," he later admitted. "They were very bad, extremely wooden" (Butts, p. 12). To learn the craft of verse drama, Wilbur began translating *The Misanthrope,* a classic comedy by Molière, the great seventeenth-century French comic dramatist.

Wilbur's fateful decision to create a rhymed English version of Molière's *The Misanthrope* began one of the greatest literary translation projects in American literature. Over the next forty years he produced lively, sophisticated, and eminently stageworthy versions of all of Molière's major comedies—*The Misanthrope, Tartuffe, The School for Wives, The Learned Ladies, The School for Husbands, Sganarelle, or The Imaginary Cuckold,* and *Amphitryon,* as well as two verse tragedies by Jean Racine—*Andromache* and *Phaedra.* From the moment his first Molière translation was staged—at the Poets' Theatre on 25 October 1955—his versions have delighted and impressed audiences. Widely produced from Broadway to college campuses, Wilbur's versions not only helped create a Molière revival across North America, but the royalties they generated eventually enabled the poet to teach only half time.

The success of *The Misanthrope* also led Wilbur into another theatrical venture inspired by a different French literary classic. Composer Leonard Bernstein and playwright Lillian Hellman approached the poet to write song lyrics for their musical comedy *Candide* (based on Voltaire's celebrated novel). Bernstein and Hellman had already been struggling with the project for five years when Wilbur joined the creative team. *Candide* became a notoriously difficult enterprise. Hellman proved temperamental, and Bernstein stubborn. Although the musical was positively reviewed with special praise for Wilbur's sparkling lyrics, the lavish production did poorly when it premiered on Broadway in December 1956. Over the next thirty years, however, Bernstein and others repeatedly revised the musical and eventually replaced most of Hellman's dialogue. Very gradually *Candide* has emerged as a classic of American musical theater, and the Wilbur/Bernstein song

The Writer

In her room at the prow of the house
Where light breaks, and the windows are tossed with linden,
My daughter is writing a story.

I pause in the stairwell, hearing
From her shut door a commotion of typewriter-keys
Like a chain hauled over a gunwale.*

Young as she is, the stuff
Of her life is a great cargo, and some of it heavy:
I wish her a lucky passage.

But now it is she who pauses,
As if to reject my thought and its easy figure.
A stillness greatens, in which

The whole house seems to be thinking,
And then she is at it again with a bunched clamor
Of strokes, and again is silent.

I remember the dazed starling
Which was trapped in that very room, two years ago;
How we stole in, lifted a sash

And retreated, not to affright it;
And how for a helpless hour, through the crack of the door,
We watched the sleek, wild, dark

And iridescent creature
Batter against the brilliance, drop like a glove
To the hard floor, or the desk-top,

And wait then, humped and bloody,
For the wits to try it again; and how our spirits
Rose when, suddenly sure,

It lifted off from a chair-back,
Beating a smooth course for the right window
And clearing the sill of the world.

It is always a matter, my darling,
Of life or death, as I had forgotten. I wish
What I wished you before, but harder.

* **gunwale** the upper edge of the side of a boat, once used to support guns

"Glitter and Be Gay" now occupies a special place in the repertory of American sopranos.

A Master of Verse Translation

Wilbur did not confine his interest in poetic translation to the theater. Every volume of his poems since *Ceremony* contains verse translations. Sometimes accounting for a quarter of the book's contents, these masterful English versions are usually drawn from French and Italian (two languages Wilbur knows well), but his translations also include poems from Russian, Spanish, Portuguese, Romanian, Latin, Hungarian, and Anglo-Saxon. A master technician, Wilbur almost always duplicates the original poem's form in English, even when translating intricately rhymed sonnets,* rondeaus,* and ballades.* Yet he never loses the literal sense or emotional force of the original.

His translation of early modernist Guillaume Apollinaire's unpunctuated but complexly musical "Pont Mirabeau," for instance, reads as if it had originally been written in English. It begins:

> Under the Mirabeau Bridge there flows the Seine
> Must I recall
> Our loves recall how then
> After each sorrow joy came back again
> Let night come on bells end the day
> The days go by me still I stay

As a translator, Wilbur has no equal among his contemporaries and stands with Henry Wadsworth Longfellow, Ezra Pound, and Robert Fitzgerald as one of the four greatest translators in the history of American poetry. Those critics who fault Wilbur for lacking poetic ambition ignore this essential and impressive part of his work.

A Religious Poet

It has been Wilbur's ironic achievement to excel at precisely those literary forms that many contemporary critics undervalue—metrical poetry, verse translation, comic verse, song

sonnet a fourteen-line poem usually composed in iambic pentameter. There are two dominant sonnet forms in English poetry, the Shakespearean and Petrarchan.

rondeau a three-stanza poem in which the first line of the first stanza is repeated as a refrain after the second and third stanzas

ballade a rhymed and rhythmic poem, usually in four-line stanzas, that tells a story and is often meant to be sung

lyrics, and perhaps foremost among these unfashionable but extraordinary accomplishments, religious poetry. A practicing Episcopalian,* Wilbur is America's preeminent living Christian poet. No other author in this neglected field has written so much over so many years with such consistent distinction.

At least a third of Wilbur's poems—light verse and translations aside—contain some conspicuous Christian element. Yet the nature of his accomplishments is both subtle and complex. Although Christianity provides the central vision of his work, he has written little devotional verse—that is, overtly pious poetry that tries to replicate the act of worship. Instead, Wilbur uses the images, ideas, and ceremonies of the Christian faith to provide perspective on the secular world. Sometimes the literal subject of the poem is religious, as in "Matthew VIII, 28ff." or "A Christmas Hymn." More often Wilbur subtly weaves his religious vision into a poem's language and imagery, as in this stanza from "October Maples, Portland," which describes the autumn foliage of New England as symbols of divine redemption in a fallen world:

> A showered fire we thought forever lost
> Redeems the air. Where friends in passing meet,
> They parley* in the tongues of Pentecost.*
> Gold ranks of temples flank the dazzled street.

Although this stanza can be read as a literal description of the October foliage in Connecticut, the natural world also becomes a sacramental* means of revealing the divine order. For example, note how the descriptive image of "showered fire" and word choice of "redeems" simultaneously portray bright red maple leaves and suggest the Pentecostal flame the Holy Spirit placed on the heads of Christ's apostles.

This stanza also demonstrates how Wilbur uses wordplay for serious ends. Few poets pun more frequently, but he rarely does so for purely comic effect. His creative obsession is to have important words serve double duty in a poem. Wilbur's best poems—like those of his mentor, Frost—often present a double structure. There is a surface plot or situation that unfolds in literal terms, but underneath that accessible level is a subtext, an unstated but implied second meaning. "October Maples, Portland" presents a New England seasonal scene, but the subtext suggests a religious vision of life, death, and eternity. What connect these two levels of meaning are Wilbur's masterful puns and wordplay.

*Episcopalian a member of the Protestant Episcopal Church, a denomination of Christianity

*parley to discuss

*Pentecost the Christian feast commemorating the descent of the Holy Spirit in the form of tongues of fire on the heads of Jesus's apostles

*sacramental relating to Christian ritual

A Sustained Career

Wilbur's late career was one of quiet but steady achievement. Wilbur retired from teaching in 1986, and in 1987 he succeeded Robert Penn Warren to become the second poet laureate of the United States. In the 1990s he divided his time between two homes—one in Cummington, Massachusetts, and the other in Key West, Florida. While many poets (like William Wordsworth) lose artistic vitality in middle age or (like Matthew Arnold) stop writing verse altogether, Wilbur is the rare poet who maintained an unbroken high standard. His style and sensibility did not change greatly after *The Beautiful Changes*—except for a slight darkening of tone in his poems of old age—but every volume contained superb new work. The special consistency of his achievement was recognized when his *New and Collected Poems* (1989) won the Pulitzer Prize, making him the only living American poet to have won the award twice. His literary stature grew even more in the late twentieth century, as a new generation of young poets interested in rhyme and meter have looked to him as mentor and model.

IF YOU LIKE the poetry of Wilbur, you might also like the poetry of Robert Frost, Edwin Arlington Robinson, or Anthony Hecht.

❧

Selected Bibliography

WORKS BY RICHARD WILBUR
Poetry

The Beautiful Changes and Other Poems (1947).

Ceremony and Other Poems (1950).

Things of This World (1956).

Advice to a Prophet and Other Poems (1961).

The Poems of Richard Wilbur (1963).

Walking to Sleep: New Poems and Translations (1969).

The Mind-Reader: New Poems (1976).

New and Collected Poems (1988).

Mayflies: New Poems and Translations (2000).

Children's Poetry

Loudmouse (1963).

Opposites (drawings by author) (1973).

More Opposites (1991).

A Game of Catch (1994).

The Disappearing Alphabet (1998).

Prose

Responses: Prose Pieces 1953–1976 (1976).

The Catbird's Song: Prose Pieces 1963–1995 (1997).

Plays

The Misanthrope. New York: Harcourt Brace, 1955. Translation of the play by Molière (premiere Cambridge, Massachusetts, 1955).

Candide (lyrics only, with others). New York: Random House, 1957. Book by Lillian Hellman, music by Leonard Bernstein, adaptation of the novel by Voltaire (premiere New York, 1956).

Tartuffe. New York: Harcourt Brace, 1963. Translation of the play by Molière (premiere Milwaukee, Wisconsin, 1964).

School for Wives. New York: Harcourt Brace, 1971. Translation of the play by Molière (premiere New York, 1971).

The Learned Ladies. New York: Harcourt Brace, 1978. Translation of the play by Molière (premiere Williamstown, Massachusetts, 1977).

Andromache. New York: Harcourt Brace, 1982. Translation of the play by Racine.

Phaedra. San Diego: Harcourt Brace, 1986. Translation of the play by Racine (premiere Stratford, Ontario, 1990).

The School for Husbands. New York: Harcourt Brace, 1992. Translation of the play by Molière.

Sganarelle; or, The Imaginary Cuckold. New York: Dramatists Play Service, 1993. Translation of the play by Molière.

Amphitryon. New York: Dramatists Play Service, 1995. Translation of the play by Molière.

Other Translations

The Whale and Other Uncollected Translations (1982).

Interviews

Butts, William, ed. *Conversations with Richard Wilbur.* Jackson: University Press of Mississippi, 1990.

WORKS ABOUT RICHARD WILBUR

Bawer, Bruce. *Prophets and Professors.* Brownsville, Oreg.: Story Line, 1995.

Bixler, Frances. *Richard Wilbur: A Reference Guide.* Boston, Mass.: G. K. Hall, 1991.

Cummins, Paul. *Richard Wilbur.* Grand Rapids, Mich.: Eerdmans, 1971.

Davison, Peter. *The Fading Smile: Poets in Boston 1955–1960.* New York: Knopf, 1994.

Edgecombe, Rodney Stenning. *A Reader's Guide to the Poetry of Richard Wilbur.* Tuscaloosa: University of Alabama Press, 1995.

Hill, Donald L. *Richard Wilbur.* New York: Twayne, 1967.

Michelson, Bruce. *Wilbur's Poetry: Music in a Scattering Time.* Amherst, University of Massachusetts Press, 1991.

Salinger, Wendy, ed. *Richard Wilbur's Creation.* Ann Arbor: University of Michigan Press, 1983.

WILLIAM CARLOS WILLIAMS

(1883–1963)

by Paul Mariani

Willi*illiam Carlos Williams was born, was raised, and died in the same town in New Jersey. He spent much of his adult life turning the inlets, rivers, vegetation, and creatures of the nearby meadowlands into our poetry and our epic. Over a lifetime as a doctor he cared for thousands of patients and delivered more than two thousand babies, yet still managed to produce nearly fifty books, including poetry, novels, short stories, plays, essays, and an autobiography. And while others ran off to Europe in search of inspiration, Williams elected to stay home, to find poetry in the everyday world where he had been born. Beauty, even great beauty, could be found in the pieces of broken green glass shining out from a cinder heap as he glanced out the window of the hospital where he worked or in an old woman munching on a plum. He would write and write, and by the time he had finished, he had changed the poetic landscape of America—as well as what constituted the poetic—forever.

Between the 1890s and the 1920s Williams traveled to Europe several times, but he always returned to America and his roots, singing his own native place in a language at once new and very much a part of the world he inhabited. "I wanted to write a poem / that you would understand," he wrote early on, addressing his readers. "For what good is it to me / if you can't understand it?" ("January Morning," *Collected Poems,* Vol. 1). But, he was quick to add, "you got to try hard."

Beginnings

William Carlos Williams was born on 17 September 1883 in Rutherford, New Jersey, a commuter suburb for people who worked across the Hudson River in New York City. His father and mother had met in St. Thomas, in the Caribbean. William George Williams, a seller of colognes who spent much of his time in Central America on business, was British. Elena Hoheb carried in her blood many of the rich strands of the Caribbean: French, Spanish, and Jewish among them. In 1882 the couple settled in Rutherford to take part in the American dream. Their first child, William Carlos, was born the following year. His middle name derived from his uncle Carlos Hoheb, a physician in the islands. Within two years there was a second son, Edward Williams, who went on to become an internationally known architect. As young men the two brothers were inseparable, but love for the same woman later drove them apart, with William eventually marrying the woman's younger sister, Florence ("Flossie").

The boys attended local public schools, played baseball on the same team—young Bill as pitcher—and lived the lives of typical suburban boys. Then their parents sent the boys to school for two years in Geneva and Paris, where they could learn French and get a taste of Europe. When they returned to the United States in the spring of 1899, they enrolled in the progressive Horace Mann School in New York City. Each morning for three years the Williams brothers took the train into Manhattan to attend classes. When it came time to graduate, not knowing what he would do other than write, William was persuaded by his mother—whom he adored and feared—to study medicine. At that time it was possible to go to medical school right out of high school, and Williams did so, attending the University of Pennsylvania in Philadelphia from 1902 to 1906, first in dentistry, then switching over to medicine. It was there that he met a young painter, Charles Demuth, as well as a poet, Hilda Doolittle (H. D.), and—most important—the flamboyant, headstrong poet Ezra Pound, two years Williams's junior but ages older in his literary sophistication.

While Pound went to England in search of the new poetry, Williams went to New York, where he interned at two hospitals. He returned to Rutherford and published his first book of poetry, called simply *Poems,* with a local publisher in 1909. Pound dismissed it as old-fashioned and romantic. In 1909, having proposed to his future wife, Williams left for Germany to do advanced work in pediatrics, stopping off in London to see Pound and the poet William Butler Yeats and to get a better sense of what was happening with contemporary poetry in Europe.

On his return home Williams opened a medical practice in Rutherford, served as a physician in the local schools, and on 12 December 1912 married Florence Herman. A few months later they moved into a house at 9 Ridge Road, which would remain their home for the rest of their lives. They had two sons, born in 1914 and in 1916.

The year 1913 saw the New York Armory Show (an influential exhibition of modern European paintings) and the arrival of Williams's second book of poetry, *The Tempers,* which Pound helped publish in London. If his first book had sounded too much like John Keats, this second book owed too much to Pound. Williams had yet to find his own voice. In 1915–1916, through his work with the Others group, a New York–based group of avant-garde writers, Williams met the painter Marcel Duchamp as well as the poets Marianne Moore, Wallace Stevens, and Alfred Kreymborg, to whom he dedicated his third book of poems, *Al Que Quiere!*—punning in Spanish ("To Al K, if he wants it"). In 1920, Williams published *Kora in Hell,* a book of wild prose improvisations,* in an attempt to shake himself free of his older style.

*improvisation a work of art, poetry, or music composed spontaneously—on the spur of the moment

Breakthrough

The real breakthrough came in 1923 with the publication of *Spring and All,* which was half prose and half poetry and unlike anything else being written at the time. Although Williams experimented with a wide range of styles, his distinctive voice is perhaps best caught in the title poem. Williams's image of the wasteland was teeming with life and hope, whereas *The Waste Land,* a poem by his contemporary T. S. Eliot, was filled with despair. "By the road to the contagious hospital," Williams's poem begins, juxtaposing the world of sickness and death with the world of spring all about him:

> under the surge of the blue
> mottled clouds driven from the
> northeast—a cold wind. Beyond, the
> waste of broad, muddy fields
> brown with dried weeds, standing and fallen
>
> patches of standing water
> the scattering of tall trees
> All along the road the reddish
> purplish, forked, upstanding, twiggy
> stuff of bushes and small trees
> with dead, brown leaves under them
> leafless vines—
>
> Lifeless in appearance, sluggish
> dazed spring approaches—
>
> They enter the new world naked,
> cold, uncertain of all
> save that they enter. All about them
> the cold, familiar wind—
>
> Now the grass, tomorrow
> the stiff curl of wildcarrot leaf
> One by one objects are defined—
> It quickens: clarity, outline of leaf
>
> But now the stark dignity of
> entrance—Still, the profound change
> has come upon them: rooted, they
> grip down and begin to awaken

It is an early spring day in New Jersey, the poet behind the wheel of his car as he drives to the hospital. Mud, bare trees, bushes just beginning to turn. The miracle of spring all about

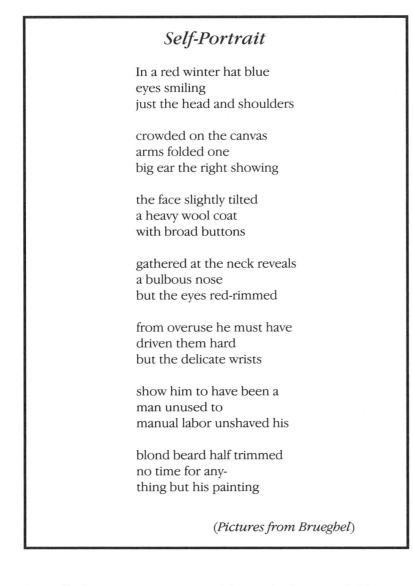

Self-Portrait

In a red winter hat blue
eyes smiling
just the head and shoulders

crowded on the canvas
arms folded one
big ear the right showing

the face slightly tilted
a heavy wool coat
with broad buttons

gathered at the neck reveals
a bulbous nose
but the eyes red-rimmed

from overuse he must have
driven them hard
but the delicate wrists

show him to have been a
man unused to
manual labor unshaved his

blond beard half trimmed
no time for any-
thing but his painting

(Pictures from Brueghel)

him, all of it entering a new world, as naked as any child entering the world, shivering, uncertain of everything except that
he is here: the profound change that life entails. And Williams
catches that shift in the way the lines push over into the following lines with a kind of expectancy and rush, one idea shifting into another, "leafless" chiming with "lifeless," the short *i*
of "still" and "grip" and "begin" played against the long *a* of
"change" and "awaken" in the rhyming position. This is subtle
music, as charged and shimmering as new life itself. Out of his

drive along a nondescript country road in spring, Williams shows us the tensed vitality of our world.

You can make a poem out of anything, Williams insisted: a pot of flowers, a young sycamore, the ritual of burning the Christmas tree, a woman walking past the window or eating a plum, great mullen, codfish, a sea elephant, a black jazz band, the falls at Paterson, a cat walking atop a jam closet, winter, a sparrow, family members, church bells ringing, clouds, a red wheelbarrow. He wrote whenever he could find the time, on any scrap of paper at hand, between house calls, at the side of the road waiting for a tugboat to pass under a drawbridge, late at night in his attic retreat.

In 1924, Williams took a six-month vacation with his wife, Flossie, to Europe. There he met the modern writers gathered in Paris—James Joyce, Ernest Hemingway, and Ford Madox Ford among them—and renewed his friendship with Pound. There, too, he continued writing his study of what was truly American about America, which he published the following year as *In the American Grain*. In 1928 he published his first novel, *A Voyage to Pagany,* based on his European trip. He returned to Europe that summer to see his sons enrolled in the same Swiss school he and his brother had attended and met the writer Gertrude Stein in Paris on his way home. Back in the states he met the poets Louis Zukofsky, with whom he maintained a lifelong friendship, and Hart Crane, just then completing his epic poem *The Bridge.*

Williams edited three magazines in the 1920s and early 1930s: *Contact* with his friend Robert McAlmon, *Pagany* with Richard Johns, and a revived *Contact* with Nathanael West, author of *Miss Lonelyhearts.* That they were short-lived ventures did not bother Williams, who saw all the little magazines and quarterlies as part of one living organism, which spread the news of what was happening in poetry to those who cared. With the American Depression his work took on an even greater sense of social urgency. In 1932 he published his first collection of short stories, *The Knife of the Times,* which focused on New Jerseyites with whom he had grown up or about whom he had heard. His first book of collected poems, covering the years 1921–1931, appeared in 1934, thanks to Zukofsky. In 1936 he published another collection, *Adam & Eve & the City.* Then, in 1937, in the person of a young American named James Laughlin, founder of New Directions Publishing Co., he met the publisher who would bring out his poems, novels, plays, and short stories for the rest of his life (except for one brief period in the 1950s) and beyond. Laughlin began by publishing *White Mule* in 1937, the first part of Williams's trilogy (a series of three books) based on the lives of his wife and her family. This was followed in 1938 by a second collection of short stories, *Life Along the Passaic River,* and *The Complete Collected Poems* and in 1941 by *The Broken Span* (new poems).

An American Epic

For twenty years Williams had dreamed of writing an epic based on his local environment; and during World War II, with his two sons in the military, the sixty-year-old doctor plunged into Paterson, the dying mill town nine miles west of Rutherford, which the founding fathers of the United States had once envisioned as a possible site for the capital of the new nation. In Paterson he had the city and the falls, the urban landscape and the pastoral. Using the city as a symbol for himself, he could explore his lifelong search for love and attempt to understand himself within the context of his place of origin. He would explore the language rising out of his world, a language forever old and forever new, as he listened to the sound of the falls calling to him in all seasons. He could also write of the debased lives of Paterson's citizens and its government. He could write a wounded poetry which rose out of a wounded place, a poetry forever changing and renewing itself against all odds. All these haunted Williams and preoccupied him throughout the 1940s and well into the 1950s. Out of this frenzy of poetic activity arose Williams's extraordinary epic, *Paterson,* which was issued in five books between 1946 and 1958. "From above," he wrote near the beginning of his epic, feeling beneath his feet the force of the great Passaic Falls:

> . . . higher than the spires, higher
> even than the office towers, from oozy fields
> abandoned to grey beds of dead grass,
> black sumac, withered weed-stalks,
> mud and thickets cluttered with dead leaves—

the river comes pouring in above the city
and crashes from the edge of the gorge
in a recoil of spray and rainbow mists—

Belated Recognition

Even as Williams began to receive the recognition he knew his
work deserved, he also began to suffer physical setbacks: a
heart attack in 1948, followed by a series of strokes beginning
in 1951, against which he fought valiantly but which returned
with increasing force, leaving his right side crippled. For the
last ten years of his life he had to type with just his left forefin-
ger, imagining himself a unicorn, that mythical one-horned
beast, hunted down by the hounds of fate. In spite of his dis-
ability, he managed to publish his collected plays, the last part
of his trilogy, *The Build-Up,* his *Autobiography,* a collection of
earlier and later poems, collected short stories, essays and letters, and a memoir of his mother. He also produced three collections of new poems, all written in distinctly new forms and
even more accessible: *The Desert Music, Journey to Love,* and
Pictures from Brueghel, for which he received, following his
death, both the Pulitzer Prize and the Gold Medal for Poetry. In
"The Sparrow," a poem remembering his long-dead father, he
wrote these "step-down" lines, which modestly and heart-
breakingly sum up his own life:

> Practical to the end,
>   it is the poem
>   of his existence
> that triumphed
>   finally;
>   a wisp of feathers
> flattened to the pavement,
>   wings spread symmetrically
>   as if in flight,
> the head gone,
>   the black escutcheon of the breast
>   undecipherable,
> an effigy of a sparrow,
>   a dried wafer only,
>   left to say

and it says it
      without offense,
            beautifully;
This was I,
    A sparrow.
          I did my best;
farewell.

In the last eighteen months of his life, unable to keep his eyes and hands coordinated, the thing he feared most happened: he was forced to give up writing. He died quietly, at home in his bed, on 4 March 1963.

Of course, many American poets knew what a treasure they had in Williams, and there is hardly a poet who wrote after him who has not acknowledged his or her debt to Williams. For Williams had as many poetic faces as his great predecessor, Whitman, influencing poets as diverse as Robert Lowell, Allen Ginsberg, Denise Levertov, and Philip Levine. It is an influence that shows no sign of abating, as young poets keep returning to him as to a great river from which to gain their sustenance.

Selected Bibliography

WORKS BY WILLIAM CARLOS WILLIAMS
Poetry

Poems (1909).

The Tempers (1913).

Al Que Quiere! (1917).

Spring and All (1923).

Collected Poems 1921–1931 (1934).

Adam & Eve & the City (1936).

The Complete Collected Poems of William Carlos Williams, 1906–1938 (1938).

The Broken Span (1941).

The Wedge (1944).

Paterson, Book One (1946).

IF YOU LIKE the poetry of Williams, you might also like the poetry of Robert Creeley or Robert Lowell.

🙐

Paterson, Book Two (1948).

The Clouds (1948).

Paterson, Book Three (1949).

Selected Poems (1949).

The Pink Church (1949).

The Collected Later Poems (1950).

Paterson, Book Four (1951).

The Collected Earlier Poems (1951).

The Desert Music and Other Poems (1954).

Journey to Love (1955).

Paterson, Book Five (1958).

Pictures from Brueghel and Other Poems (1962).

Prose

Kora in Hell: Improvisations (1920).

The Great American Novel (1923).

In the American Grain (1925).

A Voyage to Pagany (1928). A novel.

The Knife of the Times, and Other Stories (1932).

White Mule (1937). A novel.

Life Along the Passaic River (1938). Short stories.

In the Money (1940). A novel.

First Act (1945). Plays.

Make Light of It: Collected Stories (1950).

The Autobiography of William Carlos Williams (1951).

The Build-Up (1952).

Selected Essays (1954).

Yes, Mrs. Williams (1959). Memoir of Williams's mother.

The Farmers' Daughters: The Collected Stories of William Carlos Williams (1961).

Many Loves, and Other Plays (1961).

Interviews

Interviews with William Carlos Williams: "Speaking Straight Ahead." Edited by Linda Welshimer Wagner. New York: New Directions, 1976.

I Wanted to Write a Poem. Boston: Beacon, 1958. Interviews with Edith Heal.

Correspondence

The Last Word: Letters Between Marcia Nardi and William Carlos Williams. Edited by Elizabeth Murrie O'Neil. Iowa City: University of Iowa Press, 1994.

Pound/Williams: Selected Letters of Ezra Pound and William Carlos Williams. Edited by Hugh Witemeyer. New York: New Directions, 1996.

The Selected Letters of William Carlos Williams. Edited by John C. Thirlwall. New York: McDowell, Obolensky, 1957.

William Carlos Williams and James Laughlin: Selected Letters. Edited by Hugh Witemeyer. New York: Norton, 1989.

Available Collections

The Collected Poems of William Carlos Williams. Vol. 1 (1909–1939). Edited by A. Walton Litz and Christopher MacGowan. New York: New Directions, 1986.

The Collected Poems of William Carlos Williams. Vol. 2 (1939–1962). Edited by Christopher MacGowan. New York: New Directions, 1988.

Imaginations. Edited and with an introduction by Webster Schott. New York: New Directions, 1970. Includes *Kora in Hell, Spring and All, The Great American Novel,* and *The Descent of Winter.*

Paterson. Rev. ed. prepared by Christopher MacGowan. New York: New Directions, 1992.

A Recognizable Image: William Carlos Williams on Art and Artists. Edited by Bram Dijkstra. New York: New Directions, 1978. Williams on the French painters, Walker Evans, Charles Sheeler, Marsden Hartley, Alfred Stieglitz, John Marin, Constantin Brancusi, and many others.

Something to Say: William Carlos Williams on Younger Poets. Edited by James E. B. Breslin. New York: New Directions, 1985. Williams on Louis Zukofsky, David Ignatow, Robert Lowell, Allen Ginsberg, the Beats, and others.

WORKS ABOUT WILLIAM CARLOS WILLIAMS

Axelrod, Steven Gould, and Helen Deese, eds. *Critical Essays on William Carlos Williams.* New York: G. K. Hall, 1995.

Bremen, Brian A. *William Carlos Williams and the Diagnostics of Culture.* New York: Oxford University Press, 1993.

Breslin, James E. B. *William Carlos Williams: An American Artist.* New York: Oxford University Press, 1970.

Coles, Robert. *William Carlos Williams: The Knack of Survival in America.* New Brunswick, N. J.: Rutgers University Press, 1975.

Conarroe, Joel. *William Carlos Williams'* Paterson: *Language and Landscape.* Philadelphia: University of Pennsylvania Press, 1970.

Conrad, Bryce. *Refiguring America: A Study of William Carlos Williams'* In the American Grain. Urbana: University of Illinois Press, 1990.

Diggory, Terrence. *William Carlos Williams and the Ethics of Painting.* Princeton, N.J.: Princeton University Press, 1991.

Dijkstra, Bram. *The Hieroglyphics of a New Speech: Cubism, Stieglitz, and the Early Poetry of William Carlos Williams.* Princeton, N.J.: Princeton University Press, 1969.

Driscoll, Kerry. *William Carlos Williams and the Maternal Muse.* Ann Arbor, Mich.: UMI, 1987.

Fisher-Wirth, Ann W. *William Carlos Williams and Autobiography: The Woods of His Own Nature.* University Park: Pennsylvania State University Press, 1989.

Frail, David. *The Early Politics and Poetics of William Carlos Williams.* Ann Arbor, Mich.: UMI, 1987.

Kallet, Marilyn. *Honest Simplicity in William Carlos Williams'* "Asphodel, That Greeny Flower." Baton Rouge: Louisiana State University Press, 1985.

Mariani, Paul. *William Carlos Williams: The Poet and His Critics.* Chicago: American Library Association, 1975.

Mariani, Paul. *William Carlos Williams: A New World Naked.* New York: McGraw-Hill, 1981. Paperback edition, with revisions, New York: Norton, 1990.

Marzán, Julio. *The Spanish American Roots of William Carlos Williams.* Austin: University of Texas Press, 1994.

Riddel, Joseph N. *The Inverted Bell: Modernism and the Counterpoetics of William Carlos Williams.* Baton Rouge: Louisiana State University Press, 1974.

Townley, Rod. *The Early Poetry of William Carlos Williams.* Ithaca, N. Y.: Cornell University Press, 1975.

Wallace, Emily Mitchell. *A Bibliography of William Carlos Williams.* Middletown, Conn.: Wesleyan University Press, 1968.

Weaver, Mike. *William Carlos Williams: The American Background.* Cambridge, U.K.: Cambridge University Press, 1971.

Whittemore, Reed. *William Carlos Williams: Poet from Jersey.* Boston: Houghton Mifflin, 1975.

More About Williams

You can find information about Williams on the Internet at:
http://www.cwru.edu/artsci/
engl/VSALM/mod/
johnson/WCWLNX.HTM
http://www.poets.org/LIT/
poet/wcwilfst.htm

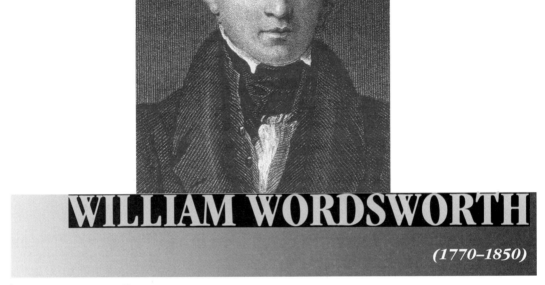

WILLIAM WORDSWORTH

(1770–1850)

by Lewis Warsh

William Wordsworth is considered by many the senior figure of English Romantic poets. The other members of this group include his friend Samuel Taylor Coleridge (1772–1834), Lord Byron (1788–1824), Percy Bysshe Shelley (1792–1822), and John Keats (1795–1821). Notice the dates: although Wordsworth was born first, he died last. In this sense he contradicts the stereotype* of the Romantic poet as a person who lived life to the hilt* and died young. But although Wordsworth lived until he was eighty, critics feel that he wrote most of his greatest poems before he was forty and spent the second half of his life revising those poems, often making them worse instead of better.

The Romantic movement flourished at the end of the eighteenth century and during the first quarter of the nineteenth century. In many ways, the Romantic poets of two hundred years ago resembled the poets of the Beat Generation—poets such as Allen Ginsberg and Jack Kerouac—who came of age in the 1950s. The poets of both groups attempted to express the immediacy of the present moment—how the poet

Quotations of Wordsworth's poetry throughout are taken from Hartman, *Selected Poetry and Prose.*

*stereotype preconceived ideas about a category of people

*to the hilt fully, to the limit

felt and what the poet was seeing at the exact moment of writing. The English Romantics were in reaction against the poets who had come before, poets such as Alexander Pope, who believed that rational thought was the key to understanding the universe. In the preface to his first book, *Lyrical Ballads,* Wordsworth says that one of the great subjects of poetry is "the essential passions of the human heart." For the Romantic poets, and for Wordsworth especially, rational thought was less important than the "elementary feelings" that everyone experienced. What counted most was the freedom of the human spirit and how it interacted with the "permanent forms of nature" (quotations are from the second edition).

Early Life

During his childhood, Wordsworth's most important influence was the countryside in northwestern England where he grew up, an area known as the Lake District. Especially important was the river Derwent, which flowed past his home in the town of Cockermouth. In his long autobiographical* poem, *The Prelude,* begun in 1798, Wordsworth says that the Derwent, "the fairest of all rivers, loved to blend his murmurs with my nurse's song." It is often said that the sight of branches outlined against the evening sky inspired him, when he was in his early teens, to become a poet, but equally important was the encouragement of his parents, John and Ann Wordsworth, who allowed their son to roam freely through the landscape. John Wordsworth was a lawyer; both he and his wife were interested in poetry and music. Their house was filled with books, and Wordsworth read avidly.* At an early age he began to memorize the poetry of Shakespeare, Edmund Spenser, and John Milton. By the time he was thirteen, he was reading such books as *Don Quixote* (Miguel de Cervantes) and *Gulliver's Travels* (Jonathan Swift). The books on the shelves of his parents' house stimulated him as much as the landscape outside.

Wordsworth, born on 7 April 1770, was the second of five children. His only sister, Dorothy, was born in 1771. His idyllic* childhood ended abruptly when his mother died in 1778. William was sent to live with his maternal grandparents but rebelled against the restrictions of their household and went to live with family friends, Ann and Hugh Tyson. He began attending school in the town of Hawkshead in 1779, and when

*autobiographical related to the author's own life

*avidly eagerly

*idyllic pleasantly simple

his father died in 1783 he went to live with his legal guardians, Richard Wordsworth and Christopher Cookson. Yet his formal education was always secondary to what he learned by observing and absorbing his natural surroundings. He enrolled at Cambridge University in 1787, graduating in 1791. It was during this time that he became devoted to writing poetry.

Among his first poetry, written during his college years, was a long poem called *Descriptive Sketches,* begun in 1790 and completed in 1792, which was influenced by a walking tour he had taken in the Swiss Alps. The long hikes he took with his friends during his college years were more important to his poetry than anything he learned in the classroom. These hikes were more than simple walks; they were quests to seek out the "power spots" of the external world. For Wordsworth, nature was like a religion. When talking about nature in his poems he is also talking about his own spiritual life. It was also during these walks, which he took until he was in his seventies, that he met many of the characters whom he depicts in his poems.

Revolutionary Years

In the early 1790s, Wordsworth was inspired by the events leading up to the French Revolution. Personal liberation and political liberation were equally important to him. For Wordsworth, being alive meant being free to act on one's instincts, to act spontaneously, to interact fully with the outside world. He was influenced in his thinking by the philosopher William Godwin, who believed that liberation and social reform should take place gradually and nonviolently.

Late in 1791 Wordsworth traveled to Paris. His goal was to learn how to speak French fluently and to observe the revolution firsthand. He visited the Bastille, the hated French prison that had recently been destroyed, but the spirit of the revolution failed to touch him as he had expected. Possibly his most important experience during the fifteen months that he lived in France was falling in love with a Frenchwoman, Annette Vallon. A daughter, Caroline Wordsworth, was born of this passionate relationship in 1792, but by that time Wordsworth had returned to England. His abandonment of his new family caused him guilt—perhaps he felt overburdened by the responsibilities of becoming a father at the age

The French Revolution was aimed at creating natural human rights based on reason rather than tradition. Those rights included equality before the law for everyone and a fairer distribution of land and wealth. The revolution also sought to limit the power of the Catholic monarchy.

of twenty-two—and is possibly the reason so many tragic children appear in the poems he wrote later.

In 1794, Wordsworth was reunited with his sister, Dorothy. The two siblings had been separated since their father's death. They decided to live together in the small town of Dorset in the south of England. Dorothy was devoted to her brother's life as a poet and spent most of her time copying his poems and keeping house. The closeness of their relationship might seem peculiar to us—most brothers and sisters, in our day, do not live together when they get older—but Dorothy was an unusual person. She spent her entire life helping others, not only her brother but the rest of her family and friends as well. In 1798 she began to keep a journal of her life with her brother. Wordsworth expresses his great debt to her in many of his poems. In "To My Sister," composed in 1798, he writes:

> Some silent laws our hearts will make,
> Which they shall long obey:
> We for the year to come may take
> Our temper from to-day.
>
> And from the blessed power that rolls
> About, below, above,
> We'll frame the measure of our souls:
> They shall be tuned to love.
>
> Then come, my Sister! come, I pray,
> With speed put on your woodland dress;
> And bring no book: for this one day
> We'll give to idleness.

In the poem "The Sparrow's Nest," he writes of Dorothy: "She gave me eyes, she gave me ears." One of his greatest poems, "Lines (Composed a Few Miles Above Tintern Abbey)," written in 1798, was addressed to his sister. Their relationship was a source of confusion to people who mistakenly assumed they were lovers.

Lyrical Ballads

In 1795, while living with Dorothy in the English town of Alfoxden, Wordsworth began a friendship with the poet Samuel Taylor Coleridge, who lived with his wife, Sara, and son, Hartley, a few miles away. Wordsworth's poems flourished as a result of the close association with the other poet. It is not hard to imagine the two of them meeting on a country road at dusk or sitting beneath a tree reading each other's new poems. At this time, Coleridge was writing his most famous poem, "The Rime of the Ancient Mariner," and Wordsworth provided him with support and advice. Both poets envisioned a new type of poetry that would be at once realistic and supernatural.

Many of the poems that Wordsworth wrote while living in Alfoxden, which he entitled *Lyrical Ballads,* are monologues in the voices of people he met while wandering around the countryside. The common trait of these people is their stubborn attempt to hold on to something that they have lost, whether it is the memory of a distant place or of someone close to them who has died. In "We Are Seven," for instance, the poet questions an eight-year-old girl about her family. The child insists that she has seven brothers and sisters, even though two of them have died and are buried "beneath the church-yard tree." For the child, her dead brother and sister are immortal—they can never really die as long as they live on in her memory. We can see how Wordsworth's relationship with Dorothy, one of the most famous brother-sister relationships in all of literature, made him extremely sensitive to the possibility of separation and loss, especially among members of the same family.

"Lines (Composed a Few Miles Above Tintern Abbey)" is considered his most important poem from this period. He was twenty-eight when he wrote it, but he already felt the loss of the excitement and innocence he had experienced when he was younger, when

> like a roe*
> I bounded o'er the mountains, by the sides
> Of the deep rivers, and the lonely streams,
> Wherever nature led . . .

*roe a type of deer

He captures a feeling that is common to everyone—returning to a place where one has lived, or where one has experienced something intensely, and remembering how it felt to be that person in the past:

> . . . I cannot paint
> What then I was. The sounding cataract*

*cataract waterfall

Haunted me like a passion: the tall rock,
The mountain, and the deep and gloomy wood,
Their colours and their forms, were then to me
An appetite; a feeling and a love,
That had no need of a remoter charm,
By thought supplied, nor any interest
Unborrowed from the eye.—That time is past,
And all its aching joys are now no more,
And all its dizzy raptures. . . .

He is no longer his younger self, the person who ran freely through the natural landscape. What makes Wordsworth's experience of returning to Tintern Abbey so inspiring to him is the companionship of his sister. When you know someone a long time, he is saying, it is easier to think about the past without regret or sadness, since the person with whom you shared the first experience is still part of your present life. Mixed with the sense of loss in "Tintern Abbey" is a profound joy of renewal and rebirth.

The Prelude

*epic a long poem that tells the story of a hero's deeds

One of Wordsworth's most ambitious writing projects was his autobiographical epic* poem, *The Prelude*. He began the poem in 1798 and spent most of his life writing and rewriting it. He completed one version in 1805 and another version just before he died in 1850. Because of its length, *The Prelude* has often been compared to great epics with historical or religious themes, but Wordsworth's epic deals primarily with his personal struggles. He gave *The Prelude* the subtitle "Growth of a Poet's Mind." It is basically an attempt to answer the mysterious question of why he became a poet.

Wordsworth was obsessed with the idea of the space between the present and the past, of returning home. For Wordsworth, home was not a place but rather a time in his past when he felt free of the burdens of responsibility. The memories of childhood were the places he wanted to return to, the spots of time that left permanent traces on his unconscious. Why do certain memories endure while others fade with the passing of time? For Wordsworth, the crucial moments are the first experiences of childhood, the feeling of freedom that accompanies innocence.

The World Is Too Much with Us

The world is too much with us; late and soon,
Getting and spending, we lay waste our powers:
Little we see in Nature that is ours;
We have given our hearts away, a sordid boon!*
This Sea that bares her bosom to the moon;
The winds that will be howling at all hours,
And are up-gathered now like sleeping flowers;
For this, for everything, we are out of tune;
It moves us not.—Great God! I'd rather be
A Pagan* suckled in a creed* outworn;
So might I, standing on this pleasant lea,*
Have glimpses that would make me less forlorn;
Have sight of Proteus* rising from the sea;
Or hear old Triton* blow his wreathèd horn.

*__sordid boon__ a shabby (sordid) blessing (boon)

*__pagan__ someone who does not accept the biblical God as the one and only god; a heathen

*__creed__ set of beliefs

*__lea__ meadow

*__Proteus and Triton__ in Greek mythology, sea gods

*__synonymous__ having the same meaning

Another major theme of *The Prelude* is the difference between life in the city and life in nature. For Wordsworth, "freedom" was synonymous* with "nature." Living in the city was for him like being in prison, yet life in nature also meant a life of solitude, while life in the city represented a life of action. In *The Prelude,* Wordsworth is trying to work out his own conflicts through writing. By the end of the poem he seems to have made a choice to live as a solitary observer of nature.

Wordsworth began *The Prelude* in his early thirties because he feared that if he waited until he was older and wiser, he would forget what it felt like to be a child. Part of his discovery is that every experience has two sides: joy is always accompanied by doubt, beauty by fear. But every experience, he seems to be saying, has a potential seed. From that seed will grow a more intense understanding of oneself and what it means to be alive.

Later Poems

Until his early thirties, Wordsworth's most important relationships were with his sister and with his fellow poet Coleridge. But he fell in love with a childhood friend, Mary Hutchinson, and in 1802, they were married. There are many stories about how Dorothy reacted to her brother's marriage: how she wore the wedding ring to bed the night before the ceremony, how she was too ill to attend the ceremony. Nonetheless, Wordsworth's marriage to Mary did not seem to change the relationship between him and his sister. After the wedding, the three of them returned to Dove Cottage in Grasmere (in the Lake District), and a year later they took a long walking tour through Scotland.

Mary and William's first child, John, was born in 1803. Four other children were born during the next few years. The stability of family life marked an end to his years of inner turmoil and restlessness. In 1807 his *Poems in Two Volumes* was published. The book contained more than one hundred poems dating from 1801 to 1807. Reviews of the book were mostly negative; critics felt that the newer poems were inferior to the poems in *Lyrical Ballads,* that Wordsworth was simply repeating the same themes and ideas, that he had not developed as a poet. Wordsworth, shaken by this response, refused to publish any new volumes of poems for the next seven years.

Some of the strongest poems in this book are in sonnet* form. Most critics feel that Wordsworth's sonnets rank among the greatest ever written. In his early poems he broke with the poetry of the past, but in the sonnets he seems concerned with placing himself firmly in the tradition of the poets who came before him, poets such as Shakespeare and Milton. "Composed upon Westminster Bridge, September 3, 1802," is one of the best:

> Earth has not anything to show more fair:
> Dull would he be of soul who could pass by
> A sight so touching in its majesty:
> This City now doth, like a garment, wear
> The beauty of the morning: silent, bare,
> Ships, towers, domes, theatres, and temples lie
> Open unto the fields, and to the sky;
> All bright and glittering in the smokeless air.
> Never did sun more beautifully steep
> In his first splendour, valley, rock, or hill;
> Ne'er saw I, never felt, a calm so deep!
> The river glideth at his own sweet will:
> Dear God! the very houses seem asleep;
> And all that mighty heart is lying still!

Notice the poem's title. Wordsworth was attempting to create a snapshot of a particular place at a particular moment and to

*__sonnet__ a fourteen-line poem usually composed in iambic pentameter (each line has five feet, each foot consisting of an unstressed syllable followed by a stressed syllable).

include within it his own emotional state. Note his use of allit-
eration—the repetition of sounds and letters—as a way of
conveying emotion. The simplicity of the language is in contrast to his depth of feeling.

In yet another sonnet, "The World Is Too Much with Us,"
Wordsworth criticizes the rampant materialism, the "getting
and spending" of the modern world. Nature is envisioned as a
force that gives the poet the strength to overcome his unhap-
piness, certainly more than any material object could do.

Possibly the most important poem in this book is "Ode:
Intimations of Immortality from Recollections of Early Childhood," composed in 1802. The poem evokes the loss of childhood innocence and bemoans the fact that as we grow older,

> Though nothing can bring back the hour
> Of splendour in the grass, of glory in the flower;
>   We will grieve not, rather find
>   Strength in what remains behind;

The Last Decades

Although most of Wordsworth's celebrated poems were written before 1810, he continued writing (and rewriting his early
works) for the next forty years of his life. Few critics feel that
the poems written after 1810 are superior to the earlier ones.
Most of the poems from the last decades sound uninspired, as
if he were trying to manufacture poetry rather than write it.

In a letter written to a friend in 1811, Wordsworth admitted that he no longer cared about "things upon which so
much of my life has been employed. I am not quite 41 years of
age, yet I seem to have lost all personal interest in everything
which I have composed." He was attempting to write another
long poem, *The Recluse,* but he did not have the energy to finish it. Somehow, as he grew older, he lost interest in the unlimited potential of poetry. Instead, he reserved his attention
for more practical matters. Two of his children died when they
were young, and Dorothy's health eventually faded. His relationship with Coleridge also changed dramatically when Coleridge separated from his wife and became addicted to opium.
The two poets eventually patched up their differences.

Despite the fact that he wrote very little new poetry, his
fame spread as he grew older. Younger poets, including Ralph

poet laureate in England, an outstanding poet once appointed for life as a paid member of the royal household and expected to write poems for certain occasions. In other countries, the term refers to a poet honored and recognized for his or her achievements.

IF YOU LIKE the poetry of Wordsworth, you might also like the poetry of John Milton, John Keats, or Samuel Taylor Coleridge.

❧

Waldo Emerson, often visited him, and Oxford University awarded him an honorary doctorate in 1839. In 1843 he was appointed the poet laureate* of England. His books sold well, and the royalties eased the financial burdens of his old age. By 1845 his reputation was higher than that of any other living poet. Shortly after an attack of pleurisy, Wordsworth died on 23 April 1850 at his home, two miles from Grasmere.

Selected Bibliography

WORKS BY WILLIAM WORDSWORTH
Available Collections

The Selected Poetry and Prose of William Wordsworth. Edited by Geoffrey H. Hartman. New York: New American Library, 1970.

The Poetical Works of William Wordsworth. 5 vols. Edited by Ernest de Selincourt and Helen Darbishire. Oxford, U.K.: Clarendon Press, 1940–1949.

The Prelude; or, the Growth of a Poet's Mind. Edited by Helen Darbishire. Oxford, U.K.: Clarendon Press, 1959.

WORKS ABOUT WILLIAM WORDSWORTH

Bateson, F. W. *Wordsworth: A Re-Interpretation.* 2d ed. New York: Longmans, Green, 1956.

Bloom, Harold. *The Visionary Company: A Reading of English Romantic Poetry.* Garden City, N.Y.: Doubleday, 1961.

Davis, Jack M., ed. *Discussions of William Wordsworth.* Boston: Heath, 1964.

Ferry, David. *The Limits of Mortality: An Essay on Wordsworth's Major Poems.* Middletown, Conn.: Wesleyan University Press, 1959.

Frye, Northrop, ed. *Romanticism Reconsidered: Selected Papers from the English Institute.* New York: Columbia University Press, 1963.

Hartman, Geoffrey H. *The Unmeditated Vision: An Interpretation of Wordsworth, Hopkins, Rilke, and Valéry.* New Haven, Conn.: Yale University Press, 1954; Folcroft, Pa.: Folcroft, 1966.

Hartman, Geoffrey H. *Wordworth's Poetry 1787–1814.* New Haven, Conn.: Yale University Press, 1964.

Knight, G. Wilson. *The Starlit Dome: Studies in the Poetry of Vision.* New York: Oxford University Press, 1941.

Lindenberger, Herbert. *On Wordsworth's Prelude.* Princeton, N.J.: Princeton University Press, 1963.

Moorman, Mary. *William Wordsworth: A Biography.* 2 vols. Oxford, U.K.: Clarendon Press, 1957 and 1965.

Rader, Melvin. *Wordsworth: A Philosophical Approach.* Oxford, U.K.: Clarendon Press, 1967.

Reed, Mark L. *Wordsworth: The Chronology of the Early Years, 1770–1799.* Cambridge, Mass.: Harvard University Press, 1967.

Woodring, Carl. *Wordsworth.* Boston: Houghton Mifflin, 1965.

Wordsworth, Dorothy. *The Journals of Dorothy Wordsworth.* New York: Oxford University Press, 1958.

More About Wordsworth

Dove Cottage, where Wordsworth lived 1799–1808, is open to the public. For information, see the Wordsworth Trust Centre for British Romanticism website at: http://www.wordsworth.org.uk/

JAMES WRIGHT

(1927–1980)

by Peter Stitt

When James Wright wrote his very first poems as a sophomore in high school, he signed his name at the bottom as "J. Wolfingham Wright." It was a self-conscious gesture and seems to suggest that he thought of poetry as an elevated activity practiced only by elderly gentlemen wearing ties and having pince-nez* glasses perched on their noses. By the time he was a senior, however, he was writing sonnets* on subjects as diverse as love and rebellion, signing the name by which he was known to all his friends, Jim Wright.

Also the president of the school's Hi-Y Club and editor of the yearbook, Wright was renowned as a poet among his classmates. And so, when he saw "a fair Calypso* in my Spanish class," he naturally decided to write a series of ardent love sonnets to her (the quotation is from one of these unpublished poems). The young lady did briefly fall under his spell, but all too soon, she grew tired of this guy who kept putting poems in her locker. The famous poet went alone to the Sweetheart Dance that year.

*pince-nez old-fashioned eyeglasses clipped to the nose
*sonnet a fourteen-line poem usually composed in iambic pentameter (each line has five feet, each foot consisting of an unstressed syllable followed by a stressed syllable).
*Calypso in Homer's *Odyssey,* an exceptionally attractive sea nymph who kept Odysseus on her island for seven years

187

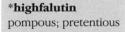
*highfalutin
pompous; pretentious

*Delphic having to do
with Delphi, in Greece,
the location of a shrine
dedicated to the god
Apollo

*Hellespont an an-
cient name for the
strait, now called the
Dardanelles, that joins
the Aegean and Mar-
mara Seas

*epithet a descriptive
phrase used along with
or in place of a per-
son's name

*iambic pentameter
five metrical feet to a
line, with two syllables
in each foot and the
accent (stress) on the
second syllable (exam-
ple: da DA da DA)

One of his best high school poems, called "Sonnet on My Violent Approval of Robert Service" (published in *Gettysburg Review* in 1990), shows how far Jim had come, by the time he was a senior, from being the highfalutin* J. Wolfingham Wright. Robert Service wrote popular poems set in the American West, often in a saloon where miners and cowboys would get into fistfights. Here is Wright's defense of liking him:

> I have not wandered far away from home,
> Nor watched the sun melt on the Delphic* shrine,
> Nor whipped the roughneck's liquor into foam,
> Nor choked on Hellespont's* bright azure brine.
> And never has it been my lot to trudge
> On equal plane with sages of deep thought,
> So (I apologise) I am no judge
> Of who is a great bard and who is not.
>
> However, ignorant jackass that I am,
> I love a man with hair upon his chest
> Who chews and spits and powerfully dares.
> Ah! I would rather do, and give a damn,
> Than dream that I might be forever blest
> If I should scorn a God-like man who swears.

And then, as if to assert his own standing as a learned man, Jim signed this poem with his full name—"James Arlington Wright"—adding an honorary epithet* at the end—"Esquire." Like most of us, he wanted to have it both ways.

In form this poem is a perfect Petrarchan sonnet, written in iambic pentameter* and having the rhyme scheme a b a b, c d c d, e f g, e f g. A question is posed in the octave (the first eight lines) and answered in the sestet (the last six lines). Maybe he did not want to admit it, but young Jim Wright was a pretty good scholar himself.

The Landscape of His Youth

James Wright was born in Martins Ferry, Ohio, on 13 December 1927. His father, Dudley Ira Wright, worked at the Hazel-Atlas Glass factory across the Ohio River and seven miles downstream in Wheeling, West Virginia. Martins Ferry was one in a whole line of factory towns spread out along the Ohio side of the river. Although people like Dudley Wright were happy (and lucky) to have jobs during the years of the Great Depression* (1929–1936), the steel mills and other factories polluted not only the river flowing by but also the air the people had to breathe.

The town sat at the bottom of a series of high river bluffs, on top of which began the unspoiled woods and peaceful farms of what James Wright later called "Beautiful Ohio" (*Above the River: The Complete Poems*). The stark contrast between the ugliness of the industrialized valley and the natural beauty of the hills and the plateau was strongly imprinted in the young poet's mind and set the pattern for much of the poetry to come.

*Great Depression
the period of economic hardship in America following the stock market crash of 1929

The Green Wall

After graduating from high school in 1946, James Wright served in the army for eighteen months, then entered Kenyon College in Gambier, Ohio. After his graduation in 1951, Wright married Liberty Kardules of Martins Ferry, and the two of them spent the next year in Vienna, Austria, where Wright studied German poetry as the recipient of a Fulbright Fellowship. Their first son, Franz, was born in Vienna; Marshall, their second son, was born two years later, while Wright was a graduate student at the University of Washington in Seattle. Wright had been writing poetry throughout this time. Even before he had earned his doctorate in English literature, the manuscript of his first book, *The Green Wall,* was chosen by the great English poet W. H. Auden to be published in the Yale Series of Younger Poets. Wright conceived of the "green wall" as a symbolic barrier between Eden and the real world, something like the barrier between "beautiful Ohio" and the industrial valley. As Wright explained later in an interview, "I tried to begin with the fall of man, and acknowledge that the fall of man was a good thing, the *felix culpa,* the happy guilt. And then I tried to weave my way in and out through nature poems and people suffering in nature because they were conscious" (Stitt, pp. 205–206). In 1957 he began teaching at the University of Minnesota in Minneapolis.

"The fall of man" refers to the biblical story in which Adam and Eve, and by extension all future generations, are banished from the paradise of Eden for disobeying God's orders.

Saint Judas

Although *The Green Wall* was favorably received by readers and critics, it is interesting that one reviewer felt the poems needed to be more formal, while another felt they were confined by their excessive formality! The poems in Wright's second book, *Saint Judas*—published only two years after his first, in 1959—are mostly just as formal as those in *The Green Wall,* though by then Wright had begun to question his own practice.

The content of both books, however, is well indicated by the title poem of the second, another sonnet, in which Wright speaks from the perspective of someone he surprisingly calls "Saint Judas":*

*Saint Judas Judas Is-
cariot, one of Jesus'
disciples, who eventu-
ally betrayed him for
thirty pieces of silver.
By calling him "Saint,"
Wright is saying that
even sinners can be
good.

> When I went out to kill myself, I caught
> A pack of hoodlums beating up a man.
> Running to spare his suffering, I forgot
> My name, my number, how my day began,
> How soldiers milled around the garden stone
> And sang amusing songs; how all that day
> Their javelins measured crowds; how I alone
> Bargained the proper coins, and slipped away.
>
> Banished from heaven, I found this victim beaten,
> Stripped, kneed, and left to cry. Dropping my rope
> Aside, I ran, ignored the uniforms:
> Then I remembered bread my flesh had eaten
> The kiss that ate my flesh. Flayed* without hope
> I held the man for nothing in my arms.
> (*Above the River: The Complete Poems*)

*flayed stripped;
skinned

Having fallen from grace into the real world of sinners and soldiers, Wright's Judas attempts to redeem himself through the brotherly love expressed by his attempt to protect the suffering man—perhaps Jesus, about to be crucified—from the blows of the angry crowd. Wright sympathizes almost always with sinners and sufferers and almost never with the authorities or others who exploit the poor.

The Branch Will Not Break: Return to the Country

By 1963, James Wright felt that he had been beaten down by the citified world of Minneapolis. His marriage had ended in divorce, and his teaching at the University of Minnesota was

Lying in a Hammock at William Duffy's Farm in Pine Island, Minnesota

Over my head, I see the bronze butterfly,
Asleep on the black trunk,
Blowing like a leaf in green shadow.
Down the ravine behind the empty house,
The cowbells follow one another
Into the distances of the afternoon.
To my right,
In a field of sunlight between two pines,
The droppings of last year's horses
Blaze up into golden stones.
I lean back, as the evening darkens and comes on.
A chicken hawk floats over, looking for home.
I have wasted my life.

(*The Branch Will Not Break*)

not going well. He was also drinking too much and had fallen into despair. When he happened upon the first issue of a new magazine called *The Fifties,* Wright wrote a nine-page letter to the editor, Robert Bly, who lived on a farm in western Minnesota. Bly—himself then a young poet—wrote back, saying simply, "Come on out to the farm," and a fruitful literary relationship began. As Wright said later of Bly and his wife, Carol, "They loved me and they saved my life. I don't mean just the life of my poetry, either" (Stitt, p. 203).

The first result of their collaboration was a series of translations of Spanish, French, and German surrealist* poems. The relationship also had a profound effect on Wright's own poetry, for he began writing in much simpler, more imagistic* forms and returned to the subject of nature and its healing powers for troubled humankind. With the publication of his triumphant third book, *The Branch Will Not Break,* Wright fulfilled a promise made to his editor when *Saint Judas* was published: "Whatever I write from now on will be entirely different. I don't know what it will be, but I am finished with what I was doing in that book" (quoted from the dust jacket of the first edition of *The Branch Will Not Break*).

The new poems were free verse,* and they depend on their images to give them both form and meaning. A small but

*surrealist** related to the literary and artistic movement surrealism, which aimed (chiefly during the 1920s and 1930s) to express the workings of the unconscious or subconscious mind

*imagistic** using words that appeal to the senses by naming things that can be seen, heard, touched, and so on

*free verse** poetry that does not follow traditional forms, meters, or rhyme schemes

significant example of both the feeling and the form of these poems is "Today I Was Happy, So I Made This Poem":

> As the plump squirrel scampers
> Across the roof of the corncrib,
> The moon suddenly stands up in the darkness,
> And I see that it is impossible to die.
> Each moment of time is a mountain.
> An eagle rejoices in the oak trees of heaven,
> Crying,
> *This is what I wanted.*
>
> (*Above the River*)

The intense love of life expressed through the eagle reflects the poet's equally intense happiness. Having traveled out of the city and away from his troubles, he had climbed back over the "green wall" and into nature once again.

Shall We Gather at the River

Unfortunately, dark clouds were gathering on the horizon of James Wright's future. In 1964 he was denied tenure* at the University of Minnesota, and in 1966 he left for New York City to teach at Hunter College. In his next book, published in 1968, he returned to the tortured landscape of his youth, the industrialized Ohio River valley where he had first learned about poverty, loneliness, suffering, and death.

Shall We Gather at the River is not a happy book, looking as it does into the very pit of blackness that epitomized* so much of human life for James Wright. Even the slightest poems in this book are heartbreaking, as Wright conflates* the life he was living when he wrote them with the spirit of the place he inhabited as a child. "The River Down Home" beautifully illustrates this technique:

> Under the enormous pier-shadow,
> Hobie Johnson drowned in a suckhole.
> I cannot even remember
> His obliterated face.
> Outside my window, now, Minneapolis
> Drowns, dark.

***tenure** permanent employment, usually in a teaching job, granted after a probationary period*

The gospel hymn from which Wright took the title *Shall We Gather* celebrates both the sacrament of baptism and the promise of an afterlife. Wright uses the title ironically.

***epitomized** exemplified*

***conflate** to combine or confuse; to condense by combining*

It is dark.
I have no life.

What is left of all of it?
Blind hoboes sell American flags
And bad poems of patriotism
On Saturday evenings forever in the rain,
Between the cathouses* and the slag* heaps
And the river, down home.
Oh Jesus Christ, the Czechoslovakians
Are drunk again, clambering
Down the sand-pitted walls
Of the grave.

(*Above the River*)

*cathouse a house of prostitution; a brothel

*slag a waste product created from melting metal

Like so much of Wright's poetry, this poem is permeated by an awareness of death, a subject that obsessed Wright, as it does so many poets. Everything in this poem is dying or gravitating toward death, including the Czechoslovakians, who represent the citizens of the river valley and who probably think they are having a good time getting drunk on a Saturday night.

Collected Poems

When James Wright married Edith Anne ("Annie") Runk on 13 June 1967, the possibility of happiness seemed to have returned to his life. The two had met at a poetry reading in New York, and they formed a strong and mutually supportive bond. In 1970, they embarked on the first of a series of trips to France and Italy, trips that were to inspire Wright's late poetry. But first there was the job of preparing the manuscript of *Collected Poems,* a volume published in 1971 that included all of his earlier poems that Wright wished to preserve.

When the book came out, Wright was hailed in the *New York Times Book Review* as "a national treasure." Most other critics agreed with this opinion, and in 1972 Wright was awarded the Pulitzer Prize for poetry. Other awards also came his way, including the Brandeis University Creative Arts Citation in Poetry and a ten-thousand-dollar fellowship from the Academy of American Poets. Some critics did suggest that there was a looseness in the form of some of the new poems published in the volume, and this perception became more pronounced with the publication of Wright's next and least successful book, *Two Citizens,* in 1973.

The European Period

The last book published by James Wright during his lifetime, *To a Blossoming Pear Tree* (1977), was more favorably received, although the level of praise did not approach that accorded some of his earlier volumes. In these poems, and in those published after his death in *This Journey* (1982), Wright finds a rich, deep, and mature sense of happiness in the middle territory offered to him by the landscapes and culture of Europe, a place standing between the American city and the raw American wilderness. *This Journey,* in particular, is full of poems in which Wright emotionally attaches himself to cultural icons, ancient sites, and sensory experiences that came to him in France and Italy.

Perhaps the best of the late poems is "The Journey." Here we seem to see Wright coming to terms, finally, with the tragic nature of life and death:

Anghiari is medieval, a sleeve sloping down
A steep hill, suddenly sweeping out
To the edge of a cliff, and dwindling.
But far up the mountain, behind the town,
We too were swept out, out by the wind,
Alone with the Tuscan* grass.

Wind had been blowing across the hills
For days, and everything now was graying gold
With dust, everything we saw, even
Some small children scampering along a road,
Twittering Italian to a small caged bird.
We sat beside them to rest in some brushwood,
And I leaned down to rinse the dust from my face.

I found the spider web there, whose hinges
Reeled heavily and crazily with the dust,
Whole mounds and cemeteries of it, sagging
And scattering shadows among shells and wings.
And then she stepped into the center of air,

*Anghiari an Italian village built in the Middle Ages

*Tuscan from or relating to Tuscany, a region of northwest Italy

Slender and fastidious,* the golden hair
Of daylight along her shoulders, she poised there,
While ruins crumbled on every side of her.
Free of the dust, as though a moment before
She had stepped inside the earth, to bathe herself.

I gazed, close to her, until at last she stepped
Away in her own good time.

Many men
Have searched all over Tuscany and never found
What I found there, the heart of the light
Itself shelled and leaved, balancing
On filaments* themselves falling. The secret
Of this journey is to let the wind
Blow its dust all over your body,
To let it go on blowing, to step lightly, lightly
All the way through your ruins, and not to lose
Any sleep over the dead, who surely
Will bury their own, don't worry.

(Above the River)

*fastidious demanding; hard to please

*filament a thread or threadlike object; the fine metal wire in a light bulb that emits the light

In both meaning and structure, the poem is carried by the progression of its imagery. Particularly noticeable is the imagery of light that becomes associated with the spider, but only *after* she has significantly cleansed herself by bathing "inside the earth" (a reference to death). This sense of light—and of lightness—is the image through which the poet expresses the heart-lifting wisdom that he has finally discovered.

James Wright died of throat cancer on 25 March 1980, in New York City.

Selected Bibliography

IF YOU LIKE the poetry of Wright, you might also like the poetry of Galway Kinnell.

WORKS BY JAMES WRIGHT
Poetry

The Green Wall (1957).

Saint Judas (1959).

The Branch Will Not Break (1963).

Shall We Gather at the River (1968).

Collected Poems (1971).

Two Citizens (1973).

To a Blossoming Pear Tree (1977).

This Journey (1982).

Prose

Moments of the Italian Summer (1976).

The Summers of James and Annie Wright (1981).

The Shape of Light (1986).

Available Collections

Above the River: The Complete Poems. New York: Farrar, Straus and Giroux, 1990.

Collected Prose. Ann Arbor: University of Michigan Press, 1983.

WORKS ABOUT JAMES WRIGHT

Dougherty, David C. *James Wright.* Boston: Twayne, 1987.

Elkins, Andrew. *The Poetry of James Wright.* Tuscaloosa: University of Alabama Press, 1991.

Roberson, William H. *James Wright: An Annotated Bibliography.* Lanham, Md.: Scarecrow Press, 1995.

Smith, Dave, ed. *The Pure Clear Word: Essays on the Poetry of James Wright.* Urbana: University of Illinois Press, 1982.

Stein, Kevin. *James Wright: The Poetry of a Grown Man.* Athens: Ohio University Press, 1989.

Stitt, Peter. *The World's Hieroglyphic Beauty: Five American Poets.* Athens: University of Georgia Press, 1985. Interview.

Stitt, Peter, and Frank Graziano, eds. *James Wright: The Heart of the Light.* Ann Arbor: University of Michigan Press, 1990.

✍

More About Wright

Wright's papers are located at:
Special Collections
Wilson Library
University of Minnesota
309 19th Avenue South
Minneapolis, MN 55455
phone: (612) 624-3855

WILLIAM BUTLER YEATS

(1865–1939)

by Christopher Merrill

A week before he died, William Butler Yeats wrote, "Man can embody truth but he cannot know it"—a maxim borne out by his long and varied experience (Ellmann, 1978, p. 289). Indeed, Yeats's life, rich in incident and irony, distilled in poems, plays, stories, autobiographies, and philosophical excursions, has become emblematic of the modern artist's search for meaning. Truth was Yeats's grail,* which he found only in his work, not in his personal life. Yet his quest for certainty, his spiritual explorations (including studies in folklore and the occult*), his desperate love for a beautiful woman, and his devotion to the cause of Irish independence all helped him become not only Ireland's greatest poet but also one of the twentieth century's literary giants. Unable to discover or create a transcendent* system of beliefs suitable for the age, he wrote instead memorable poems and plays that embody truths of a very special order: what he called "the dramatic expression of the highest man."

Quotations from Yeats's work throughout are taken from Finneran, ed., *The Collected Poems of William Butler Yeats.*

*grail the ultimate goal of life

*occult related to supernatural or supernormal powers

*transcendent rising above the normal experiences of the senses

197

Logic and Legends

Yeats was born in Dublin, Ireland, on 13 June 1865, the first child of John Butler Yeats and Susan Pollexfen Yeats. Although his paternal grandfather and great-grandfather were rectors* in the Church of Ireland, the small Protestant denomination within the largely Roman Catholic society, his father turned against organized religion; influenced by the writings of the philosopher John Stuart Mill, J. B. Yeats questioned everything, reinforcing his natural skepticism with the rules of logic. But it was no ordinary logic that prompted him to abandon a career in law and became an artist. His was a cosmopolitan* spirit, imbued* with the artistic theories of the day, and before long he had devised his own faith—in the power of poetry, especially dramatic poetry, to uncover higher truths independent of religion. "Poetry is divine," wrote J. B. Yeats, "because it is the voice of personality—this poor captive caged behind the bars" (Ellmann, 1978, p. 20).

His strong personality was to play a decisive role in his son's artistic development. He read poetry aloud to him— William Shakespeare, William Blake, Percy Bysshe Shelley, and Dante Gabriel Rossetti—and when the boy had not learned to read by the age of nine, he took over his schooling, boxing him on the ears when he could not master his lessons. In fact, the budding poet was an indifferent student; delicate, awkward, and nearsighted, he felt out of place in the classroom and on the playing fields, particularly when he was enrolled in a high school in London, where his father moved to secure artistic commissions. The young man took refuge in his Irishness and in metaphysical* speculations—two lifelong preoccupations, the roots of which may be traced to his mother, a silent, superstitious woman from Sligo, a seaport on Ireland's northwest coast. She had an altogether different influence on her son.

Yeats had spent much of his first ten years in the wilds of Sligo, a romantic setting where his mother liked to trade ghost stories with friends while he wandered by himself in thickets and caves, lost in daydreams. Childhood landscapes shape artistic destiny, and Yeats was rooted in the fairy world of County Sligo, which provided him with imagery for his poems and fueled his passion for the legends of the Irish people. The compass points of his imagination thus became Dublin and Sligo, London and the beyond. Nature and Irish folklore were

rector a church official

cosmopolitan worldly; sophisticated

inbued infused; ingrained

metaphysical relating to such concepts as being, substance, essence, time, space, and identity

set against his father's faith in reason, which the poet would associate with urban experience. Out of his father's skepticism* and his mother's belief in fairies he fashioned a singular poetic temperament, by turns fanciful and tough-minded.

*skepticism doubt, uncertainty; rational questioning

Early Work

Fancy won out when he was a young man. Like his father, Yeats attended art school, though he soon realized his gifts lay in the literary realm. In his first poems he was influenced by Pre-Raphaelite* poetry: the sensuous musicality, attention to detail, and otherworldly settings that Rossetti and the poet and artist William Morris favored in the works of Dante and Edmund Spenser, John Keats and Edgar Allan Poe. For Yeats, too, poetry could offer escape from the everyday world, as in his most famous early poem, "The Lake Isle of Innisfree." In this poem the poet's remarkable ear for the music of words is already apparent. "The bee-loud glade," for example, is surrounded by a run of *s*'s and long *e*'s, as if to set the entire stanza buzzing, and the liquid *l*'s of the oft-cited line "I hear lake water lapping with low sounds by the shore" can make the lake island in County Sligo seem close at hand. The rhyming quatrains,* languid rhythms, and repetition of key words and phrases lend

*Pre-Raphaelite related to a group of nineteenth-century English artists and writers dedicated to reviving early Renaissance ideas

*quatrain a stanza of four lines

The Lake Isle of Innisfree

I will arise and go now, and go to Innisfree,
And a small cabin build there, of clay and wattles* made:
Nine bean-rows will I have there, a hive for the honey-bee,
And live alone in the bee-loud glade.

And I shall have some peace there, for peace comes
    dropping slow,
Dropping from the veils of the morning to where the
    cricket sings;
There midnight's all aglimmer, and noon a purple glow,
And evening full of the linnet's wings.

I will arise and go now, for always night and day
I hear lake water lapping with low sounds by the shore;
While I stand on the roadway, or on the pavements grey,
I hear it in the deep heart's core.

*wattle poles interwoven with branches or reeds

the poem a songlike quality. Indeed, Yeats called many of his poems songs: "The Song of the Old Mother," "A Drinking Song," "Three Marching Songs," and so on. No wonder he titled a late sequence, "Words for Music Perhaps."

Not that he came by his musicality without hard work. Yeats served his literary apprenticeship writing poems and plays, editing anthologies of Irish verse and folktales and fairy tales as well as a collection of William Blake's work, and contributing articles and reviews to newspapers. From the beginning of his career he proved to be a painstaking craftsman. First he would describe subjects for poems in prose; then he had "to find for them some natural speech, rhythm, and syntax, and to set it out in some pattern, so seeming old that it may seem all men's speech," as he wrote in "The Bounty of Sweden," a meditation he published after receiving the Nobel Prize in literature in 1923. His labor was great, as he explains in these lines from "Adam's Curse," a poem linking his compositional methods to the labors a woman undertakes to make herself beautiful:

> I said, 'A line will take us hours maybe;
> Yet if it does not seem a moment's thought,
> Our stitching and unstitching has been naught.
> Better go down upon your marrow-bones
> And scrub a kitchen pavement, or break stones
> Like an old pauper, in all kinds of weather;
> For to articulate sweet sounds together
> Is to work harder than all these, and yet
> Be thought an idler by the noisy set
> Of bankers, schoolmasters, and clergymen
> The martyrs call the world.

Yeats was no idler—his collected works run to several volumes.

The naturalness of expression he achieved in his verse and the seeming spontaneity of his thought became a model for poets around the world. He reinvigorated traditional forms— blank verse and ballads, sonnets and ottava rima,* heroic couplets and epigraphs—by employing flexible meters, half rhymes, and the inflections of common speech. He rewrote some poems so often that he felt compelled to justify his practice in the epigraph to volume 2 of his *Collected Works* (1908):

*ottava rima a stanza consisting of eight lines that rhyme in a set pattern

The friends that have it I do wrong
Whenever I remake a song,
Should know what issue is at stake:
It is myself that I remake.

Possessed of a restless imagination, Yeats reinvented himself many times over, and his work grew suppler, more graceful, and more profound at each stage—each incarnation—of his life.

Nor would "the noisy set" have looked kindly on his occult studies. Upon his return to London in 1888 he joined the Esoteric Section of the Theosophical Society of Madame Blavatsky, a Russian-born spiritualist medium.* Her group was dedicated to spiritual evolution. Madame Blavatsky professed to believe that the world was in eternal conflict between the forces of good and evil, that Christian clergy bore a heavy responsibility for modern materialism,* and that all religions were united by a secret doctrine, which she claimed to have learned from spiritual masters in Tibet (who later tutored her by telepathy—communication through nonsensory means). The program she laid out for her followers supported Yeats's own explorations of the supernatural. Magic and mysticism became his watchwords. Two years later, even as his fellow theosophists, alarmed by his zeal, asked him to resign from the society, he was initiated into the Hermetic Order of the Golden Dawn, which demanded of its members competence in mysticism. "The mystical life is the centre of all that I do and all that I think and all that I write," Yeats confided to a friend (Ellmann, 1978, p. 97). And his interest in the hidden world never abated because he believed that the world's rebirth depended upon individual change and that the golden dawn of humanity was near at hand.

What did Yeats glean from his esoteric* investigations? "Hammer your thoughts into unity," he advised himself, and if his interest in occultism, which he called his "secret fanaticism," did not answer all his questions, he nevertheless found in it symbols useful for his poetry (Ellmann, 1978, p. 118). It was the French poet Charles Baudelaire who suggested that man can penetrate the temple of nature through symbols. Yeats took him at his word, becoming the greatest symbolist* poet of all. From his meditations on the secret significance of things, he created a poetic unity of universal significance.

*medium someone who is said to be able to communicate with spirits

*materialism preoccupation with worldly possessions

*esoteric meant to be understood only by an elite group

*symbolist belonging to an artistic movement prominent in the late nineteenth and early twentieth centuries that emphasized elusive and mysterious states of feeling and perception and sophisticated references to mythology, etc.

*unrequited not re-
ciprocated

Maud Gonne and the Irish Independence Movement

His most important symbol was Maud Gonne, whom he met in 1889. She was said to be the most beautiful woman of the day, and Yeats fell madly in love with her. He repeatedly asked her to marry him—to no avail—and his unrequited* love became a powerful stimulant for his work. In his imagination Maud Gonne, whose true passion was Irish independence, was transformed into the most beautiful woman of Greek mythology, Helen, whose abduction by her lover, Paris, led to the Trojan War:

> Why should I blame her that she filled my days
> With misery, or that she would of late
> Have taught to ignorant men most violent ways,
> Or hurled the little streets upon the great,
> Had they but courage equal to desire?
> What could have made her peaceful with a mind
> That nobleness made simple as a fire,
> With beauty like a tightened bow, a kind
> That is not natural in an age like this,
> Being high and solitary and most stern?
> Why, what could she have done, being what she is?
> Was there another Troy for her to burn?
>
> "No Second Troy"

The answer to Yeats's last question was "yes." In his mind Maud Gonne had been abducted by the Irish cause, a conviction reinforced by her decision to marry Major John MacBride, a fellow Irish nationalist who was later executed for his part in the 1916 Easter Rising. With a weary heart, Yeats, like the Greek warriors of old, went into battle on her behalf. He drew on national sentiment to help the Irish gain their freedom from the British. Yeats threw himself into dramatic work rooted in Irish themes; his favorite fairy tales acquired a political dimension when he and his friends Lady Augusta Gregory and John Synge, the author of *Playboy of the Western World,* used them to create a national theater. Together, the three playwrights ushered in a literary renaissance, galvanizing Irish nationalism until it became a force that culminated in war and independence from England. The losses were terrible, as Yeats wrote in "The Second Coming":

Things fall apart; the centre cannot hold;
Mere anarchy is loosed upon the world,
The blood-dimmed tide is loosed, and everywhere
The ceremony of innocence is drowned;
The best lack all conviction, while the worst
Are full of passionate intensity.

Never before had he spoken so publicly in his verse as he did in the aftermath of the 1916 Rebellion. Playwriting had taught him how to dramatize contradictory states of mind, and certainly the Irish civil war was rife with contradictions, which he documented in some of the finest public poems of the century. The poet fervently dreamed of independence even as he deplored its costs: bloodshed in the streets, the execution of the leaders of the uprising, and the beginning of the "Troubles" in Northern Ireland. Yeats's "Easter, 1916" memorializes not only the victims of the uprising but also its permanent effect upon the living: "All changed, changed utterly: / A terrible beauty is born."

At the Peak of His Powers

Change was afoot in Yeats's personal life as well. In 1917, having failed once again to secure Maud Gonne's hand in marriage and later that of her daughter, Iseult, he married a twenty-four-year-old aristocrat Bertha Georgina ("George") Hyde-Lees, another believer in the occult. Although his heart lay with another, George spurred him on to some of his best work. Within days of their marriage, she undertook an experiment in automatic writing,* which, over the next decade, he shaped into the strange prose book *A Vision,* a work dear to his heart. Here at last was confirmation of his intuition that correspondences existed between the hidden and the visible worlds. And it was in the pages of *A Vision* that Yeats described the sixth-century Greek city Byzantium (present-day Istanbul) as "an ideal city," where art, religion, and politics were intertwined in what he called "the artifice of eternity." It became a dominant symbol of his later poems.

His life was more settled now. He bought and restored a tower and two cottages in County Galway, near Lady Gregory's estate, and became a father. In 1922, when the Irish Free State was founded, he accepted an invitation to serve in the Irish

automatic writing writing without conscious intention, as if from the unconscious mind

senate; the next year, he was awarded the Nobel Prize. At this point in his life, he might well have rested on his laurels; instead, he wrote some of his most brilliant poems. In *The Tower, The Winding Stair and Other Poems,* and *New Poems* (published a year before he died), he extended his range, refining his language and sharpening his images. His poetic evolution continued until his death, at seventy-three, on 28 January 1939, while traveling in France. In one of his last poems, "Under Ben Bulben," he offered this advice to those who came after him:

> Irish poets, learn your trade,
> Sing whatever is well made,
> Scorn the sort now growing up
> All out of shape from toe to top,
> Their unremembering hearts and heads
> Base-born products of base beds.
> Sing the peasantry, and then
> Hard-riding country gentlemen,
> The holiness of monks, and after
> Porter* drinkers' randy* laughter;
> Sing the lords and ladies gay
> That were beaten into the clay
> Through seven heroic centuries;
> Cast your mind on other days
> That we in coming days may be
> Still the indomitable* Irishry.

*porter short for "porter's beer," a dark beer brewed from browned or charred malt

*randy coarse or lustful

*indomitable unconquerable; untamable

Suffice it to say that Yeats's work remains the source of what is indomitable in Irish poetry.

IF YOU LIKE the poetry of Yeats, you might also like the poetry of W. H. Auden
✑

Selected Bibliography

WORKS BY WILLIAM BUTLER YEATS
Poetry

Crossways (1889).

The Rose (1893).

The Wind Among the Reeds (1899).

In the Seven Woods (1903).

The Green Helmet and Other Poems (1910).

Responsibilities (1914).

The Wild Swans at Coole (1919).

Michael Robartes and the Dancer (1921).

A Vision (1925).

The Tower (1928).

The Winding Stair and Other Poems (1933).

New Poems (1938).

Last Poems (1939–1940).

Available Collections

The Autobiography of William Butler Yeats. New York: Collier Books, 1965.

The Collected Letters of W. B. Yeats. 3 vols. Edited by John Kelly. Oxford, U.K.: Clarendon Press, 1986–.

The Collected Plays of W. B. Yeats: New Edition with Five Additional Plays. New York: Macmillan, 1953.

The Collected Poems of W. B. Yeats. Edited by Richard J. Finneran. New York: Macmillan, 1989.

Essays and Introductions. New York: Macmillan, 1961.

Explorations. New York: Macmillan, 1962.

Memoirs. New York: Macmillan, 1963.

Mythologies. New York: Macmillan, 1959.

A Vision: A Reissue with the Author's Final Revisions. New York: Macmillan, 1956.

The Yeats Reader: A Portable Compendium of Poetry, Drama, and Prose. Edited by Richard J. Finneran. New York: Charles Scribner's Sons, 1997.

WORKS ABOUT WILLIAM BUTLER YEATS

Bloom, Harold. *Yeats.* New York: Oxford University Press, 1970.

Bradford, Curtis B. *Yeats at Work.* New York: Ecco Press, 1978.

Cross, K. G. W., and R. T. Dunlop. *A Bibliography of Yeats Criticism.* London: Macmillan, 1971.

Donoghue, Denis. *William Butler Yeats.* New York: Viking Press, 1971.

Ellmann, Richard. *The Identity of Yeats.* New York: Oxford University Press, 1964.

Ellmann, Richard. *Yeats: The Man and the Masks.* New York: Norton 1978.

Foster, R. F. *The Apprentice Mage, 1865–1914.* Vol. 1 of *W. B. Yeats: A Life.* New York: Oxford University Press, 1997.

Gregory, Lady Augusta. *Gods and Fighting Men.* New York: Oxford University Press, 1970.

Jeffares, A. Norman. *A New Commentary on the Poems of W. B. Yeats.* London: Macmillan, 1984; Stanford, Calif.: Stanford University Press, 1984.

Jeffares, A. Norman. *W. B. Yeats: A New Biography.* New York: Farrar, Straus and Giroux, 1990.

Kinsella, Thomas. *The Dual Tradition: An Essay on Poetry and Politics in Ireland.* Manchester, U.K.: Carcanet Press, 1995.

MacNeice, Louis. *The Poetry of W. B. Yeats.* New York: Oxford University Press, 1967.

Rosenthal, M. L. *Running to Paradise: Yeats's Poetic Art.* New York and Oxford, U.K.: Oxford University Press, 1994.

Stallworthy, Jon. *Between the Lines: Yeats's Poems in the Making.* Oxford, U.K.: Clarendon Press, 1963.

Stallworthy, Jon. *Vision and Revision in Yeats's Last Poems.* Oxford, U.K.: Clarendon Press, 1969.

Unterecker, John. *A Reader's Guide to William Butler Yeats.* New York: Noonday Press, 1959.

Vendler, Helen. *Yeats's "Vision" and Later Plays.* Cambridge, Mass.: Harvard University Press, 1968.

More About Yeats

You can write to:
The W. B. Yeats Society
of New York
c/o National Arts Club
15 Grammercy Park South
New York, NY 10003

INDIGENOUS AND ORAL POETRY

by Jerome Rothenberg

Over the past two centuries and more, many poets have raised questions about the nature of poetry and its place in the world. Poets who wrote words on paper and published them in books had long spoken of themselves as singers and of their poems as songs. They knew that their words were meant to be heard and not just seen, and this made some of them wonder if there was not a poetry—in the distant past or distant present—that existed totally apart from written words and printed books.

If so, what would such a poetry—an oral poetry—be like? Would it be called poetry by those who made it? And how would it be viewed by those who believe that poetry is the possession of a small, highly educated segment of society rather than open to all people as poets and as an audience for poetry? The attempt to answer these questions has led to a reconsideration of what is old and what is new in poetry, what is primitive and what is developed, and what are the ways that song and language lead us toward a heightened sense of living in our world.

No Language Is Primitive

Contemporary experts in languages believe that no language is primitive. There are no half-formed languages, no under-developed or inferior languages. All languages have structures of great complexity, and what is true of language in general is equally true of poetry and of the rituals of which so much poetry is a part. A study of indigenous societies*—those in particular in which writing has been absent and technological development is minimal—has shown that poetry, wherever we find it, involves an extremely complicated sense of language and structures. If *we* take poetry to be "language charged with meaning to the utmost possible degree," as the poet Ezra Pound defined it, or, more simply, as "[structures] allowing musical elements (time, sound) to be introduced into the world of words," as the composer and

indigenous societies cultures native to a given region

Quotation of Pound is taken from Pound, Ezra. *ABC of Reading.* New York: New Directions, 1960.

207

Quotation of Cage is taken from Cage, John. *Silence: Lectures and Writings.* Middletown, Conn.: Wesleyan University Press, 1961.

poet John Cage observed, we can find it even in cultures where no activity is identified as "poetry."

Indigenous Poetry

The words or sounds of this poetry are often part of a larger total work or ceremony that may go on for hours, even days. Other things that we would separate into the categories of music, dance, myth, and painting may also be part of that work—inseparable in the minds of those performing it. If this is the case, where does a poem begin and end? Is it simply the words of the song, or does it include the whole work, of which the words are just a part? The translation of such poems, as printed, may show the "meaningful" element only, often no more than a single "line":

A splinter of stone which is white (Bushman)

Semen white like the mist (Australian)

My-shining-horns (Chippewa: single word)

But, in practice, the one "line" will likely be repeated at length. (Is it "single" then?) Its sounds may be altered and the words distorted from their usual forms. Also, vocal sounds with no fixed meanings may be interspersed among the words. All of these devices create a greater and greater gap between the meaningful part of the translation and all that was actually there in the original work.

That work will probably not end with the "single" line and its repetitions and variations but will more likely be preceded and followed by other lines. All of these "lines" (each of considerable duration in performance) may be thought of as separate poems or as the component parts of a single, larger poem. In many instances, the songs develop into even longer structures, weaving many strands and images together. If sung, they are often accompanied by instrumental music and dancing. Stories may also be part of the performance, and additional paraphernalia and props may be included: masks and costumes, face and body painting, pictures showing gods or other supernatural beings depicted with colored sand or painted onto rocks or fabrics.

Such performances are a part of the rituals and ceremonies of indigenous life. They may take place in sacred natural locations or in special ceremonial structures—the underground kivas* of the southwestern American Pueblos, for example, or the theater-like buildings of the Indians of British Columbia with their hidden passageways and platforms. None of this is theater in the usual sense. Rather than entertainment, the purpose of such performances, whether by individuals or groups, is efficacy—the power to control or change one's self and one's world—from illness to well-being; from childhood to adulthood; from ordinary sight to deeper vision; from human into animal; from everyday life into a world of gods and animals and other supernatural beings; from life to death and back.

These ceremonies are enhanced by the words and gestures of the ceremonial actors, and they also become the basis for an account of tribal history, for myths of world and human origins, for tales of gods and heroes. Such songs and tales—as poetry—are central to most indigenous cultures. Many are from the distant past, while others are the work of recent, often widely known practitioners. Looking to dreams and visions for their inspiration, these practitioners, often functioning as shamans (medicine people), have been identified—from the outside at least—as healers, singers, visionaries, and, in all but name, as poets.

While it used to be common to treat the unwritten poetry of indigenous peoples as anonymous or authorless, more contemporary accounts have brought the poets and singers forward as persons with real identities and with names such as Komi Ekpe (Ewe, from Nigeria), María Sabina (Mazatec, from Mexico), Isaac Tens (Gitksan, from Canada), Eduardo Calderón (mestizo,* from Peru), Andrew Peynetsa (Zuni), Frank Mitchell (Navajo), Black Elk (Oglala, Sioux). "To say the name," says Samuel Makidemewabe, a Swampy Cree storyteller from Canada, "is to begin the story."

Some examples follow.

*kiva enclosed structure for Pueblo Indian ceremonies

*mestizo Spanish word meaning "mixed," a mestizo is a person of mixed European (Spanish) and American Indian ancestry

BLACK ELK

In 1872 the United States government was driving the Lakota (Sioux) people from their tribal lands on the American plains. A nine-year-old boy, later called Black Elk, fell sick and had a "great vision"—an extended dream in which spirit messengers, both men and horses, took him on a journey that revealed to him the future of his nation. The central vision in his dream was of a "dance" of many-colored horses filling the whole sky.

Filled with sights and sounds and many songs, Black Elk's dream stayed with him for eight years and left him sick with fear and apprehension. When he was seventeen, he heard the voices of coyotes and of crows repeating: "It is time! It is time! It is time!" Then two shamans, Bear Sings and Black Road, treated him. Black Road told him: "You must perform this vision for your people upon earth. You must have the horse dance first for the people to see. Then the fear will leave you" (Black Elk, p. 161). A great Horse Dance followed—a new and complex ceremony or performance, which was filled with charging horses and in which the many songs and voices in Black Elk's vision again were brought to life.

ISAAC TENS

Black Elk's was an elaborate version of the way in which power—and songs of power—came to traditional visionary seers. Similarly, on the Pacific Coast of British Columbia at the turn of the nineteenth century, a young Gitksan man named Isaac Tens fell into a deep trance while hunting. A large owl flew up to him and seized him by the face until he bled from the mouth and lost consciousness. When this happened several times, he was attended to by older shamans, who treated him for what was by then a raging fever. Later he said this about his experience:

> While I remained in this state, I began to sing. A chant was coming out of me without my being able to do anything to stop it. Many things appeared to me presently: huge birds and other animals. . . . These were visible only to me, not to the others in my house. Such visions happen when a man is about to become a shaman; they occur of their own accord. The songs force themselves out complete without any attempt to compose them. But I learned and memorized those songs by repeating them. (Rothenberg, *Technicians of the Sacred*, p. 51)

And, he adds, he later used the songs in one-on-one healing rituals.

The kind of spontaneous composition that Isaac Tens describes has reminded some of the French poet Arthur Rimbaud's idea, from the early days of modernism,* of the poet as a person passing through an intense personal crisis to become a visionary. It also resembles the literary idea of inspiration but with some differences of social context and function.

*modernism a series of literary movements that attempted to break with traditional styles of the past in an effort to create new means of expression and action. See also the essay "Twentieth-Century Modernism" in these volumes.

MARÍA SABINA

In the practice of another shaman-poet, María Sabina, a Mazatec Indian from Oaxaca, Mexico, the visionary state was helped along by the use of a psychedelic mushroom. Like Black Elk's vision, her first visions came early in childhood, followed by a later "great vision" in which a group of elders seated around a long table gave her a weighty tome they called the Book of Language. Although she could not read or write, she was able to understand the words in this book and to use them for the chants that formed the basis of her later practice as a healer (*curandera*). Sung continually in nightlong vigils (*veladas*), these chants celebrated her powers and the powers of the words she had been given. She summed up her experience in the following words: "I cure with language."

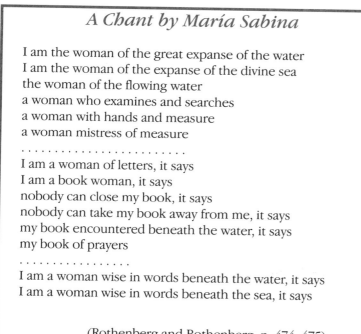

A Chant by María Sabina

I am the woman of the great expanse of the water
I am the woman of the expanse of the divine sea
the woman of the flowing water
a woman who examines and searches
a woman with hands and measure
a woman mistress of measure
· ·
I am a woman of letters, it says
I am a book woman, it says
nobody can close my book, it says
nobody can take my book away from me, it says
my book encountered beneath the water, it says
my book of prayers
· · · · · · · · · · · · · · · ·
I am a woman wise in words beneath the water, it says
I am a woman wise in words beneath the sea, it says

(Rothenberg and Rothenberg, p. 474–475)

The Night Chant

Black Elk, María Sabina, and Isaac Tens were witnesses to their own works, but many poem-songs go back to a far more distant and nearly anonymous past. The Navajo Night Chant, for example, is a ceremony that lasts for eight days and nights. Like many such traditional events, it is a multisensory performance, including monumental sandpaintings, masked dances on the final night, and hundreds of songs that are intoned by a medicine person called a *hatali* (chanter). But the entire ceremony, according to the Navajos, was the gift of a legendary figure named Bitahatini ("The Visionary"), whom the gods carried off and to whom they gave the rites for the Night Chant, along with the songs and instructions for curing. Many of these songs have become famous far outside the Navajo homeland, including the song that ends with these words:

> In beauty I walk
> With beauty before me I walk
> With beauty behind me I walk
> With beauty above me I walk
> With beauty above and about me I walk
> It is finished in beauty
> It is finished in beauty.

(Matthews, p. 145)

Other Kinds of Poetry

There were other kinds of poetry in indigenous cultures in addition to those inspired by visionary experiences. Men and women gifted in language also carried forward and sometimes reinvented the histories and mythologies of their people in memorable language, both sung and spoken. This is the kind of oral epic* that lies behind the writings of those virtually anonymous poets whom the ancient Greeks called Homer and Hesiod.

*epic a long poem that tells the story of a god's or hero's deeds, refined by the American poet Ezra Pound as "a poem including history"

In other places, specially trained singers created songs that described and celebrated rulers and other important people, as well as gods, animals, and sacred objects. This form of composition, sometimes called praise poetry, has continued with great force among many of the indigenous peoples of Africa and elsewhere. It is balanced on the negative side by forms of abuse poetry—a poetry of insult—used both for expressing anger and for calming conflicts and aggression.

Here, as in poetry everywhere, both knowledge and emotions have a role to play. For example, in the Gisaro ceremony of the Kaluli people of Papua New Guinea, the dancers and singers describe places associated with the recently deceased relatives of people in their audience. The songs aim to bring out a feeling of grief so powerful that those affected by it seize burning torches and strike and burn the bodies of the "offending" dancers. The power of the songs lies largely in the precise observations conveyed by the words—the minute particulars that the English poet William Blake claimed as the most powerful elements of his own poetry.

Magic Words

Observation and knowledge are the basis of imagination—the ability, often claimed by poets, to see what is not there. The most common medium for expressing such a form of seeing is, curiously, language. Songs and stories in both traditional and contemporary cultures are filled with accounts of magical change. An Inuit (Eskimo) account begins:

> In the very earliest time,
> when both people and animals lived on earth,
> a person could become an animal if he wanted to
> and an animal could become a human being.
> . . . .
> All spoke the same language.
> That was the time when words were like magic.
> (Rothenberg, *Shaking the Pumpkin*, p. 41)

Such a sense of "magic words" often played a role in shaping religious beliefs and views of reality. It also allowed room for the creation of "surrealist"* narratives and for the idea that poetry is, above all, the transformation of reality through language. In this vein Jacob Nibenegenesabe, a Swampy Cree from north-central Manitoba, Canada, created a cycle of stories centered on a comic figure who used the wishbone of a snow goose "to wish anything into existence." His actions, like those of other such trickster figures, often had unintended consequences—as when Nibenegenesabe tells this story, with the trickster speaking in his own voice:

*surrealist relating to the art movement surrealism, which aimed (chiefly during the 1920s and 1930s) to express the workings of the unconscious or subconscious mind, particularly as expressed in dreams

I try to make wishes right
but sometimes it doesn't work.
Once, I wished a tree upside down
and its branches
were where the roots should have been!
The squirrels had to ask the moles
"How do we get down there
to get home?"
One time it happened that way.
Then there was the time, I remember now,
I wished a man upside down
and his feet were where his hands
should have been!
In the morning his shoes
had to ask the birds
"How do we fly up there
to get home?"
One time it happened that way.

(Norman, p. 5)

Works like this, when brought forward by contemporary poets and translators, have strongly influenced the ways in which poetry is heard, read, and written. Poets experimenting with new ways of making poetry have found equally fertile possibilities in the most traditional of indigenous cultures. The connection between old and new ways of making poetry captured the imagination of the Romantic poets and influenced the theory and practice of such early-twentieth-century experimental poets as Tristan Tzara, Blaise Cendrars, Ezra Pound, and Aimé Césaire. Ethnopoetics* had a wide influence in the second half of the twentieth century, both in continuing the work of early modernism and in pointing toward a related multiculturalism that became a central concern of American poetry by the 1980s.

*ethnopoetics the opening of poetry over the whole human range (Rothenberg and Rothenberg)

IF YOU LIKE indigenous and tribal poetry, you might also like the poetry of Aimé Césaire.

ᘒ

Selected Bibliography

AVAILABLE COLLECTIONS

Berndt, R. M. *Djanggawul: An Aboriginal Religious Cult of North-eastern Arnhem Land.* London: Routledge and Paul, 1952.

Black Elk. *Black Elk Speaks: Being the Life Story of a Holy Man of the Oglala Sioux.* Lincoln: University of Nebraska Press, 1989.

Cendrars, Blaise. *The African Saga.* New York: Negro Universities Press, 1969.

Estrada, Alvaro. *María Sabina: Her Life and Chants.* Santa Barbara, Calif.: Ross-Erikson, 1981.

Finnegan, Ruth. *A World Treasury of Oral Poetry.* Bloomington: Indiana University Press, 1978.

Gleason, Judith Illsley. *Leaf and Bone: African Praise-Poems.* New York: Viking Penguin, 1994.

Matthews, Washington. *The Night Chant, a Navajo Ceremony.* New York: Knickerbocker Press, 1902; Salt Lake City: University of Utah Press, 1995.

Norman, Howard. *The Wishing Bone Cycle: Narrative Poems from the Swampy Cree Indians.* Edited by Jerome Rothenberg. Santa Barbara, Calif.: Ross-Erikson, 1982.

Rothenberg, Jerome. *Shaking the Pumpkin: Traditional Poetry of the Indian North Americas.* Albuquerque: University of New Mexico Press, 1991.

Rothenberg, Jerome. *Technicians of the Sacred: A Range of Poetries from Africa, America, Asia, Europe, and Oceania.* Berkeley: University of California Press, 1968; 1985, rev. ed.

Schieffelin, Edward L. *The Sorrow of the Lonely and the Burning of the Dancers.* New York: St. Martin's Press, 1976.

Swann, Brian. *Coming to Light: Contemporary Translations of the Native Literatures of North America.* New York: Random House, 1994.

Tedlock, Dennis. *Finding the Center: Narrative Poetry of the Zuni Indians.* New York: Dial Press, 1972.

GENERAL DISCUSSIONS

Awoonor, Kofi. *Breast of the Earth: A Survey of the History, Culture, and Literature of Africa South of the Sahara.* Garden City, N.Y.: Anchor Press, 1975.

Eliade, Mircea. *Shamanism: Archaic Techniques of Ecstasy.* Translated by Willard R. Trask. Princeton, N.J.: Princeton University Press, 1972.

Finnegan, Ruth H. *Oral Poetry: Its Nature, Significance, and Social Context.* Bloomington: Indiana University Press, 1994.

Rothenberg, Jerome, and Diane Rothenberg, eds. *Symposium of the Whole: A Range of Discourse Toward an Ethnopoetics.* Berkeley: University of California Press, 1983.

Schechner, Richard, and Willa Appel. *By Means of Performance: Intercultural Studies of Theatre and Ritual.* New York: Cambridge University Press, 1990.

Snyder, Gary. *Earth House Hold: Technical Notes and Queries to Fellow Dharma Revolutionaries.* New York: New Directions, 1976.

Swann, Brian, and Arnold Krupat. *Recovering the Word: Essays on Native American Literature.* Berkeley: University of California Press, 1987.

Tedlock, Dennis. *The Spoken Word and the Work of Interpretation.* Philadelphia: University of Pennsylvania Press, 1994.

TROUBADOURS

(1100–1350)

by Anselm Hollo

The troubadour poets flourished in the south of France between roughly 1100 and 1350. They were attached to the courts of wealthy nobles and are credited with the invention of what is known as "courtly love." Most of their lyrics, performed to musical accompaniment by either the authors themselves or by professional entertainers called *jongleurs,* were amorous and exuberant—in the words of the French scholar Henri-Irénée Marrou, "perennially adolescent" (p. 151). Some troubadours, however, also composed poems on satirical and political themes. Among the best-known troubadours are Guillem IX, duke of Aquitaine; Bertran de Born; Arnaut Daniel; Marcabru, Peire Vidal; Raimbaut de Vaquieras; and Gaucelm Faidit.

At a time when government and society were entirely dominated by men, the troubadours' courtly love poetry idealized women. The lover, enchanted by the intellectual and physical beauty of his lady, elevated her in his imagination and was obedient to her wishes. The convention* was that a knight's love ennobled him and made him worthy of his sovereign mistress. As Arnaut Daniel wrote, "The gracious thinking and the frank / Clear and quick perceiving heart / Have led me to the fort of love" (Pound, *Translations*).

*__convention__ a traditional and commonly accepted standard

Chivalry and the Celebration of Desire

The concept of courtly love was an ingredient of chivalry, an ideal of behavior that encouraged knights to leave their martial* ferocity on the battlefield and favor tenderness and refined conduct in the household and at court. If a knight acted gently toward ladies, they might grant him their love—which could consist of only a glance of approval but might also evolve into an ongoing intellectual conversation or, in a more dangerous scenario, into a secret relationship of physical intimacy. Medieval marriages were "arranged," on the basis of such practical considerations as land, possessions, and noble

*__martial__ warlike

217

extramarital outside marriage

lineage rather than romantic love, and extramarital* liaisons could have dire consequences.

This element of risk kindled a poetry that was a celebration of desire—desire understood not merely as an attraction to a member of the opposite sex but also as a powerful longing for spiritual union with that person, either actual or imagined within the framework of the poem.

Origins and Evolution

The literary origins of this development in the relationship of the two sexes have been traced to the Latin poet Ovid's *Art of Love,* published at the very beginning of the Christian era, and also to love poetry in medieval Arabic and Persian literature. Islamic love poetry may have influenced troubadours who heard it (or heard of it) while taking part in the first Crusades against the Saracens.* The songs and music of the Moors* had also been imported into the southwestern region of France.

Saracens European term for the Muslims of the Middle East

Moors the Muslim people of medieval Spain

The troubadour tradition spread to Italy, where it first influenced the works of the Italian poets Guido Guinicelli and Guido Cavalcanti. There it became known as the *dolce stil nuovo,* "sweet new style," a term first used by Dante in *Purgatorio,* the second part of his *Divine Comedy,* to describe his own literary style.

In the works of these Italian poets, woman, represented as the embodiment of God's beauty, was believed to inspire a gentle love that would lead the lover to divine love. Similarly, poetry is an attempt to reconcile, or combine, sacred and profane love. Here, however, we should consider the comments of a twentieth-century American scholar, Meg Bogin:

beatified made a saint

Beatrice Dante's beloved and the heroine of his *Divine Comedy*

mannequin a model for displaying fashionable clothing

> Desexed and beatified* (Beatrice*), definitively changed into man's spiritual redeemer, the lady of the poets became the mannequin* with which all women were compared. Perhaps the elevation of the lady was a major turning point in the history of men: to consider this development a positive one for women would be to ignore its crippling effect on the women of succeeding centuries, including our own. (*The Women Troubadours,* p. 16)

The troubadour style also became popular in northern France in the work of the *trouvères,* contemporary poets who wrote

"Ab la dolchor del temps novel"
("In the Sweetness of the New Season")

In the new season
when the woods burgeon
and birds
sing out the first stave of new song,
time then that a man take the softest joy of her
    who is most to his liking.

    But from where my joy springs
      no message comes:
the heart will not sleep or laugh, nor dare I go out
till I know the truth, if she will have me or not.

    Our love is like top
    branches that creak
    on the hawthorn at night,
    stiff from ice
    or shaking from rain. And tomorrow the sun spreads
    its living warmth through the branches and through
    the green leaves on the tree.

Remembering
the softness of that morning we put away anger,
when she gave me her love, her ring
      as sign,
    remembering the softness,
I pray to God I live to put my hands
under her cloak, remembering that.

And I
care not for the talk
that aims to part
my lady from me;
for I know how talk runs rife and gossip spreads
from empty rancid mouths that, soured
    make mock of love.
No matter. We are the ones, we have
    some bread, a knife.

                (Blackburn, *Proensa: An Anthology*
                    of Troubadour Poetry)

lyrics on similar topics. In Germany such works, always set to musical accompaniment, were created by the *Minnesingers,* and in England the troubadour style was adapted by Chaucer. But the ideals of courtly love did not really gain prominence in English literature until the sixteenth century, in Sir Thomas Wyatt's versions of sonnets written by the Italian Petrarch (Francesco Petrarca) and in the great sonnet sequences of Sir Philip Sidney, Edmund Spenser, and William Shakespeare.

Finders, Inventors, Translators

The language in which the troubadours composed their works was *langue d'oc* (or Occitan, or Provençal). It was the language of southern France and is related to Catalan (the language spoken and written today in the autonomous Spanish region of Catalonia). The troubadours themselves derived their name from the verb *trobar,* which was in turn derived from the Latin *tropare,* "to make tropes"—to invent ways of saying things in a metaphorical* way. In Occitan, *trobar* also means "to find," as does *trouver* in modern French. The troubadours were, indeed, finders and inventors: modern scholars studying the 2,700 lyrics left to us by some four hundred troubadour poets have discovered 1,001 different rhyming patterns as well as 1,422 different kinds of meters!

Such complexity of form makes the translation of troubadour poems very difficult, considerably more so than the translation of the Italian poets Petrarch and Dante, whose works have been rendered into English for five hundred years. The American poet Ezra Pound attempted to reproduce the birdsong-like quality of Arnaut Daniel's *L'aura amara* ("The Bitter Air"):

> So clear the flare
> That first lit me
> To seize
> Her whom my soul believes;
> If cad
> Sneaks,
> Blabs, slanders, my joy
> Counts little fee
> Baits

metaphorical involving poetic figures of speech that make comparisons

And their hates.
  I scorn their perk
  And preen, at ease.
Disburse
Can she, and wake
Such firm delights, that I
Am hers, froth, lees
Bigod! from toe to earring.

(Pound, Translations)

This poem inspired, among others, the contemporary modernist poet Louis Zukofsky to construct lyric poems of pure sound wedded to a meaning that is not always easy to decipher on first reading. Paul Blackburn's version of Guillem IX's "Ab la dolchor del temps novel" ("In the Sweetness of the New Season"), on the other hand, gives us the emotion and imagery of the original in plain, contemporary American English (see *boxed poem*).

The Women Troubadours

The "courtly love" of an adoring male knight and poet for his sovereign lady appears in a very different light in the work of the *trobairitz,* the women troubadours of the twelfth century. Only twenty-three poems, by nineteen poets—among them Beatriz, countess of Dia; Azalais de Porcaraiges; and Maria de Ventadorn—have survived of this undoubtedly much larger body of work. The personal note that the male troubadours were among the first to introduce into Western European literature seems even stronger in these poems. For women troubadours, the relationship of a knight to a lady was portrayed more realistically, with few of the formalities of courtly adoration, as is evident in "Estat ai en gren cossirier" ("I Have Been in Heavy Thought"), written by Beatriz de Dia:

I have been in heavy thought
over a cavalier I'd had.
I want it clear to everyone
that I've loved him to excess,
and now I see he's left me: pre-
text, I refused him my love.

*Floris and
Blancheflor** lovers in
a famous medieval ro-
mance

IF YOU LIKE the poetry of
the troubadours, you might
also like the poetry of
Dante.
◆

I seem to be mistaken, then,
as to what was going on,
dressed or in bed.

I'd love to hold my cavalier
naked one evening in my arms,
he would think he were on fire
if I'd be his pillow then.
For I burn more for him than
Floris* did for Blancheflor,*
deliver him my love, my heart, my
sensuality, my eyes, my life.
My dear and lovely friend, if ever
I come to have you in my power
and get into bed with you one night
and give you love-kiss, know it:
I'd have such a great desire
to hold you in my husband's place,
if you'd promise me to do
everything I'd want you to.

(Blackburn, *Proensa: An Anthology
of Troubadour Poetry*)

The Legacy

Caught up in the constraints and circumstances of their time,
the troubadours (and their immediate *dolce stil nuovo, trou-
vère,* and *Minnesinger* successors) stand at the beginning of
the second millennium as the first individual and intensely
personal voices of traditions still very much alive—in the patterns of courtship and civility, of love's exuberance and sorrows, of the perennial conflicts of mind and heart, and, of
course, in poetry.

Selected Bibliography

AVAILABLE COLLECTIONS

Blackburn, Paul, ed. and trans. *Proensa: An Anthology of
Troubadour Poetry.* Berkeley: University of California
Press, 1978.

Bogin, Meg, ed. *The Women Troubadours.* New York and London: W. W. Norton, 1980.

Cavalcanti, Guido. *The Complete Poems.* Translated by Mark Cirigliano. New York: Italica Press, 1992.

Goldin, Frederick, ed. and trans. *Lyrics of the Troubadours and Trouvères: An Anthology and a History.* Garden City, N.Y.: Anchor Books, 1973.

Pound, Ezra. *Translations.* Enlarged edition. New York: New Directions, 1963.

Wilhelm, James J. *Seven Troubadours: The Creators of Modern Verse.* University Park: Pennsylvania State University Press, 1970.

WORKS ABOUT THE TROUBADOURS AND THEIR TIME

Briffault, Robert. *The Troubadours.* Bloomington: Indiana University Press, 1965.

Dronke, Peter. *Medieval Latin and the Rise of European Love-Lyric.* Oxford, U.K.: Clarendon Press, 1968.

Heer, Friedrich. *The Medieval World.* New York: Mentor Books, 1962.

Lewis, C. S. *The Allegory of Love.* Oxford, U.K.: Oxford University Press, 1970.

Marrou, Henri-Irénée. *Les troubadours.* Paris: Éditions du Seuil, 1971.

RECORDINGS

Chansons des Troubadours: Lieder und Spielmusik aus dem 12. Jahrhundert. Studio der frühen Musik. Telefunken SAWT 95673, series Das Alte Werk.

Ensemble Alcatraz: Danse Royale. Elektra Nonesuch 9 79240-4. French, Anglo-Norman, and Latin songs and dances from the thirteenth century.

TUDOR AND ELIZABETHAN POETS

by Tom Clark

For sheer variety of complication and color, violent collisions of tragedy and good fortune, outrageous flamboyance and anxiety-fraught ambition, few periods in history can match the long reign (1558–1603) of the great Tudor* queen of England, Elizabeth I. Elizabeth's reign was a time of extremes—reckless geographical expansion and breakneck economic inflation; spectacular extravagance in clothing and literature reflecting the exploding growth of new commodities, new markets, and new-moneyed middle classes; far-reaching advances in technology (the "new sciences") and fantastic outcroppings of superstition and religious fanaticism. Perhaps most interesting about the period, though, is the fact that its major mover was a woman. At the center of this world of daring and brilliant men, pulling their strings for all she was worth, stood the sovereign Elizabeth I.

Tudor Tudor family, who ruled England from 1485 to 1603

Tutored by the humanist scholar and educator Roger Ascham, a proponent of the Renaissance "new learning," Elizabeth appreciated the uses of highly crafted formal language. She translated from the classics, wrote her own verses—including one poem familiarly addressing her temporary favorite, Sir Walter Ralegh, as "Wat my Pug" (Woudhuysen, p. 101)—and was as adept at handling her corps of gentlemen poets, with their high decorum* of speech, as she was at the diplomatic juggling of powerful courtiers and princes. Those poets, in turn, were largely responsible for the creation and maintenance of her glorious mythology and legend. While explorers and navigators sailed the globe to chart (and exploit for profit) the imperial reaches of her dominion, dramatic and lyric writers were surveying unexplored realms of thought and feeling to map out brave new worlds of imaginative discourse. Although the empire Elizabeth built has long since faded, the vivid words of poets like Edmund Spenser, Sir Philip Sidney, and Sir Walter Ralegh have transcended* time in their ability to engage, provoke, and captivate audiences with the cult of Elizabeth.

decorum propriety, manners

transcend to rise above normal experience of

Edmund Spenser: Constructing the Image of Elizabeth's Power

auncient ancient

The bloodline of Edmund Spenser (1552–1599) may have run back to a "house of auncient* fame" (*Poetical Works,* p. vii), as he claimed in a poem, but his family had fallen from nobility to humble circumstances. Spenser was the first great middle-class poet. Born in London, he was the son of a journeyman tailor. Spenser attended the Merchant Taylors school on a scholarship. The school was headed by a great scholar and strict teacher of classics who taught his students to play ball in Latin. Again as a scholarship boy, working to pay for his meals, Spenser went on in 1569 to Pembroke Hall, a Cambridge college noted for its large number of Puritan* students. He spent the next seven years at Cambridge, gaining a bachelor's degree in 1573 and a master's in 1576. The Catholic poet John Donne characterized the puritanism of his fellow university students as "plain, simple, sullen, young, [and] contemptuous" in his poem "Satire III." Spenser, studying logic, philosophy, and rhetoric* while doing odd jobs around the college, may have been all those things as well as industrious, curious, ambitious, clever, and a little bit neurotic. For any ambitious young intellectual these were challenging times.

Puritan a Protestant Christian who opposed the traditions and forms of the Church of England. Most Puritans opposed elaborate ceremony and church hierarchy, believing that God's will was directly revealed to individuals through Bible reading. Puritans believed that only a few "elect" were chosen in advance by God for heaven.

Spenser was already applying himself seriously to poetry, in ways that reveal the intellectual currents of the Cambridge of his time. He explored the complicated question of using Greek and Latin poetic meters in English poetry. Spenser's exploration of metrics is apparent in his first important work, the pastoral cycle* *The Shepheardes Calender,* published in 1579. Affected by the religious controversies of the time, the youthful Protestant poet put anti-Catholic (and anti-fun) sentiments into the mouths of the "innocent" shepherd speakers in that work. Classical writers like Theocritus and Virgil, as well as Continental poets of the Renaissance, used pastoral poetry, often allegorical (or "double") in meaning, to describe an idealized rural life. Spenser's pastoral work encompassed an array of subjects—love, poetry, and especially religious matters.

rhetoric the art of persuasion with written or spoken language

pastoral cycle a series of related poems dealing with rural life and tending to portray nature as sweet and beautiful

His poem for April praises only Elisa, queen of shepherds, while the one for October addresses the issue of a higher kind of poetry, turning to wars and jousts and knights. In a pair of lines from "October"—"Whither thou list in fayre Elisa rest, / Or if thee please in bigger notes to sing" (*Poetical Works*)—Spenser seems to be asking himself to choose, as ambitious young poets of the Renaissance customarily did, between a poetry of romance and praise and a poetry of knights and battle. But by the time *The Shepheardes Calender* appeared, Spenser had already embarked on a project that gave him a chance to write both kinds of poetry at once. In *The Faerie Queene* (1590, 1596) he voiced the praises of "fayre Elisa"—the queen of shepherds representing Elizabeth I, England's "Virgin Queen"—and at the same time sang in "bigger notes" about knights and battles.

Sir Philip Sidney, the poet to whom Spenser dedicated *The Shepheardes Calender,* approved of this innovative work but expressed reservations about the "old rustic language" of Spenser's rural speakers. Sidney was only the first of many critics to be troubled by Spenser's experiments with "artificial" languages.

Spenser's presentation of his groundbreaking work to Sidney was not merely a polite literary gesture. It confirmed his commitment to Sidney's literary circle, a little group of strongly Protestant poets who called themselves the "Areopagus." Spenser was familiar with these aristocratic courtier-poets through his attendance upon the household of a powerful patron, Robert Dudley, earl of Leicester, a favorite at Elizabeth's court. The Leicester connection, while providing Spenser an essential link to court, was perhaps a mixed blessing. The poet's allegiance to Leicester may have encouraged him to assert his Protestant distaste for "the French match," a proposed marriage of Queen Elizabeth to a French Catholic duke. Although ten years passed before Spenser's satirical* poem alluding to the subject, *Mother Hubberd's Tale,* appeared in print, the satire may have damaged his position at court at a much earlier date. Elizabeth did not appreciate criticism. At any rate, Spenser received a commission in 1580 as private secretary to Lord Grey of Wilton, the new Lord Deputy of Ireland.

Spenser's long stay in Ireland frustrated his courtly ambitions and was a perpetual source of disappointment to him. Ironically, the Elizabethan court, of which he dreamed from a longing distance, received its most brilliant portrayal in the poetry that exile* in Ireland afforded him time to write. It is a troubling fact that *The Faerie Queene,* an acknowledged triumph of the literary imagination, is rooted in the ruthless Elizabethan colonial policy. During his two years in service to Lord Grey—a Protestant zealot* who subjected Catholic Ireland to

*satirical bitterly and sarcasticly mocking

*exile forced absence from one's homeland

*zealot a fanatical enthusiast

devastation, bringing about the death of some thirty thousand people by starvation and slaughter—Spenser saw firsthand how Elizabethan power politics were applied. Despite the horrors he witnessed, the poet endorsed this aggressive policy unwaveringly. This is particularly clear in his *View of the Present State of Ireland* (1598), a chilling prose tract on "progressive" cultural engineering.

After Grey's recall to England, Spenser stayed in Ireland as an "undertaker," as English colonial administrators were called. For his work he received grants of thousands of acres of appropriated* Irish lands. He settled in 1587 at Kilcolman manor, near Cork. Here the wild Irish landscape became the idealized backdrop for his vast *Faerie Queene,* a work designed, as he stated to his landowning neighbor in Ireland, the adventurer-poet Sir Walter Ralegh, "to fashion a gentleman" (Kermode, 1975, p. 292)—that is, to create a picture of the ideal courtier of the Renaissance.

Spenser's *Faerie Queene*: The Deification* of Elizabeth

The adventuring knights in Spenser's romance combat terrifying beings, and their struggles define the courtly virtues they represent: Holiness, Temperance, Friendship, Justice, Courtesy, and so forth. Gloriana, a sort of dazzling absentee empress of Faery Land around whom all the knights orbit; Belphoebe, a divinely lovely and virtuous lady; and Britomart, the armor-plated female knight of Chastity, are among the poem's several symbolic characterizations of Queen Elizabeth. Britomart, a virgin warrior lifted by Spenser from an Italian heroic romance that was one of his favorite models— Lodovico Ariosto's *Orlando Furioso*—would have instantly brought to the minds of Elizabethan readers the image of the English monarch heroically encouraging her war-ready troops to confront the Spanish Armada.* Belphoebe would have evoked Elizabeth's womanly person, and the shining Gloriana would have been immediately identifiable as the radiant "Virgin Queen." These were, then, all aspects of an Elizabeth of Spenser's creation—a secular goddess bearing little resemblance to the real queen, who was, as her courtiers knew, shrewd, capricious, insincere, manipulative, jealous, cruel, and imperious. Moreover, Spenser's poem as a whole is "con-

appropriated taken over

deification the ascribing of godlike characteristics to a human being

Spanish Armada the Spanish fleet whose 1588 defeat by the British marked the decline of Spain as a world power

secrated" to the royal Elizabeth in her official capacity as the kingdom's "Magnificent Empresse." There is never any doubt that the poet has set out to propagate* the cult of the queen or that this secular goddess is the embodiment of his poem's unrestrained Protestant nationalism.

Between the lines reality presses into the escapist world of Faery Land. As an alien landowner in Ireland, Spenser feared a loss of order and control, which lent his poem an underlying tension.

It is hardly surprising that some have described Spenser's *Faerie Queene* as haunted by semihuman monsters and beasts of Celtic* origin. Do they represent the native "Other," to be suppressed and eradicated? In the poem's fifth book, the rebel-crushing Lord Grey crashes into Faery Land in the guise of Artegall, the knight of Justice, with an army allegorically embodied by the menacing warrior Talus, an impersonal agent of cosmic Justice, a kind of killing machine "made of yron mould, / Immoveable, resistless, without end" (*Poetical Works,* p. 278).

When Spencer's fears converge with his Puritan attitude toward sex, as in the Bower of Bliss episode in book two, the poem seems to push its unconscious terrors and appetites upon us in a way that belies* Spenser's apparent intentions. In that famous episode, Sir Guyon, the knight of Temperance, discovers the lair of a seductive enchantress, Acrasia, whose name means "weakness of will" in Greek. Sir Guyon not only resists this villainess's considerable temptation but actually destroys her Bower of Bliss with extreme violence and "rigour pittiless" (*Poetical Works,* p. 139). The scene fits Spenser's moral allegory of self-restraint well enough, but it leaves us wondering what this violent attack on pleasure might reflect in terms of the poet's psychology.

The power of such individual episodes makes Spenser's poem readable today partly because the deeper conflicts they hint at remain unresolved. Likewise, there may prove to be a particular fascination for modern readers of *The Faerie Queene* in its sheer variety of characters and events, many of which convey meanings on several different levels. Moreover, there is the marvelous formal progression of *The Faerie Queene,* the timeless air of dreaminess and escapism projected by its way of slowly circling around, always changing, yet always returning to itself: the poem does not end but stops uncompleted, in the mysterious *Mutability Cantos.* The slow,

*propagate to promote; to continue the existance of

*Celtic ralated to the Celts—an ethnic group native to the British Isles

*belie to contradict or work against

gliding movement, to a large extent the product of Spenser's carefully constructed nine-line stanza, has a mysterious clockwork beauty that makes us think of some celestial body's orbit. Diana, the virgin huntress and moon goddess, was Elizabeth's symbol, and there is an appealing mooniness about the movement of *The Faerie Queene.*

In 1589, Sir Walter Ralegh saw the first three books of *The Faerie Queene* and took Spenser to London to present them to Elizabeth. (The royal response, a modest pension, fell short of Spenser's extravagant expectations; it is difficult not to read personal meaning into the anticourt sentiments expressed in his allegorical pastoral *Colin Clouts Come Home Again,* written upon the poet's return to Ireland.) Published in 1590, that first installment of three books was followed by a second installment of books four through six when Spenser visited London again in 1596. In the interim he married (1594) Elizabeth Boyle, chronicling their courtship in the sonnet sequence *Amoretti* and their union in *Epithalamion,* a marriage poem following the progression of the wedding day from dawn to evening and convincingly celebrating the joys of love and of the English summer solstice. This pair of works appeared in one volume in 1595.

Spenser was still deeply caught up in *The Faerie Queene*—his original design was to carry it on through twelve books—when, in 1598, his estate at Kilcolman was sacked and burned by Irish rebels. Spenser, who had attained the position of sheriff of Cork, took refuge first in that city and then in London, where he died on 13 January 1599. Legend has him reduced to ruin at the end, dying—as the English dramatist Ben Jonson put it—"for lack of bread." It is hardly likely, in fact, that a man of Spenser's connections could have starved to death, but the expenses for his funeral in Westminster Abbey had to be picked up by a late patron, the Earl of Essex.

Sir Philip Sidney: "Worthiest Knight That Ever Lived"

Sir Philip Sidney (1554–1586) came closest of all the Elizabethans to living up to the ideal image of the aristocratic Renaissance courtier. Gentleman versifier and critical theorist, diplomat, soldier, Protestant humanist, patron of arts and learning, master of languages, moralist, political thinker, romance writer, knight-at-arms, and, by common consent of his day, the model public man, Sidney might have become more than just a symbol of the poetic brilliance of the court of Elizabeth had he had the time. As it is, his works number but a handful; he had only a few years in which to write them before he died of a fatal gunshot wound sustained in a small military skirmish in the Netherlands—where the queen, who considered him a brilliant nuisance, had sent him to get him out of her hair.

Every inch the epitome* of the new English gentry of the time, reflecting its aspirations to intellectual and spiritual as well as worldly power, Sidney came into the world at Penshurst in Kent, a crown manor bestowed on his family two generations earlier in reward for loyal service to the Tudor monarchy. Young Philip's godfather, after whom he was named, was King Philip II of Spain. His father, Sir Henry Sidney, became Elizabeth's Lord Deputy in Ireland in 1559. The boy was schooled at Shrewsbury and at Christ Church College, Oxford, which he left without taking a degree.

Sidney went abroad in 1572 and spent the next three years studying languages and traveling in high style across the Continent. This tour brought the dashing young Englishman important contacts with European scholars and theologians of the Reformation* as well as entry to the grandest of Renaissance courts. Poets across Europe dedicated verses to him, the Italian master Paolo Veronese painted him, and the great equestrian Pugliano tutored him in horsemanship. He was honored with the office of Gentleman of the Bedchamber of Charles IV, king of France. He studied astronomy in Venice and visited Padua, Genoa, Prague, Vienna, and Antwerp before returning to England in 1575.

Back in London, Sidney surrounded himself with poet friends, including Edmund Spenser, at his uncle Leicester's house. He stood in good favor now at Elizabeth's court. For Elizabeth, as for her father before her, the old-fashioned spectacle of knightly combat was a valuable instrument of political propaganda, and she encouraged the ostentatious* display of pomp in lavish tournaments held annually at her palace at Whitehall. In these costly shows, no one reflected that inflated royal purpose more magnificently than Sidney, who, sparing no personal expense, brought the Elizabethan taste for spectacular fashion to a pinnacle by presenting himself in jewel-encrusted armor atop a similarly decked steed and bearing a gleaming shield covered by painted allegorical scenes and appropriate mottos

*epitome embodiment; most typical example

*Reformation a series of changes in Christian beliefs that spread through Western Europe between the fourteenth and seventeenth centuries. Many theologians of the Reformation—such as, Martin Luther—challenged the authority of the church in Rome, and their writings and beliefs led to the establishment of new religious movements such as Lutherasism and Calvinism.

*ostentatious showy

and verses of his own composing. Sidney's most famous shield motto was *Speravi* ("I hoped"); when Elizabeth expressed her displeasure over his unsolicited advice on her short-lived French marriage plans by briefly banishing him from court, he reappeared for a Whitehall joust with the *Speravi* on his shield crossed out—meaning his hopes for her favor had been dashed.

Sidney's sense of courtly style made him an ideal ambassador. In 1577, Elizabeth sent him out on a formal mission of condolence to the Holy Roman Emperor. In the Low Countries,* Sidney met up with the militant Protestant prince of Orange and used the occasion to privately explore prospects for a Protestant league that would join England politically with states of northern Europe. But the queen did not appreciate his diplomatic freelancing.

Shadowed by royal disfavor, Sidney retired to Wilton to the country estate of his sister, Mary Sidney, countess of Pembroke. This was the site of a serene Protestant minicourt attended by aristocratic poets and progressive theologians. There, within the idyllic* park that had been made by enclosing a whole village and evicting its agricultural tenants, Sidney revised his *Arcadia* (1580), the first extended prose* pastoral. This fascinating fictional romance, written in an elaborate poetic prose interspersed with poems and songs, was at once a treatise on love, morals, and philosophy; a manual of rhetoric; and a handbook on courtly behavior. Later critics have looked at its structure of interlacing stories as a forerunner of the modern English novel.

At Wilton, Sidney also wrote his *Apologie for Poetrie* (later called *Defence of Poesie;* written 1580–1582), in which he showed the same heroic devotion to the development of poetry in the vernacular* that he had shown for the chivalric* ideal. Here he defended poetry against both contemporary Puritan pamphleteers, who found songs and poems licentious,* and the ancient Greek philosopher Plato, who described poets as agitators who could not be trusted to tell the truth. In a carefully measured "defense," Sidney argues that poetry has its own important uses: its romantic and heroic images move the heart to acts of courtesy and bravery, and its "speaking pictures" possess a special virtue, for they not only "teach" but "delight" (Ousby, p. 30). Further, Sidney argues, poetry has a unique power of "invention"; no mere slavish imitator of nature, the poet is always "making

*Low Countries the area of Western Europe bordering the North Sea; now Belgium, Luxembourg, and the Netherlands

*idyllic natural and picturesque

*prose text that is not divided into lines and that does not have rhyme and meter

*vernacular the language or dialect commonly spoken in a particular region

*chivalric related to chivalry, a code of behavior based on honor and courtesy

*licentious immoral

things either better than nature bringeth forth, or quite anew, forms such as never were in nature" (Woudhuysen, p. 1). In the case of love poetry, Sidney admits its importance but regrets the crude mimicry of Italian love poetry, suggesting that current English writers appear more ready to "read Lovers writings . . . then . . . in truth [to] feele those passions" (Sanders, p. 108).

The impersonal falseness of feeling Sidney noted stands out against the achievement of his own love poetry, *Astrophil and Stella,* a sequence of 108 sonnets and eleven songs composed around 1582. Astrophil, a lover whose name means "star lover" in Greek, addresses a distant mistress, Stella, whose name means "star" in Latin. Unlike the conventional poets criticized in his defense of poetry, Sidney defines both the lover and the beloved in dramatic terms. When Stella, who is also his muse, commands the poet-lover to "looke in thy heart and write" (sonnet 1), she is at once demanding personal authenticity of him and asserting her control over him. And when he in turn asserts, "Thus write I, while I doubt to write" (sonnet 34), he sounds like a real person, introducing an honest feeling into the usual courtly game of love poetry. Power relations in love and at court were never quite settled. Sidney identifies Stella in his poems as Penelope Devereux, the earl of Essex's daughter and a former object of his attentions, but soon after writing them he happily married another woman, Frances Walsingham (the daughter of the queen's spymaster, Sir Francis Walsingham), in 1583. In any case, it was the shining star that was Elizabeth that finally shed its overall radiance most authoritatively upon the figure of Sidney's poetic Stella.

Astrophil and Stella is the major achievement of Sidney's very brief writing career. While it is the work of an aristocratic amateur—like all his writings, these poems circulated in manuscript but were not published in his lifetime—it shows the promise of a poet of great sensitivity and skill; here verse in the vernacular takes on a new metrical poise and sophistication as well as a wit and a light, wry irony* that allows Sidney to exploit several tones of voice, as dramatists were beginning to do in plays. As the Romantic-era critic Charles Lamb affirmed, in Sidney's sonnet sequence, for the first time in English poetry, the rich drama of human emotions comes across in what seems to modern readers a "full, material, substantiated" way.

Quotations for *Astrophil and Stella* are taken from Ringler, ed.

The dazzling level of courtly decorum in Sidney's writing and in his conduct was fulfilled in 1583 when Elizabeth knighted him. Sidney nevertheless continued to yearn for a real test in the field of battle. After his unsuccessful attempts to involve himself in a privateering* raid upon Spanish holdings in the West Indies, the queen summoned Sidney to court. She awarded him a minor military appointment in the Low Countries, as governor of Flushing. It was his last posting. When he died on 17 October 1586 at age thirty-one, he left behind an unfinished metrical translation of the Psalms* (admirably completed later by his sister). There was mourning across Europe over his untimely demise—his funeral procession from Holland was followed by a grieving cortege,* and a London crowd was said to have greeted his bier* with the cry "Farewell, worthiest knight that ever lived!"

Sir Walter Ralegh: Elizabethan Reversals of Fortune

Sir Walter Ralegh (1554–1618) left behind an image of daring and arrogance, flamboyant ambition, and conflicted passion that makes him the quintessential* Elizabethan courtier. Born of an ancient family from Devon, Ralegh studied at Oxford before taking up a career as a soldier and navigator. His military exploits on the side of the Huguenots* on the Continent and against the rebels in Ireland won him the position of Elizabeth's favorite courtier—by 1584 the freewheeling Ralegh held forty thousand acres of land in Ireland, lucrative business licenses, the captaincy of Elizabeth's palace guard, and the vice admiralship of Devon and Cornwall. By then he had also taken up lyric poetry.*

In 1584, Ralegh took a seat in Parliament and in 1585 he was knighted by the queen. He lavished a small fortune on three expeditions to explore and colonize a stretch of the coast of America, which Elizabeth, the "Virgin Queen," immodestly named Virginia after herself. Tobacco was the principal commodity that resulted, but what Ralegh really sought was gold. He had his heart set on assaulting Spanish treasure ships, but Elizabeth restrained him. In 1595 he sailed up the delta of the Orinoco River in an unsuccessful search for El Dorado.* The following year he raided the Spanish port of Cádiz, but had a falling-out en route with Essex, the queen's new fa-

---

*privateering attacking an enemy's commercial shipping

*Psalms book in the Hebrew Bible, or Old Testament, containing 150 psalms, or poetic songs, that address the relationship between the individual and God

*cortege a long line of attendants

*bier a coffin stand

*quintessential representing the most typical characteristics of a category

*Huguenots French Protestants that belonged to the Reformed Church, established by John Calvin in 1550. The Huguenots fought against French Catholics in the Wars of Religion in France, 1562–1598.

*lyric poetry a kind of poetry characterized by musical and personal expression

*El Dorado a place of extreme wealth and opportunity thought by 16th-century Europeans to exist in South America

vorite. Ralegh's atheism,* skepticism, extravagance, and pride had by then earned him many enemies. After Elizabeth's death in 1603 he was arrested, tried, and found guilty of high treason and was sent to the Tower of London, where he remained until 1616. Released in order to pursue another chase for gold up the Orinoco, Ralegh was executed in June 1618, after the expedition ended in failure.

 If Spenser and Sidney fostered the cult of Elizabeth in their poetry, neither could match Ralegh's emotional dependence on the queen. Ralegh engaged Elizabeth both in her official role as ruler and in her equally formidable* capacity as a real woman; with Ralegh, therefore, the division of art and life, poetic worship and personal subjection, is unclear. Ralegh embodies the dark underside of the cult of Elizabeth. Whether he was storming and sacking a foreign port or violating Elizabeth's will by wooing and marrying Bessy Throckmorton, a girl from the queen's royal bedchamber, the adventurous, freethinking Ralegh took risks others did not take.

 He paid the price in an anxious insecurity that presses through between the lines of his poems. In Ralegh's version of the old ballad "Walsingham," Elizabeth appears in the poet's memory as a queenly nymph with an angelic face, a vision of virtuous and absent love—"who somtymes did me lead with her selfe / And me lovde as her owne" (Woudhuysen, p. 248). But in the "Booke of the Ocean to Scinthia," a strange, confessional outpouring allegedly written in the Tower while Ralegh was imprisoned briefly for his imprudent marriage, the poet wobbles between obedience and bitterness toward a queen who has rewarded him with a jail cell for his taking the trouble "to seeke her worlds, for Golde, for prayse, for glory" (Woudhuysen, p. 103), all on her behalf. The dire nature of Ralegh's plight reduces him to a deserted lover's confusion: "Shee is gonn, Shee is lost, shee is found, shee is ever faire" (Woudhuysen, p. 115).

 Only in his remarkable lyric "The Lie" was Ralegh able to trace the source of his problem back to the power game of the court, with its corrupt rules always tilting the odds in their favor—"Say to the Court it glowes / and shines like rotten wood" (Woudhuysen, p. 116). That pair of lines reveals more of what Sir Walter Ralegh learned in Elizabeth's orbit than the entirety of the unfinished work of his prison years, the *History of the World* (1614). The longing for retreat expressed in "Give me my scallop shell of quiet" (the opening line of "The Passionate Man's Pilgrimage") and the realism that enlivens "The

*atheism a belief that there is no god

*formidable awe-inspiring; impressive

Nymph's Reply to the Shepherd," Ralegh's famous response to Christopher Marlowe's poem "The Passionate Shepherd to His Love"—when time and real life set in, Ralegh suggests, idealized love goes out the window—sum up his checkered career as poet and courtier.

Fortune, often represented as a woman, was a major element in the Elizabethan understanding of the world, with its sudden ascents and equally sudden crashes. The critic F. W. Bateson has pointed out how Ralegh's fatalistic attitude about being tossed to and fro on a giddy sea of wordly ups and downs closely resembles the tragic sense in Elizabethan plays. "For conversation of particular greatness and dignity there is nothing more noble and glorious than to have felt the force of every fortune," Ralegh wrote. "He only is to be reputed a man whose mind cannot be puffed up by prosperity nor dejected by any adverse fortune" (Bateson, p. 61). Ralegh's contemporaries seemed to regard him as the age's prototype in this regard. "Fortune tossed him up of nothing and to and fro to greatness," one observer of the time noted, "and from thence down to little more than that wherein she found him" (Bateson, p. 62). The comment rings true, especially if for the word "fortune" we now read "Elizabeth."

Selected Bibliography

WORKS BY EDMUND SPENSER

Poetical Works. Edited by J. C. Smith and E. de Selincourt. London: Oxford University Press, 1912.

A View of the Present State of Ireland. Edited by W. L. Renwick. Oxford, U.K.: Oxford University Press, 1973.

WORKS BY SIR PHILIP SIDNEY

A Defence of Poetry. In *Miscellaneous Prose of Sir Philip Sidney.* Edited by Katherine Duncan-Jones and Jan van Dorsten. Oxford, U.K.: Oxford University Press, 1973.

The Poems of Sir Philip Sidney. Edited by William A. Ringler, Jr. Oxford, U.K.: Clarendon Press, 1962.

WORKS BY SIR WALTER RALEGH

The Ocean to Cynthia: His Autobiographic Poems. Omaha: Abattoir Editions, University of Nebraska, 1984.

Sir Walter Ralegh: Selected Writings. Edited by Gerald Hammond. New York: Penguin, 1986.

AVAILABLE COLLECTIONS

Kermode, Frank, and John Hollander, eds. *The Oxford Anthology of English Literature: Major Authors Edition.* Vol. 1. New York: Oxford University Press, 1975.

Woudhuysen, H. R., ed. *The Penguin Book of Renaissance Verse.* New York: Penguin, 1992.

WORKS ABOUT POETRY IN THE AGE OF ELIZABETH I

Bateson, Frederick W. *A Guide to English Literature.* New York: Anchor, 1965.

Black, John B. *The Reign of Elizabeth.* Oxford, U.K.: Clarendon Press, 1936.

Colie, Rosalie. *Paradoxia Epidemica: The Renaissance Tradition of Paradox.* Princeton, N.J.: Princeton University Press, 1966.

Empson, William. *Some Versions of Pastoral.* Norfolk, Conn.: New Directions, 1935.

Fowler, Alastair. *Spenser and the Numbers of Time.* New York: Barnes and Noble, 1964.

Fowler, Alastair. *Triumphal Forms: Structural Patterns in Elizabethan Poetry.* Cambridge, U.K.: Cambridge University Press, 1970.

Greenblatt, Stephen. *Renaissance Self-Fashioning.* Chicago and London: University of Chicago Press, 1980.

Greene, Thomas. *The Light in Troy: Imitation and Discovery in Renaissance Poetry.* New Haven, Conn., and London: Yale University Press, 1982.

Hadfield, Andrew. *Spenser's Irish Experience.* Oxford, U.K.: Oxford University Press, 1997.

Hough, Graham. *A Preface to "The Faerie Queene."* New York: Norton, 1963.

Kermode, Frank, ed. *English Pastoral Poetry.* New York: Barnes and Noble, 1952.

Lewis, C. S. *The Allegory of Love.* New York: Oxford University Press, 1936.

Lewis, C. S. *English Literature in the Sixteenth Century.* Oxford, U.K.: Oxford University Press, 1954.

Maley, Willy. *Salvaging Spenser: Colonialism, Culture, and Identity.* London: Macmillan, 1997.

Nicholl, Charles. *The Creature in the Map: A Journey to El Dorado.* London: Jonathan Cape, 1995.

Nicholl, Charles. *The Reckoning: The Murder of Christopher Marlowe.* London: Jonathan Cape, 1993.

Ousby, Ian. *The Cambridge Guide to English Literature.* 2d ed. Cambridge, U.K., and New York: Cambridge University Press, 1993.

Sanders, Andrew. *The Short Oxford History of English Literature.* Oxford, U.K.: Oxford University Press, 1994.

Thompson, John. *The Founding of English Metre.* London: Routledge and Kegan Paul, 1961.

Tuve, Rosamond. *Elizabethan and Metaphysical Imagery.* Chicago and London: University of Chicago Press, 1947.

Williams, Raymond. *The Country and the City.* New York: Oxford University Press, 1973.

Young, Alan. *Tudor and Jacobean Tournaments.* Dobbs Ferry, N.Y.: Sheridan House, 1987.

NINETEENTH-CENTURY ROMANTIC AND SYMBOLIST POETRY

by David Ball

On the evening of 25 February 1830, an amazing scene took place in Paris at the Théâtre Français, a stronghold of official culture. No sooner had the actors spoken their first lines than there was an outburst of boos and hoots from various parts of the theater and still louder applause and cheers from others. The people cheering were mostly young men with long hair and beards wearing colorful suits, among them some soon-to-be-famous poets and writers. Those who booed were mostly older, more dignified, clean-shaven men in black formal jackets. During the intermission, fistfights broke out between the two groups. The fight was about the style of the play—*Hernani,* by a twenty-seven-year-old poet named Victor Hugo (1802–1885).

Unattributed translations are by David Ball.

The "battle of *Hernani,*" as the French call it, marked the triumph of the Romantic revolution in France: the young people won, and the play was a smash hit. Five months later there was a political revolution in Paris. What could possibly have caused such passion about artistic style? To understand it, we need to understand Romanticism, the cultural and artistic movement that had swept through Europe at the end of the eighteenth century.

What Was Romanticism?

Many images and ideas we take for granted today actually come from the Romantic movement in Europe. What we call "romantic love" is one of them; so are the idea of the importance of the individual (even the very idea of an individual "personality"), the significance of childhood, the value of sincerity, the beauty of certain landscapes (high mountains, for example) and the longing to feel at one with them, and the image of a lone artist or poet heroically struggling against an unfeeling society.

239

Actually, all these notions were first powerfully expressed in the poetic prose of Jean-Jacques Rousseau, a tremendously influential French writer who lived in the eighteenth century, before Romanticism officially came into being. Rousseau's work depicts a man with an intense feeling of isolation, of aloneness (today we would call it alienation), who tries to overcome this problem through an attempt to make unity out of separation—to feel a union with nature, to imagine unity and justice in society. The Romantics, in the next generation, picked up these themes and variations in a unique poetry, drama, and art.

To express these themes, poets, writers, and artists invented new styles, new forms, and above all a new conception of art. Before this time, the "classical" idea of art claimed that it was a representation of the world; as the ancient Greek philosopher Aristotle said, art imitates nature. As for poetry, it was considered a decoration, an ornament. In opposition to this concept, the Romantics saw art and poetry as a means of personal expression, particularly of emotion. Since art was now seen as the expression of creative genius in tune with Beauty and Truth, it became enormously important. As the English poet Percy Bysshe Shelley wrote in 1821, poets not only capture "the spirit of the age" but also are "mirrors of the gigantic shadows which futurity* casts upon the present"; in fact, they are "the unacknowledged legislators of the world" ("Defense of Poetry," in *Poems and Prose,* edited by Timothy Webb, 1995 Everyman edition).

*futurity future events

These changes took place at a time of great upheaval and reveal a crisis in European culture. In 1789, the French Revolution broke out—the violent political reflection of this crisis. Then, Napoleon proceeded to conquer most of Europe, until he was defeated in 1814 and monarchy was restored in France. There were revolutions and uprisings in 1830 and again, all over Europe, in 1848. On the heels of these turbulent changes came a rapid growth of cities, capitalism, and industrial society, bringing oppressive working conditions for most. And more than in past ages, people were aware of these changes. The Romantics felt that art should change with society, that the old "rules" no longer applied.

This too was a new notion. The classical doctrine of seventeenth- and eighteenth-century Europe held that beauty never changed and that there was one timeless, fixed, correct form for poems or plays (or paintings or music). One of

Romantics, August Wilhem von Schlegel, writing in Germany around 1800 said, "Romantic poetry is still in the process of *becoming;* that is its essence, to *become,* eternally, and never be fulfilled. Romanticism is the particular spirit of modern art, in contrast to ancient or classical art" (Lagarde and Michard, *Le dix-neuvième siècle*). The great French novelist Stendhal, some twenty years later, said, "In any age, Romanticism is the art of the day; classicism is the art of the day before." And Victor Hugo wrote, "For a new people, a new art" (Lagarde and Michard). (Almost a century later, Guillaume Apollinaire and the French modernists refought some of the same battles.) The innovative style of Romanticism expressed changes in the way people viewed art and the world. It was these changes that its opponents refused to accept. The struggle played out differently in different countries.

Germany: Storm, Madness, and Greatness

Romanticism arose in Germany, in the avant-garde* movement known as *Sturm und Drang* (meaning "storm and stress"); it lasted from roughly 1760 to 1780. Two great poets, Johann Wolfgang von Goethe (1749–1832) and his friend Friedrich von Schiller (1759–1805), wrote lyrical poems and dramas glorifying individualism, liberty, and creative genius; they attacked rules and exalted emotion. (You may have heard a Schiller poem without realizing it: he wrote the "Ode to Joy" that Beethoven used in his Ninth Symphony.) Instead of decorative and conventional themes, their poetry in these years expressed personal feelings. Thus, Goethe's "Sesenheim Songs," for example, sing of his love for a real woman. Like love, nature is no longer a backdrop; it is part of our human experience. Nature became, as Goethe said, "the concrete reality of human life, becoming rhythm and melody." Goethe is as important to German poetry as Shakespeare is to English poetry. He was a novelist as well; *Die Leiden des jungen Werthers (The Sorrows of Young Werther)*, whose "Romantic" hero commits suicide, helped set off a wave of suicides in the 1780s.

Schiller's long essay "On Naive and Sentimental Poetry" (Schiller, *Essays,* German Library Vol. 17, edited by W. Hindler, 1993) grew out of the new movement but goes further. In the essay, Schiller sets up two categories that may seem bizarre to

*__avant-garde__ advanced or cutting-edge; experimental; normally applies to the arts

us today, but his ideas are the basic concepts of Romanticism. As humanity evolves, poetry does too; for this reason, what is considered great poetry changes from era to era. Schiller believed that ancient Greek and Latin poets (and Shakespeare and Goethe) are "naive" poets because they are like pure, simple facets of nature. And although nature inspires us with tenderness and longing (it represents "our lost childhood"), it "has disappeared from humanity." Contemporary culture, with its "unnaturalness" and conflicts, is more complex. Poets like Schiller are aware of this, and instead of imitating nature, they try to depict the ideal. So Schiller calls such poets "sentimental." The synthesis of "naive" and "sentimental" will give us the "maximum" of beautiful poetry, which must "be in harmony both with Nature and with the Ideal."

Among the first artists and writers to refer to themselves as "Romantics" were the von Schlegel brothers, Friedrich (1772–1829) and August Wilhelm (1767–1845). With the poet Novalis (1772–1801), they published from 1798 to 1800 the journal *Athenäum*, which was much more concerned with ideas than with actual poems. But their ideas were fertile and original; from this beginning Romanticism spread throughout Germany.

It was in this journal that Friedrich von Schlegel developed the far-reaching idea of "romantic irony"—that a poem must be conscious of itself, containing both hot passion and cold reflection, and that art must be criticism of art, playful and serious at the same time. In the next generation of German Romantics, Heinrich Heine (1797–1856) comes closer to this "romantic irony." All educated Germans know some of his beautiful lyrics. His poetry has been used in more than three thousand musical works. "Die Lorelei" ("The Lorelei") is still sung to Franz Schubert's music. Yet much of his poetry has a witty irony that undercuts the lyricism,* and he wrote searing analyses of naive romantic practices.

*lyricism music-like quality

The great lyric poet of the von Schlegels' generation was Friedrich Hölderlin (1770–1843). Almost unknown in his time, today he is a mythic figure: the insane poet stretching language to the breaking point. His "last hymns" and "hymn fragments" (1800–1806) seem modern—fragmented poems, full of "holes." Yet he expresses Romantic themes—the poetic calling (poets are holy vessels), childhood, the longing for lost unity with nature, and the value of direct intuitive knowledge.

A longing for the direct, sincere communication that was being smothered by modern society led many people to an in-

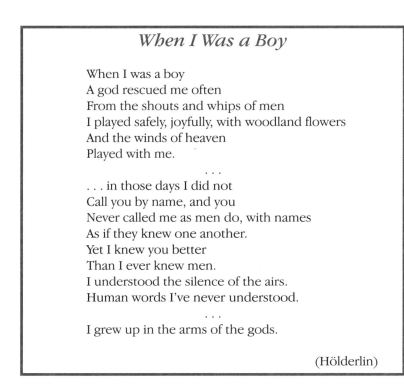

> ## *When I Was a Boy*
>
> When I was a boy
> A god rescued me often
> From the shouts and whips of men
> I played safely, joyfully, with woodland flowers
> And the winds of heaven
> Played with me.
>
> . . .
>
> . . . in those days I did not
> Call you by name, and you
> Never called me as men do, with names
> As if they knew one another.
> Yet I knew you better
> Than I ever knew men.
> I understood the silence of the airs.
> Human words I've never understood.
>
> . . .
>
> I grew up in the arms of the gods.
>
> (Hölderlin)

terest in folk lyrics. *Des Knaben Wunderhorn* ("The Boy's Enchanted Horn"), a collection of folksongs, was published at about the same time as Hölderlin's poems (and just before the Grimm brothers' fairy tales). Such writing also stirred new pride in fundamental national traditions.

The British Isles: Exaltation and Despair

When Robert Burns (1759–1796) published his *Poems, Chiefly in the Scottish Dialect* in 1786, he aroused similar feelings of national pride. By delving into the old, "natural," "common" culture of a region, making poems in simple language rather than in elevated "poetic diction," Burns was pointing the way to future Romantic writing in Britain. Schiller would have praised the book as "naive" poetry, but there is nothing really naive about these beautiful poems. *Irish Melodies,* by Thomas Moore (1779–1852), is a similar project.

Three years later, another innovative poet, William Blake (1757–1827) came out with *Songs of Innocence,* which was followed by the companion volume, *Songs of Innocence and of Experience,* in 1794. He printed them himself along with his

In this period of rising nationalism, great national poets were found throughout Eastern and Central Europe. Their poems and poetic dramas seem to embody the spirit of a country. In Poland, there was Adam Mickiewicz (1798–1855) and Juliusz Slowacki (1809–1849). In Russia, Aleksander Pushkin (1799–1837) was considered the greatest poet of this extraordinarily rich literary culture. In Hungary, there was Sándor Pëtofi (1823–1849), who was killed on the battlefield at the age of twenty-six.

own engravings—visual and verbal art formed a new synthesis. Blake's simple, direct language is even more deceptive than Burns's. Take a look at Blake's "Lamb," "The Tyger," or "The Sick Rose," for example, and you will see that this is mysterious, powerful, complex poetry. Blake also published *The Marriage of Heaven and Hell* (1793), which looks like prose but sounds like poetry. Abolishing the distinction between poetry and prose is just one striking aspect of this revolutionary work and of the great visionary poems Blake would go on to write.

A few years later, William Wordsworth (1770–1850), arguing in his preface to *Lyrical Ballads,* the collection of poems he and his friend Samuel Taylor Coleridge (1772–1834) jointly published in 1798, that poetry should be written in "language really used by men" rather than in elevated diction,* actually affirmed that there is no "essential difference between the language of prose and [poetry]." This idea later echoed through American poetry in the work of Walt Whitman and William Carlos Williams, among others. *Lyrical Ballads* contains some of the most famous poems of English Romanticism, such as "The Rime of the Ancient Mariner" and "Lines Composed a Few Miles Above Tintern Abbey." Later editions include "A Slumber Did My Spirit Seal" and many others. Wordsworth's prefaces to these editions and Schiller's essay are two of the major manifestos* of Romanticism—public statements of a new poetic program. Like the poems themselves, these prose works were ridiculed by the literary establishment.

Strangely, one of those mocking attackers was a tremendous antiestablishment figure, a man who represented, in his life and in his poems, the popular image of the Romantic poet as lone rebel—George Gordon, Lord Byron (1788–1824). But much of Byron's work, particularly his long satiric masterpiece *Don Juan* (1819–1824), does not feel "Romantic" at all. Not all writing in the Romantic period is Romantic. Thus, some critics say that the great Italian Romantic Giacomo Leopardi (1798–1837) is not really a Romantic poet.

The other two great English poets of Byron's generation are Percy Bysshe Shelley (1792–1822) and John Keats (1795–1821). Shelley's political and literary radicalism, his lyrical poetry nourished by Platonic idealism,* exaltation of music, art, and revolutionary politics, seems thoroughly Romantic to us today. So does the sensuous, magical poetry of Keats.

*elevated diction
noble, grand language, far removed from everyday speech

*manifesto a written statement of the intentions or beliefs of the author or a literary or artistic movement

*Platonic idealism
philosophy that real-world objects are copies of "ideals" existing beyond normal experience

One thing these four very different poets have in common is their alternate states of rapture and despair. Strong emotions like these often have mysterious personal roots, but they are also linked to the historical context—the hopes stirred by the French Revolution and then dashed by the Reign of Terror that followed, the terrible conditions in England during the Industrial Revolution (when children worked sixteen hours a day in mines and factories), or the political repression in Europe. An increased awareness of history, and of the self and the poet's impotence* in facing this world, often led to painful, excessive self-analysis. One critic has noted that the Romantics try to use imaginative poetry to end this self-analysis—to use imagination to go beyond analyzing oneself somehow. Wordsworth thought that he had found a solution to the problem in his inner life or imagination, but as another critic says, he had really "lost the world" (Jerome McGann, *The Romantic Ideology,* University of Chicago Press, 1993). Keats tried to find the solution in the magic of art, but that disappears, as the last line to one of his most famous poems, "Ode to a Nightingale," shows: "Fled is that music:—Do I wake or sleep?" Shelley's visionary radicalism failed him. And after creating images of doomed revolt, Byron writes in cynical despair. This drama of intensely conflicting feelings and ideas is played out, beautifully, in the poetry of these four artists.

A poet is "a man speaking to other men," said Wordsworth. But today we are beginning to rediscover the women poets of the period, some of them, like Felicia Dorothea Hemans (1793–1835), famous in their day. Perhaps Charlotte Smith (1749–1806), Ann Yearsley (1753–1806), Anna Laetitia Barbauld (1743–1825), and Laetitia Elizabeth Landon (1802–1838), among others, will become famous once again.

The French Revolution of 1789 seemed, to many, to be the beginning of a new era of freedom in Europe. Most were disillusioned in 1793, when radicals gained power and cut off the head of anyone they thought night be an enemy of the revolution.

*__impotence__ helplessness; ineffectiveness

France: Romanticism at Last

Germaine de Staël's essay "De l'Allemagne" ("On Germany"), published in 1813, hails the coming of Romanticism. (It had been printed in 1810, but Napoleon refused to let her distribute it.) In 1819, Marceline Desbordes-Valmore (1785–1859) published the first book of Romantic poetry in France; she went on to write six more over the next two decades. The value and importance of her work are gaining increasing recognition.

*Mount Parnassus in Greek mythology, the home of the Muses

*muse In Greek mythology, the nine Muses are goddesses who preside over the arts, sciences, song, and poetry. Today, a muse is a source of inspiration.

*lyre a type of harp associated with poetry

In 1820, Alphonse de Lamartine (1790–1869) published his first major collection—*Méditations poétiques* (Poetic meditations). In his preface he boasts: "I'm the first to have brought poetry down from Mount Parnassus,* the first to have changed the Muse's* conventional seven-stringed lyre* into the *very fibers of a man's heart,* plucked and moved by the shivers of nature and the soul" (italics added). "The Lake," his best-known poem, ends: "Let the groaning wind, the sighing reed . . . Everything we hear, everything we breathe / All say: 'They loved!' "

Through the late 1820s, young writers met regularly in Victor Hugo's Paris apartment; they called their group the "cenacle." The poets Gérard de Nerval (1808–1855), Théophile Gautier (1811–1872), Alfred de Vigny (1797–1863), and Alfred de Musset (1810–1857) and the novelists Honoré de Balzac, Alexandre Dumas, Prosper Mérimée were all there, excited about the new Romanticism.

From the 1830s on, Vigny wrote poems ("Moses," "The Death of the Wolf," "The Wrath of Sampson") whose heroes are huge, doomed, solitary figures. Christ on the Mount of Olives the night before the Crucifixion looks for a sign from his divine Father, sees only blackness, hears footsteps, "And then he saw the torch of Judas / Prowling in the woods."

Musset's unhappy love affair with the French novelist George Sand (pen name of the woman who was also the Polish composer Frédéric Chopin's lover) inspired some of his lyrics about love, suffering, and poetic creation in *Nights*. But he could treat Romantic themes playfully, too. Thus, in "Ballade to the Moon":

> On the yellow spire
> The moon
> Like the dot on an i.

After 1841, he continued to write lighter verse, often of great charm.

*visionary given to idealistic speculation or imaginary visions; beyond ordinary reality

Hugo's enormous poetic production is Romantic through and through and often more visionary* than most; he called one of his collections *What the Mouth of Darkness Said.* Hallucinatory seascapes, dark forests and plains, biblical scenes, love poetry, political poetry (years of struggle against Napoleon III added to Hugo's fame), poems about art and poetry, death, being a grandfather, human destiny—his range is tremendous. Thousands of French children know some of his beautiful verses by heart. His later work, less well known, is the most visionary:

> While I become a thing, I feel
> The things around me becoming beings,
> My wall is a face, and sees: my two windows
> Pale against the gray sky, watch me sleep.
> "Night of 26–27 March 1854"

France Again: Romantics, Symbolists, and Beyond

In 1857, a little poetry collection called *Les fleurs du mal* (*Flowers of Evil*)—one of the most important works of the century—was condemned for obscenity by a French court. The poet, Charles Baudelaire (1821–1867), wrote (in a letter of 18 February 1866), "I put all my thinking, all my heart, all my religion (travestied*) and all my hatred into this horrible book." Maybe that was just it: the honest exploration of a modern consciousness, with its desires (including desires usually left unspoken), anxieties, and illnesses, was too much for the bourgeois* judge. The verse was the standard meter of the Romantics, with a sensuous beauty difficult to evoke in translation. But it was new. His poetic intention, the way images were used, and his goal to make perfectly sculptured poems out of depression or anxiety attacks (creating "gold" out of "mud," "flowers" out of sickness and evil) ("Projet d'epilogue")—all of this was novel, and Baudelaire knew it. "O Death, old captain, it is time! Raise the anchor!" writes Baudelaire, in the last lines of "Le Voyage." And he goes on:

> . . . we long
> To plunge to the depths of the gulf, Hell or Heaven, no
>   matter!
> To the depths of the Unknown to find something *new*!

This last line could be the rallying cry for poetry to come, from Arthur Rimbaud to Apollinaire and beyond.

Baudelaire's images push further than the Romantics' did, leading us to what is beyond the visual; they communicate meanings. Some of his predecessors did this, too: Hugo,

***travestied** mocked or parodied

***bourgeois** middle-class; the term implies conventionality and small-mindedness

and especially Gérard de Nerval, who wrote mysterious poems in which the unexplained image is meant to communicate feelings and ideas. Baudelaire, however, really thought about this process. For him, nature does not just have forests, it has "forests of symbols" ("Correspondances"). The poet deciphers the meaning of these symbols, and, conversely, his images bear deep, complex meanings. The idea that poetry can communicate directly through images, without explanation or rhetoric,* became very influential.

*rhetoric the art of persuasion with written or spoken language

All art uses symbols. Some poets after Baudelaire—in particular, Stéphane Mallarmé (1842–1898)—developed a theory of the symbol. Here we have to be careful. "Symbolism" is a very general word. We tend to call an entire group of these poets "symbolists." As one critic said, the word "symbolist" has simply become "a convenient label for the post-Romantic era." Thus Arthur Rimbaud (1854–1891) and Paul Verlaine (1844–1896) have both been called symbolists. In Verlaine's beautiful "Clair de Lune," the soul of the loved one is the landscape described in the poem, "charmed by maskers"* who go singing a happy tune in a minor key. The poem itself was later "translated" into piano music by the French composer Claude Debussy. Since Verlaine himself wrote (in "Art poétique"), "Music over everything!" he would have been delighted. Words were too limited in meaning for the symbolists.

*masker a person who wears a mask, especially a participant in a masquerade

Mallarmé was obsessed by the inadequacy of words to convey the meanings that the material universe itself only hinted at. Sometimes he feared that meaning itself might be absent from an empty universe, like a blank white page. Certainly direct expression, ordinary language, would never make meaningful poetry. Perhaps strange language and the magic of the symbol could somehow, through its very awareness of absence, make meaning. "I say: a flower! And . . . musically arises, the idea itself and suave, the one absent from every bouquet" ("Crise de vers" in *Divagations*). Mallarmé's twisted syntax* and his desperate attempts to find and render meaning gave us, in his poetic fables of absence and whiteness, some of the most difficult—but most fascinating—poems of the nineteenth century. In his last work, "A Roll of the Dice / Never / Will Abolish / Chance," he abandons regular verse altogether and plays with typography. The arrangement of words, the blank spaces, a suggested "story" (a shipwreck), all point to a mysterious final meaning—and to the work of E. E. Cummings and Apollinaire and concrete poetry* in years to come.

*syntax the structure of a sentence; refers to word placement, as opposed to "diction," which refers to word choice

*concrete poetry poetry that looks like the thing it describes, such as a poem about a fish that is written in the shape of a fish

Mallarmé made other formal innovations, too, as did Baudelaire: they wrote prose poems. You can imagine how absurd that would have seemed in earlier times. There is no Romantic "eloquence" in these texts. And Baudelaire's subject is new, too; in his *Spleen de Paris,* the poet strolls through the modern city, fascinated by the most commonplace or "ugly" aspects of daily urban life. The surrealists* would love it.

No one of the time is closer to the surrealists than the Comte de Lautréamont, pseudonym of Isidore Ducasse. Born in Uruguay in 1846, he died twenty-four years later in Paris, completely unknown. Less than a year before his death, he had published a sort of epic* in poetic prose called *Chants de Maldoror* (*Songs of Maldoror*). Violent, hallucinatory, and amoral* (God is called "viper-faced," and the narrator makes love with a female shark), crawling with monstrous animals ("O silk-eyed octopus, your soul is inseparable from mine!"), this weird volume was hailed by the surrealists half a century later as a great precursor to their own work.

Jules Laforgue (1860–1887), another French poet identified as a symbolist (who was particularly important to the twentieth-century American poet T. S. Eliot) continued an innovation that Rimbaud may have started: free verse, or poems in lines of irregular length. Among other major symbolist poets is the Nicaraguan Rubén Darío (1867–1916), who brought French poetic practice into the Spanish domain. The Spaniard Antonio Machado Ruiz (1875–1939) became famous first as a symbolist poet and then as a defender of Spanish democracy. In Germany, Stefan George (1868–1933) translated French symbolist poetry into German (no easy feat) and wrote his own influential poems. Andrei Biely (1880–1934) and Aleksander Blok (1880–1921) both wrote symbolist poems widely praised in Russia. Blok's "The Twelve" is a famous long poem celebrating the Bolshevik Revolution—which represented a sharp break with the elitist aspect of French symbolism.

The heirs to the symbolist tradition include some of the greatest names in modern poetry: William Butler Yeats in Ireland (1865–1939), Rainer Maria Rilke in Austria (1875–1926), Wallace Stevens in the United States (1879–1955), Juan Ramón Jiménez in Spain and Puerto Rico (1881–1958), T. S. Eliot in the United States and England (1888–1965), Federico García Lorca in Spain (1898–1936), and, still more directly, the French poets who took part in the literary gatherings on Mallarmé's

Baudelaire pays tribute to Aloysius Bertrand (1807–1841), whose volume of prose poems *Gaspard de la Nuit (Gaspard of the Night)* appeared back in 1842.

***surrealist** an artist or poet involved in the art movement surrealism, which aimed (chiefly during the 1920s and 1930s) to express the workings of the unconscious or subconscious mind

***epic** a long poem that tells the story of a hero's deeds

***amoral** neither moral nor immoral; unconcerned with morality

The ideals of the Bolshevik Revolution valued cultural participation by the masses. Symbolist literature, which was intentionally obscure, aimed at reaching a small, select public.

"Tuesdays" in Paris—Paul Valéry (1871–1945) and Paul Claudel (1868–1955). Claudel once said that the great lesson Mallarmé taught him was a question: "What does that *mean?*" It is as good a way as any of summing up how the symbolists looked at the world.

Selected Bibliography

AVAILABLE COLLECTIONS

Baudelaire in English. Edited by Carol Clark and Robert Sykes. Baltimore: Penguin, 1998.

British Women Poets of the Nineteenth Century. Edited by Margaret Randolph Higonnet. New York: Meridian, 1996.

Collected Poems. Translated by H. Weinfeld. Berkeley: University of California Press, 1998. Poetry of Stéphane Mallarmé.

English Romantic Poetry: An Anthology. Edited by Stanley Appelbaum. Mineola, N.Y.: Dover, 1997.

The Flowers of Evil. Translated by J. McGowan. New York: Oxford University Press, 1993. Poems of Charles Baudelaire.

French Symbolist Poetry. Edited by C. F. MacIntyre. Berkeley: University of California Press, 1958.

German Poetry from 1750 to 1900. Translated by Robert M. Browning. New York: Continuum, 1984.

The New Oxford Book of Romantic Period Verse. Edited by Jerome J. McGann. New York: Oxford University Press, 1993.

The Nineteenth Century. Vol. 3 of *The Penguin Book of French Verse.* Edited by Brian Woledge, Geoffrey Brereton, and Anthony Hartley. Harmondsworth, U.K.: Penguin, 1975.

The Penguin Book of German Verse. Edited by Leonard Wilson Forster. Baltimore: Penguin, 1957.

Selected Poems from "Les fleurs du mal." Translated by Norman R. Shapiro. Chicago: University of Chicago Press, 1998. Bilingual edition.

GENERAL DISCUSSIONS

Abrams, M. H., ed. *English Romantic Poets: Modern Essays in Criticism.* New York: Oxford University Press, 1975.

Beer, John, ed. *Questioning Romanticism.* Baltimore: Johns Hopkins University Press, 1995.

Bishop, Michael. *Nineteenth-Century French Poetry.* New York: Twayne, 1993.

Butler, Marilyn. *Romantics, Rebels, and Reactionaries: English Literature and Its Background, 1760–1830.* New York: Oxford University Press, 1985.

Gaull, Marilyn. *English Romanticism: The Human Context.* New York: Norton, 1988.

Lagarde, André, and Laurent Michard. Le dix-neuvième siècle. Paris: Bordas, 1961.

Ruoff, Gene, ed. *The Romantics and Us: Essays on Literature and Culture.* New Brunswick, N.J.: Rutgers University Press, 1990.

Sartre, Jean-Paul. *Baudelaire.* Translated by Martin Turnell. New York: Norton, 1972.

Sartre, Jean-Paul, et al. *Mallarmé; or, The Poet of Nothingness.* Translated by Ernest Sturm. University Park: Pennsylvania State University Press, 1991.

Wilson, Carol Shiner, and Joel Haefner, eds. *Re-Visioning Romanticism: British Women Writers, 1776–1837.* Philadelphia: University of Pennsylvania Press, 1994.

TWENTIETH-CENTURY MODERNIST POETRY

by Ron Padgett

The territory of modernism in twentieth-century poetry is so vast that in this brief article there is room for only a few poets. I hope they will serve as signposts for further explorations of your own. Also note that the dates I give for literary movements are approximate. Literary movements—especially the most influential ones—don't suddenly stop; they slowly dissolve and feed into the work of the next generation of writers.

Unless otherwise noted, the translations in this article are by Ron Padgett.

The Common Bond: The Value of the New

The word *modernism* can apply to many different artistic and literary groups, movements, and individuals, but the one thing they all had in common in the twentieth century was a belief in the value of the new. As poet Ezra Pound advised, "Make it new."

Although early-twentieth-century modernist poets had a few literary heroes from the previous century, they rejected what they saw as mostly outdated art or oppressive social structures. They felt that the nineteenth century had been flowery, restricted by social class and conventional morality, hypocritical,* and too slow to change.

The new century, on the other hand, was faster and freer. Technology had provided the automobile, the express train, the airplane, the speedy ocean liner, the radio, and the telephone, opening up new feelings about the way people could live. The increasing use of electric lights allowed for changes in the traditional routines of day and night. These inventions gave many people the chance to break free of the bonds that held them firmly in their social classes, in their towns, in their countries, and in their ideas of themselves. By the beginning of the century, cultural boundaries were giving way to a sense of liberty, fragmentation, and speed, which were reflected in the poetry of the time.

Modernist poetry was also influenced by new developments in fiction, theater, visual art, dance, and music. Not only

hypocritical pretending to be virtuous or religious when you are not

253

was the world changing; writers and other artists were changing the way they—and others—looked at the world. But the impulse for many of these changes came from certain pioneering forebears, back in the nineteenth century.

Free Verse

Free verse is also discussed in the essay "Some Basic Poetic Forms" elsewhere in this volume.

One of the fathers of modernism in poetry is the American poet Walt Whitman (1819–1892). His book *Leaves of Grass,* first published in 1855, consists of poems written in long lines without a set meter or rhyme—in what is called free verse. Many readers were shocked by what they saw as his disorderly style and frank presentation of sexual themes. Whitman was the single most important poet in making free verse a major force in modernist poetry.

The Prose Poem

Two years after the death of the French poet Charles Baudelaire (1821–1867), his *Spleen de Paris* (*Paris Spleen*)—subtitled *Petits poèmes en prose* (*Little Prose Poems*)—was published. These short pieces look like ordinary prose, but they have special poetic qualities. Baudelaire had been inspired by Aloysius Bertrand's (1807–1841) book *Gaspard de la nuit* (*Gaspard of the Night*), whose short prose pieces are highly poetical. But Baudelaire took the form one step further, and then boldly claimed that such writing was poetry. Normally people thought that poetry and prose were virtual opposites, like salt and pepper. Imagine something called "peppersalt"! That's like what Baudelaire created when he blended poetry and prose.

The prose poetry of two other French writers also inspired twentieth-century modernists: Arthur Rimbaud (1854–1891) and Isidore Ducasse (1846–1870), who wrote under the name of Le Comte de Lautréamont.

The New Page

Another strong influence on modernist poetry was a poem called "Un coup de dés n'abolira le hasard" ("A Throw of the Dice Will Never Abolish Chance") by French poet Stéphane

Mallarmé (1842–1898). In this poem, the words and phrases float in fragments all over the page, and in different sizes, with lots of space around them. Sometimes it is impossible to know in what order to read the words, some of which go straight across two pages!

A Question of Tone

Any number of modernist poets, such as T. S. Eliot, Ezra Pound, Hart Crane, Valery Larbaud, and Jules Supervielle acknowledged a debt to the French poet Jules Laforgue (1860–1887). Laforgue was particularly influential in his poems that used free verse and sounded like a young man's inner (and sometimes fragmented) conversation with himself—a young man whose ironic tone suggests that he does not always mean what he seems to be meaning. Laforgue influenced T. S. Eliot's important poem "The Love Song of J. Alfred Prufrock."

A Change of Rhythm

The later poems of Gerard Manley Hopkins (1844–1889) used what he called sprung rhythm, in which each line had a fixed number of accented syllables and a varying number of unaccented ones. Actually, this technique had been used off and on for centuries, but Hopkins took it to extremes, creating lines that rhythmically lurch, pause, and leap forward with great energy, as in "Brute beauty and valor and act, oh, air, pride, plume, here / Buckle! and the fire that breaks from thee then. . . ." When these poems were finally published—in 1918, almost thirty years after Hopkins's death—they inspired other poets to experiment with rhythm too.

To read Hopkins's entire poem, see the discussion of the sonnet form in the essay "Some Basic Poetic Forms" elsewhere in this volume.

Cubism and Poetry

(ca. 1907–1918)

In the years before World War I (1914–1918), artists from all over Europe had moved to Paris. Among them were some painters and sculptors who became known as the cubists. Their art works depicted a person or scene that seemed to have been shattered and pieced back together in odd ways, or perhaps seen from many different angles all at the same time. The cubists also pioneered a technique called collage—gluing together different things to make works of art. These painters had poet friends whose writings seemed to do some of those same things. The most outstanding of those poets were Guillaume Apollinaire, Blaise Cendrars, Max Jacob, and Pierre Reverdy.

In the last part of his life, Guillaume Apollinaire (1880–1918) experimented by writing poems that had no punctuation, poems whose words were arranged to look like objects, a poem made up of bits of conversation overheard in a café, and poems that leaped from subject to subject without explaining the connections.

In 1914 Blaise Cendrars (1887–1961) wrote "Dernière Heure" ("News Flash"), which begins:

> Oklahoma, *January 20, 1914*
> Three convicts get hold of revolvers
> They kill their guard and grab the prison keys
> They come running out of their cells and kill four guards
>   in the yard
> Then they grab the young prison secretary

"News Flash" was probably the first "found" poem, that is, a poem made entirely of words from another source (in this case, a newspaper article). But Cendrars was not a plagiarist* in the usual sense of the word, because his procedure transformed the original material. Cendrars's method raised some interesting questions about originality and the ownership of words, questions that later modernists would also raise.

First published in 1917 though written some years earlier, *Le Cornet à dés* (*The Dice Cup*) by Max Jacob (1876–1944) took the prose poem a step further by introducing a tone that shifts back and forth between humor and anxiety so mysteriously that the reader is sometimes unsure whether to laugh or feel upset, as in "The Mother":

> The baby is sitting on the big paternal bed. It's morning, the grieving mother looks at him with such love.
> The child looks at her with his beautiful child's eyes and now slowly he changes into a monkey.

The use of a shifting voice became one of the principal features of modernism.

*plagiarist one who takes another person's writing and passes it off as his or her own

Soon after moving to Paris in 1910, Pierre Reverdy (1889–1960) quickly became associated with the cubist painters and the poets around them. His first book, *Prose Poems,* appeared in 1915. In general his early free-verse poetry presents fleeting glimpses of mysterious scenes and moods, using fragmented, stripped-down language that is quite musical.

The American writer Gertrude Stein (1874–1946) was a friend of the cubist painters. Some of her writing, such as *Tender Buttons* (written in 1912), can be considered prose poetry. Stein's radical style broke from conventional sentence structure and used word play and repetition in ways no one had ever done before, as in her line "A lean on the shoe this means slips slips hers."

Italian Futurism

(1909–ca. 1920)

Italian futurism was a visual art and literary movement, created in 1909 by Filippo Tommaso Marinetti (1876–1944), who wrote a number of manifestos* and speeches promoting it. He called for a rejection of the past and praised energy, speed, and machines—as well as war. He also advocated what he called *parole in libertà* ("words set free"), a kind of writing in which words and fragments of words crash and fly around the page, sideways, upside-down, every which way. (See the illustration on p. 258) Marinetti's style and ideas had a considerable influence, notably on Russian futurism and dadaism.

*manifesto a written statement citing the intentions or beliefs of the author or of a literary or artistic movement

Russian Futurism

(1912–ca. 1920)

Russian futurism had some features in common with Italian futurism, but not all. For one thing, the Russians drew on primitivism in art* and their own native folklore. Also, they had elaborate theories that justified their emphasis on the importance of sound in poetry and the creation of new words. The Russian futurists did not exalt war and speed.

*primitivism in art unsophisticated folk art

Vladimir Mayakovsky (1893–1930) is the best-known Russian futurist poet. In 1913 and 1914 he and other Futurists toured the Russian countryside, declaiming their modernist

This piece is "Parole in libertà" by Filippo Tommaso Marinetti.

*utopia an imaginary, ideal place

poems from a donkey cart. Mayakovsky performed in a bright yellow shirt, using a wooden spoon for a tie.

Velimir Khlebnikov (1885–1922) was a wild experimenter with words, but always with a conscious purpose: to create a new language that would help bring about a future utopia.* He liked to coin new words, but words that retained some relation to meaning, unlike the coinages of his fellow futurist Alexei Kruchonik (1886–1968), which were totally abstract. For example, Khlebnikov's poem "Incantation by Laughter"— which begins "Hlahla! Uthlofan, lauflings!"—consists entirely of new words derived from the word *laugh*. Khlebnikov's "supertales," such as *Zanzegi* (1922), combined poetry, fiction, drama, and essay.

Vasilisk Gnedov (1890–1978) was in some ways the most extreme Futurist poet, as in his "Poem of the End," which consisted of a blank page.

Imagism

(ca. 1910–1917)

Imagism was an Anglo-American literary movement. Ezra Pound (1885–1972), one of its promulgators,* edited the first imagist anthology, *Des Imagistes* (1914). Influenced by Japanese haiku and reacting against the flowery poetry of the late nineteenth century, the imagist poets tended to use short lines, clear images, and no abstractions. Pound said that "the natural object is always the adequate symbol," a remark reminiscent of William Carlos Williams's saying, "No ideas but in things."

> ***promulgators** people who declare or proclaim

When Pound moved on to other projects and movements, imagism was popularized by Amy Lowell (1874–1925), who smoked cigars and toured the United States giving poetry readings and lectures. Pound called it "Amy-gism."

One of the purest imagist poets was Hilda Doolittle (1886–1961), who published under the name of H. D. She had known Pound when she was in college in Pennsylvania. In 1911 she went to England, where she met other modernist writers and artists. Her first book, *Sea Garden,* was published in 1916; her last, *Helen in Egypt,* in the year of her death. Her poetry contains clear images and many references to ancient Greece, as in "Trance," which begins:

> The floor
> of the temple
> is bright
> with the rain . . .

> (H. D. [Hilda Doolittle], *Collected Poems*)

World War I and Dadaism

(1914–ca. 1924)

World War I (1914–1918) turned out to be an enormous disaster for everyone. Millions of soldiers at the front were slaugh-

*carnage brutal
slaughter

tered, while back home the leaders on both sides kept claiming victory. Disgusted by this carnage* and propaganda, a small group of artists and poets assembled in Zurich, Switzerland (a neutral country), and in 1916 invented a new artistic and literary movement, which they called dada. The dadaists used outrageous nonsense in their writing, art, and performances, as a way of breaking free from the societies that perpetuated the horrors of war. Notable among the first dadaist poets were Tristan Tzara, Richard Huelsenbeck, and Hugo Ball.

Tristan Tzara (1896–1963) had a talent for doing things to upset people who held to conventional ideas. To write a poem, he said, first cut some words out of a newspaper, put them all in a hat, shake it up, take them out at random, and glue them down. Procedures such as this are known as chance operations, a variety of which have been used by modernist writers ever since, writers such as American poet Jackson MacLow (b. 1922).

Francis Picabia (1879–1953), painter and poet, also rejected conventional ideas about art and literature. It was through Picabia's trips to New York—and his friends there, the artists Man Ray and Marcel Duchamp—that the pre-dada spirit reached the United States, as early as 1913.

In 1920 Tzara brought dada personally to Paris, enlisting young French poets André Breton, Philippe Soupault, Paul Eluard, and Louis Aragon, who had already been influenced by the poets associated with cubism.

For more on dada, see the article on Performance Poetry elsewhere in this volume.

Surrealism

(fl. 1924–1945)

By its very explosive and self-destructing nature, dada could not last long. Out of it, a new and more positive movement was born, surrealism, headed by André Breton (1896–1966). Breton's surrealist manifestos call for an art based on a deeper exploration of the unconscious mind—the irrational world of dreams, intuition, and insanity. The pioneering work of psychoanalysts Sigmund Freud and Pierre Janet influenced surrealist thinking. Other major influences were the writings of Rimbaud, Lautréamont, and Alfred Jarry (1873–1907), the author of the rambunctious play *Ubu roi* (*Ubu the King*). In looking back to writers such as these, the surrealists established their own literary lineage—an "outsider" lineage.

The poetry of Philippe Soupault (1897–1990) has a wonderful lightness of touch and a childlike innocence, as in his lines "Brave as a postage stamp / he went on his way." Soupault's novel *Last Nights of Paris* (1928) was translated into English by the American poet William Carlos Williams.

Paul Eluard (1895–1952) wrote love poetry enveloped in a mysterious dreaminess, as in his line "You are standing on my eyelids."

Robert Desnos (1900–1945) had a natural talent for automatic writing:* he could slip into a sleep-like trance and write! Using dream images, but also influenced by movies and popular radio shows, his poetry is filled with fantasy and humor. Among the surrealists, he was unusual in his use of traditional poetic forms.

Henri Michaux (1899–1984) was an explorer of the inner universe of the mind, both in his poetry and in his drawings. For a while part of the surrealist movement, he was essentially a loner whose poetry is rich in sarcasm, insults, alienation, anxiety, verbal twists, and, oddly enough, humor: "At the age of eight, I still dreamed of being granted plant status."

Many of the surrealists engaged in collaborative works. For example, as far back as 1919, Breton and Soupault had written a book (*The Magnetic Fields*) and a play (*If You Please*) together, using automatic writing. Another collaborative technique was called the "exquisite corpse," in which poems or drawings were created by three or four people together, using a single piece of paper that was folded so that each contributor did not know what the others had written or drawn. Another sign of collaboration was the surrealists' creation of what were called poem-objects—sculptures that combined objects and words. Some of the surrealist painters even wrote poetry (Jean Arp) and dreamlike prose (Giorgio de Chirico).

Just as they erased the line between the conscious and subconscious mind, the surrealists erased the line between authors, between poets and painters, between poetry and visual art.

*automatic writing
writing while in a trance or a near-trance, allowing the unconscious mind to flow onto the page

Objectivism

(1931–1984)

Inspired by imagism, the so-called objectivist poets didn't really form a literary movement, but because their work was grouped together in a 1931 issue of *Poetry* magazine under that name, these American poets were sometimes thought of as a unified group. Although their early work seems to have come from the poets' reliance on letting the form and content of their poems grow out of the poet's attention to an object (hence the name objectivist), each poet developed a different style.

Louis Zukofsky (1904–1978) wrote poetry that is considered difficult because of the ways he took language apart. In 1969 he and his wife, Celia, published a translation of the poetry of the ancient Roman poet Catullus. This unusual translation was based half on the meanings of the words and half on their sounds, as in the short poem called "106":

> Cute boy arm in elbow prize con man, kid, what do you
> see,
> quid credit, nor see (*say*) one there'd rate his procurer?

A protégé of Ezra Pound, George Oppen (1908–1984) won the Pulitzer Prize in 1968 for his *Of Being Numerous.* His other books include *Discrete Series* (1934), *The Materials* (1962), *This in Which* (1965), *Collected Poems* (1975), and *Primitive* (1978). Notice the absence of books between 1934 and 1962, a period in which more conservative tastes reigned in American poetry.

Carl Rakosi (b. 1903) seemed to disappear for decades as well; he had abandoned poetry for a while to work as a psychologist. His most accessible work combines clear images with a gentle humor.

Charles Reznikoff (1894–1976) was so neglected that for some years he had to publish his own books. In *Testimony,* Reznikoff, who worked as a law librarian, copied trial testimony from old court cases and broke it into lines, making found poems that are much stronger than the original source material. Although this technique was still considered radical, Reznikoff's use of it is mild and unthreatening.

Lorine Niedecker (1903–1970) would have been a more famous poet if she had not lived most of her life far from the American centers of literature, on Blackhawk Island, just outside of Fort Atkinson, Wisconsin. When she read the 1931 issue of *Poetry* magazine that featured the objectivist poets, it galvanized her own writing, as did the subsequent encouragement of the issue's editor, Louis Zukofsky. Niedecker's poetry uses clear, condensed language, and sharply observed details of everyday life, sometimes cast in the musical phrasing of the way people in her community talked, as in this untitled poem:

Get a load
   of April's
      fabulous

frog rattle
   lowland freight cars
     in the night.

                (Niedecker, *From This Condensery*)

Very much his own person, William Carlos Williams (1883–1963) was associated first with the imagists and later with the objectivists. His work had a tremendous influence on other American poets in the second half of the twentieth century.

American, English, and Irish Modernists

It's hard to think of any great twentieth-century American, British, or Irish poet who was not a modernist or strongly influenced by some aspect of modernism. Because many of these poets are the subjects of articles elsewhere in these volumes, I will say no more about them here. Notable examples are William Butler Yeats, Ezra Pound, T. S. Eliot, Wallace Stevens, Marianne Moore, W. H. Auden, and Langston Hughes.

Modernism in Latin America

(1885–)

You might suppose that modernism in Latin America was imported from Spain and Portugal, but in fact the Latin American modernists were first influenced mainly by the French modernists. In 1896, the Nicaraguan poet Rubén Darío (1867–1916) began a movement that he called *Modernismo,* inspired particularly by the French symbolist poets. Actually Darío's Modernism followed a previous generation of Latin American modernists. But an even more radical Latin American modernism took root a few years after Darío's *Modernismo.*

After a trip to Japan in 1900, the Mexican poet José Juan Tablada (1871–1945) introduced the haiku form into Spanish poetry. Early on he also wrote calligrams inspired by those of Apollinaire.

After going to Paris in 1916 to study, the Chilean poet Vicente Huidobro (1893–1948) began writing poetry influenced by the poets associated with cubism. When he returned to Chile, he introduced twentieth-century modernism to that country. He even founded his own movement, Creationism, which called for the creation of imaginary worlds, as he says in his poem "Altazor" (Huidobro, *The Selected Poetry of Vincente Huidobro*):

> The poet is the manicurist of the language
> And even more the magician who inflames and
>   quenches
> Stellar words and the cherries of vagabond good-byes
> Far from the hands of the earth
> And invents all that he says
> Things that move outside the ordinary world
>   (Trans. Eliot Weinberger)

The Peruvian poet César Vallejo (1892–1938) left his native country in 1923, spending the rest of his life in Paris and Madrid. Begun when he was unjustly imprisoned in Peru, his book *Trilce* (1922) is a difficult and heroic collection. Here are two lines:

> All night long I keep sticking
> out my tongue at the most mute Xes.
>   (Trans. Clayton Eshleman)

His *Poemas humanos* (*Human Poems*), edited by his wife a year after his death, is more accessible but still filled with marvelous imaginative leaps.

Pablo Neruda (1904–1973) was born in Chile. His rather surrealistic *Residence on Earth,* first published in 1933, showed the influence of Whitman, Blake, and Lautréamont. His collections of odes took that form in a surprising new direction.

The work of the Chilean poet Nicanor Parra (b. 1914) is characterized by wit and irreverence. Young readers particularly like his poem "The Teachers," which begins: "Our teachers drove us nuts / with their irrelevant questions."

The Brazilian poet Carlos Drummond de Andrade (1902–1987) helped organize Semana de Arte Moderna (Week of Modern Art), a festival that introduced modernism into Brazilian poetry in the 1920s. His first book, *Alguma Poesia* (*Some Poems,* 1930), were modernist in their use of provincial subject matter and simple language.

Modernism in Spain and Portugal

(ca. 1910–ca. 1936)

Spanish poet Juan Ramón Jiménez (1881–1958) showed that free verse can be lyrical, light of touch, and made of simple words. His poetry received the Nobel Prize in 1956.

Ramón Gomez de la Serna (1888–1963) created a form he called the *greguería,* a sort of poetic aphorism,* as in "What hurts a tree most when it is being chopped down is that the axe has a wooden handle" and "The q is the p coming back from a walk."

Federico García Lorca (1898–1936) wrote beautiful and mysterious lyric poems that used simple language and were influenced by Spanish folklore and music. After coming to New York for a visit, Lorca wrote his surrealistic book, *Poet in New York.*

In some of his poems, Luis Cernuda (1902–1963) took traditional Spanish poetic themes and gave them a surrealistic twist. His influences include Jiménez, Mallarmé, and Reverdy.

The early poetry of Miguel Hernández (1910–1942) was traditional, but under the influence of his friends Lorca and Neruda, his work moved into free verse. Brought up as a goat farmer, Hernández had a passion for poetry. The harsh conditions of his political imprisonment by the Fascist government of Francisco Franco led to his death.

The French poet Valery Larbaud (1881–1957) created a character named A. O. Barnabooth and then wrote poems "by" him (1908), but Fernando Pessoa (1888–1935), the most famous Portuguese poet of the twentieth century, took this practice to new extremes by creating multiple new identities and writing poems to go with each one.

*aphorism a brief, pithy statement of truth

A Few Unclassifiables

There are many fine twentieth-century modernists who don't fit into any literary movement. Here are just a few.

Actually, the first one—the Austrian poet Georg Trakl (1887–1914)—is often classified as an expressionist poet. Expressionism in poetry is more of a tendency—a heavy concern with themes of decay, death, and despondency, sometimes seen from an odd point of view—than it is a movement. The dreamlike flow of visual images in Trakl's poetry seems to anticipate the later developments of imagism and automatic writing.

Born in Ohio, Hart Crane (1899–1932) united modernism with the optimistic spirit of Walt Whitman. His energetic masterpiece, an epic poem called *The Bridge,* was begun around 1923 and published in 1930.

John Wheelwright (1897–1940) came from a wealthy Boston family but in the 1930s became an ardent socialist fighting for social justice. His satirical poem "You-U.S.-US" consists of fragments, verbal surprises, abrupt appearances and disappearances of themes, and takeoffs on children's songs and advertising slogans.

The American poet Kenneth Patchen (1911–1972) used free verse and fantasy. He also combined his own art and words, creating poem-pictures, in two collections, *Because It Is* and *Hallelujah Anyway.* He was one of the first poets to read his poems to jazz accompaniment.

The Romanian poet Paul Celan (1920–1970) wrote in German, the language his parents spoke at home. Unlike his parents, he escaped death in the Holocaust, though he was forced to work in a Nazi labor camp. He was influenced by these experiences, by surrealism, and by the international literature he translated.

The many books of Robert Bly (b. 1926) include *Silence in the Snowy Fields,* made of spare images from the landscape of his native Minnesota; *The Light Around the Body,* poems that are more mystical and poems against the Vietnam War; and his *Selected Poems.* Bly is also a gifted translator of Swedish, German, and Spanish poetry.

Word Play

It is likely that word play has been a part of poetry since the beginning. But certain forms of word play were taken to extremes in the twentieth century, in search of delight.

English poet Dame Edith Sitwell (1887–1964), in her book *Façade* (originally performed in 1923), wrote lines such as these, from "The Wind's Bastinado":

> . . . This corraceous
> Round orchidaceous
> Laceous porraceous
> Fruit is a lie!

(Sitwell, Collected Poems)

The poems of E. E. Cummings (1894–1962) are laid out on the page in ways that at first make them look like playful gibberish or random letters, but when read aloud usually do make sense. But an important part of the way they make sense is the way they look.

Kurt Schwitters (1887–1948) was a German artist who made beautiful collages and sculptures, and the author of poetry and a science fiction radio play. With a wry sense of humor, in 1919 he started his own one-man art movement, which he called Merz. Some of his poems are made up of words that simply indicate various sounds, but others play with recognizable words, as in his 1937 poem "When someone once said" (Schwitters, *Poems, Performance Pieces, Proses* [sic], *Plays, Poetics*):

> When someone once said
> that some friend had once said
> that some other friend said
> that I said to a third friend
> that a fourth friend had said
> that a sixth friend had said
>
> (Trans. Jerome Rothenberg)

. . . and so on.

One of the greatest word-play geniuses was the German poet Christian Morgenstern (1871–1914), who used humor, twisted syntax, invented words, old words with new meanings, and shaped poems. One of his poems, "Fish's Nightsong," has no words at all, just several rows of dashes that we recognize as fish swimming along. Most of his other work is very difficult to translate.

Subject Matter

In this article I have talked mostly about how the modernist poets explored the use of new forms and "voices" for their poems. But sometimes they also explored new and difficult subject matter: the widespread loss of religious faith; the feeling of being alone and pointless on a tiny speck (the Earth) hurtling through a cold and infinite universe; new and even disorienting ideas about the nature of time and space; war on a scale more monstrous than ever before; new onslaughts of social, economic, and political injustice; increasing dehuman-

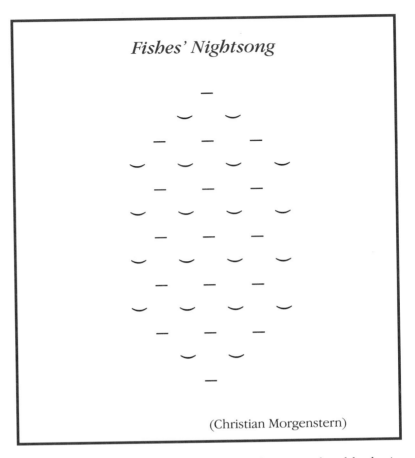

Fishes' Nightsong

(Christian Morgenstern)

ization; and the question of what role the poet should take in society. In the face of such heavy issues, the wonder is that some poets were able to express happiness, pleasure, optimism, joy, and religious faith.

Remember

The groups discussed above are not nearly so neat as they sound. Some poets were what might be called partial or temporary members of a group. Also, the work of poets in these groups changed—some modernists even renounced modernism. It is best simply to read the poetry of each individual without being concerned at first about what group the poet might have belonged to.

Some modernists went overboard in their experiments with form and language—always a danger of exploring new territory. And, as always, there were minor poets who were motivated by a shallow desire for novelty or who simply lacked talent. But the best and most brilliant modernist poets had a deep and burning desire for a new art that could express what it was like to be alive in the twentieth century.

Bibliography

Free Verse

Whitman, Walt. *Leaves of Grass.* Many editions.

The Prose Poem

Baudelaire, Charles. *Paris Spleen.* Translated by Louise Varese. New York: New Directions, 1970.

Benedikt, Michael, ed. *The Prose Poem.* New York: Dell, 1976.

Bertrand, Aloysius. *Gaspard de la Nuit.* Translated by John T. Wright. Lanham, Md.: University Press of America, 1994.

Lautréamont, Comte de (Isidore Ducasse). *Maldoror and the Complete Works.* Translated by Alexis Lykiard. Cambridge, Mass.: Exact Change, 1994.

Rimbaud, Arthur. *Complete Works.* Translated by Paul Schmidt. New York: Harper and Row, 1975.

The New Page

Mallarmé, Stéphane. "A Throw of the Dice." Translated by Daisy Aldan. In *Poems for the Millenium,* vol. 1, edited by Jerome Rothenberg and Pierre Joris. Berkeley, Calif.: University of California, 1995.

A Question of Tone

Laforgue, Jules. *Poems of Jules Laforgue.* Translated by Patricia Terry. Berkeley: University of California Press, 1958.

A Change of Rhythm

Hopkins, Gerard Manley. *Poems.* New York: Oxford University Press, 1996.

Cubism

Apollinaire, Guillaume. *Alcools.* Translated by Anne Hyde Greet. Berkeley: University of California Press, 1965.

Apollinaire, Guillaume. *Calligrammes.* Translated by Anne Hyde Greet. Berkeley: University of California Press, 1991.

Auster, Paul, ed. *The Random House Book of Twentieth-Century French Poetry.* New York: Random House, 1982.

Breunig, Leroy, ed. and trans. *The Cubist Poets in Paris.* Lincoln: University of Nebraska Press, 1995.

Cendrars, Blaise. *The Complete Poems.* Translated by Ron Padgett. Berkeley: University of California Press, 1992.

Jacob, Max. *The Dice Cup.* Edited by Michael Brownstein. Translated by Brownstein and others. New York: SUN, 1979.

Reverdy, Pierre. *Selected Poems.* Edited by Timothy Bent. Translated by John Ashbery, Mary Ann Caws, and Patricia Terry. Winston-Salem, N.C.: Wake Forest University Press, 1991.

Shattuck, Roger. *The Banquet Years.* New York: Vintage, 1968.

Stein, Gertrude. *Selected Writing.* Edited by Carl Van Vechten. New York: Modern Library, 1962.

Italian Futurism

Marinetti, F. T. *Selected Writings.* Edited by R. W. Flint. New York: Farrar, Straus and Giroux, 1972.

Russian Futurism

Khlebnikov, Velimir. *The King of Time: Selected Writings of the Russian Futurian.* Edited by Charlotte Douglas. Translated by Paul Schmidt. Cambridge, Mass.: Harvard University Press, 1985.

Mayakovsky, Vladimir. *The Bedbug.* Edited by Patricia Blake. Translated by Max Hayward and George Reavey. New York: World, 1970.

Yarmolinsky, Avrahm, ed. *An Anthology of Russian Verse, 1812–1960.* Translated by Max Eastman and others. New York: Doubleday Anchor, 1962.

Imagism

H. D. (Hilda Doolittle). *Collected Poems.* Edited by Louis L. Martz. New York: New Directions, 1983.

Lowell, Amy. *A Shard of Silence: Selected Poems.* Edited by G. R. Ruihley. New York: Twayne, 1957.

Pound, Ezra. *Personae.* Prepared by Lea Baechler and A. Walton Litz. New York: New Directions, 1990.

Dadaism

Tzara, Tristan. *Chanson Dada: Selected Poems.* Translated by Lee Harwood. Toronto: Coach House, 1987.

Tzara, Tristan. *Seven Dada Manifestos and Lampisteries.* Translated by Barbara Wright. London: Calder, 1977.

Picabia, Francis. *Who Knows.* Translated by Remy Hall. New York: Hanuman, 1986.

Motherwell, Robert, ed. *The Dada Painters and Poets.* Cambridge, Mass.: Belknap Press of Harvard University Press, 1989.

Surrealism

Breton, André. *Earthlight.* Translated by Bill Zavatsky and Zack Rogow. Los Angeles: Sun and Moon, 1993.

Breton, André. *Manifestos of Surrealism.* Translated by Richard Seaver and Helen R. Lane. Ann Arbor: University of Michigan Press, 1969.

De Chirico, Giorgio. *Hebdomeros.* Cambridge, Mass.: Exact Change, 1992.

Desnos, Robert. *Selected Poems.* Translated by Carolyn Forché and William Kulik. New York: Ecco Press, 1991.

Eluard, Paul. *Selected Poems.* Translated by Gilbert Bowen. London: Calder, 1988.

Michaux, Henri. *Darkness Moves.* Translated by David Ball. Berkeley: University of California Press, 1994.

Polizzotti, Mark. *Revolution of the Mind: The Life of André Breton.* New York: Farrar, Straus and Giroux, 1995.

Raymond, Marcel. *From Baudelaire to Surrealism.* Translated by G. M. New York: Wittenborn, Schultz, 1950.

Soupault, Philippe. *I'm Lying.* Translated by Paulette Schmidt. Providence, R.I.: Lost Roads Press, 1985.

Soupault, Philippe, with André Breton. *The Magnetic Fields.* Translated by David Gascoyne. London: Atlas, 1985.

Objectivism

Heller, Michael. *Conviction's Net of Branches.* Carbondale: Southern Illinois University Press, 1985.

Niedecker, Lorine. *From This Condensery: The Complete Writings of Lorine Niedecker.* Edited by Robert J. Bertholf. East Haven, Conn.: The Jargon Society / Inland Book Co., 1985.

Niedecker, Lorine. *The Granite Pail: Selected Poems of Lorine Niedecker.* Edited by Cid Corman. San Francisco: North Point, 1985.

Oppen, George. *Collected Poems.* New York: New Directions, 1975.

Rakosi, Carl. *Collected Poems.* Orono, Me.: The National Poetry Foundation, 1986.

Reznikoff, Charles. *The Complete Poems.* Santa Barbara, Calif.: Black Sparrow Press, 1976–1977.

Williams, William Carlos. *The Collected Poems of William Carlos Williams, Volume 1: 1909–1939.* Edited by A. Walton Litz and Christopher MacGowan. New York: New Directions, 1986.

Williams, William Carlos. *The Collected Poems of William Carlos Williams, Volume 2: 1939–1962.* Edited by A. Walton Litz and Christopher MacGowan. New York: New Directions, 1988.

Zukofsky, Celia, and Louis Zukofsky, trans. *Catullus.* London: Cape Goliard, 1969.

Zukofsky, Louis. *"A."* Berkeley: University of California Press, 1978.

Zukofsky, Louis. *Complete Short Poetry.* Baltimore, Md.: Johns Hopkins University Press, 1991.

Word Play

Cummings, E. E. *Collected Poems.* New York: Harcourt, Brace, and World, 1963.

Morgenstern, Christian. *Gallows Songs.* Translated by W. D. Snodgrass and Lore Segal. Ann Arbor: University of Michigan, 1967.

Morgenstern, Christian. *Songs from the Gallows.* Translated by Walter Arndt. New Haven, Conn.: Yale University Press, 1993.

Schwitters, Kurt. *Poems, Performance Pieces, Proses* [sic], *Play, Poetics.* Edited and translated by Jerome Rothenberg and Pierre Joris. Philadelphia: Temple University Press, 1993.

Watts, Harriett, translator. *Three Painter-Poets: Arp / Schwitters / Klee Selected Poems.* Harmondsworth, U.K.: Penguin, 1974.

Sitwell, Edith. *The Collected Poems of Edith Sitwell.* New York: Vanguard Press, 1954.

Wells, Carolyn, ed. *A Nonsense Anthology.* New York: Dover Books, 1958.

Modernism in Latin America

Caracciolo-Trejo, E. *The Penguin Book of Latin American Verse.* Harmondsworth, U.K.: Penguin, 1971.

Drummond de Andrade, Carlos. *Souvenir of the Ancient World.* Translated by Mark Strand. N.Y.: Antaeus, 1976.

Drummond de Andrade, Carlos. *Travelling in the Family: Selected Poems.* Translated by Thomas Colchie and others. New York: Random House, 1986.

Hays, H. R., ed. and trans. *Twelve Spanish American Poets: An Anthology.* Boston: Beacon, 1972.

Huidobro, Vicente. *The Selected Poetry of Vicente Huidobro.* Edited by David M. Guss. Translated by Guss, Stephen Fredman, and others. New York: New Directions, 1981.

Neruda, Pablo. *Neruda and Vallejo: Selected Poems.* Edited by Robert Bly. Translated by Bly, John Knoepfle, and James Wright. Boston: Beacon, 1971.

Paz, Octavio, ed. *Anthology of Mexican Poetry.* Translated by Samuel Beckett. Bloomington: University of Indiana, 1958.

Paz, Octavio, et al., eds. *New Poets of Mexico.* New York: Dutton, 1970.

Parra, Nicanor. *Antipoems: New and Selected.* Edited by David Unger. Translated by Lawrence Ferlinghetti and others. New York: New Directions, 1985.

Tablada, José Juan. *Obras.* Mexico City: Centro de Estudios Literarios, Universidad Nacional Autónoma de México, 1971.

Vallejo, César. *Neruda and Vallejo: Selected Poems.* Edited by Robert Bly. Translated by Bly, John Knoepfle, and James Wright. Boston: Beacon, 1971.

Vallejo, César. *Poemas humanos. Human Poems.* Translated by Clayton Eshleman. New York: Grove, 1968.

Vallejo, César. *Trilce.* Translated by Clayton Eshleman. New York: Marsilio, 1992.

Modernism in Spain and Portugal

Cernuda, Luis. *Selected Poems.* Translated by Reginald Gibbons. Berkeley: University of California Press, 1977.

Hernández, Miguel. *Miguel Hernández and Blas de Otero.* Edited by Timothy Baland and Hardie St. Martin. Boston: Beacon, 1972.

Jiménez, Juan Ramón. *Lorca and Jiménez: Selected Poems.* Edited and translated by Robert Bly. Boston: Beacon, 1973.

Lorca, Federico García. *Lorca and Jiménez: Selected Poems.* Edited and translated by Robert Bly. Boston: Beacon, 1973.

Lorca, Federico García. *Poet in New York.* Edited by Christopher Maurer. Translated by Greg Simon and Steven F. White. New York: Noonday, 1988.

Pessoa, Fernando. *Fernando Pessoa & Co.: Selected Poems.* Translated by Richard Zenith. New York: Grove, 1998.

Serna, Ramón Gomez de la. *Aphorisms.* Translated by Miguel Gonzalez-Gerth. Pittsburgh: Latin American Review Press, 1989.

A Few Unclassifiables

Bly, Robert. *Eating the Honey of Words: New and Selected Poems.* New York: HarperFlamingo, 1999.

Bly, Robert. *Selected Poems.* New York: Perennial Library, 1986.

Bly, Robert. *Silence in the Snowy Fields: Poems.* Middletown, Conn.: Wesleyan University Press, 1962.

Celan, Paul. *Poems.* Translated by Michael Hamburger. New York: Persea, 1988.

Celan, Paul. *Speech-grille and Selected Poems.* Translated by Joachim Neugroschel. New York: Dutton, 1971.

Crane, Hart. *The Complete Poems and Selected Letters and Prose of Hart Crane.* Edited by Brom Weber. Garden City N.Y.: Doubleday / Anchor, 1966.

Patchen, Kenneth. *Because It Is.* New York: New Directions, 1960.

Patchen, Kenneth. *Collected Poems.* New York: New Directions, 1968.

Patchen, Kenneth. *Hallelujah Anyway.* New York: New Directions, 1966.

Trakl, Georg. *Autumn Sonata: Selected Poems of Georg Trakl.* Translated by Daniel Simko. Mt. Kisko, N.Y.: Moyer Bell, 1989.

Trakl, Georg. *Selected Poems.* Translated by Robert Grenier and others. London: Cape, 1968.

Trakl, Georg. *Twenty Poems.* Translated by James Wright and Robert Bly. Madison, Minn.: The Sixties Press, 1961.

Wheelwright, John. *Collected Poems.* Edited by Alvin H. Rosenfeld. New York: New Directions, 1972.

Anthologies

Rothenberg, Jerome, ed. *Revolution of the World: A New Gathering of American Avant Garde Poetry 1914–1945.* New York: Seabury, 1974.

Rothenberg, Jerome, and Pierre Joris, eds. *Poems for the Millenium.* 2 vols. Berkeley: University of California, 1995, 1998.

NEW AMERICAN POETRY

by Larry Fagin

I n the years following World War II, American poetry began to flourish with a diversity of novel forms and subjects. It was a period of experimentation in language, when new poets emerged to expand the possibilities of verse. These changes developed slowly, however. In the 1950s most Americans were concerned with material goods, comfort, home, and security. The best-known poetry of the time was aimed at a small audience of academics and scholars. The tone of this "academic" poetry was dry, intellectual, and restrictive. Only a limited range of styles and contents met with the approval of the conservative literary establishment.

At the same time, the great modernists of an earlier generation were producing some of their best work. *Pisan Cantos* by Ezra Pound, *Paterson* and *The Desert Music and Other Poems* by William Carlos Williams, *Helen in Egypt* by H. D. (Hilda Doolittle), and the later poems of Wallace Stevens, Marianne Moore, and E. E. Cummings were published in the 1950s. There was also a gradual rediscovery of a second generation of avant-garde poets who had appeared in the 1930s and 1940s but who had since been neglected. They included John Wheelwright, Langston Hughes, Kenneth Patchen, Kenneth Rexroth, Louis Zukofsky, Charles Reznikoff, George Oppen, Lorine Niedecker, Edwin Denby, Elizabeth Bishop, Paul Goodman, and David Schubert.

These two generations of poets inspired a third generation, which began to challenge the limits of the prevailing academic standards. They published in hard-to-find "little" magazines and pamphlets and read their poems in coffeehouses and bars. Heeding Ezra Pound's call to "make it new," they would continue the modern movement, introducing original ideas about form and content. Their centers of activity were San Francisco and Berkeley, New York, Boston, and Black Mountain College in North Carolina.

Toward the end of the decade, signs of youthful rebellion had surfaced. Popular culture figures such as the singer Elvis Presley, the actors Marlon Brando and James Dean, the artist Jackson Pollock, and the writer Jack Kerouac caught the public imagination. In 1955, at a legendary poetry reading at the Six Gallery in San Francisco, Allen Ginsberg first read his powerful, controversial poem "Howl." Poetry readings were gaining in popularity, and soon colleges and universities—the academy—would be inviting nonacademic poets to present their strange, surprising, and sometimes shocking work.

When *Howl and Other Poems* was published in 1956, the publisher, the poet Lawrence Ferlinghetti, was arrested and tried for selling obscene material. He was acquitted, and the book has since sold more than a million copies. Ferlinghetti was one of a number of poets who read and recorded their poems accompanied by jazz musicians. Jack Kerouac was profoundly moved by the bebop* style of the jazz musicians Charlie Parker, Dizzy Gillespie, and Thelonious Monk. He performed at jazz clubs such as the Village Vanguard in New York and made several recordings with and without jazz. Modern jazz, especially the phrasing and rhythm of bop, was a key influence on the composition of the new poetry.

Another significant connection that poets made was with the painters of the period. Jackson Pollock, Willem de Kooning, Franz Kline, Philip Guston, and other artists were heroes and role models for many poets. Painters and poets often collaborated on portfolios and pamphlets; poets wrote catalog essays and reviews of art exhibits; painters attended poetry readings.

Finally, there was the attraction of Eastern philosophy and poetry. Kerouac, Ginsberg, and the poets Gary Snyder and Philip Whalen, among others, became involved in the study of Buddhism. Snyder traveled to Japan, where he practiced meditation in a Zen Buddhist monastery. Whalen ultimately became a Zen monk. The anthologist R. H. Blyth had introduced Japanese haiku* to the West in 1949 and 1950, inspiring Kerouac to write his own brand of American haiku.

A major breakthrough occurred in 1960 with the publication of *The New American Poetry, 1945–1960,* an anthology that brought national recognition to the new generation. It presented the work of forty-four poets, divided into somewhat arbitrary categories. Most of the work had been available only in limited editions or had circulated in manuscript. It is still considered to be the foremost anthology of post–World War II American poetry, summing up the accomplishments of the 1950s and looking ahead to the possibilities of the 1960s.

Important social changes took place early in the 1960s, beginning with the struggle for civil rights in the South. It was a

*bebop a style of jazz that uses dissonant notes, unusual rhythms, and fast tempos

*haiku a Japanese poetic form, usually unrhymed and consisting of three lines of seventeen syllables. A haiku often contains only a single image. See also discussion of haiku in the essay on Poetic Forms in these volumes.

time of highly charged political activity that created a communal spirit among young people. By the middle of the decade a radical "counterculture," marked by a rejection of middle-class values, was gaining momentum. After an explosion of rock music (especially the Beatles and Bob Dylan), sexual freedom, and experimentation with psychedelic drugs, the period came to a head in massive demonstrations against the Vietnam War.

Ginsberg, Snyder, Ferlinghetti, Robert Duncan, Denise Levertov, Amiri Baraka (then called LeRoi Jones), and others were writing political poetry and speaking out against censorship, racism, and war. Poetry conferences in Vancouver (1963) and Berkeley (1965) brought the new poets together for workshops, lectures, and readings. Some were still discovering each other's work and met for the first time at these events. Underground presses were multiplying. Some magazines and pamphlets were issued in elegantly designed and printed editions, but most were produced quickly and cheaply on mimeograph* machines. As the work of the third generation of modernists gained the respect of critics and mainstream publishers, a group of younger poets—a fourth generation—began to appear in print, continuing the still new tradition of the avant-garde.*

*mimeograph a duplicating machine that uses stencils to make copies. It was replaced by the photocopier.

*avant-garde advanced or cutting-edge; experimental

Black Mountain Poets

Begun in the 1930s as an experimental arts college in North Carolina, Black Mountain College attracted extraordinary teachers and students: the painters Josef Albers, Willem de Kooning, Franz Kline, and Robert Rauschenberg; the composer John Cage; the choreographer and dancer Merce Cunningham; the inventor and designer Buckminster Fuller; the prose writers Michael Rumaker and Fielding Dawson; and the poets Charles Olson, Robert Duncan, Robert Creeley, Edward Dorn, John Wieners, Joel Oppenheimer, and Jonathan Williams. The first mixed-media performances took place at Black Mountain—collaborative events that combined painting, poetry, film, music, and dance. Other poets, including Denise Levertov, Paul Blackburn, Larry Eigner, and Paul Carroll, never attended the college but were associated with the writers there.

CHARLES OLSON

The dominant figure among the poets and writers at Black Mountain was Charles Olson (1910–1970). He was a big man with a great store of knowledge about history, anthropology, geography, and many other subjects. He would sprinkle fragments of information, ideas, and memories throughout his lectures and his long, open-ended poems. He conceived of the page as a field of energy, unbounded by conventional rules. Words, phrases, and lines sprawl across the page (even diagonally) or are bunched in clusters, without depending on the left-hand margin. Large blank spaces correspond to silences. Some compositions contain random speech patterns, halting talk, stopping and starting, changing the subject in the middle of a sentence, dwelling on minute details. He often opened one parenthesis and then opened another one without closing the first one.

Olson maintained that "one perception must immediately and directly lead to a further perception" and that "a line of poetry should correspond to a unit of breath." His student Joel Oppenheimer has stated: "The poem should read on the page as I myself read it to you aloud. It should have my breath on it" (Duberman, p. 414). Olson's major work, *The Maximus Poems* (1960), is a long, continuous work, throughout which its hero, Maximus, is speaking. The poem is set in the town of Gloucester, Massachusetts, where Olson lived.

ROBERT CREELEY

Robert Creeley (b. 1926) came to study and teach at Black Mountain in 1954, where he began the *Black Mountain Review* to "admit some further possibilities" for poetry. Early issues of the magazine included important critical writing by the new poets. As opposed to Olson's expansiveness, Creeley wrote in tightly controlled short lines, using a simple vocabulary and musical phrasing. One notices the changes in the vowel sounds. He is a careful craftsman who makes the difficult look easy. With each line break a delicate transformation takes place. Creeley is like a graceful dancer, subtly changing position and direction on the dance floor. His early work is romantic and lyrical,* concerned with loneliness and love's difficulties, but the syntax, the way in which he puts together his words, is compressed, and the feeling is tense, sometimes pinched, even painful.

lyrical music-like

DENISE LEVERTOV

Denise Levertov (1923–1997), one of the few women among the new poets, was originally from England. Like Creeley she was a poet of intense lyricism and a follower of William Carlos Williams. In the late 1960s she published poems expressing her outrage with the war in Vietnam. She wrote: "There is a form in all things (and in our experience) which the poet can discover and reveal."

PAUL BLACKBURN

Although he was deeply influenced by the Black Mountain poets' concern with visual representation and breath, Paul Blackburn (1926–1971) is also remembered for his tough, humorous poems about scenes in New York City, especially the subway. He found inspiration in Pound and Williams, twelfth-century Provençal troubadour poets, and the Beat Generation. His work seems spontaneous, an off-the-cuff response to the strangeness of life, but it is the result of careful planning and composing.

LARRY EIGNER

Larry Eigner (1926–1996) suffered from cerebral palsy and spent most of his life in a wheelchair. This fact determined a lot about the forms and images of his poetry. His subjects are simply what he saw from his porch on a side street in a small Massachusetts town: people and cars passing by, trees, squirrels, birds, weather, the motion of clouds. The seeing is precise, the tone quiet. His lines are usually fragmented. Eigner's interest in detail and the importance of the line connects him to both Williams and the Black Mountain style.

EDWARD DORN

Edward Dorn (1929–1999) attended Black Mountain College but has lived mostly in the Western states. A lyricist at first, he developed into a political satirist, making fun of politics in poems full of bitter irony.* His epic work, *Gunslinger* (1972), is a poem in four volumes, containing disarming combinations of cowboy dialect,* urban slang, scientific and political jargon,* and a smattering of Elizabethan vocabulary.

JOHN WIENERS

After studying under Olson and Duncan at Black Mountain, John Wieners (b. 1934) returned to his home in Boston, where he edited *Measure* magazine. The lyricism and honesty

*irony saying the opposite of what you mean to make your point even more strongly

*dialect provincial, rural, or socially distinct variety of a language that differs from the standard language

*jargon vocabulary specific to a certain group of people and difficult for outsiders to understand

of his early work was acclaimed by his fellow poets, but his painfully direct treatment of themes of madness, drugs, and homosexuality has prevented him from attracting mainstream critical attention. His first book, *The Hotel Wentley Poems* (1958), was written in San Francisco, and he is sometimes grouped with the poets of that city.

San Francisco Renaissance

Robert Duncan, Jack Spicer, and Robin Blaser met while attending the University of California at Berkeley in the late 1940s. They shared common interests in medieval and Renaissance culture, the occult,* and modern literature. They called themselves the Berkeley Renaissance. Some years later the Berkeley group was absorbed, with a number of other San Francisco Bay Area poets, into what became known as the San Francisco Renaissance. It included Gary Snyder, Lawrence Ferlinghetti, Michael McClure, Philip Whalen, Philip Lamantia, Lew Welch, David Meltzer, and Ron Loewinsohn. These poets have sometimes been grouped with the Beats. Allen Ginsberg and Jack Kerouac were also living in San Francisco in the mid-1950s. Although they wrote in diverse styles and were often at odds with one another, the San Francisco Renaissance poets shared a love for their unique city, its physical beauty, its colorful history, and its tolerance of radical politics and nontraditional religious practices. For Robert Duncan, San Francisco was "the westward edge of dreams, / the golden promise of our days" ("Ode for Dick Brown," Robert Duncan and Jack Spicer, *An Ode and Arcadia,* Berkeley, Calif.: Ark Press, 1974).

Kenneth Rexroth, an older poet and translator, served as an important model, socially and politically, for Duncan, Snyder, and others. Rexroth, who had long been a figure in leftist politics, became a spokesperson for the Beat and San Francisco poets, helping to bring them wider recognition. Others of an earlier generation who taught, inspired, and published alongside the younger poets include Helen Adam, William Everson, Josephine Miles, James Broughton, and Madeline Gleason.

ROBERT DUNCAN

After meeting Olson in the late 1940s, Robert Duncan (1919–1988) became involved in the poetics of Black Moun-

*occult supernatural or supernormal

tain, where he taught in 1956. He was a longtime resident of San Francisco, however, and is equally associated with its group of writers and artists. Like Olson, he developed late as a poet. His first important collection was *The Opening of the Field* (1960). He was one of the most learned of all the new American poets. The sources of Duncan's inspiration include mythology, folklore, fairy tales, medieval ballads, alternative religions, mysticism,* surrealism,* psychology, Dante, the Romantic poets, Gertrude Stein, Ezra Pound, James Joyce, and H. D.

Besides experimenting with traditional poetic forms, Duncan wrote verse plays, journals, and critical essays. His *H.D. Book* functions both as an autobiography and as a study of modernism. His political engagement appears in such important works as "A Poem Beginning with a Line by Pindar" and his long collage poem "Passages." At first a dramatic poet, he became more involved in the sound of language itself. His poems are among the most musical of the post–World War II period.

JACK SPICER

Jack Spicer (1925–1965) was a difficult, hostile man but a brilliant poet and teacher. After a long friendship with Robert Duncan, he became Duncan's spiteful opponent and competitor. He argued against the Beats, accusing them of "selling out." As mentor, editor, publisher, and stern father figure (though he was only forty when he died), he attracted his own circle of fiercely loyal followers (George Stanley, Ebbe Borregaard, Joanne Kyger, Harold Dull, Stan Persky, and others) who gathered nightly in the bars of San Francisco's North Beach.

Spicer was widely read and, like Duncan, drew upon far-ranging material for his poems: medieval studies, the Oz books of L. Frank Baum, magic, baseball, the nonsense verse of the British writers Edward Lear and Lewis Carroll, folk music, Calvinism,* science fiction, the French writer and film director Jean Cocteau, and the history and geography of his beloved California. Under the influence of Cocteau's film *Orpheus* he conceived of the poet as a medium, a kind of radio broadcasting poetry that was dictated from another planet. The poem had a life of its own. For Spicer the poet's job was not to interpret but to reveal. He agreed with Duncan's statement "A poem is an event; it is not the record of an event."

*mysticism spiritual beliefs based on supernatural and unexplained phenomena that cannot be perceived by ordinary rationality

*surrealism an artistic movement that aimed (chiefly during the 1920s and 1930s) to express the workings of the unconscious or subconscious mind

*Calvinism the doctrine of John Calvin, who believed that God is present everywhere and that sinners could achieve salvation through the grace of God

GARY SNYDER

Gary Snyder (b. 1930) grew up in the Pacific Northwest. He studied anthropology and linguistics in college and did logging and forestry work. He continued his education with classical Chinese studies at the University of Californai at Berkeley. There he met Jack Kerouac and Allen Ginsberg and became associated with the Beat movement. For a good part of the 1950s and early 1960s Snyder lived in Japan, where he received formal training in Zen Buddhist meditation. His early poems, found in _Riprap_ (1959) and _Myths and Texts_ (1960), reflect his experience in the woods and mountains, hiking, hunting, and sleeping under the stars. The words are clear, concise, and carefully placed. One can feel each rock underfoot.

A fine translator of Chinese poetry of the T'ang dynasty, Snyder emulates models of Eastern literature and art in _Mountains and Rivers Without End_ (1996), a long poem that can be compared to a Chinese scroll painting. Snyder has also studied Native American song and myth and has long been committed to the politics of ecology. His many essays on ways to preserve and respect the natural world have made him one of the most popular figures among the new American poets.

MICHAEL MCCLURE

In his poems, plays, and essays, Michael McClure (b. 1932) calls on us to recognize and celebrate our own mammalian nature in order to combat the inhuman world of machines. The message dates back to the English poet William Blake in the eighteenth century. What is interesting is how McClure delivers the message. His poems are noted for their distinctive design on the page. All the lines are centered, with an extensive use of capital letters and exclamation points. In contrast to this unusual form, the lines themselves are conventional, mostly declarative sentences. McClure is direct, emotional, and sensual. In _Ghost Tantras_ (1964), he created what he called "beast language," composed of modern and ancient human speech mixed with abstract or animal sounds. There is a remarkable film of McClure reading these poems to lions at the San Francisco Zoo, as they, and he, pace back and forth.

PHILIP WHALEN

Although he became a Zen Buddhist monk in 1973, Philip Whalen (b. 1923) has long been associated with both the Beats and the San Francisco Renaissance, but his work would also fit in nicely with the New York school. He shares that group's intellectual wit and light touch. His poems are verbal collages, a diverse assembly of satirical, open, gentle wry observations and humor that pokes fun at himself. (One of his titles is "Trying Too Hard to Write a Poem Sitting on the Beach.") Scattered throughout the poems are lists, song fragments, slogans, signs, menus, recipes, handwritten doodles—whatever pops into the poet's head. Whalen delights in the moment. Above all, there are voices: comic dialogues and monologues, the poet arguing with himself. He takes notes on reality, both outside and inside his mind.

LAWRENCE FERLINGHETTI

Lawrence Ferlinghetti (b. 1919) is one of the most popular American poets. He is also an important publisher and political activist. In 1953 he opened City Lights bookstore in San Francisco and began publishing the City Lights Pocket Poets Series with his own *Pictures of the Gone World* (1955). Soon after, Ferlinghetti published Allen Ginsberg's *Howl and other Poems,* which brought the press fame and notoriety. Ferlinghetti's own poems are lyrical, dramatic, and political, influenced by modern Latin American and French poets such as Pablo Neruda and Jacques Prevert. Among his other significant achievements are his translations and his work with jazz musicians. His most well-known book, *A Coney Island of the Mind* (1958), contains poems that were written specifically for jazz accompaniment.

Beat Generation

The original Beat generation consisted of Jack Kerouac, Allen Ginsberg, and a group of intellectual "outsiders" that included the writer William Burroughs, an important influence on Kerouac and Ginsberg who became famous for *Naked Lunch* and other novels. They were joined by Neal Cassady, a young adventurer from Denver, whom Kerouac immortalized as Dean Moriarty in his novel *On the Road.* In the 1950s the group included poets Gregory Corso, Peter Orlovsky, Diane di Prima, Amiri Baraka, and others. When *On the Road, Naked Lunch,* and Ginsberg's "Howl" put the Beat generation in the national spotlight, the media responded by creating the "beatnik," a distortion of the poets' lifestyle. The public was excited by the

*iconoclastic attacking the institutions and symbolic images of society and, in particular, religion

*hipster new and unconventional; cutting-edge

forbidden subject matter and language in Beat writing, and hostile critics misunderstood iconoclastic* Beat humor, hipster* language, and the new poetry's connection with modern jazz. But the poets ignored both the public and the critical establishment. They were busy responding to each other's work, starting small publishing ventures, and, through their readings in cafés and clubs in New York, San Francisco, and other cities, reviving poetry's great oral tradition.

JACK KEROUAC

It has been pointed out that Jack Kerouac's (1922–1969) novels contain some of the finest poetry in prose ever written. Robert Creeley praised Kerouac's "ability to translate immediate sensation into immediate actual language." Kerouac described his spontaneous approach to writing as "the discipline of pointing things out directly, purely, concretely, no abstractions or explanations, wham wham the true blue song of man." In both prose and poetry, Kerouac recorded the details of American life, seen and heard on the street or from the window of a passing car—people, their way of walking and talking, their little gestures, their hats. He wrote it down quickly, in small notebooks, making few editorial changes, keeping the original syntax, trying to capture the immediate experience. His theme was always America—his wanderings out West, the people he met along the way, and especially his childhood in Lowell, a Massachusetts mill town.

Mexico City Blues (1959) contains some of his best poetry. It may be read as one long poem, divided into "choruses." Sometimes an idea or image from one chorus carries over into the next. Kerouac also wrote many small, finely crafted poems, including what he called "Western haiku":

> In my medicine cabinet,
>   the winter fly
> has died of old age.

For the most part, he abandoned conventional meter and stanzas for "non stop ad libbing."

ALLEN GINSBERG

Allen Ginsberg (1926–1997) was one of the most highly honored poets of the twentieth century, and "Howl" is perhaps the most well-known post–World War II American poem. It still has the power to shock and thrill. The same could be said for "Kaddish," Ginsberg's great elegaic* poem about his mother. Widely traveled, translated into many languages, he helped popularize poetry as performance, brought Buddhist thought to public attention, and was one of the most politically engaged writers of his time. He was known for his generosity and was a constant inspiration to his fellow poets.

Ginsberg's most important influences were William Blake, Walt Whitman, and William Carlos Williams as well as his friend Kerouac's explorations in spontaneity and jazzlike improvisation. He took to heart Blake's instruction: "First thought is best thought in art." Whitman's exclamatory, all-embracing long lines were a major inspiration. Williams himself urged the young Ginsberg to write in conventional American speech. Later, Buddhist meditation became a crucial factor in Ginsberg's development. The long line is characteristic of his work. He tried to say as much as he could for as long as one breath lasted and then go on to the next line with the next breath. He wrote a number of short, quiet, lyrical poems in long lines ("A Strange New Cottage in Berkeley," "A Supermarket in California"), but his longer poems are his most memorable: catalogs of stunning images and word combinations, rising with high energy and passionate excitement, holding nothing back.

GREGORY CORSO

Gregory Corso (b. 1930), the class clown of the Beats, had only a sixth-grade education and grew up in orphanages and foster homes. He discovered literature and began writing poems while serving time in jail for theft. In 1950, after his release, he met Allen Ginsberg, who encouraged his poetry and brought him into the circle of Beat writers. He traveled to San Francisco, Mexico—where he wrote most of the poems in *Gasoline* (1958)—and Paris. His best-known collection, *The Happy Birthday of Death* (1960), includes his great comic poem, "Marriage," about a young man anticipating the joys and pitfalls of getting married, and "Bomb," a long poem in the shape of an atomic mushroom cloud. The poems bristle with surrealistic word groupings like "penguin dust," "pipe butter," and "fried shoes." The use of archaic language in some of his work reflects his love of Greek and Latin poetry. He is also attracted to the nineteenth-century English Romantics, especially Percy Bysshe Shelley.

*__elegiac__ mournful in a way that is often pensive or sweet

AMIRI BARAKA

Amiri Baraka (b. 1934) was the only African American included in *The New American Poetry* anthology. From the late 1950s through the mid-1960s, as LeRoi Jones, he was a central figure on the avant-garde poetry scene, writing poems, plays, and essays and editing little magazines. His first books, *Preface to a Twenty Volume Suicide Note* (1961) and *The Dead Lecturer* (1964), owe something to Pound and Williams as well as to the Beats (thus his inclusion in this section). His early poems are lyrical, realistic, and ironic, with touches of African American speech. In 1968 Jones changed his name to Amiri Baraka and became part of the Black Nationalist movement, though he later turned to Marxism.* His poetry gained in persuasive power, and the influence of jazz, there at the beginning, grew in scope. He remains among the most politically and socially committed of all writers.

*Marxism a type of socialism based on the ideas of Karl Marx (1818–1883)

DIANE DI PRIMA

Diane di Prima (b. 1934) is one of the few women belonging to the third generation of modernist poets. She became associated with the Beat movement in the late 1950s with the publication of her first book, *This Kind of Bird Flies Backwards* (1958). With Baraka she co-edited the important poetry newsletter *The Floating Bear* and was the cofounder of the New York Poets Theatre. In the 1960s di Prima wrote both political and lyrical poems, and some of her work began to show her increasing interest in other spiritual traditions, such as gnosticism* and alchemy.*

*gnosticism the belief that all matter is evil and that salvation requires spiritual knowledge, called *gnosis*

*alchemy a pseudo-science/philosophy that aims to transform ordinary metals into gold, cure disease, and prolong life

New York School

The poetry of what became known as the "New York school" of poets was the most experimental, witty, and irreverent in all postwar literature. John Ashbery, Kenneth Koch, and Frank O'Hara studied at Harvard in the late 1940s. Soon after, they moved to New York, where they were joined by James Schuyler, Barbara Guest, and others. The early 1950s was an exciting time to be in New York. The great abstract expressionist painters were at their peak, and there was the stimulation of modern music, theater, dance, film, and architecture wherever one turned. The poets became friendly with young painters, and they wrote articles and reviews for the art journals and collaborated with the artists on lithographs* and collages, as well as their various literary projects. Their poems were a dizzy mixture of daily life, high and low culture, abstraction, personal references, parody,* and jokes.

*lithograph a print made with a flat surface on which the blank area is ink-repellent
*parody humorous imitation intended to ridicule

JOHN ASHBERY

For years, John Ashbery (b. 1927) was an editor at *Art News* magazine in New York, but he also lived in France for extended periods. Ashbery is a great poet of the imagination. Typical of his early poems, "The Instruction Manual" is a daydream about escaping from a boring office job and going to Mexico. The language has a fairy-tale quality. Ashbery's poems often seem to be telling a story, though it is all a little vague and dreamlike. Nothing is decided or concluded. There are sudden shifts of tone and indirect references to many things and ideas that flit through the poet's mind. In his second book, *The Tennis Court Oath* (1962), poems turn into fragmented collages, with strange combinations of words and objects, fleeting glimpses of people, and snatches of their conversations. "The Skaters," written in Paris, is perhaps Ashbery's most significant work of the 1960s. It is a long poem in four parts, like a symphony, and seems to be about everything and nothing. One scene slides into the next one. Fantasy and reality overlap and dissolve. Ashbery's work of the 1950s and 1960s was not well received by the critics. It was not until the 1970s that he became recognized as one of America's leading poets.

FRANK O'HARA

Frank O'Hara (1926–1966) died in an accident at age forty. Only two books of his poems appeared in his lifetime, *Meditations in an Emergency* (1957) and *Lunch Poems* (1964). His work was later gathered and published as *The Collected Poems* (1971). O'Hara also wrote plays and art criticism. New York was the major setting of his work. His poems can be intensely private, filled with anxiety, even angry, yet full of humor, beauty, and dazzling language. "I am the least difficult of men. All I want is boundless love." He wrote quickly, often on the run, during his lunch hour at the Museum of Modern Art, where he was a curator. He would give away his only copies of poems to friends or stick them in dresser drawers, forgetting all about them. He has often been compared to the French poet Guillaume Apollinaire, whom he admired. Like Apollinaire, O'Hara included in his poems bits of conversation overheard on the street. He was also affected by the Russian poets Boris Pasternak and Vladimir Mayakovsky. He pays tribute to Mayakovsky in his poem "A True Account of Talking to the Sun at Fire Island." O'Hara's poems, like those of the other New York school poets, are memorable for their conversational ease and their detailing of daily life. O'Hara would also include the names of his friends and his favorite hangouts, without regard for the reader's ability to recognize them. His tongue-in-cheek essay "Personism" functions both as a parody of a manifesto* and a statement of his attitude about poetry and life: "You just go on your nerve."

*manifesto a written statement of the intentions or beliefs of a literary, artistic, or political movement

KENNETH KOCH

Kenneth Koch (b. 1925) is a narrative poet (one who tells stories) and a very funny one, but humor in poetry is not considered worthy of "serious" attention, so Koch's joyful, playful poems and plays are sometimes overlooked by the critics. "Fresh Air" is a funny attack on academic stuffiness. Koch's poems are often full of wonderful characters; "Fresh Air," for example, has a "Strangler" who goes around eliminating bad poets. Koch has said, "I don't think being comic keeps one from being serious. It keeps one from being solemn." His books *Ko; or, A Season on Earth* (1959) and *The Duplications* (1977) are comic epic poems written in the tradition of the Italian poet Lodovico Ariosto's *Orlando Furioso* and Lord Byron's *Don Juan*. Koch was influenced by Apollinaire and the French surrealists, as well as by Federico García Lorca, the great Spanish poet and dramatist. The language of fairy tales and nursery rhymes and a sense of childlike wonder and simplicity are important aspects of Koch's poetry. His trailblazing work teaching poetry to children is well known.

JAMES SCHUYLER

James Schuyler (1923–1991) once wrote, "Often a poem 'happens' to the writer in exactly the same way it 'happens' to someone who reads it." Schuyler had the ability to capture the feeling of being in a room alone, looking at an object and seeing it in its totality, and writing it down—almost like drawing it—in quiet, casual language. Like Robert Creeley, he makes a hard task look easy. Schuyler was a great poet of weather, of the shifting light in the sky over Long Island, New York, where he lived for many years. His poems are full of flowers and trees. He reveals the intimate connection of people to nature. He was a late bloomer, not publishing his first collection, *Freely Espousing,* until 1969. Whether he wrote "skinny" poems of short lines and skillful line breaks or long poems of long lines, he was always the master of what he called "the pure pleasure of / Simply looking."

Selected Bibliography

Anthologies

American Poetry Since 1950. Edited by Eliot Weinberger. New York: Marsilio Publishers, 1993.

An Anthology of New York Poets. Edited by Ron Padgett and David Shapiro. New York: Random House, 1970.

From the Other Side of the Century: A New American Poetry, 1960–1990. Edited by Douglas Messerli. Los Angeles: Sun and Moon Press, 1994.

The New American Poetry, 1945–1960. Edited by Donald M. Allen. New York: Grove Press, 1960.

Postmodern American Poetry. Edited by Paul Hoover. New York: Norton, 1994.

John Ashbery

Some Trees (1956).

The Tennis Court Oath (1962).

Rivers and Mountains (1966).

Amiri Baraka (LeRoi Jones)

Preface to a Twenty Volume Suicide Note (1961).

The Dead Lecturer (1964).

Transbluesency: The Selected Poems of Amiri Baraka/ LeRoi Jones (1961–1995). Edited by Paul Vangelisti. New York: Marsilio, 1995.

Paul Blackburn

The Selected Poems of Paul Blackburn. Edited by Edith Jarolim. New York: Persea, 1989.

Gregory Corso

> *Gasoline* (1958).
>
> *The Happy Birthday of Death* (1960).

Robert Creeley

> *Selected Poems* (1991).

Diane di Prima

> *This Kind of Bird Flies Backwards* (1958).
>
> *Selected Poems* (1975).

Edward Dorn

> *Collected Poems, 1956–1974* (1975).
>
> *Gunslinger* (1972).

Robert Duncan

> *The Opening of the Field* (1960).
>
> *Roots and Branches* (1964).
>
> *Bending the Bow* (1968).

Larry Eigner

> *On My Eyes* (1960).
>
> *Selected Poems.* Edited by Samuel Charters and Andrea Wyatt. Berkeley: Oyez, 1972.

Lawrence Ferlinghetti

> *Pictures of the Gone World* (1955).
>
> *A Coney Island of the Mind* (1958).

Allen Ginsberg

> *Howl and Other Poems* (1956).
>
> *Kaddish and Other Poems* (1961).
>
> *Selected Poems, 1947–1995* (1996).

Jack Kerouac

> *Mexico City Blues* (1959).
>
> *Scattered Poems* (1971).

Old Angel Midnight (1960).

Book of Blues (1995).

Kenneth Koch

Ko; or, A Season on Earth (1959).

The Duplications (1977).

Selected Poems, 1950–1982 (1985).

Denise Levertov

Collected Earlier Poems, 1940–1960 (1979).

Poems, 1960–1967 (1983).

Michael McClure

Ghost Tantras (1964).

Selected Poems (1986).

Frank O'Hara

Meditations in an Emergency (1957).

Lunch Poems (1964).

The Collected Poems of Frank O'Hara. Edited by Donald Allen. New York: Knopf, 1971.

The Selected Poems of Frank O'Hara. Edited by Donald Allen. New York: Vintage, 1974.

Charles Olson

The Maximus Poems (1960)

Selected Poems. Edited by Robert Creeley. Berkeley: University of California Press, 1993.

James Schuyler

Freely Espousing (1969).

Selected Poems (1988).

Gary Snyder

Riprap (1959).

Myths and Texts (1960).

No Nature: New and Selected Poems (1992).

Mountains and Rivers Without End (1996).

Jack Spicer

The Collected Books of Jack Spicer. Edited by Robin Blaser. Los Angeles: Black Sparrow, 1975.

Philip Whalen

On Bear's Head (1964).

John Wieners

The Hotel Wentley Poems (1958).

Selected Poems, 1958–1984. Edited by Raymond Foye. Santa Rosa, Calif.: Black Sparrow, 1986.

Cultural Affairs in Boston: Poetry and Prose, 1956–1985. Edited by Raymond Foye. Santa Rosa, Calif.: Black Sparrow, 1988.

NATIVE AMERICAN POETRY

by Joseph Bruchac

> ### Where Songs Come From
>
> Songs are born in that stillness
> When everyone tries
> to think of nothing but beautiful things.
> Then they take shape
> in the minds of people
> and rise up like bubbles
> from deep in the sea,
> bubbles seeking the air
> so that they can burst.
> That is how poems are made.

L ong before the arrival of European colonizers, poetry was present in America. In all of the more than four hundred tribal nations of North America, oral poetry was, in fact, a central part of the culture. There were orations* and epics,* poems for healing or hunting, poems to give a person courage or lull a child to sleep. They were oral poems because most, but not all, of the indigenous cultures of this continent had no form of writing. These song poems were memorized and spoken, sung, or chanted; sometimes people would dance to them. Often they were protected by a form of ownership. If a particular poem belonged to an individual or a certain society within a nation, no one was allowed to sing or chant that poem without either permission or initiation.*

Characteristics of Native American Poetry

Powerful imagery drawn from nature was an integral part of many of these song poems. Sometimes a single individual

This essay concerns only Native poetry of the present-day United States. In Mexico and South America, writing systems were invented well over a thousand years ago. Stories, poems, histories, plays, and biographies were written on paper or carved onto flat stones, called "stelae." Most of the manuscripts were burned by Spanish priests, who thought them the work of the devil. Scholars are still learning to read what was carved onto the Mayan and Aztec stelae.

*__oration__ a formal speech

*__epic__ a long poem that tells the story of a hero's deeds

*__initiation__ instruction; admission to a group

would sing or chant a poem; sometimes poems were performed by large groups of people, usually to the accompaniment of such percussion instruments as drums, rhythm sticks, or rattles. These were not rhymed poems—rhymed poetry is an invention of western European cultures. But these song poems were carefully structured. Because they were sung or chanted, they employed the rhythms of Native American music. Repetition of words and phrases was a common device. Such structures made it easy for people to remember the poems and pass them on from person to person and from generation to generation.

Poetry had power. A Mandan buffalo song could persuade the great herds to come within the reach of human hunters. A Cherokee sacred formula could help defeat an enemy; an Abenaki love song might win another's heart. A Seneca song to the "Little People" would encourage those powerful supernatural beings to continue to care for the wild strawberries. Long ago, all Native Americans believed in the power of poetry and used it.

Although certain people in every community were known as better composers than others—the Sioux chief Sitting Bull was famed as a song-maker—poems could be made by anyone. Among many Native nations, each person had a personal death song to inspire him or her when in danger or provide courage when facing death. Human life is brief, such songs remind us, but the world around us endures. By facing our fears and avoiding self-pity, we may find courage.

Here is a translation of one such Lakota song:

> The old men say
> nothing lasts forever
> except Earth and Sky.
> You have spoken truly,
> You are right.

> *Long ago, all Native Americans believed in the power of poetry and used it.*

Among the Inuit people of Alaska, northern Canada, and Greenland, song and breath, poetry, and the very act of inhaling and exhaling were one and the same. In Native cultures, if you are alive, you are connected to breath—and to song.

Storytelling was also central to every nation. Everyone listened to stories. Everyone told them, too, although elders tended to know the most and were sought out as storytellers.

Such tricksters* and culture heroes as Gluskabe or Old Man Coyote or Raven or Iktome the Spider were as well known to Native peoples as famous movie stars or sports heroes are to us today.

> *trickster a character in folktales and legends who plays tricks

Although each of the four hundred original tribal nations was unique, they shared certain beliefs about the world, some of them central to understanding Native American poetry. Native Americans saw human beings as part of the natural world, which they needed to acknowledge and respect. Animals, plants, and even stones were thought to be as alive and aware as human beings and could be addressed as if speaking to other people. The Earth, sometimes described as "Our Mother," was considered sacred. Rather than owning land individually, Native Americans cared for it communally because it was meant to sustain the generations to come.

Day and night, the phases of the moon and change of seasons, and the growth of plants all had recurring cycles. The circle was a sacred concept, and human ceremonies made use of it. The four directions, named to correspond to the natural world itself, were another part of that circle. Even today among the Abenaki people, east is Dawn Land, south is Summer Land, west is Sunset Land, and north is Winter Land. Although three was the primary magic number in European religions and folklore, four, along with seven, held that place in most Native American cultures. The number seven included the four directions plus "above" (sky), "below" (earth), and the center of the circle, where we stand. Time was also circular, not linear. The human being did not leave the past behind but returned to it again and again in following the cycles of nature and human life.

The world was filled with spiritual power that was available to human beings through prayer and thanksgiving. The Creator was a "Great Mystery," beyond human understanding yet responsive to the needs of those humans who were humble and respectful. Finally, balance and cooperation were important and sacred. Earth and sky balance each other and work together to bring new life when rain falls to make plants grow. In a similar fashion, the roles of women and men were of equal importance. Mutual respect and cooperation were to be expected. A lack of balance was thought to lead to illness and bad fortune for the individual and disaster in the natural world. All of these beliefs remain a part of the modern Native American worldview.

A History of Native American Poetry

Native American poetry today may be seen as a contemporary example of those old ideas of balance and cooperation. Western languages and poetic forms have been blended by Native poets with the heritage of the oral tradion and traditional Native understandings about the world. This blending has a long history. One of the first things the missionaries did in North America was to teach Native people how to read and write in such languages as English, French, Spanish, and even Latin. A few Native Americans became accomplished scholars and writers three centuries ago. Many of the white scholars who translated Native American oral poetry in the nineteenth century did so with the cooperation of American Indians who spoke fluent English. American Indian poets, especially the Cherokee, were being published more than a century ago.

Most Native American poetry originally composed in English, however, comes from the last four decades of the twentieth century. In the early part of the century, most American Indians were educated at government boarding schools—paramilitary institutions where "useful" trades, not the language arts, were emphasized. This changed in the 1950s and 1960s, when Indian schools began to encourage creative writing and many future Indian poets enrolled in non-Indian schools.

The work of the first Native American poets who began to publish in the 1960s and 1970s was warmly embraced by Native Americans themselves, perhaps because that poetry mirrored the realities of contemporary Indian life. Those writers included Simon Ortiz (Acoma Pueblo), Peter Blue Cloud (Mohawk), Mary TallMountain (Athabascan) Ray Young Bear (Mesquakie), Joy Harjo (Muskogee Creek), Carter Revard (Osage), Roberta Hill Whiteman (Oneida), James Welch (Blackfeet), Luci Tapahonso (Navajo), Leslie Marmon Silko (Laguna Pueblo), N. Scott Momaday (Kiowa), Maurice Kenny (Mohawk), Wendy Rose (Hopi/Miwok), Duane Niatum (Klallam), Linda Hogan (Chickasaw), Paula Gunn Allen (Laguna Pueblo), and Lance Henson (Cheyenne).

Natives and non-Natives alike were attracted to these poems, which were usually characterized by pride in one's heritage; an ironic, sometimes hilarious vision of what it means to be an Indian in twentieth-century America; a personal awareness of the ways Native Americans suffered over the past five centuries from racism and genocide; the inclusion of trickster heroes from oral tradition; the use of charged language that drew strength from natural imagery in the same way that Indian oratory does; and a tendency toward narrative. More often than not, Native American poems told stories that Native people, whether highly educated or not, could understand.

Yet this first major generation of Native poets was a more scholarly group than many realized. Most of them had completed not only college but also graduate studies. All of them were well read in British and American poetry, aware of poetic form and history, and sometimes more fluent in English than in the tribal languages of their ancestors. In fact, some of the better-known Native American writers were raised in cities far from tribal lands.

Reclaiming an Indian identity that has been denied, either in part or entirely, by their parents is a common issue for Native writers. In reservation communities today, life is often very different from that of the past. Alcoholism and drug abuse, broken families, poverty, unemployment, and America's highest suicide rate among young people can be found on Indian reservations. The poetry of the best contemporary Native writers faces those realities. Strong social or political content was common in the work of the first major generation of Native poets, but, if anything, it is even more evident in the writing of the younger Native American writers who are now emerging.

> *Reclaiming an Indian identity that has been denied. . . by their parents is a common issue for Native writers.*

Some Contemporary Poets

Sherman Alexie (Spokane / Coeur D'Alene), born in 1966, is one of the most vital of those younger poets. His first volume of poetry, *The Business of Fancydancing*, received great praise for such lines as these from his poem "Powwow":

> of course, we all bring ourselves back
> to beauty, twenty dollar bills, bootleg
> everything, a traditional dancer
> from Montana who doesn't speak English
>
> did you ever get the feeling
> when speaking to a white American
> that you need closed captions?

The power of his writing and his Native American humor and sometimes gritty images of present-day Indian life are also evident in his prose works and his screenplay, *Smoke Signals.*

The simplicity of the language in many contemporary American Indian poems is deceptive. Lance Henson was born in Calumet, Oklahoma, in 1944 and raised by his Cheyenne grandparents. An ex-Marine and a member of the Cheyenne Dog Soldier Warrior Society and the Native American Church, he also holds a master's degree in creative writing from the University of Tulsa. Like the haiku* poets of Japan whom he has studied, he attempts more in a few lines than many poets accomplish in a page. The brevity of the songs of such Plains nations as the Cheyenne and Lakota also define his style. In the following poem, "winter back" (from *A Cheyenne Sketchbook*), he reflects the Native culture's connection to the natural world, the sacred circle, the tragedies of the past, the power of breath, and respect for elders. Henson, like a number of other Native poets, avoids punctuation or capitalization, since he believes such devices might elevate or separate the poet's voice from the natural flow of the poem:

> the old rest among forest grey
>
> somewhere
> grandmother you whisper
> a name that was never born
>
> circles of mist gather a
> moment against this breath
> on the window
> then disappear

The storytelling voice and narrative traditions are perhaps most evident in the work of Simon J. Ortiz, who comes from the Pueblo nations of the Southwest, where healing chants and ritual songs are often of great duration. Born in 1941 and raised in the Acoma Pueblo community near Albuquerque, New Mexico, Ortiz often seems to identify in his poems with Coyote, the archetypal* trickster. A master's degree graduate of the creative writing program at the University of Iowa, he was a celebrated long-distance runner in his school days. Here is a brief excerpt from his poem "Telling About Coyote" (in *Woven Stone*), in which Coyote performs such mischief as losing his skin gambling and turning the pure white feathers of the Crow black.

> ". . . you know, Coyote
> is in the origin and all the way
> through . . . he's the cause
> of the trouble, the hard times
> that things have . . ."

> "Yet, he came so close
> to having it easy.
>   But he said,
> "Things are just too easy . . ."
> Of course he was mainly bragging,
> shooting his mouth.
> The existential* Man.
> Dostoevsky* Coyote . . .

The rhythms of everyday speech and storytelling are used to create a relaxed tone. But even in this brief excerpt from a poem of 120 lines, a lot is happening. These lines begin a rhythmic structure and pattern of repetition that are followed in succeeding sections. The poet strongly reinforces the Native idea of balance by showing us how Coyote disrupts things with his meddling and lack of humility, hinting that we humans and Coyote are much the same. Ortiz also brings in existentialism and Russian literature in those last two lines, a playful blending of his college education with his traditional heritage.

Prose, poetry, and song often blend in contemporary Native writing. Joy Harjo, born in Tulsa, Oklahoma, in 1951, has written screenplays and, over the past decade, gained a reputation as a musician with her jazz fusion* group, Poetic Justice. When she is not playing the saxophone, she sings or chants many of her poems. "She Had Some Horses" (one of her best-known poems, from her collection of the same name), deals with self-assertion, Native pride, fighting back against abuse, and regaining the respect that women have always deserved. Here are a few lines:

> She had horses who waltzed nightly on the moon.
> She had horses who were much too shy, and kept quiet
> in stalls of their own making.

*existential referring to a twentieth-century philosophy that analyzes the place of the individual and individual choice in the world

*Dostoevsky, Feodor (1821–1881), Russian novelist, precursor of existentialism

*jazz fusion musical form that combines elements of jazz and rock

She had some horses.
She had horses who liked Creek Stomp Dance songs.
She had horses who cried in their beer.
She had horses who spit at male queens who made
them afraid of themselves.
She had horses who said they weren't afraid.
She had horses who lied.

The repetition of "She had horses" becomes a magical chant, like the old songs that invoked the power to make things happen. The horse was introduced to America by Europeans four centuries ago. A whole new way of life was built around the horse by the Plains Indians, who loved the animal and identified with it. That relationship is the perfect symbol of Native adaptation to European influences. For Harjo, the horse also symbolizes contemporary Indians and the confusion of modern life.

Being caught between the two worlds of white and Indian and being misunderstood or stereotyped is a common experience for Native people and a recurring theme in Native poetry. Mary TallMountain was born in Alaska in 1921 but taken from her Athabascan family at an early age after her mother became ill. Much of her adult life was spent in California, where she worked as a legal secretary. Her poem "Indian Blood" (from *The Light on the Tent Wall*) describes the painful memory of being laughed at by non-Native children when she wore traditional clothing to school. Here are the first three stanzas:

On the stage I stumbled,
my fur boot caught
on a slivered board.
Rustle of stealthy giggles.

Beendaaga' made of velvet
crusted with crystal beads
hung from brilliant tassels of wool,
wet with my sweat.

Children's faces stared
I felt their flowing force.
Did I crouch like *goh*
in the curious quiet?

> **Being caught between the two worlds of white and Indian and being misunderstood or stereotyped is a common experience for Native people and a recurring theme in Native poetry.**

The use of words in a Native language (*beendaaga'* are gloves, and *goh* means rabbit) is a device often used by Native writers as a way of emphasizing the existence of their own culture and a different viewpoint. Out of place in clothing that is necessary for survival in the Arctic but unsuitable and quaint on a school stage, the narrator asks us to identify with the experience of being an outsider and to learn from it.

One of the most powerful truths about contemporary Native American poetry is that it exists at all in the face of generations of intolerance and concerted attempts to eradicate Native culture. But there is more than mere survival to Native American poetry. It is a poetry of deep and complicated roots and of great variety, of intelligence and craft, of celebration and deep emotion. It neither romanticizes nor asks for pity. It is a poetry of purpose, a poetry that can celebrate tradition and still engage in honest reflection. It eloquently expresses philosophies that are holistic and potentially healing to a world that has forgotten the center of the spirit. The best Native poets of contemporary America remember. They have faced the fire and survived.

Selected Bibliography

WORKS BY POETS DISCUSSED IN THIS ESSAY

Alexie, Sherman. *The Business of Fancydancing: Stories and Poems.* Brooklyn, N.Y.: Hanging Loose Press, 1992.

Alexie, Sherman. *First Indian on the Moon.* Brooklyn, N.Y.: Hanging Loose Press, 1993.

Harjo, Joy. *She Had Some Horses.* New York: Thunder's Mouth Press, 1983.

Henson, Lance. *A Cheyenne Sketchbook, Selected Poems 1970–1991.* Greenfield Center, N.Y.: Greenfield Review Press, 1992.

Ortiz, Simon J. *Woven Stone.* Tucson: University of Arizona Press, 1992.

TallMountain, Mary. *The Light on the Tent Wall.* Los Angeles: American Indian Studies Center, 1990.

AVAILABLE COLLECTIONS

Bruchak, Joseph, ed. *Songs from This Earth on Turtle's Back*. Greenfield Center, N.Y.: Greenfield Review Press, 1983.

Francis, Lee, and James Bruchak, eds. *Reclaiming the Vision*. Greenfield Center, N.Y.: Greenfield Review Press, 1994.

GENERAL DISCUSSIONS

Bruchac, Joseph. *Survival This Way: Interviews with American Indian Poets*. Tucson, Ariz.: Sun Tracks and University of Arizona Press, 1987.

Rasmussen, Knud. *The Intellectual Culture of the Iguluk Eskimos*. Providence, R.I.: AMS Press, 1924.

HARLEM RENAISSANCE

by Lorenzo Thomas

The Harlem Renaissance—also known as the New Negro Renaissance—was one of the most interesting and influential artistic movements in the history of American literature. Critics generally date the movement as flourishing between publication of Jean Toomer's *Cane* (1923) and Zora Neale Hurston's *Their Eyes Were Watching God* (1937), a period during which the authentic expression of African American artists became available to a large public for the first time.

African American Cultural Heritage and Social Justice

Racial relations in the United States at this time were not good. In the South, African Americans were prevented from voting, and throughout the country their social and economic opportunities were severely limited by policies of segregation and racial discrimination. In August 1925 more than forty thousand white-robed members of the Ku Klux Klan, the white supremacist organization, paraded defiantly down Pennsylvania Avenue in Washington, D.C.

Charles S. Johnson called the Harlem Renaissance a "sudden and altogether phenomenal outburst of emotional expression, unmatched by any comparable period in American or Negro American history" (quoted in Lewis, ed., p. 207). This outburst came in the form of art, music, drama, and poetry; its purpose—carefully orchestrated by such intellectual leaders as W. E. B. Du Bois, Alain Locke, and Johnson himself—was to change the role that African Americans played in the nation's culture and everyday life. As early as 1903, Du Bois had declared that the Negro spirituals* represented America's only truly original contribution to world art and suggested that the epic experiences that had created those songs might also find expression in other art forms. Other writers suggested that in order to gain respect from other races, it would be necessary for African Americans to produce sophisticated art that matched the achievement of the spirituals.

*spiritual African American sacred song

Just as the educator Booker T. Washington felt that making an economic contribution to the nation would win respect for black people, the poet James Weldon Johnson pointed out that no race that produced great art or literature could be viewed in the viciously negative terms that proslavery propaganda and stereotyping had applied to African people in the Americas. Howard University philosophy professor Alain Locke—who had been the first black person to attend Oxford University as a Rhodes scholar—not only popularized similar ideas about art, he also made it his business to find and promote young artists who had the talent and ambition to meet that challenge. Du Bois, as editor of *Crisis* (the magazine of the National Association for the Advancement of Colored People), and Charles S. Johnson, as editor of *Opportunity: Journal of Negro Life* (put out by the National Urban League), provided the vehicles for bringing these artists and their ideas to the public. *Crisis* enjoyed a circulation of over one hundred thousand and was read by many more people than that.

Harlem: A Flourishing Urban Center

In many ways the energy of the Harlem Renaissance was youthful energy. Many of the artists and writers were members of the first generation of the twentieth century, the most adventurous representatives of the college-educated youth, a promising socially conscious intellectual elite that Du Bois called "the Talented Tenth." And while it actually was a nationwide movement that had an impact on black communities everywhere—not to mention American culture in general—part of its character derived from its central location in Harlem, a newly settled and rapidly growing district of a city that not much earlier had become the cultural capital of the United States. Furthermore, unlike the South, New York City seemed to offer African Americans previously undreamed-of opportunity and encouraged an optimistic outlook. Owing to massive migration from the South, New York had gained a large black population by the end of World War I, and these new residents brought with them the effervescent* innovation called jazz—the secular music derived from the old spirituals. Partly because of the attention directed by the music critic Carl Van Vechten and other members of the artistic avant-garde,* Harlem gained a reputation as a center of cultural activity rivaling the city's Greenwich Village.

*effervescent bubbling; lively
*avant-garde advanced or cutting-edge; experimental; normally applies to the arts

Although the young artists and writers of the Harlem Renaissance did not have a uniform aesthetic or political philosophy, they did share the "New Negro" sensibility that had emerged after the Spanish-American War in 1898—a determination that the twentieth century would not be an era of racial oppression and that any attempt to make it so would be met by an appropriately militant resistance. A banquet sponsored by the Urban League on 24 March 1924 brought together the young Harlem writers and members of New York's literary and academic establishment. Speeches by Van Vechten, James Weldon Johnson, and others declared the creative ferment to be an official cultural movement. It was a spectacular debut, as well as a carefully staged public relations event.

The Harlem Renaissance did produce a remarkable amount of excellent poetry in both traditional and innovative forms, and launched the careers of several writers who had a lasting influence on American literature. An introductory reading of Harlem Renaissance poetry should include such major figures as Claude McKay, James Weldon Johnson, Countee Cullen, and Langston Hughes. Interested students of contemporary poetry should not, however, overlook the contributions of other writers, among them, Arna Bontemps, Georgia Douglas Johnson, and Frank Horne.

The Movement's Shapers: Claude McKay and Georgia Douglas Johnson

Born in rural Jamaica, in the West Indies, to a highly literate family, Claude McKay (1889–1948) had worked as a policeman and had already published a book of dialect poems based on that experience when he immigrated to the United States in 1912. After attending Tuskegee Institute and Kansas State College, he settled in New York and became involved with the politically radical press and the literary avant-garde. A socialist and early supporter of the Soviet socialist experiment, McKay traveled for extensive periods of time in Europe. Although he was actually out of the country for most of the Harlem Renaissance period, McKay's voice was one of the movement's most dominating and influential. His best and most popular work—poems that readers memorized and recited to their friends—are bluntly political statements, such as "The White House" and his eloquent "If We Must Die," a

*sonnet a fourteen-line poem usually composed in iambic pentameter (each line has five feet, each foot consisting of an unstressed syllable followed by a stressed syllable).

sonnet* written in 1919 to protest lynching and urban mob violence against blacks.

In "The Negro's Friend," McKay bitterly assails the covert hypocrisy and political cowardice of well-intentioned but thoughtless white liberals who mistake "tokenism" for progress:

> Must fifteen million blacks be gratified,
> That one of them can enter as a guest
> A fine white house—the rest of them denied[?]

McKay's poems, written in traditional meter and rhyme, are uncompromisingly clear in their political message. In his sonnet "St. Isaac's Church, Petrograd," for example, McKay reports his sense of awe as the cathedral's "soaring arches lift me up on high." It is not religious fervor that inspires this feeling, however, but the evident skill of the workers who built the magnificent edifice, leaving behind for our appreciation and ennoblement "the sacred sight / Of man's Divinity alive in stone."

*doyenne a woman experienced or knowledgeable in some field of endeavor who gives encouragement or guidance to others (feminine form of French *doyen*, dean)

For most readers, Georgia Douglas Johnson (1886–1966) represented an extreme contrast to McKay, yet she also exerted an important shaping influence on the Harlem Renaissance movement. A classically trained musician married to an established government official, she was, according to all accounts, the literary doyenne* of black society in Washington, D.C. It might almost be said that the New Negro Renaissance was launched in her living room, since her Saturday evening literary salon brought together such figures as Alain Locke, Jean Toomer, and Jessie Fauset for readings and discussion. Her collection of poems *The Heart of a Woman* (1918) made her the most well-known African American woman writer since the abolitionist poet and novelist Frances E. W. Harper (1825–1911). Johnson's work was exquisitely crafted and racially specific, but it also followed the sentimental conventions of the late nineteenth century. Nevertheless, a lyrical* poem such as "I Want to Die While You Love Me" remains as beautiful and powerful today as the day it was written.

*lyrical having a musical quality

Countee Cullen: The Poetry of Dislocation

Countee Cullen (1903–1946), cared for by his grandmother until he was adopted by the Reverend and Mrs. Frederick A.

Cullen at age fourteen, was a brilliant student, editor of his high school literary magazine, and a contributor of poems to national publications as early as his freshman year at New York University. *Color,* his first book of poems, was published by Harper and Brothers in 1925 while he was studying for his master's degree at Harvard University. The book's critical and commercial success—with sales comparable to those of the enormously popular poet Edna St. Vincent Millay—led to prestigious magazine publications, additional book contracts, and years of lucrative speaking tours.

Personable and precocious, Cullen was something of a celebrity. His marriage in 1928 to W. E. B. Du Bois's daughter, Yolande, was a major social event, and their spectacular divorce a year later also delighted celebrity-watchers. He was married for a second time, much more happily, in 1940. Cullen's literary activities included writing a column for *Opportunity* (1926–1928), editing *Caroling Dusk: An Anthology of Verse by Negro Poets* (1927), and publishing a novel, *One Way to Heaven* (1932), but it is as a poet that he achieved fame and will be remembered.

Cullen's beautiful and important poem "Heritage," collected in *Color,* presents several themes that would be addressed by most artists of the Harlem Renaissance. Cullen's focus is both introspective and politically relevant:

> One three centuries removed
> From the scenes his fathers loved,
> Spicy grove, cinnamon tree,
> What is Africa to me?

On one level, the poem documents the African American people's historical and psychological dislocation resulting from slavery, but the Africa that Cullen invokes is a picturesque continent out of the pages of *National Geographic,* a sort of Eden, not the land that was being fought over militarily and ideologically by European colonial powers and nationalistic African intellectuals. "Heritage," in fact, is a poem about self-esteem, identity, and religious conviction. If the mythical Africa of his ancestors is a pagan paradise, the contemporary America the speaker inhabits is a society distorted by racism and a hypocritical version of Christianity that he finds difficult to accept. Even admitting that he has religious doubts, however, causes feelings of guilt. This major poem is a brilliant exploration of personal dislocation that nevertheless sounds a note of defiant resistance, voicing the poet's resolve to rediscover or create an authentic black identity. Written in the same metrical pattern found in Edgar Allan Poe's "The Raven," Cullen's poem effectively communicates a profound sense of emotional crisis that no reader is likely to forget.

A more explicit treatment of religious belief in conflict with racism is found in Cullen's poem "The Black Christ," the title poem of a collection published in 1929, which uses the Crucifixion to describe the lynching of an innocent young black man. Cullen's well-known poem "Incident" also depicts how a simple racial slur undermines a young child's self-esteem, while his sonnet "From the Dark Tower" (collected in *Copper Sun*, 1927) quietly pleads for respect. "We were not made eternally to weep," he writes. "The night whose sable* breast relieves the stark, / White stars is no less lovely being dark."

*sable black

Some readers might have regarded Cullen's blending of traditional English stanza* forms and contemporary social comment as unusual. As a poet, Cullen defined himself as "a rank conservative, loving the measured line and the skillful rhyme," but he did not feel that any poetic form should dictate his choice of subject matter. Cullen defined poetry as "a lofty thought beautifully expressed," something that "warmly stirs the emotions, which awakens a responsive chord in the human heart." A poet holding such views clearly had a great deal of confidence in poetry's power to help educate readers about racial issues.

*stanza a group of lines in a poem

Until his untimely death in 1946, Cullen continued to publish poems. He also taught French and creative writing at New York's Frederick Douglass Junior High School, where the future novelist and essayist James Baldwin was among his students.

The Blues Influence: Langston Hughes

Cullen's early fame was quickly followed by the success of Langston Hughes (1902–1967), a poet who was his opposite in many ways. "The Negro Speaks of Rivers," a poem published in 1921 in *Crisis,* bespoke the eighteen-year-old Hughes's proudly Afrocentric perspective. It was reprinted in his first book, *The Weary Blues* (1926), which announced his intention to speak poetically in the language of the common people. Born in Joplin, Missouri, Hughes grew up in Lawrence, Kansas and in Cleveland, Ohio, where quite early he demonstrated his gift for writing. He would, in time, become a widely published journalist, novelist, playwright, and one of the most beloved poets in the United States. Eventually the most popular and prolific* of all Harlem Renaissance writers, Hughes was an inventive experimentalist in both form and content. His poems were most often composed in a free verse style that includes irregular rhyme schemes and attempts to recapture the rhythms of African American speech. Hughes also wrote poems in the three-line stanza adopted from the lyrics of blues songs.

> **prolific** producing many works; fertile; productive

His ability to present social criticism within the authentic idiom of the folk blues is indicated in the poem "Po' Boy Blues" (collected in *The Weary Blues*), which begins

> When I was home de
> Sunshine seemed like gold.
> When I was home de
> Sunshine seemed like gold.
> Since I come up North de
> Whole damn world's turned cold.

That the rest of the poem addresses bad luck in love does not make the opening commentary irrelevant. In fact, the sudden change from what the reader expects to hear suggests that the speaker of the poem would rather talk about an irretrievable romance than face what really troubles him—overwhelming misfortunes connected with life in the city, real problems that he is powerless to do anything about.

Hughes was a master at presenting vivid sketches of everyday African American life in all its moods, and he was equally adept in crafting protest poems that could be either strident or subtle. In a sense, Hughes was the perfect embodiment of Alain Locke's belief that if the arts presented a complete and realistic, unstereotyped depiction of African Americans, the result could only be to defuse the hostility they faced not only in the South but throughout the country. Hughes eloquently expressed this hope in his poem "I, Too" (collected in *The Weary Blues*):

> They'll see how beautiful I am
> And be ashamed—
>
> I, too, am America.

In a career that spanned four decades and brought him international renown, Hughes never tired of spreading that message.

The Rhythm of Speech: James Weldon Johnson, Sterling Brown, and Frank Horne

James Weldon Johnson (1871–1938), best known for his masterpiece *God's Trombones: Seven Sermons in Verse* (1927), was also interested in using the African American vernacular as a medium for literary art. In such poems as "The Creation," Johnson successfully combined the regional dialect of the old-time Southern preacher with a modernist free verse style that anticipated the "breath units"* explored by avant-garde American poets in the 1960s.

Howard University professor Sterling A. Brown (1901–1989) pursued a similar poetic project. A folklorist as well as a literary critic, Brown adapted forms from traditional ballads, the blues, and African American folktales to produce vibrant poems first collected in his volume *Southern Road* (1932). During his lifetime Brown's poetry was overshadowed by his scholarly writings and only recently have critics begun to assess the full measure of his achievement. Brown's most delightful poems are those that recount the adventures of a character named Slim Greer, a traveling man and gifted conversationalist "With always a new lie / On the fire" ("Slim Greer").

A member of Brooklyn's black upper-middle class, Frank Horne (1899–1974)—the popular singer Lena Horne's uncle—was trained as an optometrist but became a college administrator and an adventuresome poet. His work, written in an avant-garde free verse style, includes the series "Letters Found near a Suicide" (in *Haverstraw,* 1963), poems full of passion, regret, and sensuous imagery. Some of these poems explore the ultimately self-defeating satisfaction of revenge:

> You pricked the iridescent* bubble
> Of my dreams
> And so to make
> Your conquest more sweet
> I tell you now
> That I hated you
>
> (section subtitled "To Jean")

breath units a style of poetry practiced by Charles Olson and others in which each line represents a complete utterance and the end of each printed line functions as punctuation, indicating that a breath should be taken

iridescent shining with colors like a rainbow

Interestingly, the elegiac* tone of these poems also allows Horne to celebrate the carefree days of adolescence and to recall the camaraderie shared with such friends as Llewellyn Johnston and football or track-team buddies. In their unadorned directness, they have the tone of valedictory sadness marking the beginning of adulthood, a quality that makes them continue to appeal to new readers.

*elegiac mournful in a way that is often pensive or sweet

Poems of Protest and Pride: Arna Bontemps, Gwendolyn Bennett, and Helene Johnson

Arna Bontemps (1902–1973), born in Louisiana and raised in Los Angeles, California, was a talented poet and fiction writer who later became head librarian at Fisk University in Nashville, Tennessee, and collaborated with Langston Hughes on such projects as the anthology *The Poetry of the Negro: 1746–1964* (1965) and *The Book of Negro Folklore* (1951). Unlike Hughes's work, Bontemps's poems demonstrate skill with traditional rhyme and meter as well as an inclination toward conventional poetic subjects, such as youth, love, and biblical themes. One of his best-known lyrics, written when he was twenty-two years old, "A Black Man Talks of Reaping," combines racial protest and a tone that recalls Old Testament stories:

> for my reaping only what the hand
> can hold at once is all that I can show.
>
> Yet what I sowed and what the orchard yields
> my brother's sons are gathering stalk and root;
> small wonder then my children glean in fields
> they have not sown, and feed on bitter fruit.

As with Countee Cullen, racial protest in Bontemps's work is never strident and never disrupts the elegance of his carefully controlled poetic diction.

A graduate of Pratt Institute, Gwendolyn Bennett (1902–1981) was active both as a poet and as a visual artist. Although she never published a book-length collection, her poems frequently appeared in such magazines as *Opportunity* and *Crisis,* and she taught art at Howard University, the Harlem Community Art Center, and elsewhere. Brilliantly managing both free verse and traditional stanza forms, Bennett produced bright and elevating poems. In "To a Dark Girl," she sings:

> Oh, little brown girl, born for sorrow's mate,
> Keep all you have of queenliness,
> Forgetting that you once were slave,
> And let your full lips laugh at Fate!

No less skilled than Bennett, Helene Johnson (1907–1995) offered a different perspective. Instead of a defiant racial pride, her poems contrast the repressed and regimented mainstream American society and a carefree and colorful hedonism* associated with Africa. "Sonnet to a Negro in Harlem," for example, addresses a person (whom other writers might have thought oppressed) from Johnson's unique (but possibly naive) point of view:

> you are incompetent
> To imitate those whom you so despise—
> Your shoulders towering high above the throng,
> Your head thrown back in rich, barbaric song,
> Palm trees and mangoes stretched before your eyes.
> Let others toil and sweat for labor's sake
> And wring from grasping hands their meed* of gold

A Vibrant Diversity

Helene Johnson's street singer is, to say the least, a far cry from the cynically percipient* blues singers who inhabit the poems of Langston Hughes. Comparing these two poets does, however, show the range of styles and attitudes represented by the Harlem Renaissance poets. There were many differences that distinguished the Harlem Renaissance writers from one another. On one hand, there is Frank Horne's downbeat stream of consciousness and the vigorous modernism of Langston Hughes. Contrasted to their poetry is the work of Countee Cullen and Claude McKay—stylistically resistant to modernism while concerned with subject matter quite different from that of the traditional British poetic forms the two admired and mastered.

The excitement created by the poets of the Harlem Renaissance has had a wide and lasting influence. In Texas, for example, J. Mason Brewer edited *Heralding Dawn* (1936), a small

sidebar notes:

*hedonism lifestyle devoted to pleasure

*meed reward

*percipient perceptive

anthology of that state's African American poets. Elsewhere, younger poets, such as Frank Marshall Davis, Margaret Walker, Melvin B. Tolson, Robert Hayden, and Gwendolyn Brooks, experimented with both the modernist idiom and the revitalization of traditional forms. In Europe during the 1930s, French-speaking students at the Sorbonne, the major center of learning in Paris, also discovered the works of the Harlem Renaissance poets. As a result, Aimé Césaire, Leon Damas, and Léopold Sédar Senghor founded the negritude movement to adopt and promote the values of black civilization. A similar discovery by Portuguese-speaking African students in Lisbon inspired Francisco-José Tenreiro, Noemia da Sousa, and others to embark on successful careers as poets dedicated to celebrating the lives and documenting the vibrant traditions of their people.

While the Harlem Renaissance might have lost its original energy during the Great Depression, many of its talented participants continued to pursue extraordinarily successful literary careers and—as Alain Locke and W. E. B. Du Bois had hoped—permanently changed the way that African American people and culture were perceived. The enthusiastic popular audience for African American poetry and the plenitude of gifted writers that emerged during the Harlem Renaissance have, however, been paralleled only by the Black Arts movement of the late 1960s.

America

Although she feeds me bread of bitterness,
And sinks into my throat her tiger's tooth,
Stealing my breath of life, I will confess
I love this cultured hell that tests my youth!
Her vigor flows like tides into my blood,
Giving me strength erect against her hate.
Her bigness sweeps my being like a flood.
Yet as a rebel fronts a king in state,
I stand within her walls with not a shred
Of terror, malice, not a word of jeer.
Darkly I gaze into the days ahead,
And see her might and granite wonders there,
Beneath the touch of Time's unerring hand,
Like priceless treasures sinking in the sand.

(Claude McKay, *Harlem Shadows*.
New York: Harcourt, Brace and Company, 1922)

Selected Bibliography

WORKS BY INDIVIDUAL POETS DISCUSSED IN THIS ESSAY

Available Collections

Cullen, Countee, ed. *Caroling Dusk: An Anthology of Verse by Negro Poets.* New York: Harper and Brothers, 1927. Reprinted as *Caroling Dusk: An Anthology of Verse by Black Poets of the Twenties.* New York: Citadel Press, 1993.

Johnson, James Weldon, ed. *The Book of American Negro Poetry.* New York: Harcourt, Brace, 1931. Reprinted San Diego, Calif.: Harcourt, Brace, Jovanovich, 1983.

Lewis, David Levering, ed. *The Portable Harlem Renaissance Reader.* New York: Viking, 1994.

General Discussions

Bontemps, Arna, ed. *The Harlem Renaissance Remembered: Essays.* New York: Dodd, Mead, 1972.

Buckley, Gail Lumet. *The Hornes: An American Family.* New York: Knopf, 1986.

Levy, Eugene. *James Weldon Johnson: Black Leader, Black Voice.* Chicago and London: University of Chicago Press, 1973.

Lewis, David Levering. *When Harlem Was in Vogue.* New York: Knopf, 1981.

Honey, Maureen, ed. *Shadowed Dreams: Women's Poetry of the Harlem Renaissance.* New Brunswick, N.J.: Rutgers University Press, 1989.

Hutchinson, George. *The Harlem Renaissance in Black and White.* Cambridge, Mass.: Harvard University Press, 1995.

Perry, Margaret. *A Bio-Bibliography of Countee Cullen, 1903–1946.* Westport, Conn.: Greenwood Publishing, 1971.

Wintz, Cary D. *Black Culture and the Harlem Renaissance.* Houston, Tex.: Rice University Press, 1988.

SPANISH POETRY

by Rafael Ocasio

With the fall of the Roman Empire in the fifth century, Latin lost its influence as the official language of the arts. The degeneration of Latin produced the Romance languages, such as Spanish and French, spoken by the masses. In the Iberian Peninsula (Spain and Portugal) some of these languages, such as Castilian, Galician-Portuguese, and Catalan, became vehicles for oral literature. Spanish literature originated from the strong popular entertainment traditions that developed in these languages.

The Middle Ages

The Moslems first came to the Iberian Peninsula from northern Africa in 711 and ruled much of the peninsula until the mid-twelfth century, when the Christian kingdoms began to reconquer. During this period, known as the Middle Ages, love poetry took on greater importance, especially in the eastern and western areas of the peninsula. Influenced by the troubadours of France, works written in Galician-Portuguese helped set the conventions of love poetry for centuries to come. The first literary texts written in what became Spanish are known as "*jarchas*," short poems written in a Mozarabic dialect, a hybrid* form of Romance dialects spoken in the territories occupied by Islamic groups. The *jarcha* combines traditional Arabic poetic forms and the themes popular among the bilingual speakers of Arabic and the local Romance languages. The *jarcha* is a fairly short poem that praises love and friendship or laments the loss or absence of a loved one. These documents are the oldest surviving literary texts of a booming poetic production in southern Spain. In fact, the *jarcha* is the oldest written text produced in an emerging Romance language.

Amid the bustling commercial trade between the Christian and Moslem kingdoms, the political tensions between the Islamic and Catholic societies led to constant military battles. Epic* poetry records these battles in rather graphic detail and

See the article on Troubadours in this volume.

*hybrid** blended from two or more cultures or backgrounds

*epic** having the characteristics of poetry that tells the story of a hero's deeds

317

with historical accuracy. The first surviving epic poem in Spanish, the *Poema del Cid,* which dates from about 1140, sings of the military campaigns of a renowned fighter, Rodrigo Díaz de Vivar (ca. 1043–1099), known as El Cid. This narrative poem follows closely the actual events that led to the taking of the city of Valencia from Moorish control in 1094. Originally sung in Castilian Spanish by an anonymous bard, the *Poema del Cid,* stands out for its incorporation of popular, oral elements into learned, written poetic forms. This epic was mostly lines of fourteen syllables, with a pause in the middle of each line. El Cid himself represents the chivalrous* qualities necessary for the establishment of a fair Christian society: faith in God, a balance between courage and generosity, and fidelity to a just authority.

*chivalrous knightly, honorable, courteous

In the thirteenth century, the emergence of authors as an intellectual class promoted literary production on a much larger scale. The first identified poet of significant reputation was Gonzalo de Berceo (ca. 1195–ca. 1264). Berceo, who wrote in Castilian Spanish, a language that became the official, dominant language of Spain, produced his literary work under the protection of monasteries. Although Berceo drew from popular religious tales, he wrote his poetry for a more intellectual population. As he was writing for the church, his work was highly instructional. He used a fixed form, consisting of stanzas of four rhymed lines, each with fourteen syllables.

Another poet writing within the church was Juan Ruiz (ca. 1283–ca. 1351). Like Berceo, Ruiz wrote from a religious-pedagogical* point of view. Ruiz's major work, *El libro del buen amor* (The book of good love; 1330), dealt, however, with more secular subjects. In his attempt to warn his readers against the dangers in providing the body with earthly pleasures, Ruiz offered rather detailed examples of sin's many disguises. His descriptions came alive with rich metaphors* and symbols.

*pedagogical relating to teaching or education

*metaphors poetic figures of speech that make comparisons

The Fifteenth to the Eighteenth Centuries

There were also identifiable poets writing outside the church, such as Jorge Manrique (ca. 1440–1479), who stands out among the considerable number of nobles who produced poetry in Castilian Spanish. Manrique wrote poems on various themes, particularly love. He is best known for the long poem "Coplas por la muerte de su padre" (Verses about the death of his father). The poem brings forward themes characteristic of the Middle Ages: the shortness of life; the need to live on good terms with God, the church, and political institutions; and the promise of heaven. By the fifteenth century, structural changes in the epic poem were noticeable. The lines were shortened to eight syllables and used rhyme. Known as "romances" or ballads, these new poems were printed in large numbers and distributed throughout Spain. The ballads also became more sophisticated by stressing poetic devices, such as the metaphor, but these changes did not lessen their popularity.

THE RENAISSANCE

With the decisive military victory of the Catholic monarchy over the Moslems and the discovery of the Americas in 1492, Spain was united and entered a new intellectual phase. The poet Garcilaso de la Vega (ca. 1503–1536) is representative of the new humanist intellectual in Spain. Military expeditions outside the confines of the Iberian Peninsula brought new literary forms back to Spain. Garcilaso, both a poet and a distinguished man of arms, was influenced by Italian poetic forms, especially the sonnet.* He is especially known for his lyric* and love poems, which incorporate Italian love motifs. He is also responsible for an increased popularity of bucolic poems, or poetry inspired by the beauty of nature. The bucolic poem praises life in the countryside by stressing its strong soothing effects on human behavior. His "carpe diem" ("seize the day") poems, which call for the enjoyment of pleasures in the face of life's shortness, made him tremendously popular throughout Spain.

Spain's unification under one language, Castilian, resulted in increasingly diverse poetic movements. Among these movements, a mystical* religious group stands out for its use of poetry as means to religious education. Three religious poets representative of Spanish mysticism are Fray Luis de León (1527–1591), Saint Teresa of Avilà (1515–1582), and Saint John of the Cross (1542–1591). They are outstanding in their ability to write fairly uncomplicated poetry that speaks of highly sophisticated philosophical and religious thoughts in a language accessible to most lay readers. This is the case of Saint John of the Cross's poem "La noche obscura del alma," (The dark night of the soul), which many consider one of the best mystic poems of all time.

*sonnet a fourteen-line poem usually composed in iambic pentameter

*lyric a kind of poetry characterized by musical and personal expression

*mystical spiritual; going beyond the ordinary senses

A la noche

Noche, fabricadora de embelecos,
loca, imaginativa, quimerista,
que muestras al que en ti su bien conquista
los montes llanos y los mares secos;

habitadora de cerebros huecos,
mecánica, filósofa, alquimista,
encubridora vil, lince sin vista,
espantadiza de tus mismos ecos:

la sombra, el miedo, el mal se te atribuya,
solícita, poeta, enferma, fría,
manos del bravo y pies del fugitivo.

Que vele o duerma, media vida es tuya:
si velo, te lo pago con el día,
y si duermo, no siento lo que vivo.

To the Night

Night, you fabricator of deceptions,
insane, fantastic, and chimerical,*
who show those who derive delight from you
the mountains flattened and the seas gone dry;

inhabitor of hollow, empty brains,
mechanic, alchemist,* philosopher,
a vile concealer, lynx* that cannot see,
you are of your own echoes terrified:

darkness, fear, and evil are your works,
cautious, poetess, infirm and cold,
with ruffian's hands and feet of fugitive.

Whether I sleep or wake, half my life's yours:
if I'm awake, I pay you the next day,
and if I sleep, I sense not what I live.

(Lope de Vega, translated by Alix Ingber)

*chimerical imaginary

*alchemist in the Middle Ages and Renaissance, someone believed to have the ability to transform base metals into gold

*lynx bobcat

THE BAROQUE

The three most famous poets of what is known as the Spanish golden age are Lope de Vega (1562–1635), Luis de Góngora (1561–1627), and Francisco de Quevedo (1580–1645). Lope de Vega was also a prolific playwright, and his poetry appealed to mass audiences. He is also known for promoting a strong nationalist spirit against classical* and foreign influences.

Luis de Góngora's poetry is characteristic of the best of a highly intellectual movement known as *culteranismo*. Because of its emphasis on "culture," understood by the poets as the exploration of classical knowledge and the rediscovery of obscure mythical figures, *culteranismo* produced sophisticated poetry. *Culteranista* poetry uses abstract* language and complex linguistic forms. For *culteranista* poets, such as Góngora, the message is subordinated to form and style.

The "culteranista" style was challenged by poets who demanded a return to a more accessible poetry. Francisco de Quevedo's campaign against Góngora's *culteranismo* produced an opposite literary movement—*conceptismo*. Quevedo's poetry promotes a concept or an idea based on strong philosophical thinking. The poetic structure supports the concept by using clear and clever language. Góngora sings particularly of human virtues, such as charity and neighborly love, and rejects the vices of the Spanish nobility.

ENLIGHTENMENT

After Quevedo's death Spain entered a phase of literary stagnation. Spanish literature, once a center of international attention, began to imitate foreign models, especially French literature. This was the case in the eighteenth century, known in Spain as "Siglo de las Luces," or "Age of Enlightenment." In Spain the Enlightenment* was a sober and highly rational movement that rejected the golden age's rich literary forms. The movement produced few poets of importance. One, José Cadalso (1741–1782), is better known for his essays, a genre that dominated that literary movement.

The Nineteenth Century

The nineteenth century in Spain began with failed military confrontations with European powers. In 1805, Spain, allied

classical relating to ancient Greece or Rome

abstract not concrete; without narrative or pictorial content

Enlightenment intellectual and cultural movement of the eighteenth century characterized by emphasis on reason and criticism of tradition

with France, lost to England in a naval battle at Trafalgar. Three years later Napoleon invaded Spain and named his brother Joseph king of Spain. This internal disorganization prompted several Spanish American colonies to demand political independence, and by 1825 Spain had lost most of its American territories. Political instability caused a migration of Spanish intellectuals and writers to France and England.

ROMANTICISM

The return of these exiled intellectuals after the French Revolution (1789–1799) brought back the literary movement called Romanticism. Romantic poetry explored human feelings, often from extreme points of view, such as sublime love or raging jealousy. The Spanish Romantics were also interested in showing the impact of nature and the Spanish landscape on the development of Spanish character. Although Spanish Romanticism is best represented in drama, Romantic poetry became a genre of considerable importance. José de Espronceda (1808–1842), José Zorilla (1817–1893), Rosalía de Castro (1837–1885), and Gustavo Adolfo Bécquer (1836–1870) are perhaps the best-known Spanish Romantic poets. Romanticism developed another trait—exoticism, or enthusiasm for the remote in time and space. Zorilla's poetry illustrates his interest in the Orient. Bécquer and de Castro are known for their love poems. Their work shows a softness of lyrical language and a direct style. José de Espronceda lived a short but intense life, full of adventures. His poem "La canción del pirata" (The pirate's song) presents the pirate, a marginal outlaw, as representative of a free spirit against the conservative attitudes of an outdated society. The pirate, like the Romantic hero-author, responds to his desire to achieve fulfillment of his extreme emotions.

THE GENERATION OF '98

Spain's turn-of-the-century literature is represented by a group of writers known as the "generation of '98." This generation received its name from Spain's last international confrontation, the Spanish American War of 1898, fought against the United States, in which Spain lost Cuba and Puerto Rico, its last colonies in the New World. The generation of '98 produced literature that analyzed the reasons for Spain's collapse as a world power. Although most of these writers were novelists and essayists, some of them also wrote poetry, including Miguel de Unamuno (1864–1936) and Ramón del Valle-Inclán (1866–1936). Other poets related to the generation of '98 achieved international stature, such as Juan Ramón Jiménez (1881–1958), who received the Nobel Prize in literature in 1956.

Unamuno's interest in the powerful role of the Catholic Church in the formation of the Spanish character led him to produce poetry heavily influenced by contemporary philosophical trends. Valle-Inclán preferred a more direct, critical view of contemporary Spain, including the impact of Spanish institutions on the present conditions of Spanish America.

The Twentieth Century

The generation of '98 gave way to the highly sophisticated "generation of 1927," a group of gifted and experimental young writers including Federico García Lorca (1898–1936), Vicente Aleixandre (1898–1984), and Luis Cernuda (1902–1963), who joined forces in 1927 to celebrate the three-hundredth anniversary of the death of the *culteranista* poet Góngora. Their poetry reflects the diversity of critical thinking and the literary experimentation that took place between the two world wars. The generation of 1927 brought the world's attention to Spanish literature. Some of its members were caught amidst the horrors of the Spanish Civil War (1936–1939). Federico García Lorca was assassinated by right-wing elements. Other poets, such as Antonio Machado (1875–1939), Juan Ramón Jiménez, and Luis Cernuda left the country as political exiles. Concha Espina (1877–1955) and Miguel Hernández (1910–1942) suffered imprisonment.

After the civil war, Spain was left in considerable turmoil and under the totalitarian military government of Francisco Franco, whose regime was highly moralistic* and exercised severe censorship. In the early 1950s, Franco's regime began to open Spain's economy to the world. Although censorship was still at work, more poets wrote socially or politically committed literature, calling for democratic government. This phenomenon occurred particularly in drama, which produced a rich underground movement of unlicensed performances highly critical of Franco's government.

Post-Franco literature presented a variety of social and political themes and trends. With complete liberty of expression, writers disclosed graphic details of national history dealing

*moralistic overly concerned with morals; preachy

with the civil war. Their autobiographical memories included accounts of growing up under Franco's regime or coming of age under his collapsing dictatorship. The emergence of other Romance languages as strong literary languages may be one of the most innovative characteristics of contemporary Spanish literature. Castilian Spanish is just one of the historic languages used in literary expression in Spain. Its prominence as an official language is political. With the lessening of requirements to use Castilian Spanish, the various regional languages were revived. Representatives of this multilingual literary production included poets Arantza Urretabizkaia (b. 1947), who writes in Basque; Xohaha Torres (b. 1931), a Galician poet, novelist, actress, and radio journalist; and Maria Angels Anglada (b. 1930), a Catalan novelist and poet.

The emergence of a considerable number of poets, especially women, fostered numerous poetry contests organized by various regional political centers, such as Catalonia and the Basque country. Poetry had always played an important social and political role in Spain. Released from the strong Franco dictatorship, Spanish poetry continued to serve these purposes on a larger, international scale.

Selected Bibliography

Barnstone, Willis, ed. *Spanish Poetry, from Its Beginnings Through the Nineteenth Century: An Anthology*. New York: Oxford University Press, 1970.

Cohen, J. M., ed. *The Penguin Book of Spanish Verse*. Harmondsworth, U.K.: Penquin, 1988.

Crow, John A., ed. *An Anthology of Spanish Poetry: From the Beginnings to the Present Day, Including Both Spain and Spanish America*. Baton Rouge: Louisiana State University Press, 1979.

Flores, Angel, ed. *Spanish Poetry: Poesia Española: A Dual-Language Anthology, 16th–20th Centuries*. New York: Dover, 1998.

SPANISH AMERICAN POETRY

by Rafael Ocasio

The term "Spanish America" refers to those parts of America colonized by Spain shortly after the arrival of Columbus in 1492. Most historical accounts of the development of Spanish American literature begin with works in Spanish written at the time of the conquest of the New World in the sixteenth century. This approach ignores, however, a strong literary tradition of various native empires flourishing in Central and South America at the time of the Spanish conquest. Today the oral literature of indigenous* groups, such as the Aztecs in Mexico, the Incas in Peru, or the Mayans in Guatemala, has come under serious study in its own right.

Spanish America includes South America, except Brazil and the Guianas; Central America, except Belize; Mexico; Cuba; Puerto Rico; Dominican Republic; and some islands of the West Indies.

*indigenous relating to the earliest human inhabitants of a place. See also essay on Indigenous and Oral Poetry in these volumes.

Conquest and Colonialism

Not long after the arrival of Christopher Columbus on 12 October 1492, the clash of Spanish and indigenous American cultures began. Early in the sixteenth century, the Caribbean native groups rebelled against Spanish rule. These military confrontations were described in prose by eyewitnesses, some of whom were historians. At the time of the American conquest, epic* poetry had lost its interest for readers in Spain. The news of the discovery of fabulous cities in the New World and of the bloody confrontations of the Spanish expeditions against the indigenous peoples revived the epic genre. The first of such texts, based on historical military battles in Latin America, was *La araucana,* by Alonso de Ercilla y Zúñiga (1553–1594). This epic poem recounts the final defeat of the Araucan Indian group in Chile.

*epic a long poem that tells the story of a hero's deeds

One of the most important writers during the colonial period (1600–1750) was the Mexican nun Sor Juana Inés de la Cruz (1651–1695), who represented a new generation of Spanish American–born colonists who preferred their native lands over Spain. De la Cruz's poetry has elements and images of particular interest to a Mexican readership. She was a woman of extensive knowledge, but social restrictions limited her intellectual development. She therefore joined a convent, where she wrote poetry that rivaled the best in Spain or elsewhere in Spanish America. In the twentieth century, feminist readings of her poems brought her international fame.

The Baroque, Romanticism, and Modernism

The baroque* movement was a literary movement of major intellectual experimentation. The Mexican Carlos de Sigüenza y Góngora (1645–1700), faithful to the scientific trends of the movement, wrote extensively and in detail about anthropology, astronomy, and advanced mathematics. Although he was a gifted poet, he is better known for his fiction. The poetry of the baroque writers demonstrated their ability to keep up with Spanish trends in spite of legal and political restrictions, and it forecast a rich poetic tradition after Spanish America's independence from Spain.

When the fight for political independence began, following Napoleon's invasion of Spain (1808), Spanish American poetry found new inspiration in the local patriotic figures, such as the South American liberator Simón Bolivar (1783–1830), who worked to establish the various independent countries. The independence movement (1810–1826) coincided with Romanticism,* an artistic movement that emphasized a love of one's homeland. Spanish American poets sang of the new national figures and of the American landscape, characterized as free-spirited and majestic in its intensity and exuberance.* In Argentina, the national spirit was embodied by the *gaucho,* the Argentine cowboy. José Hernández (1834–1886), in his epic poem *Martín Fierro,* expressed the fervor of local Argentine customs. The maturity of Spanish American poetry immediately after the wars of independence is notable.

The publication of *Azul,* by Nicaraguan poet Rubén Dario (1867–1916), launched a new literary movement from Spanish America—modernism.* Although modernism is a local version of a similar French movement, Spanish American modernism reached Spain before French modernism. The impact of modernism on Spanish American poetry can be seen especially in the use of images and metaphors. Among the most renowned Spanish American modernist poets are the Cuban José Martí (1835–1895) and the Mexicans Manuel Gutiérrez

Nájera (1859–1895) and Amado Nervo (1870–1919). Martí's lyrical verses, inspired by the Cuban landscape, became popular songs throughout Spanish America. Gutiérrez Nájera is well known for somber, nostalgic poetry. Nervo puts the modernist interest in symbolic language to religious and philosophical use.

The Twentieth Century

In the period between World War I and World War II, a movement of Spanish American poetry known as the avant-garde* began to secure a worldwide reputation. A dominant characteristic of this movement was emphasis on the creation of new aesthetic forms. In 1918 the Chilean poet Vicente Huidobro (1893–1948) presented his own poetic movement, *creacionismo* (creationism), which promoted the concept that the poet is a creator, a "small god" of unlimited creative abilities. As part of this *creacionismo,* Huidobro proclaimed the liberty to invent words that let him describe his newly created reality.

*avant-garde ad-vanced or cutting-edge; experimental; normally applies to the arts

Other poets participated in the European avant-garde movements, including Argentine poet Jorge Luis Borges (1899–1986), whose contributions to Spanish American poetry are significant. Borges expressed a strong interest in the use of metaphor, which he related to metaphysical* considerations. The Peruvian poet César Vallejo (1892–1938) stands out for his refined and unconventional poetry. Unlike Borges, Vallejo took a more personal and politically committed approach, as in his volume *España aparta de mi este cáliz,* about the bloody Spanish Civil War (1936–1939). Commitment to left-wing social and political causes is also present in the poetry of the Chilean poet Pablo Neruda (1904–1973). Neruda received the Nobel Prize in literature in 1971.

*metaphysical relating to such concepts as being, substance, essence, time, space, and identity

Originating in France in the 1920s, the surrealist* movement encouraged Spanish Americans to explore their own folklore. The Puerto Rican Luis Palés Matos (1898–1959) and the Cuban Nicolás Guillén (1902–1989) began the so-called *negrismo* movement. Intended to give voice to native African rhythmic forms preserved in Caribbean music, *negrismo* poetry also became a political poetry. The Mexican Octavio Paz (1914–1998) wrote religious and philosophical poems that dealt with spiritual questions that arose after World War II. Inspired by Aztec motifs, his poetry attempts to find a cosmic

*surrealist an artist or poet involved in the art movement surrealism, which aimed (chiefly during the 1920s and 1930s) to express the workings of the unconscious or subconscious mind

Entre irse y quedarse

Entre irse y quedarse duda el día,
enamorado de su transparencia.
La tarde circular es ya bahía:
en su quieto vaivén se mece el mundo.
Todo es visible y todo es elusivo,
todo está cerca y todo es intocable.
Los papeles, el libro, el vaso, el lápiz
reposan a la sombra de sus nombres.
Latir del tiempo que en mi sien repite
la misma terca sílaba de sangre.
La luz hace del muro indiferente
un espectral teatro de reflejos.
En el centro de un ojo me descubro;
no me mira, me miro en su mirada.
Se disipa el instante. Sin moverme,
yo me quedo y me voy: soy una pausa.

Between Going and Staying

Between going and staying the day wavers,
in love with its own transparency.
The circular afternoon is now a bay
where the world in stillness rocks.
All is visible and all elusive,
all is near and can't be touched.
Paper, book, pencil, glass,
rest in the shade of their names.
Time throbbing in my temples repeats
the same unchanging syllable of blood.
The light turns the indifferent wall
into a ghostly theater of reflections.
I find myself in the middle of an eye,
watching myself in its blank stare.
The moment scatters. Motionless,
I stay and go: I am a pause.

(Octavio Paz)

order, as in his poem "Piedra de sol" (Sun stone), inspired by the Aztec calendar (whose astronomical accuracy still surprises scientists). Paz received the Nobel Prize in literature in 1990.

After World War II, international readership discovered sophisticated poetry by Spanish American women. The first was the Chilean Gabriela Mistral (1889–1957). Her poetry examines social injustices, particularly abuses against children, from a female perspective. Mistral received the Nobel Prize in literature in 1945. Other poets who were early defenders of women's rights are the Uruguayans Juana de Ibarbourou (1892–1979) and Delmira Agustini (1886–1914), the Argentine Alfonsina Storni (1892–1938), the Puerto Rican Julia de Burgos (1917–1953), and the Mexican Rosario Castellanos (1925–1974). Unable to cope with the tight gender restrictions of her time, Storni drowned herself. The poetry of these women is highly symbolic because the social taboos of the time restricted the poets' freedom to express themselves openly.

After the triumph of the Cuban Revolution in 1959, Spanish American poetry returned to demands for social changes. Seasoned poets, such as Nicolás Guillén, offered their political readings of Latin American colonialism. The Nicaraguan Ernesto Cardenal (b. 1925), a priest, achieved international attention when he was named minister of culture after the victory of the Sandinista Revolution in 1979. His poetry differs from that of other political activists in that it works with biblical images, akin to what is called "liberation theology.*" Cardenal's poetry blended indigenous mythology and biblical imagery.

Opposition to the Cuban Revolution produced anti-revolutionary poetry as well. Heberto Padilla (b. 1932) is among the best known of the disaffected Cuban poets; in 1971 he was imprisoned because of his poetry collection *Fuera del juego* (Out of the game). Beginning with a symbolic title that announces his intention to stop playing the revolutionary game, this collection deviated from the political views imposed by the Cuban Revolution.

Cuban poetry exerted a strong influence on Spanish American poets, but the political tone became diversified. Women poets continued to fight for rights equal to those of men, though less directly than the early feminist poets. The Nicaraguan Gioconda Belli (b. 1948) is outstanding for her feminist poetry that, although inspired by the Sandinista Revolution, provides a voice for women speaking on the issues of particular interest to them. Other poets, such as the Argentine

*liberation theology a social and intellectual movement formulated in the late 1960s by Latin American theologians and social scientists. The movement interprets the Bible and other Christian doctrines through the experiences of the poor, and champions a social system based on equitable treatment for poor people.

Alejandra Pizarnik (1936–1972), the Puerto Rican Rosario Ferré (b. 1942), and the Cuban Nancy Morejón (b. 1944), represent an increasingly popular trend toward using sensual images and language reflective of women's experiences.

Latino Poetry

With the Treaty of Guadalupe Hidalgo in 1848, the expanding United States incorporated one-third of Mexico's territory, and more than eighty thousand Mexicans suddenly lived in American territory. As a result of the Spanish American War of 1898, Cuba and Puerto Rico came under the economic and political jurisdiction of the United States. People of Latin American descent who live in the United States are collectively called Hispanics, and their culture is referred to as Latino.

Latin America refers to all of the Americas south of the United States.

ORIGINS

The first Latino poetry came out of strong connections with the working class. Popular poetic forms, such as folk songs (the Mexican *corrido,* for example), were entertaining. They acted as a way of preserving events of importance to the community. In nineteenth-century California, a considerable number of Mexicans retained their attachment to Mexican culture and thus preserved poetic forms associated with traditional music.

A formal literary phase of Latino poetry began with poetry written in Spanish by Spanish American visitors to the United States. The Cuban José Maria Heredia (1803–1839), fleeing Cuba because of his political activities against the Spanish government, found himself in Boston in 1823. His poem "Niágara," inspired by Niagara Falls, incorporated the United States into the Spanish American community. Another renowned Cuban political exile was José Martí, who lived in New York City at various times after 1881. He was an important politician; his 1889 letter to the *Evening Post,* for instance, shows Martí as the prototype of the activist immigrant who defends himself against the xenophobia* of American society.

The Puerto Rican Pachín Marín (1863–1897) is representative of the first Latino poetic generation shaped in the United States. In 1891 he settled in New York City, where he joined José Martí's intellectual fight to promote the independence of Cuba. In 1892 Marín published his first collection of poetry and started

*xenophobia fear of foreigners

to write for Spanish newspapers. A true nationalist, like Martí, he died in Cuba fighting for that country's independence.

TWENTIETH CENTURY

As Hispanic poets began to write in English in the twentieth century, their poetry became well known outside the Latino community. Piri Thomas (b. 1928) achieved success with his poetry written in a combination of Spanish and English that depicts life in a Puerto Rican neighborhood. Víctor Hernández Cruz (b. 1949), also a bilingual poet, drew poetic inspiration from the so-called *negrista* (black) movement. His poetry offers commentaries of the racial oppression encountered by Puerto Ricans born in New York City (Nuyoricans), but his work can be quite witty as well. Other distinguished poets include Miguel Algarín (b. 1941), Tato Laviera (b. 1950), and Iván Silén (b. 1944).

Along with hundreds of thousands of exiles from the Cuban Revolution, distinguished dissident poets made the United States their permanent home. In spite of their literary reputation in Cuba, however, these poets, because of their limited knowledge of English, found at first no formal recognition of their talents by mainstream American publications. Heberto Padilla, after his arrival in the United States in 1980, experienced that cultural isolation. Having worked for many years for Cuban journals, he started his own literary journal, *Linden Lane Magazine*. This publication promoted up-and-coming Cuban and Latino poets. Other distinguished Cuban poets include Dolores Prida (b. 1943), Matías Montes Huidobro (b. 1931), and José Sánchez-Boudy (b. 1928).

Poets of Mexican descent have also shown a marked inclination for political poetry. This is the case of Rodolfo "Corky" Gonzáles (b. 1928), whose poem "I Am Joaquín" offers a succinct history of his Mexican ancestry. This poem, a cry to return to ancient Aztec and Mexican traditions, leads to the concept of "Aztlán," the mythical promised land inherited by contemporary Mexican Americans (Chicanos). The poem was well known among Chicanos throughout the United States and was used in political rallies and presented in dramatic readings. Similar commitment to political causes is present in the poetry of Alurista, the pen name of Alberto Baltazar Urista Heredia (b. 1947). Like the poetry of Corky Gonzáles, Alurista's poetry is inspired by Aztec folklore and religious beliefs.

Latina poets helped promote the acceptance of Latino poetry by mainstream readers, particularly in the late twentieth century. The Chicana poets Gloria Anzaldúa (b. 1942), Cherríe Moraga (b. 1952), Lorna Dee Cervantes (b. 1954), Helena María Viramontes (b. 1954), and Sandra Cisneros (b. 1954), for instance, came to national attention through their feminist and political poetry. This was also the case of the Puerto Rican poet Judith Ortiz Cofer (b. 1952), whose poetry expresses the Puerto Rican values associated with women's culture.

In the 1990s significant connections between Spanish American and Latino poetry were evident in the ample market serving a large bilingual community that read poetry by Spanish American and Latino poets either in Spanish or in English. The increasing number of Spanish American poets translated into English reflected the demand for Spanish American poetry in the United States. The constant struggle to improve social and political orders continued to be an important theme for the Spanish American poet. This fighting spirit was also present in Latino poetry. Social causes, such as achieving a society free from racism, xenophobia, or sexism, were important for all Latino poets.

The closeness between Spanish American and Latino poetry also resulted in experimentation with poetic structure. Linguistic games—in the use of English by Spanish Americans, or of Spanish, or of such hybrid forms as Spanglish by Latino poets writing in English—offered new possibilities of expression. Readers of Spanish American and Latino poetry found writing of a transnational character. New cultural material and new uses of language made Spanish American and Latino poetry highly innovative.*

*innovative** new and original

Selected Bibliography

Crow, John, ed. *An Anthology of Spanish Poetry: From the Beginnings to the Present Day, Including Both Spain and Spanish America.* Baton Rouge: Louisiana State University Press, 1979.

Tapscott, Steven, ed. *Twentieth-Century Latin American Poetry: A Bilingual Anthology.* Austin: University of Texas Press, 1996.

Zeller, Ludwig, ed. *The Invisible Presence: Sixteen Poets of Spanish America, 1925–1995.* Translated by Beatriz Zeller. Buffalo, N.Y.: Mosaic Press, 1996.

CONTEMPORARY ASIAN AMERICAN POETRY

by Kimiko Hahn

How useful is the term "Asian American"? This group, containing nationalities from such different countries as Sri Lanka, Korea, and the Philippines, is amazingly diverse. Every Asian country has distinct, though sometimes related, cultures, languages, and histories. In China alone there are numerous cultures and dialects. To consider such a heterogeneous* grouping as a "community" is symbolic of how twentieth-century Western powers carved up the globe into categories. For Asian Americans the corraling of nationalities over time has caused both conflict and unity and, above all, has highlighted their diversity.

*heterogeneous diverse; made up of dissimilar parts

For artists and audiences from this so-called community, "diversity" contains the usual meaning of differing ethnic peoples, and as generations pass there are increasing mixtures of nationalities, Asian and otherwise. My own mother, born in Hawaii, was of Japanese descent; my father was born in Wisconsin of mainly German ancestry. I could be categorized either as Eurasian or Asian American.

In some cases, even for artists, the ethnic differences among Asian Americans have caused problems, as can be seen among some immigrants from Japan and the Philippines. Because Japan brutally dominated the Philippines during World War II, the resulting scars still create occasional conflicts between these peoples. Sometimes these conflicts are carried across geographical borders and generations.

On the other hand, during the civil rights movement in the 1960s and 1970s, some Asian Americans were inspired by the African Americans who were demanding equality. This social change made it necessary for the different groups to find strength in numbers—power in their diverse experiences. This was the beginning of Asian Americans' identifying themselves as a unified group that could work together for a common cause. One of the causes became culture. During this era numerous writers began creating from their own experiences and seeing their work produced. In the words of Elaine Kim, one of the pioneers of this literature, "Anglo-American literature does not tell us about Asians. It tells us about Anglos' opinions of themselves, in relation to their opinions of Asians" (p. 20). Writers of Asian ancestry needed to see themselves refelcted in American culture and pushed to find publishers.

A number of Asian American writers also began searching for their literary roots, which took them back to the entire cultures from which they were descended—whether or not they had ever even seen their ancestors' homelands. In other cases, some early texts by immigrants to the United States were discovered and published in literary journals and books; still others were found carved into the walls of immigration detention cells, as seen in *Island: Poetry and History of Chinese Immigrants on Angel Island, 1910–1940*. Similarly, poems written in the Japanese internment centers during World War II were collected and translated in a volume called *Poets Behind Barbed Wire*. These nonliterary works became intermingled with the poetry taught to all Americans, such as the verse of those remarkable literary "parents" Emily Dickinson and Walt Whitman.

Thus, the literary influences themselves are also varied. My own influences include mainstream American poets and the anonymous poems on the walls as well as such poets as the Japanese poets Ono no Komachi (ca. 850) and Bashō (1644–1694). Other influences have to do with my own taste and personal history. For example, the political lyrics of the singer Marvin Gaye played a vital role in my understanding that the words in poetry did not need to sound "poetic."

The Effects of Immigration

The time when one immigrates has a great effect on one's writing. The daughter of plantation workers who left Japan at the turn of the 1800s had a different view of the world than that of someone who is fifth-generation Chinese living in the suburbs or a Korean born in Seoul in the 1980s but brought up in Los Angeles. Some writers have parents who cannot read their work because they do not understand English. Still others may be from a country such as India and educated in English, so the language was learned at an early age. Jessica Hagedorn (b. 1949) is a Filipina who grew up in Manila. When she was a teenager, her family moved to California, where she became involved in the heady rock / theater / poetry scene of the 1960s. "Motown/Smokey Robinson" (in *Danger and Beauty*) is an early poem:

hey girl, how long you been here?

did you come with yr daddy in 1959 on a second-class
   boat

cryin' all the while cuz you didn't want to leave the
   barrio*

the girls back there who wore their hair loose

lotsa orange lipstick and movies on sundays

quiapo* market in the morning, yr grandma chewin' red
   tobacco

roast pig? . . . yeah, and it tasted good . . .

hey girl, did you haveta live in stockton with yr daddy

and talk to old farmers who emigrated in 1941?

did yr daddy promise you to a fifty-eight-year-old
   bachelor

who stank of cigars . . . and did you

run away to san francisco/go to poly high*/rat your hair/

hang around woolworth's/chinatown at three in the
   morning

go to the cow palace* and catch SMOKEY ROBINSON*

cry and scream at his gold jacket

Dance every friday night in the mission/go steady with
   ruben?

(yr daddy can't stand it cuz he's a spik*)

and the sailors you dreamed of in manila with yellow
   hair

did they take you to the beach to ride the ferris wheel?

Life's never been so fine!

you and carmen harmonize "be my baby" by the
   ronettes*

and 1965 you get laid at a party/carmen's house

and you get pregnant and ruben marries you

and you give up harmonizing . . .

hey girl, you sleep without dreams

and remember the barrios and how it's all the same:

manila/the mission/chinatown/east l.a./harlem/
   fillmore st.

and you're gettin' kinda fat and smokey robinson's
   gettin' old

   ooh baby baby baby
   ooh baby baby
   ooh . . .

but he still looks good!!!

i love you

*barrio a Spanish-speaking neighborhood

*Quiapo district of the city of Manila, Philippines

*Poly High a high school in San Francisco

*cow palace The Cow Palace, a hall south of San Francisco used for expositions, entertainment events, and sporting events

*Robinson, Smokey rhythm-and-blues singer, writer, and producer of the 1960s to the 1980s

*spik variant of "spick," derogatory term for a Hispanic person

*Ronettes the Ronettes, an all-female rock group of the 1960s

i need you
i need you
i need you
i want you
ooh ooh
ooh

In this poem Hagedorn displays a young woman's preoccupations, her curiosity about sex and the world outside her family, and the problem with dating someone who is different. Her experience is very different from that of, say, Li-Young Lee (b. 1957). Lee's family had to flee Indonesia as Chinese political refugees. In "For a New Citizen of These United States" (in *The City in Which I Love You*), Lee recalls, for himself and a stranger, the other "new citizen," the details and feelings that exile can bring:

Forgive me for thinking I saw
the irregular postage stamp of death;
a black moth the size of my left
thumbnail is all I've trapped in the damask.*
There is no need for alarm. And

*damask richly patterned satin fabric

there is no need for sadness, if
the rain at the window now reminds you
of nothing; not even of that
parlor, long like a nave,* where cloud-shadow,
wing-shadow, where father-shadow
continually confused the light. In flight,
leaf-throng and, later, soldiers and
flags deepened those windows to submarine.

*nave part of the interior of a church

But you don't remember, I know,
so I won't mention that house where Chung hid,
Lin wizened, you languished, and Ming—
Ming hush-hushed us with small song. And since you
don't recall the missionary
bells chiming the hour, or those words whose sounds
alone exhaust the heart—*garden,*
heaven, amen—I'll mention none of it.

After all, it was just our life,
merely years in a book of years. It was
1960, and we stood with

the other families on a crowded
railroad platform. The trains came, then
the rains, and then we got separated.
And in the interval between
familiar faces, events occurred, which
one of us faithfully pencilled
in a day-book bound by a rubber band.
But birds, as you say, fly forward.
So I won't show you letters and the shawl
I've so meaninglessly preserved.
And I won't hum along, if you don't, when
our mothers sing *Nights in Shanghai.*
I won't, each Spring, each time I smell lilac,
recall my mother, patiently
stitching money inside my coat lining,
if you don't remember your mother
preparing for your own escape.

After all, it was only our
life, our life and its forgetting.

The region to where a family moves also creates a different experience. Lois-Ann Yamanaka (b. 1961) was raised in
Hawaii and writes of that particular experience, often in what
is known as pidgin, a combination of English, Hawaiian, Chinese, Japanese, Portuguese, Filipino, and probably other languages as more immigrants settle in that island state. In the
opening of "Yarn Wig" (from *Saturday Night at the Pahala
Theatre*), the speaker complains about the short haircut her
mother has given her:

My madda cut our hair so short.
Shit, us look like boys, I no joke you.
I mean mo worse than cha-wan cut.
At least cha-wan cut get liddle bit hair
on the side of your face.
Us look almost bolohead
and everybody tease us, *Eh, boy,
what time?* or *Eh boy,
what color your panty?*

Such word usage creates an interesting texture, enriching the
English.

Playing with Language, and Other Factors

Foreign words also create an interesting visual and oral texture, whether or not the average reader can understand them. Take, for example, this excerpt from "Cosmography" in *Dura,* by the experimental poet Myung Mi Kim (b. 1957):

First flute cut from bamboo

First fabric dye from snails

Five tone and seven tone scales

시조 ——a short lyric poem or, the founder of a family

신 보 ——an ancestral tablet

신세계 ——a new world

시래기 ——dried radish leaves

The four Korean characters add a dimension to the poem. Similarly, the Filipino poet Nick Carbo (b. 1964) sometimes uses Tagalog (the main indigenous Filipino language), as when he juxtaposes* a refrain from a children's song with a narrative presenting political atrocities in his poem "When the Grain Is Golden and the Wind Is Chilly, Then It Is the Time to Harvest":

A soldier recognized him at a military

checkpoint and he pointed his gun at Ramon,
yelled at him to step out with his hands up in the air.

Leron-leron sinta, umakyat sa papaya
Dala-dala'y buslo', sisidlan ng bunga

No questions were asked.

Sometimes Carbo uses Spanish, as in the title of his book *El Grupo McDonald's.* Such mixtures are increasingly common.

*juxtaposes places next to or in close proximity

Other writers choose to write in English, and many do not speak or understand the language of their ancestors.

Some Asian American poets choose to write poems that are identifiably ethnic such as Janice Mirikitani (b. 1940s) in her elegy to her Japanese American uncle who was confined in an internment camp during World War II:

> We will not leave your memory
> as a silent rancid rose.
> Our tongues become livid with history and
> demands for reparations*. . . .
> Our tongues are sharp like blades,
> we overturn furrows of secrecy.
> "In Remembrance" (*Shedding Silence*)

*reparations payments made to compensate a group or nation for injury or damage

In its expression of political ideas, Mirikitani's work is akin to African American poetry of the 1960s.

There are also many poets writing in a more experimental vein, such as John Yau (b. 1950), who also writes fiction and art criticism.

> The motorcycle was saved when the driver's head
> was etched by lightning
>
> She spends a weekend on a beach in Crete
> without opening her eyes
>
> They kiss as if tomorrow is an island
> trickling into the sea
> "Paradise" (*Radiant Silhouette*)

Yau's work plays with language—at times nearly dismissing meaning—and has a surreal* vision. At the same time, he is serious about this playfulness. The point is not merely to be humorous, but to recreate in art his experience of the world, which is often both offbeat and melancholy.

*surreal dreamlike

You can see how different these poets are in subject matter and style. Further, from its content Yau's poem is not identifiably Asian American. In the past this would have led some to question whether the poet was part of the Asian American community. Today there is greater acceptance of all content and form.

Timothy Liu (b. 1965) is another poet who rarely writes about ethnic identity. His material often comes from his life as a gay man, as suggested in "Leaving the Universe":

> Can't go back
> to his body. That wilderness.
>   A time he would let me
> rest there, no other place to go.
>   A bedroom
> full of star charts, planets tearing
>   free from orbit, a belt
> of asteroids flying apart.
>   In that space
> between us, the gravity
>   of my bed unable
> to keep his body from floating
>   out the door.
>
> *(Vox Angelica)*

You can see that Liu's style is very different from Yau's—it is more conventional, but that does not mean it is more or less meaningful or important.

Transcending Categories

Asian American poets write in as many styles as there are in the poetry scene, and they write about whatever is affecting their lives, whether it has to do with their ethnicity or not. So it is not easy to identify or categorize these writers. Each has a different background, and these differences lead to different work.

My own life and poetry are a case in point. I was born in 1955 near New York City. Although I inherited a love for Japanese language from my mother, much of my interest in Asian culture came from my father, who is Caucasian. Because my mother was second-generation Japanese (second-generation children often reject their parents' homeland), and because of World War II and the propaganda against the Japanese, she rejected her culture, until we lived in Japan for a year while my father studied Japanese painting and calligraphy there. Aside from folktales I heard as a child, this period was the beginning of my Japanese studies. In high school I hung around students involved in the Civil Rights movement and began to identify myself as a Japanese American. Instead of my nickname, "Kim," I began to use my full name, Kimiko, because it is Japanese. I studied writing in college and Japanese literature in graduate school. Here I developed an intense interest in the Heian period of Japanese culture (794–1185), during which the women were the dominant writers. During this time I became more involved in identity issues and read Asian American literature on my own.

Most of my poems are about my Asian American roots and issues of patriarchy and feminism. I do not *try* to write on these issues—they are just so essential to me that they emerge naturally. Here are two poems that use one image in two very different ways—one "Asian" and the other not.

> Watching the day lilies
> shrivel by afternoon,
> the buds behind them
> swollen from green to orange,
> I think of our wedding
> two years ago.
> Mother brought armfuls
> from the woods near their home.
> She told me
> in China they dry the blossoms
> and eat them in soup.
> I imagine the spent lilies
> opening a second time
> in the hot broth.
>
> "Day Lilies on the Second Anniversary
>   of My Second Marriage" (*Earshot*)

In the train an hour along the Sound, distant from the
      details of grief
I look up from the salt marshes
clumped beneath a snow we thought we would not see
      this year;
snow fallen twice this past week since mother died, in-
      stantly, 10:35 pm.
broadsided by an Arab kid fleeing a car of white kids
      with baseball bats;
a snow only matched by my father's head as I reach to
      touch him

as I have never touched him. He wishes
he could see her once more, to say goodbye,
as Ted and I said goodbye to the body that was mother's.
Grief comes in spasms: the smell of banana bread, I
    think of the rotting fruit
my sister and I tossed before father came home from
    Yonkers General.
A flashlight. The flashlight she bought my youngest
    daughter
who always rummaged for one under grandpa's side of
    the mattress.
The orange day lilies the florist sent to our apartment:
the lilies from the woods she brought to my wedding.
And after I told my six-year-old, grandma died in the ac-
    cident,
after tears and questions she suggested, maybe now is a
    good time
to explain what the man has to do with babies.
So I chose one perfect lily from that vase
and with the tip of a paring knife slit open the pistil
to trace the passage pollen makes to the egg cell—
the eggs I then slipped out and dotted on her fingertip,
    their greenish-white
translucent as the air in this blizzard that cannot cool the
    unbearable heart.

As I write this, I still demand your attention, mother.

And now that she's gone how do we find her—
especially my small daughters who will eventually recall
    their grandmother
not as a snapshot in the faults of the mind
but as the incense in their hair long after the reading of
    the Lotus Sutra.*
      "The Unbearable Heart" (*The Unbearable Heart*)

*Lotus Sutra a sacred Buddhist text

You can see the way these poems are essentially Asian Ameri-can—but like any poet who hopes to transcend pigeonholes, I hope that anyone can relate to the themes of rebirth and loss in these poems.

    As the number of Asian immigrants increases in the United States, there are expanding intraethnic conflicts and rifts. Some members of this "community" wonder why all these different peoples continue to be categorized in a single grouping. In any case, it remains essential to celebrate the differences and similarities as well as the vast growing number of Asian American writers and books.

Selected Bibliography

WORKS BY POETS DISCUSSED IN THIS ESSAY

Carbo, Nick. *El Grupo McDonald's.* Chicago: Tia Chucha Press, 1995.

Hagedorn, Jessica. *Danger and Beauty.* New York: Penguin, 1993.

Hahn, Kimiko. *Earshot.* Brooklyn: Hanging Loose Press, 1992.

Hahn, Kimiko. *The Unbearable Heart.* New York: Kaya Productions, 1995.

Kim, Myung Mi. *Dura.* Los Angeles: Sun and Moon Press, 1998.

Lee, Li-Young. *The City in Which I Love You.* Brockport, N.Y.: Boa Editions, 1990.

Liu, Timothy. *Vox Angelica.* Cambridge Mass.: Alice James Books, 1992.

Mirikitani, Janice. *Shedding Silence.* Berkeley, Calif.: Celestial Arts, 1987.

Yamanaka, Lois-Ann. *Saturday Night at the Pahala Theatre.* Honolulu: Bamboo Ridge Press, 1993.

Yau, John. *Radiant Silhouette.* Santa Rosa, Calif.: Black Sparrow Press, 1994.

AVAILABLE COLLECTIONS

Nakano, Jino, and Kay Nakano. *Poets Behind Barbed Wire.* Honolulu: Bamboo Ridge Press, 1983.

GENERAL DISCUSSIONS

Kim, Elaine. *Asian American Literature.* Philadelphia: Temple University Press, 1982.

Lai, Him Mark, Genny Lim, and Judy Yung, eds. *Island: Poetry and History of Chinese Immigrants on Angel Island 1910–1940.* San Francisco: Chinese Culture Foundation, 1980.

✍

More About Asian American Poets

You can write to:
Asian American Writers
   Workshop
37 St. Marks Place
New York, NY 10003
phone: (212) 228-6718
fax: (212) 228-7718
e-mail: aaww@panix.com

CALLIGRAMMATIC AND CONCRETE POETRY

by Emmett Williams

"We see eggs, balls, wings, battle-axes...," and the widely read sixteenth-century philosopher Michel de Montaigne might well have added to his list an array of Latin, Greek, and Hebrew "picture poems" in the shape of pyramids and diamonds; of mythical beasts and talking trees; of altars, chalices, and crosses; of lutes,* viols, and panpipes; and of labyrinths and magical circles and squares. Although the outspoken Montaigne dismissed all such language games as trivial, they have persisted for thousands of years.

Calligrams (from the Greek *kalli* and *gramma,* "beautiful writing") and concrete poems are distinct twentieth-century types of poems whose roots stretch back at least into classical antiquity. (Similar poems exist in Chinese, Sanskrit, Arabic, and other literatures.) Despite their ancient lineage, these "shaped poems" remained largely outside the mainstream of European literature until the second half of the twentieth century, principally because most of these sometimes ingenious and often fascinating creations were the inventions of antiquarians and pedants, of mystics and divines, and of dilettantes and eccentric typographers with little or no literary distinction or popular appeal.

An Explosion of Words

In the turbulent decade before World War I, a literary revolution was in the air. Language began to invade the still lifes and collages* of the cubist* painters, and letters and words in all shapes, sizes, and colors were used as the raw material of art and transformed into vibrant visual images on poster poems. The Italian F. T. Marinetti and his futurist* colleagues exhorted poets and painters to "treat words like torpedoes and to hurl them forth at all speeds: at the velocity of stars, clouds, aeroplanes, trains, waves, explosives, molecules and atoms."

One of the "bombs" that provoked a call to arms for a renewal of language was concealed in a poem by the highly

*lutes etc. early musical instruments

*collage a work of art (or a method of composition) in which bits and pieces of different objects and media are used together

*cubist a movement in art characterized by a separation of the subject into cubes and planes rather than a "realistic" representation of nature.

*futurist an Italian artistic movement of the early 20th century that embraced, and even glorified, new machines and mechanization.

345

Il pleut

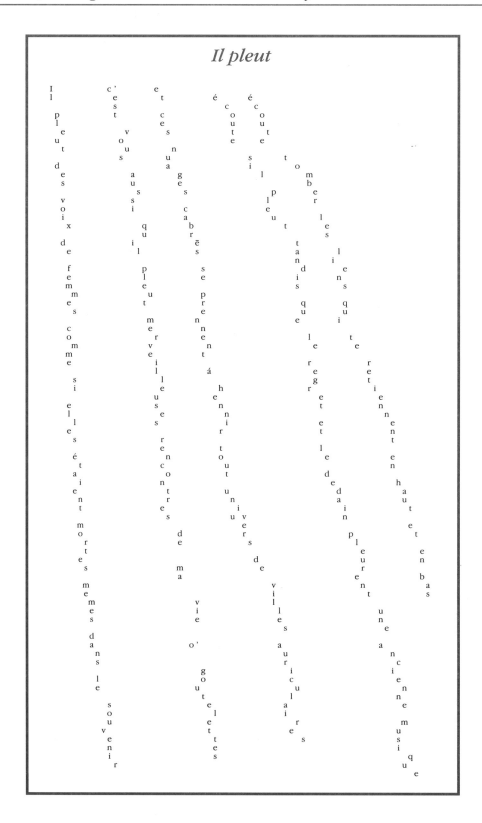

Il pleut des voix de femmes comme si elles étaient mortes même dans le souvenir

c'est vous aussi qu'il pleut merveilleuses rencontres de ma vie ô gouttelettes

et ces nuages cabrés se prennent à hennir tout un univers de villes auriculaires

écoute s'il pleut tandis que le regret et le dédain pleurent une ancienne musique

écoute tomber les liens qui te retiennent en haut et en bas

It's Raining

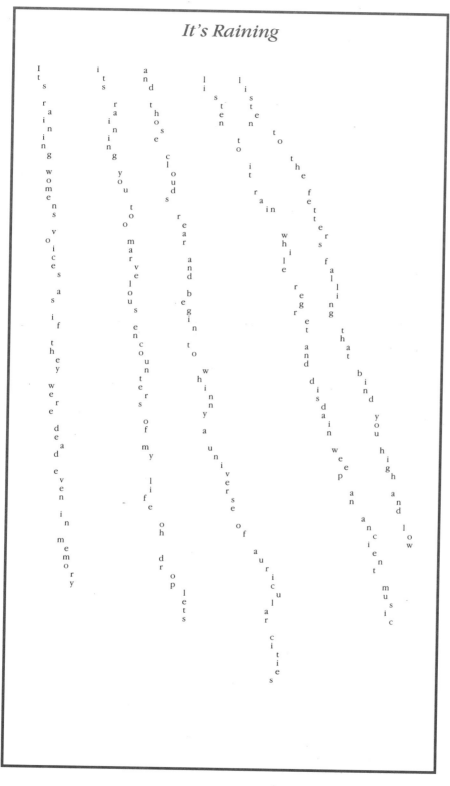

It's raining womens voices as if they were dead even in memory

its raining you to marvelous encounters of my life oh droplets

and those clouds rear and begin to whinny a universe of auricular cities

listen to it rain while regret and disdain weep an ancient music

listen to the fetters falling that bind you high and low

respected French poet Stéphane Mallarmé (1842–1898), a shy schoolteacher. The poem, "Un coup de dés" (A throw of the dice), had appeared in a literary magazine only a year before the poet's death. By the time it was republished to his exacting typographical specifications seventeen years later, in 1914, it had become a kind of battle cry among the avant-garde artists and writers in Paris, then the capital of European culture, and helped break down the barriers between poetry and the visual arts.

It was a new and startling kind of composition. In it, Mallarmé put into practice his own advice to his fellow poets: "Let us have an end to these incessant, back and forth motions of our eyes, traveling from one line to the next and beginning all over again." In his poems punctuation is abolished. Words and phrases are freed from the rules of traditional syntax* and, in effect, float about the page in clusters or "constellations." The open double-page spread, not the foot, line, or stanza,* is the unit of the poem. The reader plays a new role, a creative role, concentrating not only on *what* is expressed in words but also on *how* and *where* it is expressed, much in the way a conductor "reads" the superimposed notes of a musical score all at once. The new reader activates and completes the poem.

Apollinaire and the Calligram

An early and fervent admirer of "Un coup de dés" was the flamboyant "poet among the painters," Guillaume Apollinaire. Poet, novelist, playwright, art critic—and pornographer—Apollinaire was a prime mover, interpreter, and propagandist for the modernist movements in Europe. He called for a language of "visual lyricism" that would be a blending of all the arts, a dream more fully realized by the following generations of poets, artists, and composers after Apollinaire's early death in 1918.

Apollinaire's calligrams, which he sometimes called "lyrical ideograms," present modern subject matter at a literary and pictorial level simultaneously—the outline of a woman's breasts, a vase with flowers, a cognac bottle, a heart pierced by an arrow, a boxer, a gun, a watch, the Eiffel Tower. One of his best-known calligrams is "Il pleut" (It's raining), in which words and phrases evocative* of the poet's nostalgic memories streak down the page letter by letter, word by word, raindrop by raindrop, teardrop by teardrop.

*syntax the structure of a sentence; refers to word placement, as opposed to "diction," which refers to word choice

*stanza a group of lines in a poem

*evocative likely to cause an emotional response

If concrete poetry has a patron saint it is Mallarmé rather than Apollinaire, for concrete poetry is far more than a simple return to the poem as picture. The Swiss poet Eugen Gomringer, acknowledged "father" of the international concrete poetry movement, called his first book *Constellations,* a word borrowed from Mallarmé. A concrete poem, Gomringer wrote in his first manifesto (1954),

> disposes its groups of words as if they were clusters of stars. The constellation is a system, it is also a playground with definite boundaries. The poet . . . designs the playground as a field of force and suggests its possible workings. The reader, the new reader, accepts it in the spirit of play, then plays with it. With each new constellation something new comes into the world. Each constellation is a reality in itself and not a poem about some other thing. The constellation is a challenge, it is also an invitation.

It was a challenge and an invitation readily accepted by poets and artists worldwide: the Noigandres poets in Brazil, the Austrian Ernst Jandl, Ian Hamilton Finlay in Scotland, Pierre Garnier in France, Franz Mon in Germany, Seiichi Niikuni in Japan, and many other poets seeking a new poetics. They would all agree with Gomringer's warning that

> since our Concrete Poetry should actually be a genuine constituent of contemporary literature and contemporary thought, it is important that it should become not merely playful, that the element of play which we advocate should not result in a facetious kind of poetry. Concrete Poetry has nothing to do with comic strips. In my view it is fitted to make just as momentous statements about human existence in our times and about mental attitudes as other forms of poetry did in previous periods. It would be unfortunate if it were to become an empty entertainment for the typographer.

Selected Bibliography

ANTHOLOGIES

An Anthology of Concrete Poetry. Edited and compiled by Emmett Williams. New York: Something Else Press, 1967.

Concrete Poetry: An International Anthology. Edited and compiled by Stephen Bann. London: London Magazine Editions, 1967.

Concrete Poetry: A World View. Edited and compiled by Mary Ellen Solt. Bloomington: Indiana University Press, 1968.

Imaged Words and Worded Images. Edited and compiled by Richard Kostelanetz. New York: Outerbridge and Dienstfrey, 1970.

Pattern Poems: Guide to an Unknown Literature. Edited by Dick Higgins. Albany: State University of New York Press, 1987.

Poesia totale 1897–1997. Edited by Enrico Mascellone and Sarenco. Mantua, Italy: Palazzo della Ragione, 1998.

Speaking Pictures: A Gallery of Pictorial Poetry from the Sixteenth Century to the Present. Edited and compiled by Milton Klonsky. New York: Crown, 1975.

Typoésie. Edited by Jérôme Peignot. Paris: Imprimerie Nationale, 1993.

WORKS BY INDIVIDUAL POETS

Apollinaire, Guillaume. *Calligrammes: Poems of Peace and War (1913–1916).* Translated by Ann Hyde Greet. Berkeley: University of California Press, 1980.

Gomringer, Eugen. *The Book of Hours and Constellations.* Translated by Jerome Rothenberg. New York: Something Else Press, 1974.

Mallarmé, Stéphane. *Oeuvres completes.* Vol. 1. Edited by Bertrand Marchal. Paris: Bibliothèque de la Pléiade, Éditions Gallimard, 1998.

PERFORMANCE POETRY

by Anne Waldman

The term "performance poetry" is of recent origin, but the performed word goes back many thousands of years and is rooted in ancient ritual or religious traditions. It is a mistake, then, to think of poetry as just another branch of written literature. Poetry is also a branch of the performing arts, with a special relationship to theater.

Origins of Theater

Theater also has its origins in ancient rituals, and it draws on poetic language. In addition to dance, music, costumes, and masks, rituals include vocalization or singing of words. Many of the world's religious traditions use the power of the voice in invocations,* supplications,* hymns, prayers, mantras,* spells, and chants of all kinds. The idea seems to be that by naming your hopes and your fears, you can have power over your world.

*invocation pleas for help or divine intervention

*supplication prayer of asking or begging

*mantras mystical formulas or chants

Epic and Lyric Poetry

The epics* of Homer—the *Illiad* and the *Odyssey* (eighth century B.C.)—are based on a long tradition of heroic poetry that was created and transmitted orally. These epics were composed specifically for recitation. Lyric* poetry, which developed in Greece in the seventh century B.C., was sung to the accompaniment of a lyre, an ancient stringed instrument. Sappho (flourished ca. 600 B.C.), a poet from the island of Lesbos, worked with monodic (one voice) lyrics. The choral ode often used a chorus* of up to fifty voices.

*epic a long poem that tells the story of a hero's deeds

*lyric a kind of poetry characterized by musical and personal expression

*chorus in ancient Greek drama, a group of singers or dancers

Greek Odes and Drama

Ancient Greek odes (from the word *aeidein,* "to sing") were often written in praise of sports heroes and victorious warriors.

Greek drama, which came out of this sung "ode" tradition, was supposed to be "cathartic," meaning that you would have a liberating experience from viewing the performance.

In the sixth and fifth centuries B.C.E., Greek drama began to flourish. The Greek tragedies can also be traced to ritual—in this case to rituals primarily choral in form, in honor of the god Dionysus. The three great Greek tragic dramatists were Aeschylus (525–456 B.C.), Sophocles (c. 496–406 B.C.), and Euripides (484–406 B.C.). Aristophanes (c. 450–c. 388 B.C.) was the great comic playwright. The Romans had an early tradition of rude farces* and possibly were the originators of the satyr plays* before this form heavily influenced by Greek models.

*rude farces simple dramas written for common folk

*satyr plays rites involving dressing up as part beast

Mystery and Miracle Plays

Forms of performed poetry and theater that developed in the Middle Ages are the mystery and miracle plays, which began inside churches in many parts of Europe and were originally written in Latin. A mystery play was based on stories from the Bible, which were dramatized during special parts of the church service; this practice went on from the ninth to the sixteenth centuries. The story of the Passion of Christ (his suffering, death, and Resurrection) became popular toward the end of the twelfth century, and the name shifted from "mystery" to "passion" play. In the early fourteenth century Corpus Christi plays* were acted as single scenes on wagons that were drawn in order around a city or town. Miracle plays focused on the lives of Christian saints, and it is thought that these plays greatly influenced secular (nonreligious) drama during the medieval period. Four early miracle plays deal with Saint Nicholas, the patron saint of boys in school, who was the forerunner of Santa Claus.

*Corpus Christi plays plays performed during the Christian religious festival of Corpus Christi ("body of Christ")

Morality Plays

The morality play is a dramatized story with a message or moral in which the characters symbolized, and were named for, such concepts as the seven deadly sins—Lust, Avarice, Gluttony, Pride, Wrath, Sloth, and Envy. A character might simply be named Death. Morality plays were performed in various parts of Europe; one of the most famous is *Everyman.* A later one was entitled *The Longer Thou Livest, the More Fool Thou Art.*

Renaissance Poetic Drama

Renaissance poetic drama developed from the religious drama of the Middle Ages and was particularly successful in England. The great period of English drama began around 1580 with the work of John Lyly (1554–1606), George Peele (1556–1596), Robert Greene (ca. 1558–1592), and Thomas Kyd (1558–1594), all skilled versifiers. Christopher Marlowe (1564–1593) is the most important of these early dramatists; William Shakespeare (1564–1616) remains the genius of the age. He was able to adapt blank verse* to every conceivable purpose, and the beauty of his language, images, and sound is unrivaled. For a time, he was also an actor. Shakespeare's younger contemporaries and followers include Ben Jonson (1572–1637) and John Webster (ca. 1580–ca. 1625).

*__*blank verse__ unrhymed verse in iambic pentameter*

Masques

A unique type of poetic drama that also developed at this time was the court masque, composed in lyric meters* and set to music. Many native folk traditions and foreign traditions contributed to this form, including "morris dancing,"* mummers' pageants,* "disguisings,"* ballets, and morality plays. The masque was a royal and courtly entertainment in which a procession of masked figures would play out a plot, interspersed with speeches and songs. In the concluding dance the masks would be shed, and the players would take partners from the audience. Some of Shakespeare's plays incorporate the masque; it appears as a little play within the play in *The Tempest, The Winter's Tale,* and *Romeo and Juliet.*

*__*meter__ in poetry, the rhythmic pattern within each line*

*__*morris dancing__ vigorous traditional English dance*

*__*mummers pageants__ pantomime performances by disguised merrymakers*

__"disguisings"__ masquerades*

Dada

A long leap in time takes us to the Cabaret Voltaire in Zurich, Switzerland, in 1915, during World War I, where the dada movement was born. Hugo Ball (1886–1927), the German poet who ran this cabaret beer hall; his wife, Emmy Jennings;

*nihilistic belief that traditional values are unfounded and that existence is useless

and various artists and poets improvised very strange entertainment, which they called dada. Dada became an artistic movement that was both playful and nihilistic.* It attracted many artists and writers who considered themselves independent—beyond war and nationalism, living for other ideals.

In his cabaret, Ball tried out what he called his "new species of verse"—"verse without words," or sound poems constructed of nonsense syllables. He wore a special costume designed especially for the occasion. His legs were covered with boots of luminous blue cardboard. Around his neck, he wore a huge cardboard collar, scarlet inside and gold outside and attached so that it could be manipulated like wings. A blue-and-white-striped top hat completed the outfit. Ball described his role as a "magical bishop." He chanted:

> *gadji beri bimba*
> *glandridi lauli lonni cadori*
> *gadjama bim beri glassala*
> *glandridi glassala tuffm i zimbrabim*
> *blassa galassasa tuffm i zimbrabim. . .*

Another important member of this group was Tristan Tzara (1896–1963), the inventor of the "cut-up" technique for writing a poem: Cut out a newspaper article, cut out each word, put them all in a bag, shake. Tzara wrote a series of manifestos, one of which included these lines:

> Here is the great secret:
> *The thought is made in the mouth.*
> I still consider myself very charming.

(Motherwell, p. 87)

Kurt Schwitters (1887–1948), an important visual artist, also composed sound poems. In one of his demonstrations he showed the audience a sheet of paper containing one letter—*W.* Then he started to recite it in a slowly rising voice. His voice went from a whisper to the sound of a wailing siren to a shout. Another sound poem by Schwitters, "priimiitittiii," begins like this:

> *priimiitittiii   tisch*
> *tesch*
> *priimiitittiii   tesch*
> *tusch*

(Motherwell, p. xxii)

The dadaists were reacting against the European culture that had allowed World War I to arise, against conformity, and against standard language. Dada moved on to Paris in 1919 and developed into an international movement called surrealism.

Surrealism

The leader of surrealism was the poet André Breton (1896–1966). The use of dreams and hallucinations and the practice of automatic writing under the dictation of the subconscious were all surrealist methods of composition. The term "surrealist" was first used in the subtitle of a play by Guillaume Apollinaire (1880–1918). The play was called *Les mamelles de Tiresias** (The Breasts of Tiresias), subtitled "A Surrealist Drama." Surrealism influenced the movies and theater considerably, most notably the work of Antonin Artaud (1896–1948), who developed "theater of cruelty," and that of some playwrights of the "theater of the absurd."

***Tiresias** in Greek myth, a blind male seer of Thebes who was changed into a woman for seven years and then changed back again

Russian Futurism

In Russia, Vladimir Mayakovsky (1894–1930), wearing a bright yellow shirt and with his face bizarrely painted, declaimed the Russian Revolution's praise to dumbfounded peasants. One of his poems, "The Cloud in Trousers," has one of the best lines for a performer in any context: *"Can you hear me in the back?"*

Velimir Khlebnikov (1885–1922) wrote sound poems that have influenced new generations of American performance poets. For decades dramatic Russian poetry readings drew audiences of thousands.

Other Modernist Poets

Sound poetry events in the early part of the twentieth century influenced several generations of poet-performers and poets who wrote for theater. Poets of the modernist period often broke away from the usual three-act structure of drama. Gertrude Stein (1874–1946) wrote the libretto* for the "opera" *Four Saints in Three Acts* by the composer Virgil Thomson (1896–1989). She begins with the heading "Act One"; several

***libretto** the text of the words of an opera or other musical narrative

lines later she writes, "Repeat Act One," and then we are confronted with three consecutive scenes III, and so on. This opera was first performed in 1934 with an all-black cast, singing such lines as these:

Pigeons on the grass alas
Pigeons on the grass alas.
Short longer grass short longer longer shorter yellow
*   grass. . . .*

(Van Vechten, p. 609)

Vachel Lindsay (1879–1931), a populist* showman of poetry, traveled all over the United States trading poetry readings for room and board. During his readings, he often accompanied himself with a drum. The Welsh poet Dylan Thomas (1914–1953) offered dramatic incantations* at his readings and enjoyed quite a reputation for his grand vocal style. The Vienna group in Austria in the 1950s carried the dadaist and surrealist experiments forward. This group featured the sound poet Ernst Jandl (1891–1976) and the lyrical, dreamlike poetry of Friederike Mayröcker (b. 1924).

*incantation a spell or chant

The Beats, Poets' Theater

Since the 1950s the public poetry reading has proliferated in America. The beats*—reading primarily in coffeehouses in San Francisco and New York—often spoke with jazz accompaniment. The writing of Jack Kerouac (1922–1969) was heavily influenced by bebop* music. In one recording Kerouac reads his haiku* accompanied by jazz musicians Zoot Sims and Al Cohn. Beginning in the 1960s, the poet Allen Ginsberg (1926–1997) wrote and performed songs, accompanying himself on a portable organ. The Poet's Theater, started in New York by the poet Diane diPrima (b. 1934), presented plays by the poets Frank O'Hara, James Schuyler, and John Ashbery, among others.

*beats beatniks; rebellious nonconformist young people, especially artists, musicians, and writers of the 1950s

*bebop jazz a style of jazz that uses dissonant notes, unusual rhythms, and fast tempos

*haiku a Japanese poetic form, usually unrhymed and consisting of three lines of seventeen syllables. A haiku often contains only a single image. See also discussion of haiku in the essay on Poetic Forms in these volumes.

Happenings

"Happenings," which began in the 1950s, were a kind of performance that involved a wide range of dancers, musicians, artists, and poets. An early happening took place in the dining room at the innovative Black Mountain College in North Carolina. All the chairs for the audience were placed in the middle of the room, and the performances took place in and around the audience. These included the experimental composer John Cage (1912–1992) in a black suit and tie reading a visionary text while another poet—M. C. Richards (1916–1999)—recited standing on a ladder. The poet Charles Olson (1910–1970) stood up in the audience and recited a line or two. Movies were projected on the ceiling. The painter Robert Rauschenberg (b. 1925) operated old records on a hand-cranked phonograph, and the choreographer and dancer Merce Cunningham (b. 1919) improvised a dance around the audience.

Poetry Centers

Several literary centers that encourage and highlight poetry in performance include the St. Mark's Poetry Project in New York, the Nuyorican Poets' Cafe in New York (which features regular poetry contests), and the Jack Kerouac School of Disembodied Poetics at the Naropa Institute in Boulder, Colorado. At the Poetry Project, the avant-garde musicians John Cage and Yoko Ono, as well as the poet rockers Lou Reed, Patti Smith, and Jim Carroll have performed.

Rap

Rap emerged from black urban centers in the 1970s. Rap gets much of its power from its gripping, skillfully rhymed language. Particularly "strong" lyrics—referred to as "gangsta rap"—are often political in content and violent, reflecting the concerns of urban youth. Rap has probably reached more people through popular media and recordings than any other type of poetry performance.

Poetry Bouts and Slams

Poetic contests go back to ancient times. From the fourteenth to sixteenth centuries, the minnesingers* of Germany engaged in poetic combat, as did the Academy of the Joc Florals in Toulouse, France. This was the time of the roving troubadours,*

*minnesinger German singer, usually of love lyrics, of the Middle Ages

*troubadour a traveling poet. Troubadours were common in France in the Middle Ages. See also article "Troubadours" in this volume.

The poet Ed Sanders (b. 1939), who began the poetry rock group the Fugs in the 1960s and who performs with instruments of his own design, including a "talking tie," wrote this charming poem that extols the virtues of performance poetry ("perf-po") and invokes the sense of lineage and relationship to ancient theater and ritual.

*__Logos__ Greek word for "word" or "divine wisdom"

The Time of Perf-po Is Now

The time of perf-po is now
The time of perf-po is now

How beautiful is the
unification
of word & melody throb & vision
sky & thrill perf & joy
in the 4-dimensional poem zone

All the components that
Aristotle listed:
Plot, diction, Character, Meter/Melody,
Thought and Spectacle
fly into the zone
with Music, Motion, Logos.*
    Percussion, Bird Songs,
    Clogs, Images
    Story & Theme Events

    & speckled-throated lilies
    soft on the face

The time of perf-po is now
The time of perf-po is now

(Thirsting for Peace in a Raging Century)

---

*__jongleur__ a wandering entertainer of the Middle Ages

trobairitz (female troubadours), and jongleurs,* who "sang for their supper" in the courts of France, Italy, and Spain. The first competition of the Joc Florals took place in 1334, and the prize was a violet made of gold. It is not clear who won that first "bout," but one of the participants was a woman, Clemence Isaura. This contest was imitated in Barcelona shortly thereafter and continued in the Catalan dialect into the twentieth century. The main event of the contemporary Taos Poetry Circus in New Mexico is the World Heavyweight Champion Bout. The bout consists of ten rounds of poetry with a referee, a ring girl, a bell, and a trophy. The audience members are free to behave as they might at an actual boxing match—shouting, jeering, booing, whistling. Bout champions have included Victor Hernández Cruz (b. 1949), Anne Waldman (b. 1945), and Ntozake Shange (b. 1948).

Poetry slams are a modern-day competition involving both team and individual poets. The audience usually decides the winner. Slams began in the United States in the 1970s and are now catching on in Europe.

One-Poet Show

The poet-librettist Kenward Elmslie (b. 1929), long associated with the New York school, is perhaps the contemporary poet who best carries on in the dadaist tradition; he wears a strange painted "naked lady" costume and a painted crown of hair. Elmslie is a seasoned performer who travels around the country giving his one-man shows with taped music, occasional musicians, and slides. He has collaborated with visual artists and composers to create wacky but provocative visual and musical settings for his poems and songs. His creations—a fusion of poetry, musical comedy, and dreams—are unique, imaginative, even nostalgic journeys through the states of mind of various oddball characters. Some of his performances have titles that take the audience beyond the typical poetry reading: "Squeegee Bijou," "Palais Bimbo Lounge Show," and "Postcards on Parade."

Selected Bibliography

Brogan, T. V. F., ed. *The Princeton Handbook of Multicultural Poetries.* Princeton, N.J.: Princeton University Press, 1996.

Elmslie, Kenward. *Routine Disruptions: Selected Poems and Lyrics, 1960–1998.* Minneapolis, Minn.: Coffee House Press, 1998.

Gates, Henry Louis, and Nellie Y. McKay, eds. *The Norton Anthology of African American Literature.* New York: W. W. Norton, 1997.

Harrison, Jane Ellen. *Epilegomena to the Study of Greek Religion and Themis: A Study of the Social Origins of Greek Religion.* New Hyde Park, N.Y.: University Books, 1962.

Kirby, Michael. *Happenings.* New York: E. P. Dutton, 1965.

Motherwell, Robert. *The Dada Painters and Poets: An Anthology.* Cambridge, Mass.: Belknap Press, 1989.

Padgett, Ron, ed. *Handbook of Poetic Forms.* New York: Teachers and Writers Collaborative, 1987.

Preminger, Alex, and T. V. F. Brogan, eds. *The New Princeton Encyclopedia of Poetry and Poetics,* 3d ed. Princeton, N.J.: Princeton University Press, 1993.

Rothenberg, Jerome, ed. *Technicians of the Sacred.* Berkeley: University of California Press, 1985.

Sanders, Ed. *Thirsting for Peace in a Raging Century: Selected Poems, 1961–1985.* Minneapolis, Minn.: Coffee House Press, 1987.

Schechner, Richard, and Willa Appel, eds. *By Means of Performance: Intercultural Studies of Theatre and Ritual.* New York: Cambridge Univesity Press, 1990.

Van Vechten, Carl, ed. *The Selected Writings of Gertrude Stein.* New York: Random House, 1946.

Waldman, Anne. *Fast Speaking Woman.* San Francisco: City Lights, 1975, 1996.

Waldman, Anne, ed. *The Beat Book.* Boston: Shambhala, 1996.

SOME BASIC POETIC FORMS

by Ron Padgett

A poetic form is a pattern that organizes words in a way that can be beautiful, interesting, and satisfying. There are many poetic forms, each with its special virtue, and they all have rules, some strict, some loose. Putting words in a particular order or shape creates a feeling of unity, which is a feeling that all good poetry has, no matter how odd, difficult, or disorganized it may appear at first. There are many different ways to create an orderly shape with words, such as using a particular rhythm, using words that rhyme, making the lines have a similar length, and putting lines into groups (called "stanzas"). This orderly arrangement of words can produce poems that, when read aloud, have an appealing sound, what is called their "music." Until the twentieth century, most poets used what are called fixed forms (ones with fairly definite rules).

Order and musicality are not the only virtues of fixed forms. Another virtue is surprise: sometimes the restrictions of a form will cause the author to write things that he or she had not expected (there is an example of this in the discussion of the acrostic form below). In this way, forms can inspire writers, just as strong feelings can.

The relationship between the form and content of a poem is a subject that scholars and poets have discussed for centuries, but two things are sure: first, a form can help generate the content of a poem, and, second, content can generate a suitable new form. In good poems, the form and content seem inseparable. As the Irish poet William Butler Yeats asked in his poem "Among School Children," "How can we know the dancer from the dance?"

For information about poetic meter, see Appendix 1 in this volume.

The Most Enjoyable Way to Learn About Poetic Forms

Poetics* reference books define poetic forms, but most of them do not give you a feel for how the form works. But poetic forms are like games—they both have rules—and it is a lot more fun to play a game than to read about its rules. The same

*poetics the theory of poetry

361

applies to poetry. That is why I suggest you use the information below to write a few poems yourself, to learn from the inside out how they work. If you prefer not to write, the information will be useful to you anyway.

I have picked seven poetic forms that are interesting for anyone to learn about and to try, especially young people who might not have a lot of experience with poetry. These forms are inviting, and together they suggest the wide range of possibilities in poetry. I have arranged them in a sequence that would be good to follow, but feel free to try them in any order you like. And keep in mind that it is okay to bend poetic rules. Poets have done it for many centuries, sometimes expanding the definition of a particular form by doing so.

Only one of the forms below—the traditional sonnet—follows a prescribed system of rhymes and rhythms. Using rhyme well in the English language is not easy. So if you are a beginning writer, you should not be too concerned with trying to rhyme. As for rhythm, you will find that if you like music or dancing, you already have a knack for it. Besides, almost everything we say has a rhythm. If you read a poem aloud, you will notice when the rhythm sounds good and when it sound clunky. The main thing, though, is not to worry about whether your writing is "correct." Think of trying these poetic forms as an experiment, as an active way of learning about them, as a way of opening yourself up to the magic of poetry.

The Acrostic

The acrostic is one of the easiest and most amusing poetic forms. To write a basic acrostic, choose any word (such as your own name) or short phrase and write it *down* the page instead of *across* the page, as I do here with my name:

R
O
N
P
A
D
G
E
T
T

... Keep in mind that it is okay to bend poetic rules. Poets have done it for many centuries. ...

Then go back and fill out the lines. For example:

> Run all
> Over the world and you will
> Never find the lost
> Paradise that
> A
> Delicious
> God
> Established even for
> The
> Termites!

Until I wrote that poem (a minute ago, off the top of my head), I had never imagined a delicious god. I do not know what a delicious god is, but I like the way it makes me feel, and without the acrostic form, I might never have thought of it. One of the beauties of the acrostic is the way that it prompts you to come up with such surprises, if you let your mind go and accept what it offers you, even something silly or weird. Of course, an acrostic can be quite serious too (parts of the Bible were originally written in acrostic form). An acrostic can have any tone you like. In acrostics, there is no rule for the number of words per line, though lines with a huge number of words would probably defeat the purpose of the form. My example of an acrostic happens to consist of only one sentence, but acrostics can have several shorter ones, or simply a series of phrases or images.

There are many possible variations on the basic acrostic form. One of them involves having a word or name along the left edge of the poem (as in the basic form) and another one along the right edge. "A Valentine to __ __ __" by Edgar Allan Poe (1809–1849) is another variation. In it he used the name of his beloved, with the first letter of her name as the first letter of the first line, the second letter of her name as the second letter in the second line, and so on, so that her name formed a diagonal cutting down through the finished poem. Only someone who knew he used that method would know to whom he addressed his love poem. In fact, the same is true of all acrostics: the original word or name is camouflaged in the poem—another part of the fun.

The Haiku

The haiku (commonly pronounced "HI-coo") is a popular poetic form that has been used in Japan for hundreds of years by

Until I wrote that poem. . . I had never imagined a delicious god.

famous poets and by ordinary people. It has become quite popular in America and the rest of the world as well. Some people say that the haiku form consists of three lines and that the first one has five syllables, the second has seven, and the third has five, for a total of seventeen syllables. This is not quite true, since the Japanese syllable and the English syllable are not the same. Although most contemporary American haiku have three short lines, sometimes the number of syllables in them varies a lot.

There are other things that make a haiku a haiku. Often the haiku describes the experience of a single moment, using simple words to focus clearly on something in nature. Haiku do not use similes, metaphors, explanatory language, or hidden meanings to be puzzled over; rather, they simply present moments of clear perception that give the reader pleasure. Here are some examples (translated by William J. Higginson), the first by one of the early great Japanese haiku masters:

> *Haiku do not use similes, metaphors, explanatory language, or hidden meanings to be puzzled over. . . .*

old pond . . .
a frog leaps in
water's sound

—Matsuo Bashō (1644–1694)

oh, don't swat!
the fly rubs hands
rubs feet

—Kobayashi Issa (1763–1827)

Japanese women are also great haiku writers:

fresh-washed hair
everywhere I go
making trickles

—Hashimoto Takako (1899–1963)

Here are a few contemporary Japanese and North American examples:

autumn salmon
the flipping leaping
one I catch

—Takahashi Kazuo

Listening . . .
   After a while
      I take up my axe again.

—Rod Wilmot

red flipped out
chicken lung
in a cold white sink

—Anita Virgil

buzzZ
  slaP
buzzZ

—Alan Pizzarelli

As you can see, these modern haiku—especially the last one—do not have anywhere near the seventeen syllables of traditional haiku.

If you want to try writing haiku, it is a good idea to write several of them quickly. If the first few do not sound very good, just keep writing. This way you will loosen up and eventually find that you are writing them with ease. Keep the ones you like. Improve the others later.

The Ode

There are so many types of odes that no single strict definition can describe them all. Different poets have used different stanza sizes and rhythm and rhyme patterns. In general, though, an ode is a serious poem about a single subject, treated with dignity. Sometimes the ode is addressed to a person or a thing. Another way an ode gets to be an ode is when the author calls his or her poem "Ode"!

The earliest odes we know of were written by the ancient Greek poet Pindar (522–442 B.C.). His odes followed complicated patterns of rhythm and stanza shapes and were written to be sung and danced by a chorus. The only surviving odes by Pindar are his victory odes, in which he praises the winners of athletic events in an exalted and intense tone and with expansive feeling.

[One] way an ode gets to be an ode is when the author calls his or her poem "Ode"!

The ancient Roman poet Horace (65–8 B.C.) wrote quieter, more philosophic odes, usually shorter than Pindar's. Horace would pick a stanza form and then repeat it throughout his ode. One English poet who wrote odes of this type was Alexander Pope (1688–1744; see his "Ode on Solitude").

The English Romantic poets excelled in writing odes. Among the most famous of them are "Ode on a Grecian Urn" and "Ode to a Nightingale" by John Keats (1795–1821), "Ode to the West Wind" by Percy Bysshe Shelley (1792–1822), and "Ode: Intimations of Immortality from Recollections of Early Childhood" by William Wordsworth (1770–1850). All these poems continue the ode's classical tradition of treating a serious subject in a dignified manner.

In the twentieth century, poets redefined the ode in various ways. The American poet Frank O'Hara (1926–1966) wrote odes—such as "Ode to Joy," "Ode to Willem de Kooning," and "Ode to Michael Goldberg('s Birth and Other Births)"—that have no set patterns of rhyme, meter, or stanza but that have an expansive energy reminiscent of Pindar's. The Chilean poet Pablo Neruda (1904–1973) gave the form a surprising twist by writing odes addressed to everyday objects, as in his "Ode to My Socks," "Ode to Salt," and this, his "Ode to the Watermelon":

> The tree of intense
> summer,
> hard,
> is all blue sky,
> yellow sun,
> fatigue in drops,
> a sword
> above the highways,
> a scorched shoe
> in the cities:
> the brightness and the world
> weigh us down,
> hit us
> in the eyes
> with clouds of dust,
> with sudden golden blows,
> they torture
> our feet
> with tiny thorns,

with hot stones,
and the mouth
suffers
more than all the toes:
the throat
becomes thirsty,
the teeth,
the lips, the tongue:
we want to drink
waterfalls,
the dark blue night,
the South Pole,
and then
the coolest of all
the planets crosses
the sky,
the round, magnificent,
star-filled watermelon.

It's a fruit from the thirst-tree.
It's the green whale of the summer.

The dry universe
all at once
given dark stars
by this firmament of coolness
lets the swelling
fruit
come down:
its hemispheres open
showing a flag
green, white, red,
that dissolves into
wild rivers, sugar,
delight!

Jewel box of water, phlegmatic
queen
of the fruitshops,
warehouse
of profundity, moon
on earth!
You are pure,

rubies fall apart
in your abundance,
and we
want
to bite into you,
to bury our
face
in you, and
the soul!
When we're thirsty
we glimpse you
like
a mine or a mountain
of fantastic food,
but
among our longings and our teeth
you change
simply
into cool light
that slips in turn into
spring water
that touches us once
singing.
And that is why
you don't weigh us down
in the siesta hour
that's like an oven,
you don't weigh us down,
you just
go by
and your heart, some cold ember,
turned itself into a single
drop of water.

(Translated by Robert Bly)

Odes are good to write when you have a strong positive feeling about a particular person or idea or object. No matter what type of ode you write, the attraction between you and the subject is crucial. A good way to learn about the ode is to read examples of it, starting with the contemporary (Neruda's, for example) and working your way back to the ancient (Pindar's). Even if you cannot explain every word in these poems, you will absorb things from them just by reading them. For one thing, you will begin to get a "feel" for their forms.

The Pantoum

The pantoum (pronounced "pan-TOOM") is a wonderful form that first appeared in Malaysian literature in the fifteenth century, although as an oral form it goes back further than that. In the nineteenth century, French poets learned about pantoums and began writing them. English poets then picked up the form, and, since the 1950s, some American poets have used it.

In pantoums, rhyme and a set meter are not necessary, and there is no definite length. The only requirement is that the poem have stanzas of four lines each, with the lines repeated according to the following pattern.

First you write one stanza. That makes four lines.

Lines 2 and 4 must now be repeated as lines 1 and 3 of the second stanza. Copy them into the second stanza, and then create new lines 2 and 4 for it.

Now lines 2 and 4 of the second stanza become lines 1 and 3 of the third stanza, which you fill out with two new lines.

This pattern continues for as long as you want (though most pantoums have at least five or six stanzas, allowing the repetitions to work their magic). A neat way to end a pantoum is to have lines 3 and 1 of your first stanza—the only ones not repeated in the poem so far—come back as lines 2 and 4 of the final stanza. That way, all the lines are repeated, and the first line of the poem is also the last. The pattern sounds complicated, but it really is not, especially if you look at an example, my previously unpublished poem "The Shooting Star":

> With the brevity of a shooting star,
> I look at my memory of you:
> The light falls on your face
> And I wish for it to happen.
>
> I look at my memory of you.
> It is only one inch high
> and I wish for it to happen,
> and then it happens:
> It is only one inch high,

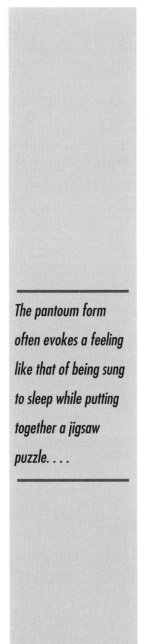

The pantoum form often evokes a feeling like that of being sung to sleep while putting together a jigsaw puzzle. . . .

the book with the king inside it.
And then it happens—
the king steps out of the book.

The book with the king inside it
is shining like a movie star.
The king steps out of the book
and my mind

is shining like a movie star
who knows me well
and my mind,
just below where thoughts fly up.

Who knows me well?
The dark puts its heavy paw on my shoulder
just below where thoughts fly up
and the invisible flower explodes again.

The dark puts its heavy paw on my shoulder,
saying "I am another you,
and the invisible flower explodes again
because of the accident you have become."

Saying "I am another you,"
the light falls on your face
because of the accident you have become
with the brevity of a shooting star.

Writers of pantoums find themselves thinking ahead in the poem so that some repeated lines will take on a different feeling or meaning because of the lines around them. The pantoum form often evokes a feeling like that of being sung to sleep while putting together a jigsaw puzzle—a wonderful, interlocking dreaminess.

The Sonnet

The sonnet is probably the most famous poetic form in the English language, though it was an Italian named Giacomo da Lentini (ca. 1200–1250) who is believed to have invented it.

The word "sonnet" comes from the Italian *sonnetto,* which means "little sound" or "song." There are several different types of traditional sonnets, but they all have fourteen lines. Until the twentieth century, sonnets also had definite patterns of rhyme and rhythm.

The most common type of sonnet is the Italian, or Petrarchan, sonnet, which consists of two parts, of eight lines and six lines (called the octave and sestet). In the following example of this type of sonnet ("Mee thought I saw my late espoused saint"), John Milton (1608–1674) describes a dream in which his deceased wife (his "late espoused saint") appears. If you read the poem aloud, its old-fashioned spelling will not seem so strange. In the margin is a paraphrase* of the poem, but it is okay if you do not understand everything in the poem. (Few people do.) Just focus first on noticing the poem's form:

> Mee thought I saw my late espoused saint
> > Brought to me like Alcestis* from the grave
> > Whom Jove's* great son to her glad husband gave
> > Rescu'd from death by force though pale and faint.
> Mine as whom washt from spot of child-bed taint,
> > Purification in th' old law did save,
> > And such, as yet once more I trust to have
> > Full sight of her in heav'n without restraint,
> Came vested all in white, pure as her mind:
> > Her face was veil'd, yet to my fancied sight,
> > Love, sweetness, goodness in her person shin'd
> So clear, as in no face with more delight.
> > But O, as to embrace me she inclin'd,
> > I wak'd, she fled, and day brought back my night.

The rhyme scheme here is *abbaabba cdcdcd* (some poets—including Milton—varied this scheme). The rhythmic pattern (meter) of his lines is called iambic pentameter. That is, each line has ten syllables, with an accent on the even-numbered syllables.

The second type of sonnet is the Spenserian (named after the sixteenth-century English poet Edmund Spenser). This type has four sections (stanzas), with a rhyme scheme of *abab bcbc cdcd ee.* Below is an example, "Sonnet LXXV," from Spenser's collection of sonnets, *Amoretti* (1595). I have modernized the spelling.

*paraphrase a restatement of something using different wording from the original

*Alcestis in Greek myth, the wife of Admetus, who dies for her husband and is brought back to life by Heracles

*Jove the supreme god among Roman pagan deities, also known as Jupiter

Here is a paraphrase of this poem: I thought I saw my saintly, dead wife, brought to me the way the son of the god Jove revived Alcestis and returned her to her husband. My wife was purified, the way I hope to see her in heaven, and dressed in pure white, and although she was wearing a veil, I felt I could see clearly her radiant beauty and goodness. But when she bent down to embrace me, I woke up, she disappeared, and the daylight plunged me back into my dark depression.

*strand beach

*vain foolish

*in vain unsuccess-
fully

*assay try

*like to this like this

*eek also

*quod I I said

*baser lower

*whenas when

One day I wrote her name upon the strand*
But came the waves and washéd it away:
Again I wrote it with a second hand,
But came the tide, and made my pains his prey.
"Vain* man," said she, "that doest in vain* assay*
A mortal thing so to immortalize,
For I myself shall like to this* decay,
And eek* my name, be wipéd out likewise."
"Not so," quod I,* "let baser* things devise
To die in dust, but you shall live by fame:
My verse your virtues rare shall eternize,
And in the heavens write your glorious name.
Where whenas* death shall all the world subdue,
Our love shall live, and later life renew."

The third type, the Shakespearean sonnet, follows a rhyme scheme of *abab cdcd efef gg*, using more rhymes than the previous two types. Here is an example from Shakespeare himself, his sonnet xxx:

*session a sitting of
the royal court

*with old woes new
wail cry out in grief
again

*dateless endless

*expense loss

*grievances fore-
gone old causes for
grief

*tell count

*o'er over, again

*iambic pentameter
verse that has five met-
rical feet to a line, with
two syllables in each
foot and the accent
(stress) on the second
syllable (example: da
DA da DA)

When to the sessions* of sweet silent thought
I summon up remembrance of things past,
I sigh the lack of many a thing I sought,
And with old woes new wail* my dear time's waste:

Then can I drown an eye, unused to flow,
For precious friends hid in death's dateless* night,
And weep afresh love's long since cancell'd woe,
And moan the expense* of many a vanish'd sight:

Then can I grieve at grievances foregone,*
And heavily from woe to woe tell* o'er*
The sad account of fore-bemoanéd moan,
Which I new pay as if not paid before.

But if the while I think on thee, dear friend,
All losses are restored and sorrows end.

Shakespeare varies the iambic pentameter* pattern, so it does not sound mechanical or monotonous.

In addition to patterns of rhyme and meter, the sonnet has other characteristics. It is usually about one theme, such as love or death, and typically treats that theme thoughtfully and seriously. Also, in most cases the sonnet presents its

theme, reveals the complexity of the theme, and then resolves the complexity or says something that sounds conclu-
sive. Look at the example from Shakespeare: in the first four
stanzas, the poet talks about how depressed he gets when he
thinks about the past, and in the final two lines he resolves
the issue. Those final two rhyming lines, called the couplet,
have a satisfying effect, like dessert at the end of dinner. In addition to length, rhyme, and rhythm, this tendency to present
an unresolved situation and then resolve it is at the heart of
the sonnet.

Some poets have continued to write strictly traditional
sonnets, but others have expanded the possibilities of the
form. The rhythmic variations of the sonnets of Gerard Manley
Hopkins (1844–1889) give them great energy, as in the following poem about a bird. Read the poem aloud, and you will see
what I mean, even if you do not understand all the words:

The Windhover: *
    (TO CHRIST OUR LORD)

I caught this morning morning's minion,* king-
    dom of daylight's dauphin,* dapple-dawn-drawn Fal-
    con, in his riding
    Of the rolling level underneath him steady air, and
      striding
High there, how he rung upon the rein* of a wimpling*
    wing
In his ecstasy! then off, off forth on swing,
    As a skate's heel sweeps smooth on a bow-bend: the
      hurl and gliding
    Rebuffed the big wind. My heart in hiding
Stirred for a bird,—the achieve of, the mastery of the
    thing!

Brute beauty and valour and act, oh, air, pride, plume
    here
    Buckle*! AND the fire that breaks from thee then, a bil-
    lion
Times told lovelier, more dangerous, O my chevalier*!

    No wonder of it: shéer plód makes plough* down sil-
    lion*
Shine, and blue-bleak embers, ah, my dear,
    Fall, gall* themselves, and gash gold-vermilion.

windhover a falcon

minion a follower; a servant

dauphin royal suc-cessor; son of the king of France

rung upon the rein circled, like a horse on a rein circling around a trainer

wimpling rippling

buckle bend or col-lapse under a heavy weight

chevalier a knight; a cavalier

plough plow

sillion a furrow, a strip of arable land

gall rub; chafe; irritate

Notice how, from the very first line, Hopkins makes one line run over into the next. This technique—called "enjambment"—gives poems more forward momentum.

The American poet Edwin Denby (1903–1983) allowed some of his sonnets to be quick and sketchy. In his later sonnets, he does not use a regular rhythm, and sometimes he abandons rhyme, but he does keep to a single theme or feeling, as in this untitled sonnet that compares the way he saw the world when he was fifteen with the way his life actually turned out:

Inattentively fortunate
Having been pausing at lunchcounters
While what I most like, art that's great
Has been being painted upstairs
No homebuilder, even goofy
To virtue have been close as that
It I love and New York's beauty
Both have nodded my way, up the street
At fifteen maybe believed the world
Would turn out so honorable
So much like what poetry told
Heartbreak and heroes of fable
And so it did; close enough; the
Djin* gave it, disappeared laughing

*djin genie

The sonnets of Ted Berrigan (1934–1983) dispense with rhyme and meter; they seem to be about many things all at once. Most of his sonnets have fourteen lines, but a few have as many as twenty-three! This does stretch the definition of sonnet a bit far. If you saw one of his fourteen-line sonnets, you might not recognize it as a sonnet until you learned that he collected these poems in a book called *The Sonnets*.

In addition to the poets quoted here, there are many others who wrote wonderful sonnets; among them are Dante, the sixteenth-century English poet Thomas Wyatt, William Wordsworth, John Keats, Elizabeth Barrett Browning, Edna St. Vincent Millay, Rainer Maria Rilke, and John Berryman. Some poets have written a series of connected sonnets, called a sonnet cycle.

At first, writing a sonnet can seem hard. To practice, you might want to begin by picking the rhyme words first and writing them down the right-hand edge of a piece of paper. Then go back and fill in the lines. The result might be silly or odd, and you might find yourself adding unnecessary words ("padding") just to maintain the rhythm, but at least you will start to have a better sense of the sonnet form. You might prefer to start from scratch. Once you have a first draft, it is interesting to go back and tinker with it, to smooth out the rhythm, to change a word here and there, to rewrite a line that sounds phony. It is satisfying to improve any poem, but the sonnet, like a beautifully made little machine, gives special pleasure when its parts are all working together efficiently and in harmony.

Shaped Poetry (and Its Variations)

In shaped poetry, the written words form the shape of an object or animal, such as a cross, a tree, or a horse. This type of poetry goes back as far as ancient Greece and can be found all over the world, including particularly beautiful examples in Arabic. Shaped poetry (also called "pattern poetry") is a hybrid of written language and visual art. Although it sacrifices rhythm, it opens up new possibilities for writing and reading poetry.

Two of the most famous shaped poems in English are "Easter Wings" and "The Altar" by George Herbert (1593–1633). Shaped verse became more widespread in the twentieth century with the publication of Guillaume Apollinaire's collection of poems, *Calligrammes*. Here is an example:

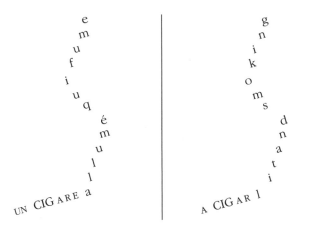

Much of the pleasure of this simple poem comes from its arrangement on the page; if these same words were written out in the usual way (left to right), the poem would lose most of its charm.

*futurist adherent of an Italian artistic movement of the early 20th century that embraced, and even glorified, new machines and mechanization. See also section on futurism in the essay on Twentieth-Century Modernism in these volumes.

*dada a movement in art and literature that emphasized chance and the irrational

Apollinaire wrote "calligrams" in the shape of a valentine heart, a pistol, the Eiffel Tower, a necktie, a house, a mandolin, a bird, a train, and so forth. He even wrote one that did not look like anything in particular: its lines just fly all over the page. This poem is like those of a group called the Italian futurists,* who, about the same time as Apollinaire, were advocating a kind of writing they called "words set free," in which words and phrases were placed around the page, some larger than others, crooked, upside down, any which way. One futurist work used invented words, such as "SCRABrrRrraaNNG" and "GRAAAAG," wildly flying around among other such explosions, to describe a battle scene in World War I. Both Apollinaire and the futurists (as well as the dada* poets who followed) felt that because modern life was radically different, it could be described only in a radically new way.

This liberation of words led to a related type of poetry called "concrete poetry," which became popular in the 1950s. With the development of the personal computer and better computer programs, it became easy to generate words in different typefaces, sizes, and positions on the page and to combine words and pictures (this combination is sometimes called "collage").

Of course, it can still all be done by hand, the way the modern American poet Kenneth Patchen (1911–1972) did it. You can use a pencil, ink, or paint; you can cut words out of magazines and newspapers and glue them together in new combinations. You can assign colors to words and phrases, the way the French poet Arthur Rimbaud (1854–1891) did when he assigned colors to the vowels of the alphabet. The possibilities are vast.

Free Verse

Free verse is hard to describe because, as its name suggests, it has no set patterns to follow. Good free verse does, however, have a sense of unity, which can be achieved in a great variety of ways. Modern free verse got its start in France in the nineteenth century, but the father of free verse in English is Walt Whitman (1819–1892), whose *Leaves of Grass* not only showed a whole new way to write, but is also a great book filled with boundless energy, an expansive spirit, and colorful and interesting details. Whitman's big, roomy poems are held together by unity of tone and theme and by the momentum of his long lines and lists. Read his poem "Song of Myself," and you will get an idea of how his free verse works.

Whitman created a type of free verse that was right for him. Other poets have done the same for themselves, which is why there are as many types of free verse as there are people who write it. We might even go so far as to say that in the best free verse a new form is created with each poem, a unique fusion of meaning, sound, and shape that can be right only for that poem. Because free verse has no rules for rhyme, meter, or length, it is easier than fixed forms, but in another sense it is harder because in writing it you must create the rules as you write, to give the poem a feeling of unity. It is not quite so "free" as it sounds.

Free verse eventually became the dominant form in the twentieth century. To get an idea of its range, look at the work of William Carlos Williams, Guillaume Apollinaire, the American poet H. D. (Hilda Doolittle), Robert Creeley, Elizabeth Bishop, Allen Ginsberg, John Ashbery, Langston Hughes, and Anne Porter.

. . . In writing [free verse] you must create the rules as you write, to give the poem a feeling of unity. It is not quite so "free" as it sounds.

Conclusion

People like freedom, but they also like order. The order in poetic forms comes in many shapes and sizes, but in all cases it is most pleasing when it is neither too tight nor too loose, like a glove that fits your hand perfectly: the container (the poetic form) and the contained (the words) seem to be made for each other. In these cases, the poem begins, develops, and ends, giving us the feeling that it is just the right shape and length. The best use of poetic forms provides this satisfying sense of unity and shapeliness.

Different poetic forms have different effects; for example, a good pantoum is hypnotic, a good haiku wakes you up. There are many other wonderful forms, such as the ballad, the blues poem, the cento, the chant, the eclogue, the elegy, the epistle, the found poem, the ghazal, the list poem, the nonsense poem, the prose poem, the rap poem, the renga, the sestina, and the villanelle. Each one brings its own little world. Each has its challenges and pleasures. Each has its own way of leading you deeper into the fascinating connections among words, poetic structures, and the imagination.

Selected Bibliography

POETIC FORMS HANDBOOKS

Padgett, Ron, ed. *The Teachers & Writers Handbook of Poetic Forms.* New York: Teachers & Writers Collaborative, 2000. Nineteen poets helped assemble this collection of articles on traditional and modern poetic forms. Each article defines the form, tells something of its history, quotes examples, and gives advice on how to use the form. The handbook is designed for high school and college students and teachers.

Preminger, Alex, and T. V. F. Brogan, eds. *The New Princeton Encyclopedia of Poetry and Poetics.* Princeton, N.J.: Princeton University Press, 1993. Considerable detail in an authoritative and sometimes scholarly book, with discussions of just about everything you would want to know about poetry. It is more suitable for advanced high school students and college students.

ACROSTIC

Collom, Jack, and Sheryl Noethe. *Poetry Everywhere.* New York: Teachers & Writers Collaborative, 1994. Written by two poets, with good information on lots of poetic forms and writing ideas.

HAIKU

Higginson, William J. *The Haiku Handbook.* Tokyo: Kodansha International, 1989. The best book ever written about the haiku form, including a history of haiku and many examples as well as advice on teaching and writing haiku.

Van den Heuvel, Cor. *The Haiku Anthology.* 3d ed. New York: Norton, 1999. An excellent international anthology of haiku.

ODE

Neruda, Pablo, and Cesar Vallejo. *Selected Poems.* Translated by Robert Bly and others. Boston: Beacon Press, 1971.

PANTOUM

Jouet, Jacques. *Echelle et papillons: Le pantoum.* Paris: Belles Lettres, 1998. The best book on this form, but in French. For good but smaller discussions of this form, see the entries in the books listed under Poetic Forms Handbooks.

SONNET

Bender, Robert M., and Charles L. Squier. *The Sonnet: A Comprehensive Anthology.* New York: Washington Square Press, 1965.

Berrigan, Ted. *The Sonnets.* New York: Penguin Books, 2000.

Denby, Edwin. *The Complete Poems.* Edited by Ron Padgett. New York: Random House, 1986.

Negri, Paul, ed. *Great Sonnets.* New York: Dover, 1994.

Shakespeare, William. *Sonnets.* Available in many editions. This is the most famous book of sonnets in the English-speaking world, if not the entire world.

SHAPED POETRY (AND ITS VARIATIONS)

Apollinaire, Guillaume. *Calligrammes.* Translated by Anne Hyde Greet. Berkeley: University of California Press, 1980. A bilingual edition, with excellent notes.

Marinetti, F. T. *Selected Writings.* Translated by R. W. Flint and Arthur A. Coppotelli. New York: Farrar, Straus and Giroux, 1972.

Motherwell, Robert, ed. *The Dada Painters and Poets.* 2d ed. Cambridge, Mass.: Harvard University Press, 1989. An exciting anthology of writings and illustrations, many featuring experimental typography and combinations of words and pictures.

Morice, Dave. *The Adventures of Dr. Alphabet.* New York: Teachers & Writers Collaborative, 1995. More than one hundred inventive ways to write poetry, such as creating a poetry robot or taping a roll of paper all the way around a school building and having everyone contribute to the one long line that goes all the way around to meet itself at the beginning.

Patchen, Kenneth. *Because It Is.* New York: New Directions, 1960.

Patchen, Kenneth. *Hallelujah Anyway.* New York: New Directions, 1966.

Williams, Emmett, ed. *An Anthology of Concrete Poetry.* New York: Something Else Press, 1967. The best selection of this type of poetry.

FREE VERSE

See the entries in the books listed under Poetic Forms Handbooks.

ADVICE ON WRITING POETRY

by Kenneth Koch and Kate Farrell

Writing poetry is interesting and exciting. Why would poets write it if it weren't? But writing poetry for a classroom assignment often seems difficult and boring and embarrassing. Students think that they won't write well enough, that they won't be able to get started writing—to find a first line, to find something to write about, to find enough to say. They're afraid that they won't be inspired, that they have no ideas that are right for poetry. One reason for this difficulty in writing poetry is probably that the way many people think that poetry should be written has been very much influenced by various old-fashioned and false ideas about poetry—ideas that can make poetry writing seem like an unrewarding struggle. Reading modern poetry can inspire you to be rid of useless worries and restrictions and to write in freer and more experimental ways.

And so the poems you write are likely to be different from the ones you have written before. And the way of writing may seem different from the way you thought poems were written. But you will probably end up liking to write and liking your poems.

Although your poetry may be freer, this does not mean that there is no work involved in writing it. But it is a kind of work that you discover how to do while you're writing. And it seems that it can best be discovered by beginning with freedom and pleasure and ease and by being attentive to your own inclinations and open to many different possibilities.

For a beginning writer the usual kind of thinking, in fact, can get in the way. This is because it is not mainly your intellect that you use to write poetry, but what might be called your imaginative intelligence, which is different. In writing poetry, you think more the way you do when you daydream or make a joke or talk with your friends than the way you do when you write an essay or punctuate a sentence. It is a natural kind of thinking, but since it is not often talked about or specifically required in school, it is perhaps strange to find out how valuable and important it is.

When you are going to write a poem, you don't have to think too much before you begin, or worry about how to begin, or wonder how to make the poem right. How you start the poem isn't likely to be crucial. There is no right answer when you write a poem. To create something means to make something that wasn't there before, so how can there be a right answer? Try writing down the first thing that comes into your mind and whatever else comes after that, even if it's not connected. When ideas are connected in usual ways, what is said can end up being the usual thing, which may be uninteresting. Sometimes you have to get away from the usual connections in order for new ones to appear. That is one of the things inspiration is about. Try making impossible, untrue statements or being funny, crazy, or silly. You could try writing in a way that seems very unlike you. You do not have to end your poem with something general or abstract. "And then I woke up" and "but it wasn't really true" kinds of endings are often boring. Be as free and particular at the end as you are in the middle. If you want to give the poem a title, you don't have to give it one that describes the poem. When a baby girl is born, you don't name her Baby Girl. You name her Jill, or some other name you like. Give your poem a title that adds something to it.

It is often good to write even when you don't feel inspired. Inspiration may come after you start to write, but in any case writing and trying new things will make you a better writer. The first person to please is yourself. It is a sign of success if you write something you like—or if you write in a way that you have never written before, if you say something you've never said or didn't know you knew, if you find out something, or if you've put words together in a way that seems beautiful or new or exciting. You'll like some poems better than others, some parts of a poem better than other parts. After you write a few poems, you'll probably begin to be more particular about what you want in your poems; you'll want to change words or lines or add things or leave things out. That's fine. Revision is an interesting part of writing.

If you already write poetry, you may have the idea that being influenced by another poet will make your poem less your own. You may want to write always in a style that you feel is completely yours. It is helpful to know that poets have always been inspired and influenced by other poets. It is natural when you read a good poem to feel like writing one a little bit like it. It is natural to learn to do things from others who do them well. Actually, the way you write poetry now is probably mainly the result of poems you've read, songs you've heard, things people have said to you about poetry. It's impossible not to be influenced. Think about the way you play tennis or dance or sing. Obviously, the best people to be influenced by are people who do something really well. For writing poetry, those are good poets. It is important, particularly for young poets, to try out all kinds of ways of writing and thinking about writing. It may seem risky to give up, even temporarily, writing a kind of poem you feel successful at and to write instead something unfamiliar, but if you want to write well, it is worth it.

Most young writers don't write poetry as well as they could because of what they think poetry has to be like—that poetry has to have rhyme and meter,* or that it has to be about something profound, or that it has to use special language. They may think, too, that everything has to be worked out in advance and that it's important to stay on the subject they start with. The poets in this book will probably change such ideas, if you have them, as will writing poems inspired by them. There are, though, a few general things it may be helpful to know right away.

*meter in poetry, a regular pattern of stressed and unstressed syllables in a line

Some poetry rhymes, but most of the poetry that has been written in the world doesn't rhyme. Rhyme is just one kind of sound that poets have liked, one way of helping them write their poems. It can sometimes be inspiring, but most young poets find it too limiting, and most write better poetry without it. Meter is usually limiting too, and it is equally unnecessary.

There aren't really subjects that are less appropriate for poetry than others. You can write about anything you want— about talking on the phone, looking out the window, dreaming, anything you imagine, think, see, or hear. Certain subjects have seemed right at various times, but now poets feel free to write about everything.

Sometimes young poets make the mistake of writing about things they think they ought to care about. Or they try to transform what they care about into something poetic; they write about "friendship" and "peace" and the "avenues of life" instead of about a certain friend, a certain day, a certain street. Making your poem general or abstract won't make your subject more worthy of poetry. It will probably overwhelm what

Planning may get in the way of inspiration

you're really feeling and thinking, maybe even keep you from knowing what it is. The simple and particular way you talk with your friends is most likely the way you can best say what you want to, so try that way first. Using old-fashioned poetical words can falsify what you write and take you away from what you mean. The word "baby" probably means more to you than, say, the word "infant," and "blue" may have more color and be more full of music and memories than, say, "azure." Of course "infant," "azure," "damsel," "shimmering," and other such words have their appeal, too. But any word you use, you should use because it's what you mean, not because it's supposedly poetic. Part of the pleasure of writing is being free to use all words.

For most people planning everything in advance is not a good way to write a poem. Often poets get some of their best ideas after they've started a poem. They hardly ever know in advance all they're going to say. They may start with a few words that sound good together, maybe with a line or two, maybe just with a feeling. Then other words and other ideas come to them while they write. Planning may get in the way of inspiration. And so may a deliberate decision to stay on the subject with which you started. Both can limit the different things that might be good in your poem. A good poem can have more than one subject.

Some planning and organizing, of course, can be very useful. But probably even more important for you as a beginning writer is having enough nerve and persistence to try out new ways of writing before you feel sure of them; to talk about what you care about even though you risk feeling silly; to let yourself be inspired as you go along, even though that means losing control, a little, of where the poem is going; to write not to please someone else but to get the poem so that it seems right to you.

You can be completely free in your first version of a poem—you can always revise it. There is nothing in a poem that can't be changed. A poem isn't like a painting, where the change you make covers what was there before. You can always change a poem and change it back. You can revise by cutting things out, by replacing things, by changing the way you say something, by changing the lines around, by adding new lines.

Sometimes a poem seems too short. Sometimes you may want to change the ending. Whatever you do in revising, try to be as easy and free about it as you were in writing the poem in the first place. Keep the first version, though. You may decide later that you want to go back to it, at least partly. You can change a poem while you're writing it, right afterward, or, of course, anytime after that. Sometimes, after you write a poem and then don't think about it for a while, when you look at that poem again in a few weeks or in a month, you may get some ideas about how to make it better.

The best things for a young poet to do are to read a lot of poetry and to write a lot of poetry. It's very good to have some friends who also write poetry, people you can talk about poetry with and show your work to and read theirs. Some writers like to keep some sort of journal in which they write down their thoughts and feelings, maybe even their dreams. One good thing to write, in a journal or elsewhere, is what's called "stream of consciousness." That means writing, say, for a half hour or even an hour whatever comes into your head, without stopping. Don't try to make sense, and forget about spelling, punctuation, complete sentences, and everything like that. You could start by thinking about something in the past—your old room, a former friend, a park you played in. You could also try writing to music. Turn on some music (preferably without words) and write whatever the music makes you think of or see. Anything that gets you involved with writing in new ways is good. Try collaborating on a poem with a friend, for example—you write the first line, he or she writes the next, and so on. You can make rules, such as that each line has to have a color in it and the name of a city. If you know another language, even a little, do some translations. If you find any kind or form of poetry that appeals to you, try writing it yourself.

Young poets tend to worry about whether or not they're working in the right way. It is helpful to know that different poets work in different ways. Some have fixed schedules; some have erratic ones. Some write easily and write a lot; for others it is more difficult. Some poets are always beginning new poems; others work hard revising old poems. It is possible to write, in a short period, a good many poems you like a lot. At other times, maybe, you will not write anything, for a while, you really like. And then, just as unpredictably, you will start writing well again. It is good to be ambitious, to want to write very good poetry, to keep trying new ways of doing it. After you write for a while, you'll find the way of working that is best for you.

Try collaborating on a poem with a friend.

Lea Baechler Assistant Dean of Academic Affairs at Columbia University, where she is finishing her dissertation on modern American elegies. She has published articles on Joyce, Yeats, Stevens, and Berryman, and has taught at the University of Idaho, Columbia University, Princeton University, and Barnard College. She co-edited the most recent edition of Ezra Pound's *Personae* as well as a number of critical-biographical volumes, including Scribner's *Modern American Women Writers* and *African American Writers*.
JOHN BERRYMAN; THEODORE ROETHKE

David Ball Poet, translator, and Professor of French and Comparative Literature at Smith College. His writings on European poets, playwrights, and novelists have appeared in many scholarly journals. His translations of modern French poetry have been widely published. *Darkness Movers: An Henri Michaux Anthology 1927–1984,* selected, presented, and translated by David Ball, won the Modern Language Association's Scaglione Prize for outstanding translation in 1996. Ball's own poems have appeared in *Locus Solus, The World, The Atlantic Monthly, Bombay Gin*, and in four small books.
NINETEENTH-CENTURY ROMANTIC AND SYMBOLIST POETRY

Coleman Barks Poet, translator, and Professor Emeritus of English at the University of Georgia in Athens. For twenty-four years he has collaborated with various Persian scholars to bring over the poetry of the thirteenth-century mystic Jelaluddin Rumi into English. This work has resulted in sixteen volumes, culminating in the best-selling *Essential Rumi,* an appearance on Bill Moyers's PBS special *The Language of Life,* and inclusion in the prestigious *Norton Anthology of World Masterpieces*. Barks taught poetry and creative writing in various universities for thirty-four years.
RUMI

Catherine Barnett Poet, journalist, teacher, and editor. Her essays, interviews, and book reviews have appeared in national magazines and newspapers. She teaches writing in the New York City public schools with Teachers & Writers Collaborative, at the Children's Museum of Manhattan, and at New York University.
ADRIENNE RICH

Judith Baumel Associate Professor of English at Adelphi University and Senior Lecturer in Poetry in the graduate program at the City University of New York. The author of two books of poems—*The Weight of Numbers,* which won the 1987 Walt Whitman Award of the Academy of American Poets, and *Now*—Judith Baumel has published poems in such magazines as *The New Criterion, The New Yorker,* and *The Threepenny Review,* as well as several anthologies.
ELIZABETH BARRETT BROWNING

Bill Berkson Poet, critic, and Professor of Art History at the San Francisco Art Institute. He is the author of fourteen books and pamphlets of poetry, including *Saturday Night, Shining Leaves, Hymns to St. Bridget* (with Frank O'Hara), *Serenade,* and *Fugue State*. He is a corresponding editor for *Art in America* and a regular contributor to many other art journals and literary magazines.
FRANK O'HARA

Anselm Berrigan Poet and critic. Author of *Integrity and Dramatic Life,* a book of poems. His poems and reviews have appeared in *Explosive, Talisman, Lungfull!, Tripwire: A*

Journal of Poetics, The Germ, and other small magazines and journals. Berrigan lives in Brooklyn, New York, and coordinates readings at The Poetry Project.
SAMUEL TAYLOR COLERIDGE; PERCY BYSSHE SHELLEY

Jay Bochner   Writer, editor, and educator. Jay Bochner was born in Buffalo, New York, and raised in the United States and in France. Since 1969 he has taught in the English Department at the Université de Montréal. Bochner has written on Walt Whitman, Henry James, John Dos Passos, Henry Miller, and, most frequently, on the Swiss-French poet and novelist Blaise Cendrars: *Blaise Cendrars: Discovery and Re-creation.* He recently edited *American Modernism Across the Arts* and is presently working on a study of the New York photographer and patron of modern American artists Alfred Stieglitz.
BLAISE CENDRARS

Joseph Bruchac   Poet and founder of the Greenfield Review Press, one of the leading publishers of contemporary Native American writing. His own writing, for adults and young readers, often reflects his Abenaki Indian ancestry. His most recent book of poetry, *No Borders,* was published in 1998.
NATIVE AMERICAN POETRY

Tom Clark   Poet, biographer, critic, and teacher, a member of the Core Faculty in Poetics at New College of California. He has written biographies of Jack Kerouac, Charles Olson, and Robert Creeley, as well as a poetic re-creation of the life of the English poet John Keats.
ROBERT HERRICK; JOHN KEATS; TUDOR AND ELIZABETHAN POETS

Angus R. B. Cochran   Educator and author. He has written widely on Scottish and modern literature and has taught courses on many different aspects of twentieth-century English, Scottish, and Irish literature, most recently at Bowdoin College in Maine.
ROBERT BURNS

Katharine Coles   Assistant Professor of English at the University of Utah, where she teaches literature and creative writing.
MAY SWENSON

William Corbett   Poet and critic; currently Writer-in-Residence at the Massachusetts Institute of Technology. He has published books on literary New England, on New York City, and on the late work of the painter Philip Guston. Author of *Furthering My Education* (a memoir) as well as *New and Selected Poems* and *Boston Vermont* (poetry).
WILLIAM BLAKE; HENRY WADSWORTH LONGFELLOW

Robert Cording   Professor of English and Poet-in-Residence at Holy Cross College. He has published three collections of poems, *Life-list* (Ohio State University Press/Journal Award, 1987), *What Binds Us to This World,* and *Heavy Grace,* and has received fellowships from the National Endowment of the Arts, the Connecticut Commission of the Arts, and Bread Loaf. In 1992 he was Poet-in-Residence at the Frost Place in Franconia, New Hampshire. His poems have appeared in *The Nation, Poetry, Double Take,* and *The New Yorker.*
GEORGE HERBERT

Michael Davidson   Professor of English at the University of California, San Diego. He is the author of eight books of poetry, most recently *The Arcades,* and two critical books on modern poetry: *The San Francisco Renaissance* and *Ghostlier Demarcations: Modern Poetry and the Material Word.*
GARY SNYDER

Jordan Davis   Editor and teacher. Jordan Davis attended Columbia College, where he edited the arts section of the *Spectator* and hosted a poetry program on WKCR. Since graduating, he has edited two magazines, *Skylab* and the *Poetry Project Newsletter.* With Anna Malmude, he is the host of Poetry City, a weekly reading series at the Teachers & Writers

Collaborative's Center for Imaginative Writing. He has worked with Teachers College's Institute for Learning Technologies to invent ways to use computers to teach writing, and currently teaches eighth-graders at School for the Physical City.
EMILY DICKINSON; D. H. LAWRENCE; MARIANNE MOORE

Connie Deanovich   Writer and recipient of a Whiting Writers Award and a G.E. Award for younger writers. Based in Chicago, she is the author of *Zombie Jet* and *Watusi Titanic.*
GWENDOLYN BROOKS; RUSSELL EDSON

Christopher Edgar   Poet, translator, and Publications Director of Teachers & Writers Collaborative, a nonprofit arts organization in New York City. His poems have appeared in *Transfer, The Germ, Shiny,* and *Best American Poetry 2000,* and he is an editor of *The Hat,* a literary magazine. Edgar is the translator of *Tolstoy as Teacher: Leo Tolstoy's Writings on Education* and has also translated works by Mayakovsky, Khlebnikov, and Gumiliev. He has co-edited a number of books on teaching writing, including *Classics in the Classroom: Using Great Literature to Teach Writing.*
VLADIMIR MAYAKOVSKY; BORIS PASTERNAK

Andrew D. Epstein   Critic, poet, and teacher at Columbia University, where he is completing his doctorate in English. His thesis is a study of friendship and individualism in twentieth-century American poetry that focuses on Frank O'Hara, John Ashbery, Wallace Stevens, and William Carlos Williams. His poems and essays have appeared in *Raritan, Keats-Shelley Journal, Verse, The Review of Contemporary Fiction,* and *Brooklyn Review.*
GERARD MANLEY HOPKINS, ANDREW MARVELL

Clayton Eshleman   Poet, translator, editor, and Professor of English at Eastern Michigan University. His published titles include *From Scratch, Under World Arrest,* and *Hotel Cro-Magnon.* Twelve collections of his poetry have been published. Besides Aimé Césaire, he has

also translated the poetry of César Vallejo and Michel Deguy and the poetry and prose of Antonin Artaud. Eshleman founded and edited twenty issues of the literary magazine *Caterpillar* (1967–1973) and also founded and edited the literary magazine *Sulfer.*
AIMÉ CÉSAIRE

Larry Fagin   Founder of the Danspace project and director of Danspace (1975–1980); faculty member in the Poetics Department at Naropa Institute in Boulder, Colorado, since 1975; director of the Naropa Poetics program (1982–1984). He has been teaching creative writing to public school children and teachers since 1963, when, with Ron Padgett and others, he established a regular series of writing workshops at the Brooklyn Children's Museum (MUSE). He has been poetry consultant in Brooklyn's District 22 since 1972 and was co-director of the St. Mark's Poetry Project in New York City (1971–1976).
NEW AMERICAN POETRY

Kate Farrell   Poet and editor. She has taught at Columbia University and elsewhere, and has edited illustrated poetry anthologies including *Time's River: The Voyage of Life in Art and Poetry; Art & Love; Art & Nature*; and *Art & Wonder.* With Kenneth Koch, besides writing *Sleeping on the Wing,* she co-edited *Talking to the Sun: An Illustrated Anthology of Poetry for Young People.*
ADVICE ON WRITING POETRY

Alan Feldman   Professor and former Chair of English at Framingham (Massachusetts) State College. He is the author of *Frank O'Hara, Lucy Mastermind,* and several collections of poems, including *The Happy Genius,* which won the Elliston Book Award. He is a former fellow of the National Endowment for the Arts, the National Endowment for the Humanities, and the Massachusetts Artists Foundation, and a member of the faculty of the Radcliffe Seminars.
ROBERT LOWELL

Ed Folsom   F. Wendell Miller Distinguished Professor of English at the University of Iowa, where he has edited the *Walt Whitman Quarterly Review* since 1983. He is the author, editor, or co-editor of numerous books on Whitman, including *Walt Whitman: The Measure of His Song*; *Walt Whitman and the World; Walt Whitman's Native Representations;* and *Walt Whitman: The Centennial Essays.* He is co-director of the Walt Whitman Hypertext Archive and co-editor of *Major Authors on CD-ROM: Walt Whitman.*
WALT WHITMAN

James Gibbons   Editor at the Library of America and M. A. from Rutgers University. He lives in Brooklyn, New York.
VACHEL LINDSAY; EDWIN ARLINGTON ROBINSON; VIRGIL

Dana Gioia   Poet, critic, translator, and anthologist. He is the author of two collections of poetry, *Daily Horoscope* and *The Gods of Winter.* His critical book *Can Poetry Matter?* was a finalist for the 1992 National Book Critics Award. Gioia is the editor of several best-selling literary anthologies and a frequent commentator for the British Broadcasting Corporation. He lives in northern California.
RICHARD WILBUR

Loren Goodman   Poet and doctoral candidate in Poetics under Robert Creeley at the State University of New York at Buffalo. Formerly a lifeguard in Kansas, a driver in Iowa, and a poetry instructor in Arizona, he is the author of *Remembering Werner Heisenberg* and was a finalist for the Academy of American Poets Walt Whitman Award in 1996 and 1999. He began writing poetry as a student of Kenneth Koch at Columbia University. Goodman recently accepted a Japanese Government scholarship to conduct research on boxing in Japan.
E. E. CUMMINGS; A. E. HOUSMAN

Rachel Hadas   Rachel Hadas is the author of more than twelve books of poetry, essays, and translations, including *Halfway Down the Hall.*

She teaches English at the Newark campus of Rutgers University and has also taught at Columbia and Princeton. She lives in Manhattan with her husband, the composer George Edwards.
ALFRED LORD TENNYSON

Kimiko Hahn   Poet and Associate Professor of English at Queens College, City University of New York. She is the author of five collections of poetry: *Mosquito and Ant*; *Volatile; The Unbearable Heart,* which received an American Book Award; *Earshot,* which was awarded the Theodore Roethke Memorial Poetry Prize and an Association of Asian American Studies Literature Award; and *Air Pocket*. In 1995 she wrote ten portraits of women for the MTV special "Ain't Nuthin but a She-Thing," for which she also recorded the voiceovers. She is a recipient of fellowships from the National Endowment for the Arts, the New York Foundation for the Arts, and the Lila Wallace–Reader's Digest Writer's Award.
CONTEMPORARY ASIAN AMERICAN POETRY

Lynn Hejinian   Poet and essayist. She has published more than twenty volumes, including *Writing Is an Aid to Memory*, *My Life*, and *Happily*. She is the codirector of *Atelos*, a literary project commissioning and publishing cross-genre work by poets. Other projects include a composition entitled *Qûê Trân,* with music by John Zorn, a mixed media book entitled *The Traveler and the Hill and the Hill* created with the painter Emilie Clark, and the award-winning experimental documentary film *Letters Not About Love*, directed by Jacki Ochs.
GERTRUDE STEIN

Alba Delia Hernández   Teacher and Program Coordinator for Teachers & Writers Collaborative. In addition to teaching poetry and fiction in the schools, she has published short stories in *Quarto Magazine*.
NICOLÁS GUILLÉN

Robert Hershon   Poet and Executive Director of The Print Center, a nonprofit facility providing printing services to literary publishers and

other arts organizations. He is the author of eleven books of poetry, including *The German Lunatic*. His work has appeared in more than forty anthologies and in such journals as *Poetry Northwest, The World, The Nation, TriQuarterly, Talisman, Verse, Chicago Review* and *New American Writing*. Among his awards are fellowships from the National Endowment for the Arts and the New York Foundation on the Arts. Hershon also has a long history of publishing and editing poetry and fiction. Hanging Loose Press has published a magazine since 1966 and books since 1972, presenting the work of numerous contemporary writers. He lives in Brooklyn, New York, with his wife, Donna Brook, a poet and children's book author.
OGDEN NASH

Geof Hewitt   Poet and edcucator. His most recent book is *Today You Are My Favorite Poet: Writing Poems with Teenagers.* Hewitt often travels the country, conducting poetry-writing workshops for people of all ages, leading discussions of Robert Frost, and performing his own work in schools, colleges, and at poetry slams. He lives in Calais, Vermont.
ROBERT FROST

William J. Higginson   Poet. Born in New York City, he studied Japanese at Yale University. Since 1967 he has been as active member of the North American Haiku Community, publishing his first collection of translations of Japanese haiku in 1968. He is the co-author, with his wife, Penny Harter, of *The Haiku Handbook: How to Write, Share, and Teach Haiku*, and the author of *The Haiku Seasons: Poetry of the Natural World* and *Haiku World: An International Poetry Almanac.* He lives and writes in Santa Fe, New Mexico.
MATSUO BASHŌ

David Hinton   Translator and poet. His translations from Chinese include *Mencius, The Analects* of Confucius, *Chuang Tzu: Inner Chapters, Forms of Distance* by Bei Dao, *The*

Selected Poems of T'ao Ch'ien, and *The Selected Poems of Tu Fu, The Selected Poems of Li Po,* Bei Dao's *Landscape Over Zero*, and *The Late Poems of Meng Chiao*. He has received fellowships from the Witter Bynner Foundation, the Ingram Merrill Foundation, the National Endowment for the Arts, and the National Endowment for the Humanities.
LI PO; TU FU

Daniel Hoffman   Poet, critic, and Felix Schelling Professor of English Emeritus at the University of Pennsylvania. The author of *Poe Poe Poe Poe Poe Poe Poe*, he served as Poet Laureate of the United States in 1973–1974, the appointment then called Consultant in Poetry of the Library of Congress. His literary studies include *Form and Fable in American Fiction* and *Faulkner's Country Matters.* Among his nine books of poems are *Brotherly Love, Hang-Gliding from Helicon,* and the novel in verse, *Middens of the Tribe.* Hoffman is Poet in Residence at the Cathedral of St. John the Divine, New York City, where he administers the American Poets' Corner.
EDGAR ALLAN POE

Anselm Hollo   Associate Professor at the Jack Kerouac School of Poetics, the graduate Writing and Poetics department at Naropa University, a Buddhist-inspired nonsectarian liberal arts school in Boulder, Colorado. He has published many books of poetry, most recently *Corvus* and *AHOE (And How on Earth)*. His book of essays is *Caws and Causeries: Around Poetry and Poets.* Hollo's work has been widely anthologized, and some of it has been translated into Finnish, French, German, Swedish, and Hungarian.
TROUBADOURS

Carol Howard   Assistant Professor of English at Warren Wilson College in Asheville, North Carolina. She holds the Ph.D. from Columbia University. Her publications include essays on contemporary African-American women writers and eighteenth-century British women writers.

She has co-edited two volumes in the Scribner *British Writers* series.
Lucille Clifton

Lisa Jarnot Assistant Professor of English at Long Island University. Her first collection of poems, *Some Other Kind of Mission*, was published in 1996. A second, *Ring of Fire*, is forthcoming. She lives in New York City, where she is writing a biography of the American poet Robert Duncan.
Robert Creeley

Paul Kane Poet, critic, and Professor of English at Vassar College. He has published seven books, including *Ralph Waldo Emerson: Collected Poems and Translations, Poetry of the American Renaissance: A Diverse Anthology from the Romantic Period*, and *Ralph Waldo Emerson: Essays and Poems*. He was a Fulbright scholar at the University of Melbourne in 1985. His other awards include fellowships from the National Endowment for the Humanities and from the John Simon Guggenheim Memorial Foundation.
Ralph Waldo Emerson

David Scott Kastan Professor of English and Comparative Literature at Columbia University. He is a specialist on Shakespeare and Renaissance literature and culture. Among his publications are *Shakespeare and the Shapes of Time, Staging the Renaissance* (ed. with Peter Stallybrass), *Critical Essays on Shakespeares's "Hamlet," The New History of Early English Drama* (ed. with John Cox), *A Companion to Shakespeare,* and *Shakespeare After Theory*. Professor Kastan is also the general editor of the Arden Shakespeare (the first American ever to serve in this capacity in the Arden's hundred-year history), and he is editing *1 Henry IV* for that series.
William Shakespeare

Claudia Keelan Poet and critic. Among her collections of poetry are *Refinery*, which won the Cleveland State Poetry Prize in 1994, and *The Secularist*. Her essays and reviews have appeared

in numerous publications, including *Denver Quarterly, Pequod, American Letters,* and *Commentary*.
James Tate

Edmund Keeley Poet, translator, and former Charles Barnwell Straut Professor of English at Princeton University, where he taught for forty years. He has published seven novels, nine volumes of nonfiction, and fourteen volumes of poetry in translation. His latest books are *An Albanian Journal: The Road to Elbasan; George Seferis and Edmund Keeley: Correspondence, 1951–1971; Inventing Paradise: The Greek Journey, 1937–47;* and *On Translation: Reflections and Conversations.*
C. P. Cavafy

Hugh Kenner Professor Emeritus of English at the University of Georgia. He first met Ezra Pound in 1947 and since then has written numerous books on modern poetry, notably *The Pound Era*. Born in Peterborough, Canada, he attended the University of Toronto and then Yale University (Ph.D. 1950) and has taught at many universities.
Ezra Pound

Nathan Kernan Poet and editor. He attended the University of California, Los Angeles, and the San Francisco Art Institute, studying photography and painting. His poems have appeared in little magazines and in the portfolio *Poems*, a collaboration with the painter Joan Mitchell, published by Tyler Graphics in 1992. Kernan became friends with James Schuyler near the end of Schuyler's life, and subsequently edited his *Diary*, which was published by Black Sparrow Press in 1997. He lives in New York City.
James Schuyler

Kenneth Koch Poet. His most recent books of poetry are *Straits, One Train,* and *On the Great Atlantic Rainway: Selected Poems 1950–1988.* For these last two books, he was awarded the Bolligen Prize in poetry. A new book of poems, *New*

Addresses, will be published in 2000. His *Making Your Own Days: The Pleasures of Reading and Writing Poetry* was published in 1998. He also writes fiction and plays. His most recently produced dramatic work, the opera *The Banquet* (with music by Marcello Panni), was produced in Bremen, Germany, in 1998. Born in Cincinnati, Koch attended Harvard University and Columbia University (Ph.D., 1953). He lives in New York City.
ADVICE ON WRITING POETRY

John Koethe   Poet and Professor of Philosophy at the University of Wisconsin–Milwaukee. He has published five books of poetry: *Blue Vents; Domes,* which won the Frank O'Hara Award; *The Late Wisconsin Spring; Falling Water*, which won the Kingsley Tufts Award; and *The Constructor,* which was nominated for the New Yorker Book Award. He is also the author of *The Continuity of Wittgenstein's Thought* and *Poetry at One Remove,* a collection of essays.
WALLACE STEVENS

Herbert Kohl   Writer and Director of the Center for Teaching Excellence and Social Justice at the University of San Francisco. His books include *36 Children, I Won't Learn from You, The Discipline of Hope,* and *A Grain of Poetry.*
VICTOR HERNÁNDEZ CRUZ

Ann Lauterbach   David and Ruth Schwab III Professor of Language and Literature at Bard College. She has taught poetry and poetics at Brooklyn College, Columbia, and elsewhere, and has published five collections of poetry, including *Clamor, And for Example*, and *On a Stair*.
JOHN ASHBERY

Michael Leddy   Poet and critic. He teaches in the Department of English at Eastern Illinois University at Charleston. Leddy's essays, reviews, and poems have appeared in *Cather Studies, Contemporary Literature, The Gertrude Stein Awards in Innovative American Poetry, Modern Fiction Studies, Talisman, World Literature Today,* and other publications.

GUILLAUME APOLLINAIRE; KENNETH KOCH; RON PADGETT

Brad Leithauser   Poet, novelist, critic, and graduate of Harvard Law School. He is the author of a book of essays, *Penchants and Places,* as well as four books of poetry and four novels. Leithauser has lived in Japan, England, Italy, France, and Iceland. He and his wife, the poet Mary Jo Salter, now live in Massachusetts.
ANTHONY HECHT

Gary Lenhart   Poet, critic, teacher, and editor. His three books of poems are *Father and Son Night, Light Heart,* and *One at a Time,* along with many reviews and essays. He edited two literary magazines: *Mag City* (1977–1984, with Gregory Masters and Michael Scholnick) and *Transfer* (1986–1991). He also edited *The Teachers & Writers Guide to William Carlos Williams* and *Clinch: Selected Poems of Michael Scholnick*, with Gregory Masters, Bob Rosenthal, and Steve Levine. He has taught writing at the Poetry Project, Columbia University, the Community College of Vermont, and Dartmouth College.
GEOFFREY CHAUCER; THOMAS GRAY; JOHN MILTON

Joel Lewis   Poet and critic, recipient of the Ted Berrigan Award.
STEPHEN VINCENT BENÉT; EDGAR LEE MASTERS

Kenneth Lincoln   Educator and critic at the University of California, Los Angeles. Lincoln has taught Contemporary and Native American Literatures at for thirty years. He developed the American Indian Studies curriculum, chaired the first interdisciplinary Master's Program in American Indian Studies, and published widely: *Native American Renaissance; The Good Red Road: Passages into Native America; Indi'n Humor: Bicultural Play in Native America; Men Down West; A Writer's China: Bridges East and West;* and *Sing with the Heart of a Bear: Fusions of Native and American Poetry 1890–1999.*
N. SCOTT MOMADAY

Lisa Hermine Makman   Doctoral candidate in English and Comparative Literature at Columbia University, where she teaches. Makman writes about children and the culture of childhood and has published articles on Beatrix Potter, Roald Dahl, and A. A. Milne for the Scribner *British Writers* series. Her dissertation, "Childhood Lost and Found," explores representations of child's play and the child's imagination in Victorian and modern writings for and about children.
HOMER; EDWARD LEAR

Anna Malmude   Co-host of *Poetry City,* a weekly reading series at the Teachers & Writers Collaborative's Center for Imaginative Writing.
D. H. LAWRENCE

Paul Mariani   Poet, critic, and Distinguished University Professor at the University of Massachusetts, Amherst. He is the author of five collections: *The Great Wheel; Salvage Operations: New and Selected Poems; Prime Mover; Crossing Cocytus;* and *Timing Devices.* He has also published much prose, including *A Useable Past: Essays 1973–1983; William Carlos Williams: The Poet and His Critics;* and *A Commentary on the Complete Poems of Gerard Manley Hopkins;* and four biographies: *The Broken Tower: A Life of Hart Crane; Lost Puritan: A Life of Robert Lowell; Dream Song: The Life of John Berryman*; and *William Carlos Williams: A New World Naked.* The last won the New Jersey Writers Award and was short-listed for an American Book Award. His honors include fellowships from the Guggenheim Foundation, the National Endowment for the Arts, and the National Endowment for the Humanities.
WILLIAM CARLOS WILLIAMS

A. Michael Matin   Professor of English at Warren Wilson College. He has published articles in the *Journal of Modern Literature* and *Studies in the Novel*, and his work is appearing as well in the forthcoming Norton Critical Edition of Rudyard Kipling's *Kim.* He is currently writing a book whose working title is *Securing Britain: Invasion-Scare Literature Before the*

Great War. He has contributed essays on David Lodge and Anita Desai to the Scribner *British Writers* series.
W. H. AUDEN; T. S. ELIOT

Christopher Merrill   Poet and translator. His books include three collections of poetry, *Workbook, Fevers and Tides,* and Watch *Fire;* translations of Alej Debeljak's *Anxious Moments* and *The City and the Child*; several edited volumes; and several works of nonfiction, including *The Grass of Another Country: A Journey Through the World of Soccer; The Old Bridge: The Third Balkan War and the Age of the Refugee*; and *Only the Nails Remain: Scenes from the Balkan Wars.*
WILLIAM BUTLER YEATS

Ange Mlinko   Poet, educated at St. John's College and Brown University. Her poems are collected in *Matinees.* She lives in New York City.
ANNE BRADSTREET; GEORGE GORDON, LORD BYRON; ALEXANDER POPE

Charles North   Poet and teacher. As a youth he was an active musician (clarinet). He has degrees from Tufts and Columbia Universities, has worked as an editor and art reviewer, and has published seven poetry collections (most recently *New and Selected Poems*) and a book of critical essays, *No Other Way.* With James Schuyler he edited the anthologies *Broadway* and *Broadway 2.* Poet-in-Residence at Pace University, he has received an NEA Fellowship, a Poets Foundation award, and three Fund for Poetry awards.
ELIZABETH BISHOP

Odetta Norton   Executive Director of the West African Eye Foundation and and a scholarship student of Garth Fagan Dance. Norton received a Fulbright Fellowship to study in Senegal and an M.F.A from the University of Michigan. She worked as a writer in residence with the Teachers & Writers Collaborative and taught as an adjunct professor at Parsons School of Design. Her poetry

has appeared in *Eclipse, The Yalobusha Review,* and *Beyond the Frontier.* Her essays have been published in *African Form and Imagery: Detroit Collects.*
ROBERT HAYDEN

Alice Notley   Author of over twenty-five books of poetry. *Mysteries of Small Houses* won the *Los Angeles Times* Book Award for Poetry and was a finalist for the Pulitzer Prize. *The Descent of Alette* is an epic poem based on a measure of Notley's invention and has received increasing acclaim. Another long poem, *Disobedience,* is scheduled for publication in 2001. Notley lived for many years in New York City on the Lower East Side, but now resides in Paris, where she teaches creative writing and co-edits the journal *Gare du Nord.*
TED BERRIGAN

Rafael Ocasio   Associate Professor of Spanish at Agnes Scott College, where he teaches the Latin American novel and Cuban literature.
PABLO NERUDA; SPANISH POETRY; SPANISH AMERICAN POETRY

Karen Odden   MacCracken Fellow at New York University. Dissertation: *Broken Trains of Thought: The Railway, Trauma, and Narrative in the British Novel, 1848–1906.* She has published essays on popular fiction and Eavan Boland; short pieces have appeared in women's magazines and the *New York Times.* Her research interests include the history of medicine, psychoanalysis, and law.
MATTHEW ARNOLD; ROBERT BROWNING

Douglas Oliver   Poet and novelist. His most recent book is the political prose/poetry work, *A Salvo for Africa.* His American *Selected Poems* came out in 1996, and he was featured in *Penguin Modern Poets 10* that same year. His *Penniless Politics* is a satire on U.S. politics. Oliver, who is British, is married to the American poet Alice Notley, and they co-edit *Gare du Nord* magazine from their home in Paris, France.
DYLAN THOMAS

Ron Padgett   Poet and teacher; for nineteen years Padgett was Publications Director of the Teachers & Writers Collaborative, for which he edited *The Teachers & Writers Handbook of Poetic Forms.* His many books include *New and Selected Poems; Creative Reading: What It Is, How to Do It, and Why: Blood Work: Selected Prose; The Straight Line: Writings on Poetry and Poets,* and a translation of *The Complete Poems of Blaise Cendrars.* His honors include Fulbright and Guggenheim fellowships and an award from the American Academy of Arts and Letters.
SOME BASIC POETIC FORMS; TWENTIETH-CENTURY MODERNIST POETRY

Mark Polizzotti   Writer, translator, and publishing director at the Boston Museum of Fine Arts. His books include *Revolution of the Mind: The Life of André Breton, Lautréamont Nomad, The New Life* (poems), and the collaborative novel *S.* His essays and reviews have appeared in *The New Republic, The London Review of Books, ARTnews, The Partisan Review, Agni,* and elsewhere. He has also translated works by Breton, Jean Echenoz, Patrick Chamoiseau, Marguerite Duras, Maurice Roche, and others.
ANDRÉ BRETON

Arnold Rampersad   Professor of English at Stanford University. Trinidad-born, Rampersad holds degrees from Bowling Green State University and Harvard University and has taught at Rutgers, Columbia, and Princeton. He has published several books, including biographies of Langston Hughes and Jackie Robinson. He was also co-author, with Arthur Ashe, of *Days of Grace: A Memoir.*
LANGSTON HUGHES

Nelly Reifler   Writer living in Brooklyn, New York. Her plays have been performed both abroad and in the United States, and her short stories may be read in journals including *Florida Review* and *Mississippi Mud.*
GREGORY CORSO; CARL SANDBURG

Bob Rosenthal Writer, teacher (City University of New York), and co-trustee of the Allen Ginsberg Trust. Formerly secretary to Allen Ginsberg. Rosenthal founded both the Yellow Press and Frontward Books and published a series of mimeograph poetry volumes. He has written and coproduced six plays. His poetry includes *Rude Awakenings* and *Viburnam;* prose: *Cleaning Up New York* (1976).
ALLEN GINSBERG

Jerome Rothenberg Poet and editor. He has published over sixty books of poetry and numerous assemblages of tradtional and contemporary poetry such as *Technicians of the Sacred* and *Shaking the Pumpkin* (American Indian poetry). He has also been involved with various aspects of poetry performance, including radio soundplays written and performed for Westdeutscher Rundfunk (Cologne) and theatrical and musical works with the Living Theater and the Bread and Puppet Theater. Founder of the movement called ethnopoetics, his latest collection (with Pierre Joris) is *Poems for the Millennium,* a two-volume global anthology of the twentieth-century avant-garde.
INDIGENOUS AND ORAL POETRY

Hardie St. Martin Editor as well as contributing translator of two anthologies: *Root and Wings, Poetry of Spain 1900–1975* and also *Small Hours of the Night: Selected Poems of Roque Dalton.* He has also translated Pablo Neruda's *Memoirs,* several novels, and many short stories by Latin American and Spanish authors.
FEDERICO GARCÍA LORCA

Paul Schmidt Critic, translator, and playwright (deceased). His plays have been performed at the Brooklyn Academy of Music, Thalia Theatre in Hamburg, and Institute for Contemporary Art in London. Dr. Schmidt, who held a Ph.D. in Slavic Literature from Harvard, was a Professor of Russian Literature at the University of Texas and at Wellesley College. He taught at Harvard, Cornell, and Yale and lectured widely in this country and abroad. A recipient of a fellowship from the National Endowment for the Arts, Dr. Schmidt was the author of *Meyerbold at Work* and editor of *The Complete Works of Arthur Rimbaud* and *The Collected Works of Velimir Khlebnikov.*
ARTHUR RIMBAUD

Jeffrey T. Schnapp Pierotti Professor of Italian Studies at Stanford University. He is the author of five books and nearly one hundred essays on topics ranging from ancient patchwork poetry to art and architecture during Italy's Fascist decades.
DANTE

Peter Sears Poet and educator. He is the author of *Tour: New and Selected Poems*; *Secret Writing;* and *Gonna Bake Me a Rainbow Poem: A Student Guide to Writing Poetry.* He has taught creative writing at, among others places, Reed College. At Bard College he served as Dean of Students. Sears also worked for the Oregon Arts Commission, founded the Oregon Literary Coalition, a statewide advocacy group, and served as the first director of the Friends of William Stafford. He works for the magazine *Rubberstampmadness* and lives with his wife in Corvallis, Oregon.
WILLIAM STAFFORD

David Shapiro Professor at William Paterson College; author of many books of poetry and critical studies of John Ashbery and Jasper Johns.
ANNE PORTER

Eleni Sikelianos Poet. The author of *The Book of Tendons, The Lover's Numbers,* and *The Blue Guide,* Sikelianos has traveled extensively in Africa, Europe, and the Near East. Awards include a National Endowment for the Arts fellowship in poetry, a James D. Pohelan Award, and a Fulbright grant to Greece. She lives in New York City, where she works as a Poet-in-Residence for the Teachers & Writers Collaborative and as co-curator of a reading series at the St. Mark's Poetry Project.
SAPPHO

Mark Statman Poet, translator, and educator. Statman's poetry, fiction, articles, and translations have appeared in numerous journals and collections. He has taught writing at Eugene Lang College of the New School and for Teachers & Writers Collaborative since 1985. Forthcoming are *Down the Lane* and a book on teaching nature writing.
Gabriela Mistral

Peter Stitt Poet, critic, and editor of *The Gettysburg Review*. He has published two volumes of literary criticism: *The World's Hieroglyphic Beauty* and *Uncertainty and Plenitude: Five Contemporary Poets*. With Frank Graziano he has co-edited two books: *James Wright: The Heart of the Light* and *James Wright: A Profile*. He is working on the authorized biography of Wright.
James Wright

Lorenzo Thomas Professor of English at the University of Houston–Downtown. Panama-born, Thomas is a widely published poet and literary critic. His books include *Extraordinary Measures: Afrocentric Modernism and Twentieth-Century American Poetry* and *Sing the Sun Up: Creative Writing Ideas from African American Literature*.
Amiri Baraka; Harlem Renaissance; Sonia Sanchez

Paul Vangelisti Poet and Chair of the Graduate Writing Program at Otis College of Art and Design. He is the author of some twenty books of poetry, as well as numerous translations from the Italian. From 1971 to 1982 he co-edited the award-winning literary magazine *Invisible City,* and since 1993 he has edited the visual and literary arts annual *Ribot.* He has received National Endowment for the Arts fellowships for translation (1981) and for poetry (1988)
Giacomo Leopardi

Karen Volkman Poet and teacher. Her book of poems, *Crash's Law*, was published in 1996. She has received grants and awards from the National Endowment for the Arts, the Poetry Society of America, the Academie Schloss Solitude, and

elsewhere. Her poems appear in a number of journals and anthologies, including *Best American Poetry* and *The KGB Bar Book of Poems*. She has taught at New York University, the New School, and the University of Alabama, as well as in the New York City schools with Teachers & Writers Collaborative.
Sylvia Plath; Rainer Maria Rilke; Charles Simic

Anne Waldman Distinguished Professor of Poetics at the Jack Kerouac School of Disembodied Poetics at the Naropa University in Boulder, Colorado, a program she co-founded with Allen Ginsberg in 1974. She is the author of over thirty books of poetry including, most recently, the twentieth-anniversary edition of *Fast Speaking Woman; Iovis: All Is Full of Jove: Books I & II; Kill or Cure;* and *Marriage: A Sentence*. She is the editor of *The Beat Book* and co-editor of *Disembodied Poetics: Annals of the Jack Kerouac School*. Formerly director of the St. Mark's Poetry Project (1968–1979), she has also been on the guest faculty of the Institute of American Indian Arts in Santa Fe, and the Schule für Dichtung in Vienna. She is featured on the video *Battle of the Bards* and is the recipient of grants from the National Endowment of the Arts and the Poetry Foundation and is a winner of the Shelley Memorial Award for poetry.
Performance Poetry

James Wanless Teacher and scholar. For the past thirty years he has been teaching creative writing, literature, and composition in the Detroit area, since 1984 at Henry Ford Community College in Dearborn, Michigan. His primary scholarly interests are European culture since ancient times, French language and literature, and modern American poetry. James Wanless is married, co-caretaker of numerous pets, and a gardener, cook, and squash player.
Ovid

Lewis Warsh Editor and Publisher of United Artists Books and Adjunct Professor of Writing and Literature at Long Island University. His writings include *Agnes and Sally* and *A Free Man*

(novels), a volume of stories, *Money Under the Table*, and numerous books of poems, including *Dreaming as One*, *Blue Heaven*, and *Avenue of Escape*. He has received grants for his writing from the National Endowment for the Arts, the New York Foundation for the Arts, and the Fund for Poetry.
JOHN DONNE; EDNA ST. VINCENT MILLAY; WILLIAM WORDSWORTH

Emmett Williams   Poet, painter, and printmaker. He is the author of many innovative volumes of concrete poetry in both English and German, including the book-length poem cycles *sweethearts*, *the boy and the bird*, and *the voyage*. His *Anthology of Concrete Poetry* remains the best introduction to the international movement. His autobiographical book *My Life in Flux—and Vice Versa* explores his active role as a performance artist in Fluxus, the radical international art movement of the sixties. He lives and works in Berlin.
CALLIGRAMMATIC AND CONCRETE POETRY

Bill Zavatsky   Poet and teacher at the Trinity School in New York City. He has published two books of poems, *Theories of Rain and Other Poems* and *For Steve Royal and Other Poems*, as well as articles on creative writing and writers, including Walt Whitman, William Carlos Williams, and Ramón Gómez de la Serna. His co-translation of *Earthlight*, poems by André Breton, won the PEN/Book-of-the-Month Club Translation Prize for 1993. His work has been anthologized in *Up Late: American Poetry Since 1970; Reading Jazz; For a Living;* and *Sports in Literature*.
CHARLES REZNIKOFF

Richard Zenith   Writer, translator, and researcher in the Pessoa archives; recipient of the PEN Award for Poetry in Translation for his translation of *Fernando Pessoa & Co.* from the original Portuguese.
FERNANDO PESSOA

Lee Zimmerman   Professor of English at Hofstra University. He is the author of *Intricate and Simple Things: The Poetry of Galway Kinnell* and of many essays about modern and contemporary poetry, Romantic poetry, and psychoanalysis and literature. He is also the editor of the academic journal *Twentieth Century Literature*.
GALWAY KINNELL

POETIC METER

A traditional poetic rhythm, or meter, comes from the pattern of stressed and unstressed syllables in the poem. If the pattern is repeated, its unit is called a foot. Free verse poetry, however, has no repeating pattern; its rhythm often approximates that of everyday speech.

Below are the five most common metrical feet in English poetry and some examples of them. The symbol ∪ indicates an unstressed syllable, while the symbol / indicates a stressed syllable.

iamb: ∪ /
    Examples: *undo; trombone*

trochee: / ∪
    Examples: *exit; package*

anapest: ∪ ∪ /
    Examples: *on a whim; understand*

dactyl: / ∪ ∪
    Examples: *harmony; elephant*

spondee: / /
    Examples: *calm down; full house*

When someone talks about a poem's meter, that person is normally referring to two pieces of information about the poem: (1) the type of foot (iamb, trochee, etc.) and (2) the number of feet per line. The terms below are used to indicate the number of feet per line.

	Feet Per Line
monometer	1
dimeter	2
trimeter	3
tetrameter	4
pentameter	5
hexameter	6
heptameter	7
octometer	8

One of the most common meters in English is iambic pentameter, that is, in lines made up of five iambs each. Here is an example:

∪ /   ∪ /   ∪ /   ∪ /   ∪ /
I can't | unglue | this trom | bone from | my head.

399

Poet Laureates of England

The position of poet laureate is a royal appointment and is considered the greatest official honor that England can bestow on one of its poets. But in the history of this institution, the quality of the poetry of the laureates has varied considerably. The first officially titled poet laureate was John Dryden, but in effect the position began when Ben Jonson received a royal pension in 1616. The list below gives the names of the poet laureates and the years they received their appointments. Incidentally, the terms *poet laureates* and *poets laureate* are both correct.

Ben Jonson	1616
William Davenant	1638
John Dryden	1668
Thomas Shadwell	1689
Nahum Tate	1692
Nicholas Rowe	1715
Laurence Eusden	1718
Colley Cibber	1730
William Whitehead	1757
Thomas Warton	1785
Henry James Pye	1790
Robert Southey	1813
William Wordsworth	1843
Alfred Tennyson	1850
Alfred Austin	1896
Robert Bridges	1913
John Masefield	1930
Cecil Day-Lewis	1968
John Betjeman	1972
Ted Hughes	1984
Andrew Motion	1999

Consultants in Poetry and Poet Laureate Consultants in Poetry to the Library of Congress

The positions of Consultant in Poetry and Poet Laureate Consultant in Poetry are the American equivalents of England's poet laureate. In the United States, the title Consultant in Poetry was used from 1937 until 1986, when it was changed to Poet Laureate Consultant in Poetry, commonly shortened to Poet Laureate.

Joseph Auslander	1937–1941
Allen Tate	1943–1944
Robert Penn Warren	1944–1945
Louise Bogan	1945–1946
Karl Shapiro	1946–1947
Robert Lowell	1947–1948
Léonie Adams	1948–1949
Elizabeth Bishop	1949–1950
Conrad Aiken	1950–1952
William Carlos Williams	Appointed in 1952 but did not serve
Randall Jarrell	1956–1958
Robert Frost	1958–1959
Richard Eberhart	1959–1961
Louis Untermeyer	1961–1963
Howard Nemerov	1963–1964
Reed Whittemore	1964–1965
Stephen Spender	1965–1966
James Dickey	1966–1968
William Jay Smith	1968–1970
William Stafford	1970–1971
Josephine Jacobsen	1971–1973
Daniel Hoffman	1973–1974
Stanley Kunitz	1974–1976
Robert Hayden	1976–1978
William Meredith	1978–1980
Maxine Kumin	1981–1982
Anthony Hecht	1982–1984
Robert Fitzgerald	1984–1985 Appointed and served in a health-limited capacity
Reed Whittemore	1984–1985 Interim Consultant in Poetry
Gwendolyn Brooks	1985–1986
Robert Penn Warren	1986–1987
Richard Wilbur	1987–1988
Howard Nemerov	1988–1990
Mark Strand	1990–1991
Joseph Brodsky	1991–1992
Mona Van Duyn	1992–1993
Rita Dove	1993–1995
Robert Hass	1995–1997
Robert Pinsky	1997–

National Book Award Winners in Poetry

1950	*Paterson: Book III* and *Selected Poems*. William Carlos Williams
1951	*The Auroras of Autumn*. Wallace Stevens

1952	*Collected Poems.* Marianne Moore
1953	*Collected Poems, 1917–1952.* Archibald MacLeish
1954	*Collected Poems.* Conrad Aiken
1955	*The Collected Poems of Wallace Stevens.* Wallace Stevens
1956	*The Shield of Achilles.* W. H. Auden
1957	*Things of This World.* Richard Wilbur
1958	*Promises: Poems, 1954–1956.* Robert Penn Warren
1959	*Words for the Wind.* Theodore Roethke
1960	*Life Studies.* Robert Lowell
1961	*The Woman at the Washington Zoo.* Randall Jarrell
1962	*Poems.* Alan Dugan
1963	*Traveling Through the Dark.* William Stafford
1964	*Selected Poems.* John Crowe Ransom
1965	*The Far Field.* Theodore Roethke
1966	*Buckdancers Choice: Poems.* James Dickey
1967	*Nights and Days.* James Merrill
1968	*The Light Around the Body.* Robert Bly
1969	*His Toy, His Dream, His Rest.* John Berryman
1970	*The Complete Poems.* Elizabeth Bishop
1971	*To See, to Take.* Mona Van Duyn
1972	*Selected Poems.* Howard Moss
	The Collected Poems of Frank O'Hara. Frank O'Hara
1973	*Collected Poems, 1951–1971.* A. R. Ammons
1974	*The Fall of America: Poems of These States, 1965–1971.* Allen Ginsberg
	Diving into the Wreck: Poems 1971–1972. Adrienne Rich
1975	*Presentation Piece.* Marilyn Hacker
1976	*Self-Portrait in a Convex Mirror.* John Ashbery
1977	*Collected Poems, 1930–1976.* Richard Eberhart
1978	*The Collected Poems of Howard Nemerov.* Howard Nemerov
1979	*Mirabell: Book of Numbers.* James Merrill
1980	*Ashes.* Phillip Levine
1981	*The Need to Hold Still.* Lisel Mueller
1982	*Life Supports: New and Collected Poems.* William Bronk
1983	*Selected Poems.* Galway Kinnell
	Country Music: Selected Early Poems. Charles Wright
1984–1990	No awards given
1991	*What Work Is.* Phillip Levine
1992	*New & Selected Poems.* Mary Oliver
1993	*Garbage.* A. R. Ammons
1994	*Worshipful Company of Fletchers.* James Tate
1995	*Passing Through: The Later Poems, New & Selected.* Stanley Kunitz
1996	*Scrambled Eggs & Whiskey, Poems, 1991–1995.* Hayden Carruth
1997	*Effort at Speech: New & Selected Poems.* William Meredith
1998	*This Time: New and Selected Poems.* Gerald Stern
1999	*Vice: New and Selected Poems.* Ai

Pulitzer Prizes in Poetry

In 1918 and 1919, the awards were made possible by gifts from the Poetry Society. In 1922, the Pulitzer Board assumed full responsibility.

1918 *Love Songs.* Sara Teasdale
1919 *Old Road to Paradise.* Margaret Widdemer
       Corn Huskers. Carl Sandburg
1922 *Collected Poems.* Edwin Arlington Robinson
1923 *The Ballad of the Harp-Weaver; A Few Figs from Thistles;* eight sonnets in *American Poetry, 1922: A Miscellany.* Edna St. Vincent Millay
1924 *New Hampshire: A Poem with Notes and Grace Notes.* Robert Frost
1925 *The Man Who Died Twice.* Edwin Arlington Robinson
1926 *What's O'Clock.* Amy Lowell
1927 *Fiddler's Farewell.* Leonora Speyer
1928 *Tristram.* Edwin Arlington Robinson
1929 *John Brown's Body.* Stephen Vincent Benét
1930 *Selected Poems.* Conrad Aiken
1931 *Collected Poems.* Robert Frost
1932 *The Flowering Stone.* George Dillon
1933 *Conquistador.* Archibald MacLeish
1934 *Collected Verse.* Robert Hillyer
1935 *Bright Ambush.* Audrey Wurdemann
1936 *Strange Holiness.* Robert P. T. Coffin
1937 *A Further Range.* Robert Frost
1938 *Cold Morning Sky.* Marya Zaturenska
1939 *Selected Poems.* John Gould Fletcher
1940 *Collected Poems.* Mark Van Doren
1941 *Sunderland Capture.* Leonard Bacon
1942 *The Dust Which Is God.* William Rose Benét
1943 *A Witness Tree.* Robert Frost
1944 *Western Star.* Stephen Vincent Benét
1945 *V-Letter and Other Poems.* Karl Shapiro
1946 No award given
1947 *Lord Weary's Castle.* Robert Lowell
1948 *The Age of Anxiety.* W. H. Auden
1949 *Terror and Decorum.* Peter Viereck
1950 *Annie Allen.* Gwendolyn Brooks
1951 *Complete Poems.* Carl Sandburg
1952 *Collected Poems.* Marianne Moore
1953 *Collected Poems, 1917–1952.* Archibald MacLeish
1954 *The Waking.* Theodore Roethke
1955 *Collected Poems.* Wallace Stevens
1956 *Poems—North & South.* Elizabeth Bishop
1957 *Things of This World.* Richard Wilbur
1958 *Promises: Poems, 1954–1956.* Robert Penn Warren
1959 *Selected Poems, 1928–1958.* Stanley Kunitz

1960   *Heart's Needle.* William Snodgrass
1961   *Times Three: Selected Verse from Three Decades.* Phyllis McGinley
1962   *Poems.* Alan Dugan
1963   *Pictures from Breughel.* William Carlos Williams
1964   *At the End of the Open Road.* Louis Simpson
1965   *77 Dream Songs.* John Berryman
1966   *Selected Poems.* Richard Eberhart
1967   *Live or Die.* Anne Sexton
1968   *The Hard Hours.* Anthony Hecht
1969   *Of Being Numerous.* George Oppen
1970   *United Subjects.* Richard Howard
1971   *The Carrier of Ladders.* William S. Merwin
1972   *Collected Poems.* James Wright
1973   *Up Country.* Maxine Winokur Kumin
1974   *The Dolphin.* Robert Lowell
1975   *Turtle Island.* Gary Snyder
1976   *Self-Portrait in a Convex Mirror.* John Ashbery
1977   *Divine Comedies.* James Merrill
1978   *Collected Poems.* Howard Nemerov
1979   *Now and Then: Poems 1976–1978.* Robert Penn Warren
1980   *Selected Poems.* Donald Rodney Justice
1981   *The Morning of the Poem.* James Schuyler
1982   *The Collected Poems.* Sylvia Plath
1983   *Selected Poems.* Galway Kinnell
1984   *American Primitive.* Mary Oliver
1985   *Yin.* Carol Kizer
1986   *The Flying Change.* Henry Taylor
1987   *Thomas and Beulah.* Rita Dove
1988   *Partial Accounts: New and Selected Poems.* William Meredith
1989   *New and Collected Poems.* Richard Wilbur
1990   *The World Doesn't End.* Charles Simic
1991   *Near Changes.* Mona Van Duyn
1992   *Selected Poems.* James Tate
1993   *The Wild Iris.* Louise Gluck
1994   *Neon Vernacular.* Yusef Komunyakaa
1995   *Simple Truth.* Philip Levine
1996   *The Dream of the Unified Field.* Jorie Graham
1997   *Alive Together: New and Selected Poems.* Lisel Mueller
1998   *Black Zodiac.* Charles Wright
1999   *Blizzard of One.* Mark Strand

ILLUSTRATION ACKNOWLEDGMENTS

Cover

VOLUME 1

Boris Pasternak: Archive Photos.
Walt Whitman: Library of Congress.
Sonia Sanchez: © 2000 Nancy Crampton.
Percy Bysshe Shelley: Library of Congress.
Edna St. Vincent Millay: Library of Congress.
Geoffrey Chaucer: Library of Congress.

VOLUME 2

Amiri Baraka: Library of Congress.
Gertrude Stein: Library of Congress.
Edgar Allan Poe: Library of Congress
Federico García Lorca: Archive Photos.
Matsuo Bashō: Master Bashō Memorial Museum.
Emily Dickinson: Library of Congress.

VOLUME 3

Arthur Rimbaud: Library of Congress.
Aimé Césaire: © Ph.Bourgade/GLMR.
Anne Bradstreet: Painted by LaDonna Gulley Warrick.
Sappho: Staatliche Antikensammlungen und Glyptothek München.
William Butler Yeats: Alice Boughton/Library of Congress.
E. E. Cummings: Library of Congress.

Interior

Guillaume Apollinaire: Corbis-Bettmann.
Matthew Arnold: Library of Congress.
John Ashbery: UPI/Corbis-Bettmann.
W. H. Auden: George Cserna/Library of Congress.
Amiri Baraka: Library of Congress.
Matsuo Bashō: Master Bashō Memorial Museum.

Stephen Vincent Benét: UPI/Corbis-Bettmann.
Ted Berrigan: Sharon Guynup.
John Berryman: UPI/Corbis-Bettmann.
Elizabeth Bishop: UPI/Corbis-Bettmann.
William Blake: Library of Congress.
Anne Bradstreet: Painted by: LaDonna Gulley Warrick.
André Breton: Library of Congress.
Gwendolyn Brooks: Library of Congress.
Elizabeth Barrett Browning: © Hulton-Deutsch Collection/CORBIS.
Robert Browning: H. H. Hay Cameron; Library of Congress.
Robert Burns: Library of Congress.
George Gordon, Lord Byron: Corbis.
C. P. Cavafy: Manuscripts Division. Department of Rare Books and Special Collections. Princeton University Library.
Blaise Cendrars: Archive Photos.
Aimé Césaire: © Ph.Bourgade/GLMR.
Geoffrey Chaucer: Library of Congress.
Lucille Clifton: © Christopher Felver.
Samuel Taylor Coleridge: Library of Congress.
Gregory Corso: Harold S. Chapman/Corbis-Bettmann.
Robert Creeley: © Christopher Felver.
Victor Hernández Cruz: © Christopher Felver.
E. E. Cummings: Library of Congress.
Dante: Corbis.
Emily Dickinson: Corbis-Bettmann.
John Donne: Corbis-Bettmann.
Russell Edson: © Nancy Crampton.
T. S. Eliot: UPI/Corbis-Bettmann.
Ralph Waldo Emerson: Library of Congress.
Robert Frost: Library of Congress.
Allen Ginsberg: Library of Congress.
Thomas Gray: Corbis-Bettmann.
Nicolás Guillén: Archive Photos/Hector Sardinas.
Robert Hayden: Pach/Corbis.
Anthony Hecht: UPI/Corbis-Bettmann.
George Herbert: Archive Photos.
Robert Herrick: Library of Congress.
Homer: Library of Congress.

Gerard Manley Hopkins: Archive Photos/Popperfoto.
A. E. Housman: Corbis-Bettmann.
Langston Hughes: Jack Delano/Library of Congress.
John Keats: Corbis-Bettmann.
Galway Kinnell: Alan Caruba/Archive Photos.
Kenneth Koch: Daily Mirror/Corbis-Bettmann.
D. H. Lawrence: UPI/Corbis-Bettmann.
Edward Lear: Library of Congress.
Giacomo Leopardi: Library of Congress.
Li Po: Jeffrey H. Chen.
Vachel Lindsay: Library of Congress.
Henry Wadsworth Longfellow: Corbis-Bettmann.
Federico García Lorca: Archive Photos.
Robert Lowell: Library of Congress.
Andrew Marvell: Library of Congress.
Edgar Lee Masters: Library of Congress.
Vladimir Mayakovsky: Courtesy Howard Schickler Fine Art.
Edna St. Vincent Millay: Library of Congress.
John Milton: Library of Congress.
Gabriela Mistral: Marcos Chaundes/Library of Congress.
N. Scott Momaday: © Nancy Crampton.
Marianne Moore: Library of Congress.
Ogden Nash: UPI/Corbis-Bettmann.
Pablo Neruda: Library of Congress.
Frank O'Hara: Renate Ponsold.
Ovid: Corbis-Bettmann.
Ron Padgett: © Christopher Felver.
Boris Pasternak: Archive Photos.
Fernando Pessoa: Courtesy of Assírio & Alvim II (Lisbon).
Sylvia Plath: UPI/Corbis-Bettmann.
Edgar Allan Poe: Library of Congress.
Alexander Pope: Library of Congress.
Anne Porter: Fairfield Porter, (America, 1907–1975), *Anne in a Striped Dress,* oil on canvas, 1967. The Parrish Art Museum, Southampton, N.Y. Gift of the Estate of Fairfield Porter, 1980.10.176.
Ezra Pound: Arnold Genthe/Library of Congress.
Charles Reznikoff: Photo by Gerard Malanga. Courtesy of Black Sparrow Press.
Adrienne Rich: Thomas Victor/Library of Congress.
Rainer Maria Rilke: Corbis-Bettmann.
Arthur Rimbaud: Library of Congress.
Edwin Arlington Robinson: Corbis-Bettmann.
Theodore Roethke: UPI/Corbis-Bettmann.
Rumi: Michael Green.
Sonia Sanchez: © 2000 Nancy Crampton.
Carl Sandburg: Courtesy of National Park Service & Carl Sandburg Home NHS.
Sappho: Staatliche Antikensammlungen und Glyptothek München.
James Schuyler: UPI/Corbis-Bettmann.
William Shakespeare: Library of Congress.
Percy Bysshe Shelley: Library of Congress.
Charles Simic: Sara Barrett.
Gary Snyder: UPI/Corbis-Bettmann.
William Stafford: Kim Stafford.
Gertrude Stein: UPI/Corbis-Bettmann.
Wallace Stevens: Corbis-Bettmann.
May Swenson: Rozanne Knudson (Estate of May Swenson)/Corbis-Bettmann.
James Tate: James Tate Collection, Special Collections Department, Pittsburg State University.
Alfred Lord Tennyson: Library of Congress.
Dylan Thomas: Library of Congress.
Tu Fu: Jeffrey H. Chen.
Virgil: Corbis-Bettmann
Walt Whitman: Library of Congress.
Richard Wilbur: Photo Credit: Constance Stuart Larrabee.
William Carlos Williams: Library of Congress.
William Wordsworth: Library of Congress.
James Wright: Layle Silbert.
William Butler Yeats: Alice Boughton/Library of Congress.

Guillaume Apollinaire, excerpt from "Annie," translated by Ron Padgett, from *Sulfur* 42 (spring 1998). Excerpt from "Zone," translated by Ron Padgett, from *Sleeping on the Wing: An Anthology of Modern Poetry with Essays on Reading and Writing,* edited by Kenneth Koch and Kate Farrell. Excerpt from "The Windows," translated by Ron Padgett, from *Blood Work: Selected Prose.* Copyright © 1993 by Ron Padgett. Excerpt from "The Pretty Redhead," translated by Ron Padgett (unpublished manuscript, 1998). All reprinted with the permission of the translator.

John Ashbery, "The Painter" and excerpts from "The Instruction Manual" from *Selected Poems* (New York: Viking, 1985). Copyright © 1985 by John Ashbery. Excerpt from "The New Spirit" from *Three Poems* (New York: The Ecco Press, 1989). Copyright © 1989 by John Ashbery. Reprinted with the permission of Georges Borchardt, Inc. for the author.

W. H. Auden, "The Unknown Citizen" and excerpts from "1929," "Lullaby" ("Lay your sleeping head, my love"), "Musée des Beaux Arts," "In Memory of W. B. Yeats," "The Shield of Achilles," "New Year Letter," "August 1968," "Doggerel by a Senior Citizen," "Spain 1937," and "Thank You, Fog" from *Collected Poems,* edited by Edward Mendelson. Copyright 1934, 1940, 1941, 1952, © 1969 and renewed © 1962, 1968, 1969 by W. H. Auden. Copyright © 1974 by the Estate of W. H. Auden. Reprinted with the permission of Random House, Inc.

Amiri Baraka (LeRoi Jones), excerpts from "Letter to E. Franklin Frazier," "Hymn for Lanie Poo," *It's Nation Time,* and "A Poem for Deep Thinkers" from *The LeRoi Jones/Amiri Baraka Reader* (New York: Thunder's Mouth Press, 1991). Copyright © 1991 by Amiri Baraka. Excerpts from "Ostriches & Grandmothers!" and "In the Tradition" from *Transbluesency: Selected Poems 1961–1995* (New York: Marsilio Publishers, 1995). Copyright © 1991 by Amiri Baraka. All reprinted with the permission of Sterling Lord Literistic, Inc.

Matsuo Bashō, haiku "Old Pond," translated by William J. Higginson, from William J. Higginson and Penny Harter, *The Haiku Handbook: How to Write, Share and Teach Haiku* (Tokyo: Kodansha International, 1985). "on a leafless branch" and "Summer Moon" (excerpt), translated by William J. Higginson, from William J. Higginson, *The Haiku Seasons: Poetry of the Natural World* (Tokyo: Kodansha International, 1996). "ill on a journey—" and "Clear Cascade . . ." Excerpt and haiku "the stillness . . ." from *Narrow Road to the Interior,* translated by William J. Higginson. All reprinted with the permission of the translator.

Ted Berrigan, excerpts from "Tambourine Life" from *Many Happy Returns.* Copyright © 1969 by Ted Berrigan. Excerpt from "The Joke & The Stars" from *Easter Monday* (previously unpublished). "Wind" and excerpts from "Red Shift" from *So Going Around Cities: New and Selected Poems 1958–1979.* Copyright © 1980 by Ted Berrigan. All reprinted with the permission of Alice Notley, The Estate of Ted Berrigan. "Sonnet XV" and excerpts from "Personal Poem #9" from *The Sonnets.* Copyright © 2000 by Alice Notley. Reprinted with the permission of Viking Penguin, a division of Penguin Putnam Inc.

John Berryman, "Henry's Confession" and excerpts from "Dream Song 1," "Dream Song 76," "Dream Song 241," "Dream Song 384," and "Dream Song 157" from *The Dream Songs.* Copyright © 1959, 1962, 1963, 1964, 1965, 1966, 1967, 1968, 1969 by John Berryman. John Berryman, excerpts (6 lines) from "The Ball Poem" from *Collected Poems 1937–1971.* Copyright © 1989 by Kate Donahue Berryman. All reprinted with the permission of Farrar, Straus & Giroux, LLC.

T. S. Eliot, all poetry from *Collected Poems 1909–1962*. Copyright 1922, 1925, 1927 1941 by T. S. Eliot. Copyright 1936 by Harcourt, Inc., renewed © 1964 by T. S. Eliot. Reprinted with the permission of Harcourt, Inc. and Faber and Faber Limited.

Robert Frost, all poetry from *The Poetry of Robert Frost*, edited by Edward Connery Lathem. Copyright 1916, 1936, 1942, 1944, 1951, © 1956, 1958 by Robert Frost. Copyright © 1964, 1967, 1970, 1975 by Lesley Frost Ballantine. Copyright 1916, 1923, 1928, 1930, 1939, 1947, © 1969 by Henry Holt and Co., Inc. Reprinted with the permission of Henry Holt and Co., LLC.

Allen Ginsberg, "A Supermarket in California" and excerpts from "Howl," "Kaddish," and "A Lover's Garden" from *Collected Poems 1947–1980*. Copyright © 1955 by Allen Ginsberg. Reprinted with the permission of HarperCollins Publishers, Inc.

Nicolás Guillén, excerpts from "Tengo," and from "No Sé Por Qué Piensas Tú" (original and translation) from *Patria o Muerte! The Great Zoo and Other Poems*, translated and edited by Robert Márquez (New York: Monthly Review Press, 1972). Reprinted by permission.

Guillem IX, "In the Sweetness of the New Season" from *Proensa: An Anthology of Troubadour Poetry*, edited and translated by Paul Blackburn. Copyright © 1978 by The Regents of the University of California. Reprinted with the permission of the University of California Press.

Kimiko Hahn, "Day Lilies on the Second Anniversary of My Second Marriage" from *Earshot*. Reprinted with the permission of Hanging Loose Press. "The Unbearable Heart" from *The Unbearable Heart* (New York: Kaya Productions, 1996). Copyright © 1996. Reprinted with permission.

Hashimoto Takako, haiku ("fresh-washed hair"), translated by William J. Higginson. Reprinted with the permission of the translator.

Robert Hayden, "Names" and excerpts from "The Ballad of Sue Ellen Westerfield," "Elegies for Paradise Valley," "Those Winter Sundays," "A Ballad of Remembrance," "For a Young Artist," "Summer-time and the Living . . . ," "Homage to the Empress of the Blues," "Sphinx," "Stars," "Middle Passage," "The Tattooed Man," "from THE SNOW LAMP," and "October," from *Collected Poems of Robert Hayden*, edited by Frederick Glaysher. Copyright © 1966 by Robert Hayden. Copyright © 1985 by Emma Hayden. Reprinted with the permission of Liveright Publishing Corporation.

Jessica Hagedorn, "Motown/Smokey Robinson" from *Danger and Beauty*. Copyright © 1981 by Jessica Hagedorn. Reprinted with the permission of Viking Penguin, a division of Penguin Putnam Inc.

Joy Harjo, excerpt from "She Had Some Horses" from *She Had Some Horses*. Copyright © 1983, 1997 by Thunder's Mouth Press. Reprinted with the permission of the publisher, Thunder's Mouth Press.

Anthony Hecht, "Giant Tortoise" and excerpts from "A Hill," "The Deodand," "The Lull," and "The Venetian Vespers" from *Collected Earlier Poems*. Copyright © 1996 by Anthony E. Hecht. Reprinted with the permission of Alfred A. Knopf, a division of Random House, Inc.

Lance Henson, "winter black" from *A Cheyenne Sketchbook: Selected Poems 1970–1991*. Copyright © 1991 by Lance Henson. Reprinted with the permission of Greenfield Review Press.

Homer, excerpt from *The Iliad*, translated by Richmond Lattimore. Copyright 1951 by The University of Chicago, renewed © 1979 by Richmond Lattimore. Reprinted with the permission of The University of Chicago Press.

A. E. Housman, "XXIII" from *More Poems* from *The Collected Poems of A. E. Housman*. Copyright 1939, 1940 by Henry Holt and Company, renewed © 1967 by Robert E. Symons. Reprinted with the permission of Henry Holt and Company, LLC.

Langston Hughes, "The Negro Speaks of Rivers," and excerpts from "Mother to Son," "The Weary Blues," "Harlem," "Dream Boogie," "Po' Boy Blues," and "I, Too" from *The Collected Poems of Langston Hughes,* edited by Arnold Rampersad and David Roessel. Copyright © 1994 by the Es-

William Stafford, "Time for Serenity, Anyone?" from *The Methow River Poems*. Copyright © 1995 by William Stafford. Reprinted with the permission of Confluence Press. "Ask Me" and "Traveling Through the Dark" from *The Way It Is: New and Selected Poems*. Copyright © 1987, 1998 by the Estate of William Stafford. Reprinted with the permission of Graywolf Press. St. Paul, Minnesota.

Gertrude Stein, excerpt from "Lifting Belly" from *Bee Time Vine Bee Time Vine and Other Pieces 1913–1927* (New Haven, Conn.: Yale University Press, 1953). "A Handkerchief," excerpt from Stanza XV from *Stanzas in Meditation and Other Poems*. Copyright © 1956 by Alice B. Toklas. Copyright © 1980 by Calman A. Levin, Executor of the Estate of Gertrude Stein. Excerpt from *4 Saints in Three Acts*. All reprinted with the permission of the Estate of Gertrude Stein.

Wallace Stevens, "As You Leave the Room" and excerpts from "Sunday Morning" and "The Auroras of Autumn" from *Selected Poems*. Copyright 1947, 1954 by Wallace Stevens. Copyright 1957, 1959 by Elsie Stevens and Holly Stevens. Reprinted with the permission of Alfred A. Knopf, a division of Random House, Inc.

May Swenson, excerpt from "October," "Pure Suit of Happiness," and "Looks" from *New and Selected Things Taking Place* (Boston: Little, Brown, 1978). Copyright © 1978 by May Swenson. Reprinted with the permission of The Literary Estate of May Swenson. "Painting the Gate," "Living Tenderly," and excerpts from "The Centaur" "Pure Suit of Happiness," "Looks" from *The Complete Poems to Solve*. Copyright © 1993 by The Literary Estate of May Swenson. Reprinted with the permission of Simon & Schuster Books for Young Readers, an imprint of Simon & Schuster Children's Publishing Division.

Mary TallMountain, excerpt from "Indian Blood" from *This Earth on Turtle's Back,* edited by Joseph Bruchac (Greenfield Center, NY: Greenfield Review Press, 1983). Reprinted with the permission of M. Catherine Costello, TallMountain Literary Executor.

James Tate, excerpt from "The Lost Pilot" from *The Lost Pilot*. Copyright © 1978 by James Tate.

Reprinted with the permission of HarperCollins Publishers, Inc. "Dear Reader" and excerpts from "Up Here" and "Bennington" from *The Oblivion Ha-Ha*. Copyright © 1970 by James Tate. Reprinted with the permission of Little, Brown and Company. Excerpt from "Absences" from *Absences*. Copyright © 1972 by James Tate. Reprinted with the permission of Little, Brown and Company. Inc. Excerpt from "Happy as the Day Is Long" from *The Worshipful Company of Fletchers*. Copyright © 1994 by James Tate. Reprinted with the permission of HarperCollins Publishers, Inc.

Dylan Thomas, all poetry from *The Poems of Dylan Thomas*. Copyright 1939, 1946 by New Directions Publishing Corporation. Reprinted with the permission of New Directions Publishing Corporation and David Higham Associates, London, as agents for the Trustees of the Copyrights of Dylan Thomas.

Tu Fu, "Impromptu," "Dreaming of Li Po," "Moonlit Night Thinking of My Brothers," "The River Village," "Night at the Tower," "Returning Late," and "8th Month, 17th Night: Facing the Moon" from *The Selected Poems of Tu Fu*, translated by David Hinton. Copyright © 1988, 1989 by David Hinton. Reprinted with the permission of New Directions Publishing Corporation.

Cesar Vallejo, excerpt from *Trilce*, translated by Clayton Eshleman. Copyright © 1968 by Clayton Eshleman. Reprinted with the permission of Grove/Atlantic, Inc.

Virgil, excerpts from *Virgil's Eclogues*, translated by Barbara Hughes Fowler. Copyright © 1997 by The University of North Carolina Press. Reprinted with the permission of the publisher. Excerpts from *The Georgics*, translated by L. P. Wilkinson. Copyright © 1982 by L. P. Wilkinson. Reprinted with the permission of Penguin Books, Ltd. Excerpt from *The Aeneid*, translated by Robert Fitzgerald. Copyright © 1980, 1982, 1983 by Robert Fitzgerald. Reprinted with the permission of Random House, Inc.

Richard Wilbur, excerpt from "Pont Mirabeau" from *New and Selected Poems*. Copyright © 1988 by Richard Wilbur. Excerpt from "Ceremony" from *New and Selected Poems*. Copyright 1949 and re-

Page numbers in **boldface** refer to the main discussion of a subject.